WHERE WE MUST STAND

Ten Years of Feminist Mormon Housewives

Edited by

Sara K. S. Hanks and Nancy Ross

Cataloging-in-Publication Data

Names: Ross, Nancy, 1980- editor. | Hanks, Sara K. S., 1987- editor.
Title: Where we must stand : ten years of Feminist Mormon Housewives / edited by Sara K. S. Hanks and Nancy Ross.
Description: United States : Feminist Mormon Housewives, 2018.
Identifiers: ISBN 9781717433527
Subjects: LCSH: Feminism--Religious aspects--Mormon Church--Blogs. | Feminism--Religious aspects--Church of Jesus Christ of Latter-day Saints--Blogs. | Mormon women--Religious life--Blogs. | Feminist Mormon Housewives (blog)
Classification: LCC BX8643.W66 W44 2018

CONTENTS

PREFACE

When I first proposed the idea of creating a ten-year anniversary book for Feminist Mormon Housewives (FMH), I thought it would take a year. When I inched past that self-imposed deadline and then found out I was pregnant with my second baby, I promised myself that I'd be done before my due date. As I'm writing this now, that baby girl is sleeping upstairs, and I'm looking at a tentative publication date that will fall just before her second birthday. All things considered, the timeline has quadrupled. So let that be a lesson in what God thinks of our plans.

I began my time as an FMH blogger in 2013. When the tenth anniversary rolled around in August of the following year, I still had enough Mormon feminist fire in me to not only believe that this commemorative book needed to exist, but that I was completely capable of making it all by myself, despite my lack of editing or publishing credentials. The size of the undertaking dawned on me slowly. I was fine with reading all the posts (4,167 of them, to be exact) and narrowing them down to the absolute essentials; I didn't know I'd have to take that bare-minimum list and hack it down thrice more, and I certainly didn't know how much it would break my heart each time. I was fine with the idea of self-publishing in theory, but I had no idea what that actually entailed. And while I understood on some level that there would be tense or awkward moments with a number of people along the way, I didn't really appreciate the way relationships would be tested and forced to evolve through the process of making this book. Basically, I didn't have the faintest idea of what I was getting myself into, and I both love and pity my younger self for her innocent faith and confidence in taking on this project.

And what is this project, exactly? What are its goals, and what is its vision? Heck if I know for sure, but I'll take a stab at it: *Where We Must Stand* is a collection of valuable posts published on the Feminist Mormon Housewives blog from August 2004 to August 2014. I hope it's an accurate representation of the blog in those years, and to whatever extent possible, I hope it's an accurate representation of the Mormon feminist community as a whole in those years. But of course, there are varying levels of accuracy, and this book isn't perfect or whole. It couldn't possibly be. For every post you'll read in these pages, there were 35 more originally published on the blog, and probably five or six of those 35 would have been strong contenders for final inclusion. We had to make tough decisions and consider many factors in assembling this final text. The following questions were among the many we asked ourselves:

What topics need to be covered, and how much space does each one merit? How many posts should come from resident bloggers vs. guest bloggers? And for the resident bloggers, or permabloggers, what's the appropriate number of posts to include proportional to her or his overall contribution to the blog? What's an ideal length for the posts that are included? Is it worth it to include this very long post if it means we have to remove three other short posts in order to stay within our designated word count? Are there certain posts that absolutely must be included because of their original impact? Are there certain posts that should NOT be included because of their original impact, or because of how they come across now with the benefit of 20/20 hindsight? What are the minimum expectations for literary merit? Can we secure author permissions for all the posts we want to include? What's the correct balance of faith-promoting vs. faith-critical posts? Of posts that relate personal stories vs. document important community events vs. get deep into theory or doctrine vs. reflect on relevant history? And finally, is this just a jumbled-up smattering of favorite posts, or does each post contribute to the overall arc of the story we're telling? How does each post develop the book's important themes?

There were dozens of posts I loved and wanted to keep, but finally, I just had to kiss them goodbye and leave them in the blog archives. I hope that won't be read as any slight or disrespect to those authors. I'm sure another person could come up with a completely different table of contents, with no overlap at all, and make a gorgeous book out of it. (If you'd like to try it, please, please do. Just know it might take you four years.)

I'm proud of this book. It's precious to me, and it has been a labor of love, but I understand fully that it is an imperfect book. It is an imperfect representation of an imperfect blog from an imperfect community. I believe in celebrating our triumphs and also in looking honestly at our failings, in reckoning with our sins. The Mormon feminist community has all of those in spades. I think that, for a long time, many of us were so immersed in how we'd been hurt that we were blind to how we perpetuated other kinds of hurt, especially towards those on the margins. We succeeded in loving one another, and we also fell short in loving one another, and we *still* fall short today. Our words and actions have been healing for many and have also caused pain for many. We are a long way from Zion, but it is a beautiful destination, and as much as I hope this book is a worthwhile read in its own right, I hope it will also be, in some small way, evidence of our progress and motivation in our onward journey.

Here's what I can say for certain: in this book, we have a complete story. It started with a woman in Boise who wanted to talk with other Mormon women about the stuff that mattered to her. It gathered steam as more and more voices joined the chorus. It's a story of individuals connecting to community, finding confidence, speaking their truths, and developing faith in God and themselves. It's a story of personal and group evolution. And it's a story of great hope and disappointment. The sequence of events that took place in these exact ten years is almost too synchronistic to be believed, but it's all true, and thousands of Mormon feminists witnessed it in real time. I hope this book does justice to all it meant.

I'd like to thank my husband, Craig, for his regular encouragement in this process and for his insistence that I pursue anything that makes me feel alive and whole. Thanks to my kids, Soren and Freya, for being consistent nappers and good playmates to one another whenever I've had to sneak off and work on the book. You inspire me not only as my children but as my friends and teachers. Thank you to my parents (and grandparents, aunts, uncles, cousins, brothers, neighbors) for surrounding me with such a welcoming spiritual world. And thank you to my absolute best friend forever, Chelsea Campbell, for just being the greatest in every way and for introducing me to Feminist Mormon Housewives way back in 2007.

Thank you to my friends and mentors in the world of Mormon feminism. For the sake of word count, I can't list you all by name, but you are dear to me. Endless love and hugs to my fantastic bwords, and special thanks to Tresa Brown Edmunds and Meredith Hartley for their wholehearted belief in this project, as well as to Joanna Brooks for her shepherding wisdom and to Lisa Patterson Butterworth for starting this whole gorgeous mess in the first place. Thank you to my co-editor Nancy Ross; the reason you're reading this book right now is because she swooped in with new energy and focus when I was emotionally over it and made it happen. And of course, thank you to all those who contributed to Feminist Mormon Housewives over the years, in both posts and comments. I hold your words as sacred.

A final thank you and a dedication: to Mormon women of all kinds, feminist or not, living or dead or still to be born. You are my people. You are the loves of my life. I am honored to be among you.

—Sara Katherine Staheli Hanks

LOOKING BACK

By Lisa Patterson Butterworth

As I write this, 2018 has just begun and I have just received news that Thomas Monson has passed away. This year will mark fourteen years from the time I started Feminist Mormon Housewives, and ten years since my father passed away. Each time an LDS leader dies, my father grief shows up again, my relationship to Mormonism and my relationship to my father are metaphorically inextricable to me. My father loved me very much, I felt safe and warm as his beloved daughter, and he never really understood me, not the real me, the feminist me. That is very painful. This year will also mark about four years since I began slowly and unofficially moving away from being a daily contributor to the Feminist Mormon Housewives community (and online Mormonism generally).

I very much still feel like a Mormon Feminist, and in that core identity I face a very Mormon struggle, what does it mean to be a Mormon feminist? This is a particularly Mormon struggle because of its sister question what does it mean to be a Mormon? The way my Mormon belonging was taught to me (at least outwardly) was very much about community markers. One of the most important markers being engagement in Mormon community, specifically weekly attendance and doing the check lists. All of the checklists: earrings, haircuts, underwear, the temperature of our drinks, the mission, and the temple marriage and never expressing (and barely admitting to) doubts about truth.

Can I be Mormon without all of these things? Can I be a Mormon with doubt? Can I be a Mormon who skips church? How about a Mormon who loves being Mormon some days, and other days doesn't want to be Mormon, but can't help but think and act like a Mormon 90% of the time anyway? Can I be a feminist Mormon who loves my mother church at the same time I am angry and hurt by so much that is broken here? Can I be a Mormon when they don't seem to want me, the real me, the feminist me?

In my essay "Faithful and Feminist" from October 2010 I was reaching for a definition of what it meant to be a Mormon Feminist. After six years of blogging about everything from cloth diapers to polygamy, we had moved from being a tiny personal blog to a vibrant community full of people with vastly different relationships with Mormonism and Feminism and Housewifery (take that last bit with a smidge of uncomfortable oxymoronic indulgence). We were trying to make space for 'baby feminists" who were just waking up to the fact that it might not be fair that the Young Men's budget was double that for Young Women but who still fully committed to the checklist. At the same time, we were trying to make space for the "angry feminists" who were rightly furious with the church for every abuse laying at its feet. We were trying, with mixed success, to stand in this impossible middle ground and we hadn't even yet begun to grasp the challenges that still lay ahead. Many of us (though certainly not all) were writing from a place of white privilege, able-bodied privilege, cis-hetero privilege. We were (and often still are) so rooted in and not addressing this overlapping privilege, the layers of oppression we inherited from our broken systems and blindly brought with us as we strived and fumbled toward something better. We had no idea the waves of technology, growth, activism and retrenchment that were ahead of us.

As I re-read the eight-year-old essay and try to remember the then-me who wrote it, I think I was making the argument that the thing that made us Mormon Feminists was our commitment to being with each other in the complicated journey through liminal Mormon spaces, a commitment to seeing the best in each other and making space for a wide variety of approaches and beliefs. To embody the very Mormon message of universal love and abandon the very Mormon fear of the impure lost sinful "other." While our (my) execution of that vision is certainly up for debate, I feel like that is still a vision I can get behind.

I think it is in death and grief that I most clearly learn over and over to unmake the illusion of the "other." All my logical reasons for rejecting everything the patriarchy stands for shatters in the face of my love for my father and the grief I feel every time I lose one of these men that feel so much like him in my heart. My love for them does not excuse the systems of abuse they perpetuate, but it does deny me the refuge of othering them, of reducing them to my enemy, it denies me moral superiority, and it balances me on the knife edge between unconditional love and complicity.

Thomas Monson often counseled us to "Stand in Holy Places,"[1] and I have often experienced the awesome uplifting sanctity when the air shifts and the light shimmers and the power of a holy place overwhelms me, I experienced it when my father laid his hands upon my head and gave me a blessing, and I experienced it around a campfire singing suffrage songs with feminists our voices ringing through the trees in four part harmony, I have felt it in stables and in temples, and I have come to believe that this power to stand in holy places is something we carry inside ourselves.

Standing as a metaphor speaks to our desire to be unchanging and unchanged, and yet we cannot cease our progression, eternally walking toward greater light and knowledge. Mormonism is rife with paradoxes like this one, obedience and agency, the meek shall inherit, standing in holiness and walking toward progression. Over the last decade, my Mormon

Feminist sisters and brothers have come to stand in a beautiful mélange of holy places, for some the questions of Mormon identity are simple, they are or they are not, but most of us wear our Mormon feminist identity like a complicated garment that we can neither discard nor wear with an uncomplicated joy of belonging. A messy garment that can be particularly difficult to wear to funerals, where our love and sorrow, our doubt and faith, our joy and pain, come into sharp focus and no easy answers or simple fixes arrive.

I am a Mormon feminist, full of doubt and faith, full of love for my sister feminists, longing for my literal father, and hope for my metaphorical mother church. And Feminist Mormon Housewives is the place where I learned to sit and stand and walk in the complicated messy unresolvable paradox that is Mormon feminism.

A BRIEF HISTORY OF FEMINIST MORMON HOUSEWIVES AND ONLINE MORMON FEMINISM

By Nancy Ross

When Lisa Patterson Butterworth founded the Feminist Mormon Housewives (FMH) blog in 2004, aging Mormon feminist organizations did not have a substantial pool of younger women to draw on. The LDS Church publicly excommunicated several prominent Mormon feminist authors and other intellectuals in 1993 and this series of events rocked the Mormon feminist community, creating a widespread fear of Church discipline and a reluctance to speak out.[2] Many women who were prominent in the Mormon feminist movement at this time reported that their daughters left the Church during the 1990s. *Exponent II* struggled to find people to take over the editing of its magazine, and the *Mormon Women's Forum*, once a quarterly newsletter, supported only an annual conference. In a *Salt Lake Tribune* article from 2003, religion writer Peggy Fletcher Stack asked the poignant question "Where have all the Mormon feminists gone?"[3]

Butterworth created the FMH blog without a knowledge of those other Mormon feminist structures, thinking that she might be the only Mormon feminist.[4] Her decision to create the blog, write consistently, and then add other voices changed the trajectory of the whole movement. Before this, Mormon feminism was difficult to access, hard to find or bump into. Some Mormon feminists talked with each other through email listservs, but those were not accessible to the general public.[5] The FMH blog was different in that it invited an interested public into a very specific kind of conversation. Readers could participate in the comments, with nearly everyone using pseudonyms to feel safe from prying eyes. The movement found new life as a younger generation of Mormon feminists gathered online and restarted the old conversations anew.

The following year, the Exponent women formed their own blog, and other group and individual Mormon feminist blogs followed. This momentum created a series of networked conversations on important subjects, with bloggers reading and responding to posts on other blogs and generating new blog content. Readers and commenters followed the links and discovered new authors and new material. Several media outlets ran stories on the FMH blog, drawing attention and new readers to the community. FMH responded by taking on new bloggers and new topics.

While other blogs contributed to the growth of the Mormon feminist community at this time, the FMH blog was the central hub of the online movement for more than a decade. It had a higher readership, received more comments, and produced more posts than any other Mormon feminist blog at this time.[6] Once Facebook groups became an important location for Mormon feminist discussion in late 2012, the Feminist Mormon Housewives Society group dominated the landscape. For about four years, it had a much higher membership than any other Mormon feminist group.[7] The conversations happening in the Feminist Mormon Housewives Society (FMHs) Facebook group seeded ideas for activism and offered a sympathetic crowd for support. By the time that Mormon feminists started wearing pants to church in December 2012, there was momentum in the online movement backed by thousands of participants, readers, and allies.

Studying the Mormon feminist community has shaped my own perception of it. Starting in the summer of 2013, Jessica Finnigan and I conducted several surveys of Mormon feminists. Our earliest studies followed the internet-as-a-disruptive-innovation line of thinking, noting the work of Harvard business professor (and Mormon) Clayton Christensen.[8] The results of a 2015 survey gave more insight into how Mormon feminists benefitted from participation in the online movement.[9] Specifically, participants noted that they had a supportive community where they could bring questions and problems and expect answers and support. Many Mormon feminists said that participation in the online community helped them to stay active in the LDS Church, as it gave them a space to ask and offer advice about navigating difficult situations and setting boundaries at church.

The second survey also highlighted the ways in which the community provided an education in Mormon history, feminist theory, and feminist critique. This happened in part because the community circled around to discuss many of the same topics over and over again, and some Mormon feminists expressed frustration that the same 10–15 issues kept resurfacing.[10] In the long run, this process of continually revisiting common themes helped individuals to deepen their knowledge on matters that impacted them, such as motherhood, mental health, gender equality, polygamy, The Family: A Proclamation to the World, the discomfort of questions, Mormon women's history, women and the priesthood, the role of Jesus at church, women's experiences in the temple, Heavenly Mother, LGBTQIA people at church, and activism. Numerous blog posts at FMH and other blogs in the Mormon feminist community, together with the Facebook groups and podcasts, educated the community and helped individuals practice engaging in feminist discourse. Interestingly, members of the online community were largely unaware of the ways in which they were retreading similar ground that had been discussed in the 1970s, 80s, and 90s.

In 2013, 81 percent of more than 1,800 Mormon feminists replied to a survey telling us that they attended church at least two to three times per month.[11] Participants in the movement hoped for positive change for women in the Church, and many framed their engagement in activism as an extension of their own faith. The excommunication of Kate Kelly, one of the founders of Ordain Women, in June 2014 changed this framing. This event crushed that hope and clarified to Mormon feminists the negative ways in which they were perceived by the LDS Church. A survey from early 2015 showed a sharp decline in church activity rates, with just 65 percent of respondents reporting that they attended church at least two to three times per month.[12] Anecdotal evidence suggests that the activity rate dropped further after the leak of the Exclusion Policy in November 2015, which outlined that same-sex married couples should be charged with apostasy and experience Church discipline. The policy also limited their children's access to ordinances. If a child's primary residence was with a parent in a same-sex marriage or cohabitating relationship, the child could not receive baptism or ordination to the priesthood until the age of 18—and then only if the child disavowed the same-sex relationship.

The online community remained through these challenges, but the conversations about race in the aftermath of the police shooting of Michael Brown in Ferguson, Missouri in August 2014 changed FMH fundamentally. Prior to this event, white Mormon feminists had not tackled race in the LDS Church in substantial ways, nor was there a recognition that the movement largely operated from the social location of whiteness, together with privileged positions of class, sexual orientation, gender identity, and ability. For months, the community wrestled painfully with education and conversation on race, intersectionality, and inclusion. This moved the FMH community beyond a comfortable space of being welcoming and accessible to new, budding (and primarily white) feminists, but also into conversations that the Mormon feminists of previous generations had not engaged with. The whiteness of Mormonism and the whiteness of feminism is still something that the community is in the early stages of addressing.

In the last year, new questions have emerged about the longevity, purpose, and future of FMH. I sat with Lisa Patterson Butterworth at a Mormon feminist retreat in July 2017, and she wondered aloud if FMH was over and if it was time to retire. I nodded, understanding some of the ways in which the organization was exhausted from activism, excommunication, changing relationships, scandal, and education. Ultimately, things have not gone that way, and there have been feelings and movements toward renewal. Early this month (December 2017), Lisa and Kalani Tonga announced that FMH would be relaunching the blog in early 2018. The organizational tagline is changing from "A Safe Place to be Feminist and Faithful" to "Preaching Christ's Message of Radical Inclusion." In this process of restoration, FMH continues to push its own community and the larger Mormon feminist movement to do the challenging work of social justice while recognizing that we, collectively, are a long way from mastering any of it.

NOTES FROM THE EDITORS

We hope that people from a variety of backgrounds will be drawn to this book and find useful things in it. To aid an understanding of the text, we have included a number of explanatory notes and references. We also encourage readers who are not familiar with Mormonism or Mormon feminism to consult a glossary such as the one in *Mormon Feminism: Essential Writings* (Oxford University Press, 2015), edited by Joanna Brooks, Rachel Hunt Steenblik, and Hannah Wheelwright.

One of the difficulties of translating blog posts into a book is the handling of the links to other content. In traditional publishing, these references would be handled by footnotes or endnotes, but in the internet age, authors just create a hyperlink to the source being referenced. Many links from the early years of the blog no longer work today. Where links are still functional, we have included the link destination in a note. There remain a number of instances where the text indicates that a link should exist, but it has not been possible to find a current link for the referenced content. In these cases, we have not included a note. We have also added some explanatory notes and additional citations.

Many posts originally published at Feminist Mormon Housewives were written under pseudonyms or only the author's first name. With the permission of the authors, we have revised most of the posts to be attributed under the author's actual full name. Some authors preferred to keep their identities obscured, and we have respected their wishes.

In order to honor the informal nature of the blog, only minimal edits have been made, mostly related to spelling and punctuation. Heartfelt thanks to Christa Baxter for her work on this.

2004

In 2004, the LDS Church published *Preach My Gospel: A Guide to Missionary Service*, which represented a shift for those serving as proselytizing missionaries. Prior to the new resource, the Missionary Training Center used a teaching model based on memorized discussions. These were scripted, carefully ordered lessons that were consistent regardless of language, culture, or the needs of the person being taught. *Preach My Gospel*, on the other hand, emphasized a less structured approach and reliance on the Spirit.

In April, Marjorie Pay Hinckley passed away at the age of 92. She was the author of three inspirational books for Mormon audiences and the beloved wife of President Gordon B. Hinckley. In October, the First Presidency released a statement that said that sexual relations between people of the same gender undermine the family and that the Church supported a definition of marriage as "the union of a man and a woman." The Church supported the Federal Marriage Amendment, which used similar language.

This year marked a subtle but important shift in the Mormon feminist trajectory. A *Salt Lake Tribune* article published on October 4, 2003 by journalist Peggy Fletcher Stack asked, "Where have all the Mormon feminists gone?"[13] Following the fervor of the fight for the Equal Rights Amendment in the 1970s and 80s and the fear that followed the public discipline of several Mormon feminists in September 1993, the movement had diminished. The article quoted Mormon feminist historian Claudia Bushman, who said, "Feminism as a movement within Mormonism 'is dead or dying with our generation.'" All signs indicated that Bushman was correct in her assessment.

At that same time there was a surge of personal blogging in the larger world that was also present in Mormonism. Group blogs like Times and Seasons, started in 2003, and By Common Consent, started in 2004, both featured posts for a thoughtful, intellectually inclined, and less orthodox Mormon audience. Lisa Patterson Butterworth was an interested reader of both blogs and decided to start one of her own in August. Butterworth had the specific intention of addressing topics of interest to Mormon women.[14] Her solo project soon grew to include guest writers and an additional permablogger, Laurie Burk/Not Ophelia. By the end of the year, the blog had published 74 posts on such varied topics as children's animated films, polygamy, sexual choices, cultural conceptions of modesty, motherhood, and the 2004 US presidential race. Butterworth reignited the conversation on Mormon feminism in social media.

"THE F-WORD" BY LISA PATTERSON BUTTERWORTH (OCTOBER 11, 2004)

Feminist. Oh, I love that word. I'll be teaching my daughter to call herself one tomorrow. (BTW, she tells me I'm gorgeous all the time. I wonder who taught her that?) Maybe I'll tattoo "Feminist" on my bum. I'd like that much better than a rose, or a ship, or "mom."

Seriously, I've always loved the f-word. Even while being raised a small-town Utah conservative, I always liked the word feminist. It felt strong and smart, and most of all I think it validated my differences from the rest of the mo[15] girls. I was interested in women-centered topics, fascinated with underdog stories. Human rights, civil rights, and women's rights. And these were topics covered in a negligent/dismissive/vaguely-negative way in my experience, and yet I really wanted to know this stuff.

And being interested often made me a topic of derision from kids who thought these interests were nerdy and adults who thought they were suspect. I remember being taught in seminary that "nothing good came out of the women's rights movement" and it made me feel horrid. That a man I respected, who I felt had taught me lots of really valuable things, could believe such a thing. Could teach such a thing.

And I wondered if he was right. Was I wrong to think that the world seemed to be a better place for women now? Was I wrong to be such a strong-willed, loud, opinionated woman? Was I wrong that a world where men rule everything and women submit made me sad and uncomfortable and angry?

But labeling myself with "feminist" freed me from that. I was able to love my loud, opinionated self. "Feminist" validated the importance of women, not just as wives and mothers and bodies, but as individuals. Meek, quiet, sweet women have value, but so do loud, obnoxious, cranky women.

As a teenager I always admired the nice girls, the ones who talked softly, the ones who didn't frighten boys, the ones who always seemed so sweet. As much as I admired them, I was genetically incapable of being one of them. The women in my family are seriously strong. My mom, my auntie, my sisters, tough as nails, scary smart, and blunt as sledge hammers. And the women in my family have been regularly smacked down by mo men. (Though not by the husbands, we've got them trained up right, don't we Beth?) I think it's probably because many men find strong women disturbing and improper, maybe even threatening. And in the case of the older generation, my mom and auntie, they generally blame themselves for being too blunt. They admire those women who can keep their mouths shut and who seem to enjoy speaking in a soft voice and obeying their husbands.

But I'm of a new generation. I wish my mom and my auntie could love themselves. I want them to see how amazingly powerful they are, how they shaped me to be strong and independent and happy. I want them to love their own voices and not wish to be some hyper-feminized ideal. And "feminist" encapsulates that for me. It says it's okay to be a strong woman and to love yourself for it.

Yes, it can mean that women who pursue nontraditional roles are doing a legitimate and useful thing, both for them and the community. That women who work, women who remain childless, women who don't marry, women who don't even like kids are important too. And of course "feminist" says that we need to value women more for their brain size than their boob size.

But as I get older and wiser, I also hope it means that all girl stuff is important. That naturally sweet girls are important too. And housewives are important. And all the icky love stuff, the building of communities, the friendships, talking about our feelings, making homes, the things that women invest in, ALL the things that women do (things that are often dismissed as frivolous, silly, embarrassing) are just as important as making lots of money and playing blood sports.

To me, feminism says that girls matter, we have choices and we have worth. And feminism says that we need to put more value on women as individuals and appreciate our individuality. It says we need to emphasize our sisterhood and support each other in our diversity of choices and needs and hopes and temperaments and boob sizes. And most important, we need to recognize our contributions and our worth and demand that they be seen as important. Because sisterhood is powerful.

"BITTER IS NO FUN" BY LISA PATTERSON BUTTERWORTH (OCTOBER 17, 2004)

In case you were wondering, being an angry activist, a good Mormon, and a happy person is a delicate balancing act. I'm working on it.

To show you what I mean, I'd like to discuss some experiences at church today and show you the inner workings of my brain.

Today in Relief Society[16] our bishop came in for a question & answer session. He handed out sheets of paper for questions so they could be anonymous. This was a really great use of our time, and there was some really great discussion. Our bishop is not only a really good man, but he's a great guy. Good social skills, good leadership skills, good hearted, smart. He is very well suited to his position and clearly a great example of the Lord's anointed.

His demeanor was humble, he was there as our servant. And yet, as he introduced his lesson and told us his purpose in coming, while it was clear that he was here to make sure that our needs were being met and our questions answered (which I appreciate soooo much), something within me just could not ignore the little naggy voice that pointed out that his very presence as our priesthood leader felt paternal. Paternal both in a pleasing protective way and an annoying patronizing way.

Again let me stress that his demeanor was in no way patronizing. All this baggage came from me, because I couldn't help but feel a little insulted when he explained that he likes to use this same question/answer format with the young women and young men. So now, though unintentional and (I guess) subtle, the bishop had lumped women & children together as those who must follow counsel rather than give it.

And I wonder if I should just not feel these things. If I am somehow to blame for these feelings of bitterness that seep into an otherwise very uplifting and enlightening lesson. But I don't think that is right. I refuse to hate myself and my natural pathways of thought. I know there is danger in dwelling on unhappy thoughts about the state of things in the church, but I also feel there is danger in blindly yielding my intellect. Neither extreme would be appropriate, so I continue with my delicate balancing act.

I believe that many women never have these thoughts, they submit happily. In fact they are uncomfortable with thoughts like mine, which is why I rarely voice them. I don't want to make anyone uncomfortable. I don't want to challenge anyone's delicate testimony. Everyone has their own balancing act going on. If they're not struggling with male authority, then they're struggling with something.

So while I don't want to be throwing my baggage onto people who don't need more baggage, I think we need more paradigms for being a faithful member. Because people like me, who cannot just "not think about" things that aren't "faith promoting"—people like me, who feel the need to question everything and pray about everything and discover for myself the truth of everything before I submit myself in faith to it, have no paradigm to follow.

And I don't foresee that I will ever submit myself to the idea of male authority and female submission. It feels too wrong to me to the very core of my moral self. The very idea of it makes me cross eyed with moral outrage. But neither will I allow this belief to make me bitter or unbalanced or faithless. Because that would be wrong too.

I sometimes feel tempted to follow the bitterness wherever it leads; it would be so much easier than this tightrope I walk between faith and logic. I think being an agnostic would be very intellectually comfortable for me. But I cannot throw away my faith in the gospel. And I also refuse to believe that my faith in the gospel dictates that I throw away my logic, my desire for knowledge, and my bone-deep belief in humanism and feminism.

I'm sure we must all have similar struggles. Life is an endless wrestling match. The bitterness can also be a tool, a clarifier, a contrast. My bishop loves us. He couldn't have been more clear on that in both word and deed. And in the end, that is what really matters.

"CAREER AS PERSONAL PROGRESS" BY LISA PATTERSON BUTTERWORTH (OCTOBER 26, 2004)

I knew there was something wrong at the core of my career post from a few days ago,[17] but I couldn't put my finger on it. The comments (from Heidi, Beth, Kristine) filled in some of the gaps, but after some contemplation, I think I was to some degree missing the whole point. The big forest-for-the-trees point.

See, when I talk about women and careers, I come from a lifetime of being told, and believing to a degree, that a woman's ultimate experience and purpose is to be a mother. And at present, my entire life is all motherhood and baby poo.

But the thing this motherhood emphasis often misses, and the thing that bothers me about that emphasis, is that we women are more than just potential mothers. We are valuable people, with lives valuable of their own accord.

I think it is misguided to imply that the only way a woman's life can have value, purpose, and fulfillment is through motherhood. And Mormon culture is guilty of perpetuating that belief. I think this is harmful for many reasons. The most obvious is that not every woman can become a mother, and it is deeply wrong to demean these women's rich lives. But less obviously, I think this hurts mothers too. I know so many mothers, many in my immediate family, who do not think they matter except when they are nurturing someone else. They see no purpose to enriching their inner lives, their personal souls, their own needs and wants and pleasures, except as it serves others.

I'm not advocating for an end to serving others, a license to selfishness. But the Lord loves each of us, he created us that we might have joy. And joy is an inner thing, a soul thing. We can't give it away, it is within us. And as noble as wiping baby butts is, it doesn't do much for uplifting my soul, for challenging my mind, for engaging my inner self.

Independent of my children, I matter, and that is not selfish, that is okay. My inner search for joy, in and of itself, independent of anything else, is part of my purpose. Children can be one source of joy, a husband another, and service of course, but too often I think women believe that these are the only options, and anything else is selfish.

Ultimately, I am all I have. I cannot choose the path my children will take, I cannot foresee the choices my husband will make. I do not know where this journey will lead me, and I am the only thing that I can control. So forming and nurturing my inner self should be one of my greatest priorities, not the last "to do" on the list. And for many women, a career is a great tool for inner development, for learning and growth. And that matters immensely.

"Moral Authority" by Lisa Patterson Butterworth (November 8, 2004)

I'm having an angry feminist moment. I followed a link from T&S[18] over to this Moral Politics Test. It's a fun (if sometimes poorly worded) test. You should try it. And anyway, I got to this question and had to pause:

6. About men and women:
- A. Men and women are equal. (Society should treat men and women in the same way in all domains and actively prevent disparities.)
- B. Men and women are different. (Men and women should play different roles in families and society.)
- C. Men have moral authority over women. (Men should have a very important or final say in women's lives.)
- D. Men and women are different, but equal. (Men and women are equal but biological differences suggest that they can play different roles in certain contexts.)

I believe D. Both A & B are ... incomplete. And C I find repugnant. And yet ... C is my life. As a Mormon, in ways both implicit and explicit, C is my life.

You can couch it in whatever kind of language you want, you can justify it however you like. But if you boil Mormon gender belief down to one simple statement, C is that statement, and that makes me ill.

How do I reconcile this?

Consider the Proclamation on the Family's[19] statement: "By divine design, fathers are to preside over their families." And the all-male priesthood and its clear-cut "Moral Authority." Both absolutely, explicitly firm on where "Moral Authority" presides within my religion.

I hear "equally yoked." I hear "righteous dominion." But frankly, right now that does not satisfy. It rings hollow. It sounds like a sorry excuse. And it changes nothing.

I used to say that I could accept my husband's presiding authority only because he was the most perfect man in the universe. Any other man, and NO WAY IN HELL. But I don't believe that any more. My husband is still the most perfect man in the universe, but he does not preside here. There is nothing about his maleness, his priesthood, his role as father that gives him the last word or one more speck of authority in this house than I have. Nothing. Nor do I have that last word for that matter.

If we ever got to a point of disagreement where compromise and negotiation could not solve the problem, I would not submit to him. I do not foresee this ever happening. After eleven plus years together, the give and take runs so smoothly around here that we hardly even notice it anymore. But the point is, I would not submit, and I think he would find it as ridiculous as I that I should be expected to.

I'm sure most of us would agree that this is the way things should work. Healthy marriages do not require nor ask for submission. So then why give authority to preside at all? If that authority cannot be used righteously (and I dare you to think of an example where a husband could justly demand that a wife submit), then the power should not be given at all. Church authority is somewhat different. The gospel is based on having the proper authority. I know submission to this authority is cornerstone. I've heard all the arguments about why this authority is solely in the hands of men. Frankly, so far as I've ever heard, they're not very persuasive.

All those people who point out that if you feel you have to elaborately justify a behavior then that behavior is probably wrong—think about that for a moment. All this elaborate justification: what does it signify?

Of course I'm power-grubbing and selfish for pointing this out. But the thing is, I'm not. My ambition-o-meter hovers somewhere near zero. Most of the time I don't have strong feelings about women getting the priesthood. It's right there in my "whatever" file of things I don't feel like worrying about because I'm lazy and busy and I'd rather spend my time reading romance novels.

I refuse to believe that God would want men to have moral authority over women. And how do I reconcile that with my belief in the Gospel?

And don't make this into a semantics game about the meaning of "moral authority." Bill Clinton already tried that and it's lame. And I know all about the "I'd be fine with women getting the priesthood if the Lord revealed it" argument that releases you from having an opinion on the matter. If that's how you feel, and you've no interest in thinking for yourself, then sit on your hands. I've heard you before.

Would you, in good conscience, check C? And if not, how can you say you believe in the male-only priesthood?

"CULTURE SHOCK" BY LISA PATTERSON BUTTERWORTH (NOVEMBER 8, 2004)

My post last night[20] was pretty harsh, and I can understand why it made a lot of people feel uncomfortable. I'm about as subtle as a brick and I seem to have a gift for using language powerfully. Someone even commented that I'm an evil spirit, which is also pretty harsh, but I can sympathize with her discomfort.

If you don't feel comfortable here, I'll be sad to see you go, but we all are in different places in our lives. I can't watch the news right now. As sad as I am about what's happening in Darfur, I can't face the stories that come out of there. A woman with a handful of rice to feed her five children, but no wood to cook it with. And the risk of looking for very scarce fuel is the risk of being gang raped by thugs. The cold hard truth of it is too much for me right now and my spirit isn't strong enough to deal with it.

I can understand if you feel that way about my opinions. It's okay to avoid the questions if they hurt you too much right now. Or ever. And certainly never do anything that will drive you away from the church.

I don't think I'm evil or that my thoughts (while they could have been more balanced, the risks of posting at two in the morning I suppose) are inspired by Satan. They're just my honest facing of the truth as I see it. Blunt is my culture, and it's not so much the culture of the church.

I suspect what many of you are feeling is not a spirit of evil, but the discomfort of culture shock. I experienced it too, when I discovered I had questions I couldn't ignore anymore and opinions that were no longer mainstream. It was not easy for me to find a place where I could have both my faith and my honest questions. I guess maybe I hoped this would be a place where we could explore that territory together. But I will not believe that my belief in the value of hard questions and my belief in the divine and overlooked worth of women is based in the spirit of evil.

Have you ever taken note of the intense discomfort you feel in the midst of a different culture? I know I've felt it, surrounded by Mexicans, surrounded by Muslims, surrounded by Baptists. Not knowing quite what to say, not feeling like I fit in, wanting to go back to where I feel safe and comfortable and welcome. But that feeling is just one of human nature, Mexicans and Muslims and Baptists are not evil. The discomfort I sometimes feel isn't based in the fact that their cultures are wrong, it's just that I don't know how to navigate myself there, I don't know how welcome I am, I don't know if I will be accepted, or how these new people and ideas fit into my already formed worldview.

Yes, please avoid evil influence. But also be careful that you don't confuse evil influence with plain old human discomfort at brushing up with the unknown. It's for you to decide. Pray about it, avoid me, do whatever you need to do to feel okay with yourself.

I for one will be working on my social skills, once again. I've driven off my friends at an alarming rate and I just don't like that. Time for me to go off and grow.

This year marked 200 years since the birth of LDS Church–founder Joseph Smith. Brigham Young University and the United States Library of Congress co-sponsored a conference titled "The Worlds of Joseph Smith," which took place in Washington, D.C. in May. Later that year, the inaugural season of the Nauvoo Pageant in Nauvoo, Illinois, was part of that celebration. The performance depicted various scenes from the Nauvoo Period of Church history and honored Smith's prophetic mission. The course of study for adult Gospel Doctrine classes throughout the world focused on the teachings of Joseph Smith.

Richard Bushman published his definitive biography, *Joseph Smith: Rough Stone Rolling.*[21] It won the Best Book Award in 2005 from the Mormon History Association and changed the direction of the conversation surrounding Smith within the LDS Church. On July 26, *The Salt Lake Tribune* published an article titled "Keeping Members a Challenge for LDS Church," written by Peggy Fletcher Stack. The article documented available research on the growth of Church membership and rates of retention. Low estimates of church attendance and engagement demonstrated that the days of rapid growth were over.

Mormon feminists published the first issue of *Segullah* in the spring, with a mission "to encourage literary talent, provoke thought and promote greater understanding and faith."[22] Founded by Kathryn Soper, Kylie Turley, and Justine Dorton, this addition to the Mormon feminist landscape featured essays, poetry, and visual art from Mormon women. John Dehlin launched and hosted Mormon Stories, a podcast featuring in-depth interviews with newsworthy Mormons and wide-ranging examinations of controversial aspects of Mormon history and culture. These were both significant additions to the Mormon blogosphere, known as the bloggernacle.

Over the course of 2005, Feminist Mormon Housewives published over 300 new blog posts. Most of the content continued to be written by founder Lisa Patterson Butterworth (under the pseudonym fmhLisa). The blog added five new permabloggers: Kris, Rebecca, Rachael Lauritzen/Artemis, Emily Summerhays/Athena (later amended to EmilyS), and LisaB. The blog's popularity escalated in March, when FMH was featured in a *New York Times* piece on the growth of religiously themed blogs. Reporter Debra Nussbaum Cohen identified "the universal challenges of mothering young children"[23] as an emerging theme at FMH.

This focus was due largely to the fact that fmhLisa, founder and most significant contributor, was tending to her three small children at the time. This prompted her to write such classic posts as The Poop Chronicles, which documented some of the most frustrating and yuck-inducing moments of parenthood. Other writers, however, brought their own experiences to bear, and the conversations ranged widely in both topic and tone.

"DESPERATE HOUSEWIVES"[24] BY LISA PATTERSON BUTTERWORTH (JANUARY 7, 2005)

I've never seen it. Not that I'm one of those snooty I'm-too-erudite-to-watch-the-trash-on-TV types. No, I like trash quite a bit, I've got low-brow tastes aplenty. It's just that my kids don't really allow me to watch TV. So I've never seen it.

However, did anyone else hear Terri Gross's (I heart TG) interview with the guy who writes this show? It was really interesting. He was talking about his inspiration for the first script and it's pretty dark, but it held a lot of truth for my own life. He was sitting with his mother when he heard the news about Andrea Yates drowning her five kids. He commented, "What could drive a woman to do that?" And his mother replied, "I've been there."

My reaction at the time was much the same. I haven't "been there" exactly, but I've been a few miles down the road. Close enough that I can sympathize with the mental state that could get to that point. I've been in some pretty dark, postpartum, too-many-toddlers-and-I'm-not-okay places. I never got to a really scary place because I have a truckload of fabulous resources, a sympathetic husband, supportive parents, sisters, friends, doctors, financial resources, kickboxing. But take away all those supports, give me five rowdy homeschooled boys, some fundamentalist Christian propaganda, and . . . well, it scares the hell out of me.

Anyway this writer guy went on to say how the seeds of that idea grew into *Desperate Housewives*. Because like many housewives of that era (and this one), his mother was living her dream. A nice husband, a lovely home, beautiful children. She had everything she had ever hoped for and she was still desperately miserable. He talked about how that is a really special kind of desperation. Not the desperation of dreams unfulfilled, but of a dream fulfilled and found to be empty.

I'm not sure I ever really had the goal to be a housewife. I don't think I did. I'm here because it's practical, because I couldn't make enough money to put my three kids under four in day care. And only to a lesser degree because the thought of them being raised by someone else for ten hours a day hurts my stomach. I'm here because I'm lucky enough to have a husband who will do the daily grind and be miserable in his yuck job so that our kids can have their mom at home. So when I feel unfulfilled by this role, which is the case 98.5% of the mind-numbing-drudgery time, it's not that big a crisis for me in the unfulfilled dreams sense, because this was never my dream to begin with. And in a sick way, it also helps that the dear husband hates his job too. I think I'd be bitter if he went off and enjoyed himself everyday while I clean up poop.

This has me wondering:

Are all housewives miserable? Because I'm pretty sure that most of the ones I know are. And I always suspect in my heart of hearts that the ones that seem to like it are faking.

"PROCLAMATION CONFESSION" BY LISA PATTERSON BUTTERWORTH (JANUARY 21, 2005)

Oh goodness. Now the kids are in bed, the baby is done crying, I've cleaned up ten pee spots off the floor (why couldn't she just pee in one spot?), still have to do the dishes and clean the blue finger paints the four-year-old found and blue-man-grouped all her dolls with. But now I will take a second to answer Julie's question.[25]

Hum, what do I despise about the Proclamation? Oh how do I hate thee, let me count the ways.

Let's start with the whole preside thing. Preside? Nope, I don't think so. I'm not even interested in debating this because it'll just make me insane and I'm already crazy enough.

That's enough really. I don't need more reasons, the preside bit alone is enough.

I didn't come to the decision to hate it easily btw, and I do believe this is the first time I've expressed my feelings. But I cringed the first time I heard it, even before I took on the feminist mantle, and I haven't stopped cringing since. And now that I consider myself a full-fledged fire-breathing feminist with an agenda, I've given myself permission to *hate* it. It's kinda freeing actually, to admit I think the preside crap is pure stinky yucky ugliness.

I like to think that if I'd been old enough to hate the black priesthood ban with equal voracity, I would have done so. And knowing myself, I think that's a distinct possibility. I certainly hate it that much now. Also a bunch of pure stinky yucky ugliness.

Come on people. Did any of you read that preside thing and not cringe? In your gut, admit it, you felt it: that clenching up of the stomach muscles, the tightening of the skin on the back of the neck, perhaps a little tingling along the scalp. Yup, I thought so.

And you know what I hate most of all? The thought of all you priesthood-holding men reading this right now, most of you excellent and thoughtful husbands and fathers who never in actual practice preside. You respect your wives, trust and admire them, are for all practical purposes "equally yoked." But you sit here with smug assurance that you naturally come by that preside right by way of your Y chromosome.

And I wonder, how would that be? To just know, your whole life, that you're the one who gets to make the choices? You're the one who gets to preside? And how did you earn that privilege exactly? It's not earned then? It's granted by God. Oh that's nice, so why do *you* get it? Because let me let you in on a little secret, fellas: you can preside and nurture and not one soul will fault you for it. But not me. Nope, I only get one half of that pie.

And I'm ungrateful and misinformed and unfaithful and (gasp) ambitious because I don't like it. Because I don't believe it. Well, let me tell you what I think. It's crap. Amen.

The rest of the proclamation I'm more ambivalent about, I don't exactly love it, but there's more room for not hating it. I guess maybe I could go into more detail, but not tonight. I've got dishes and they're making the place stink like old Mexican food. Which I suppose is better than "stink like old Mexican foot," which is what I wrote the first time.

"COMMEMORATING THE FOUNDING OF RELIEF SOCIETY AND THE PROBLEM OF MORMON WOMEN'S HISTORY" BY KRIS WRIGHT (MARCH 20, 2005)

March 17th was the anniversary of the founding of the Relief Society. It seems there wasn't much mention of it around the bloggernacle, including here.

About a month ago, our Relief Society President announced to the RS board the plans for our Relief Society Commemorative Dinner. Each member of the board was going to be assigned a General Relief Society President, read up on her (with materials provided), come in character, and give a 3 minute address about each woman after the meal. I sat nervously, waiting to get my assignment. Would I be Sister Smoot? Sister Winder? Eliza R. Snow? As Sister C. read through the names, I thought to myself, "Please let me be Emmeline B. Wells. Please let it be Sister Wells." Sure enough, when my name was called, I was given a package of articles on the very person I had hoped to be. (More on this later.) As I looked over the articles, I couldn't help but wonder if a train wreck was coming.

On Friday afternoon, I was talking to one of my friends and asked, "So, are you all ready to be Eliza R. Snow tomorrow night?"

"No!" came the emphatic reply. "What am I supposed to talk about? Women giving healing blessings? Eliza's polygamous marriages to both Joseph and Brigham? Heavenly Mother?"

"Well, I'm not sure that's what Sister C. had in mind."

"Did you know about this kind of stuff?"

"Like what? The healing blessings?"

"Yes!"

"Um, yeah, I do and-"

"Well, what am I supposed to do with this? This makes me feel really uncomfortable! I've been freaking out all week!"

"Like how? Uncomfortable because the women were giving healing blessings, or uncomfortable because we don't do it now?"

"Uncomfortable because I don't understand why women still don't have those kind of experiences."

"Well, I understand that. Do-"

"Why haven't I heard of this before?"

"I don't know. It just doesn't seem to be the kind of thing we talk about in Relief Society or other meetings. For some reason, it seems to be, well, sort of taboo. . . ."

Our conversation continued for quite a while. Among many things I came away with was the idea that there are many problems in how we approach Mormon women's history. In 1993, Jan Shipps wrote an article that was published in *The Christian Century* titled, "Dangerous History: Laurel Ulrich and Her Mormon Sisters"[26] (also included in Shipps's recent book *Sojourner in the Promised Land: Forty Years among the Mormons).*[27] Shipps seems to be saying that Mormon women's history is "dangerous" because of the feminist theology that flows from it, and she claims that Mormon women do not have the "authority" to interpret their own history. She states that LDS leaders have a

> concern about how Mormon women's history is being used to call into question the church's conservative stance on the role of women, and also how history seems to be driving the development of an LDS feminist theology centered on the Mormon concept of a Mother in Heaven, a deity (consort to God the Father) whose existence was described in an 1845 poem written by Eliza R. Snow (arguably the most notable female Mormon in the history of the movement).[28]

How do we teach the history of women in the church without glossing over these issues? Have things changed much since 1993 when this piece was written? Is it important for LDS women to know their history? Could Mormon women's history actually be dangerous?

"POWER HUNGRY" BY LORIE WINDER STROMBERG (APRIL 14, 2005)

In "Why Don't Women Hold the Priesthood? A Brief but Insightful Interview," Betina Lindsey[29] wrote:

> On a June morning in 1988, I was cooking pancakes for my eleven-year-old son and his friends after a sleep-over. Twelve-

24

year-old David had recently been ordained to the priesthood and the other boys were asking how many times he'd passed the sacrament. While slapping a few more pancakes on their plates, I asked, 'Why don't women hold the priesthood?' Their answers were as follows:

DAVID: (age 12) 'Men have better looks.'

ROBERT: (age 13) 'Some women have their priorities wrong and men are more distinguished.'

STRYDER: (age 11) 'My sister's Sunday School teacher said giving women the priesthood would be like giving them an open-ended credit card.'

RICKY: (age 11) 'My grandpa says maybe they'll get it in heaven.'

ROBERT: 'Women aren't strong enough because it would fatigue them like when Jesus blessed people he would get weak.'

DAVID: 'Yea, if women had the priesthood they might beat the men up.'

ROBERT: 'And women have their times when they aren't cooperative and I give you my permission to quote me.' (He's a lawyer's son.)

ERIC: (age 8—interrupting impatiently) 'Hey, you guys, let's go play Power Lords.'

RICKY: (Hurriedly stuffing the last bit of pancake into his mouth) 'Well, I think (long pause with a shake of his head) I don't know why.'

End of pancakes. End of interview. Exit Power Lords.

David's comment, "Yea, if women had the priesthood they might beat up the men," is revealing. In David's mind, and the minds of countless others, power is perceived as devouring, as dominating and coercive. This is why feminists are derisively accused of being power hungry, as if wanting power were necessarily a bad thing.

And it is, if it is only seen as coercive and controlling. But I've spent too many years on the defensive. It's time I owned the term. Perhaps I am power hungry.

And my question is: Why aren't we all?

If by power hungry you mean I desire the ability not only to accept responsibilities in the institutional Church but to be part of defining what those responsibilities are, then, yes, I'm power hungry. Over the years, many Church leaders have asserted that we should be talking more about taking responsibility than exercising or demanding rights.[30] This privileging of responsibility over rights for women is problematic. In a discussion with Margaret Toscano, she suggested that Mormon women seem to have plenty of delegated responsibilities. It is their right within the organization to oversee and establish their responsibilities that is lacking. Responsibility devoid of rights is servitude.

I'm weary of the false dichotomies that are set up for women in the Church. Both former Relief Society General President Barbara B. Smith and Russell M. Nelson have suggested that Mormon women ought to choose integrity over visibility, charity over charisma.[31] What is wrong with having both integrity and visibility, both charity and charisma? Obviously, members of the Church's male hierarchy don't have to make such choices, so why should women?

If by power hungry you mean I believe women must have a voice in the Church, then, yes, I'm power hungry. In a panel discussion on working with women presented at the 1993 BYU Women's Conference, several male panelists admitted that they were never forced to take women seriously until they became colleagues.[32] While their emphasis was on a secular setting, the question and answer period exploded with faithful, mainstream Mormon women wondering how they could get their Church leaders to listen to them. It was obvious to me, and I said so during the session—women in the Church would never have a voice until, as in the secular arena, they were seen as colleagues, in this case spiritual colleagues, within the power structure of the Church.

If by power hungry you mean I believe that women should not only be represented but should be an integral part of every major decision-making body of the Church, then, yes, I'm power hungry. I've often said that I'm passionately ambivalent about priesthood. I'm not fond of hierarchies and am leery of structures that promote them because they are almost always abusive. However, having power within an institution is preferable to institutional powerlessness, particularly if we are able as women to bring the consciousness of what it is like on the margins to the center of our religious community.

Positional power in the Church is granted primarily to those who hold the priesthood. This is particularly true above the local level. While a charismatic woman might have significant influence on the ward or, perhaps, even the stake level, thereafter positional power for women in the Church evaporates. Since, for the most part, we no longer recognize charismatic power in the Church—only positional power—can women have equal status to men in the Church without being ordained to the priesthood?

Recognizing the inequity inherent in an all-male priesthood, Bruce Hafen[33] tried to minimize its importance. In a keynote address at the 1985 BYU Women's Conference titled "Women, Feminism and the Blessings of the Priesthood,"[34] Hafen listed several of the blessings that were available to both men and women in the Church. As if it were a mere trifle he added,

> The one category of blessing in which the role of women is
> not the same as that of men holding the priesthood is that of
> administering the gospel and governing all things.

How could Hafen deliver this line with a straight face, and, perhaps even more disturbing, how could his audience of women listen to it in silence?

If by power hungry you mean I would welcome a heightened ability to bless the lives of others, then, yes, I'm power hungry. Aside from its administrative function, if priesthood is merely a sort of temporal permission to tap spiritual resources already available to the faithful, then it is superfluous. If, however, it truly is a real, bestowed power that can enhance our ability to bring comfort and peace and joy into the world, then, yes, I'm power hungry and unambivalently so. Who would not righteously want it?

Finally, if by power hungry you mean I want the ability to participate in a model of power based on partnership rather than patriarchy, based on empowerment rather than domination, then, yes, I'm power hungry. Scott Bartchy, UCLA professor of Christian origins and early Church history, gave a presentation at Sunstone[35] in which he declared that Christ came to overthrow traditional models of power, which were based on domination, coercion, and control. In their place, he offered a model of power in which power is used to empower. Power used to dominate, coerce, or control will always burn itself out, asserted Bartchy. Only power used to empower is everlasting.

By now I've given sufficient weight to the word power in the term power hungry. Alas, I've neglected the word hungry. Just as by power I do not mean domination or coercion, but rather voice and influence and empowerment, so by hungry I do not mean gluttony. I'm talking about sustenance. I'm talking about a soul-deep yearning for a life-sustaining, sacramental meal to which all are invited.

"IN SEARCH OF MORMON FEMINISM: A CONVERSATION WITH LORIE WINDER STROMBERG" BY KRIS WRIGHT (APRIL 20, 2005)

For the first in a series of interviews called "In Search of Mormon Feminism," we asked Lorie Winder Stromberg a few questions. Lorie graduated with a M.A. in humanities from Brigham Young University. She was the editor of the *Mormon Women's Forum Quarterly* for seven years. Her essay "Power Hungry" can be read here.[36]

1. How did you come to identify yourself as a feminist?

I date my feminism from 1973 when I was invited by a BYU Family Home Evening sister to attend a meeting of the Utah Valley Chapter of the Women's Political Caucus. The discussion focused on The Equal Rights

Amendment, which had passed Congress in 1972 and was being ratified by the States. I was converted. However, it took me a few years to transfer my new-found feminist sensibilities from the secular to the religious arena. When the LDS Church came out against the ERA, I initially questioned my commitment to the controversial amendment. However, after reexamining all the arguments, I decided I could not in good conscience adopt the Church's position on this issue. This process freed me to question other issues, beliefs, and practices, including the Church's patriarchal underpinnings.

When I finished my master's degree, I moved to Boston, in part because I wanted to work with Exponent II and get to know other LDS feminists. I moved back to Utah a few years later and became acquainted with a whole network of Mormon feminists, in addition to the Boston group, who were rediscovering Mormon women's history, sponsoring retreats and public forums, and publishing essays that challenged traditional views of gender, history, theology and social mores. These associations and avenues of discussion were very important in shaping my feminism, particularly because I finished college a few years before the explosion of feminist theory and scholarship.

2. Within LDS culture, many feel that "faithful" and "feminist" are opposite terms. What is your personal definition of a Mormon feminist?

Quite simply, a Mormon feminist is a woman or man who self-identifies as Mormon and feminist, whatever their attachment to the Church or definition of feminism might be. There are all sorts of feminists, just as there are all sorts of Mormons. I'm careful not to make judgments about the faithfulness of either.

3. You were the editor of the *Mormon Women's Forum Quarterly* for seven years. What are some of the more memorable experiences and impressions that you came away with from working in that position?

I loved working with the women and men who founded and supported the Mormon Women's Forum. I'm especially proud of the issues we tackled in public lectures and discussions and in the *Mormon Women's Forum Quarterly*, such as Sonja Farnsworth's dissection of the priesthood/motherhood concept; the Carol Lynn Pearson, Rodney Turner, Paul Toscano and Kathleen Woodbury panel on the worship of God the Mother; Lavina Fielding Anderson's chronologies of issues and events affecting contemporary Mormon women and the Church; Kristin Rushforth's essay on feminist activism at BYU during the late 1980s and early 1990s and VOICE, BYU's Committee to Promote the Status of Women; Alison Walker's feminist interpretation of the atonement; Marion B. Smith and Linda King Newell's insights with regard to the syndrome of silence surrounding sexual abuse in the Church and Church history, respectively; Lynn Matthews Anderson's witty "Questions to Gospel

Answers" column; Margaret Toscano's presentation on human and divine images of the female body and how they affect the ways Mormon women see themselves; Janice Allred's wrenching account of her excommunication for refusing to be silent; Nadine Hansen's paper "Women, Priesthood and the RLDS Experience"; Arta and Rebecca Johnson's insightful look at the patriarchal imperatives in personal and Church discourse; and interviews with Kelli Frame and Lee Partridge on being Mormon and lesbian, Utah's Episcopal Bishop Carolyn Tanner Irish, and Marti Bradley and Bill Evenson on academic freedom at BYU. I'm also proud of a couple of things I did while editor of the *MWF Quarterly*, including putting together a panel with Nadine Hansen and John Tarjan on ecclesiastical sexual harassment and compiling a sort of reader's theater piece featuring posts excerpted (with permission) from various Mormon feminist lists called "The Sacred and the Mundane: Mormon Feminism on the Internet."[37]

The downside of being engaged in Mormon feminist activism in the 1990s was that the spate of excommunications made the whole Mormon feminist community skittish. Out of that skittishness there seemed to emerge a sense that there were "good feminists"—those who were more like the women of *Exponent II*, none of whom had been excommunicated— and "bad feminists"—those who were a little more likely to push the envelope and put their membership on the line. Having been involved with both groups, I think the characterization was false. However, the issue that seemed to be the flashpoint was the question of women and priesthood ordination.

4. What do you feel are the main issues that LDS feminists are facing today?

Years ago I predicted that if the LDS church didn't abandon patriarchy, ordain women and integrate them into its power structure, it would lose a generation or more of bright, young women and some older ones who valued their Mormonism but were tired of waiting. As the gap between Church norms and societal norms for women grew, I opined, many women would leave, and we would be left predominantly with a female membership that was frustrated and depressed and didn't know why or more conservative and, thus, more accepting of the status quo.

Because of the threat of Church disciplinary action following Sonia Johnson's excommunication[38] and those of a decade ago, feminists who stay in the Church are often afraid to speak out. How can we expect change if we are silent? Are we willing to live with the possible consequences in either case?

5. "Power Hungry" is a forthright and potent essay. How did you come to "own" this term?

I suppose I got tired of taking a defensive posture, of feeling that I somehow had to justify my feminism to members of the Church. I no longer feel that way. It is clear to me that underlying such ridiculous comments as, "Women are more spiritual than men and, therefore, don't need the priesthood," is a tacit recognition of, but unwillingness to face, the inequity of women's position in the Church. Using "power hungry" was a rhetorical device, a way of playfully re-appropriating a negative term so often flung at feminists, much like gays have re-appropriated the term "queer."

6. You have noted that an article by Peggy Fletcher Stack, which raises the question, "Where have all the Mormon feminists gone?"[39] overlooks the Internet and the place of electronic lists. What are your impressions of the role and importance of the Internet to LDS feminists?

Dialogue, Sunstone, the Sunstone Symposium, *Exponent II* and the *Mormon Women's Forum Quarterly* have provided an invaluable, though by their very nature limited, public platform for the discussion of Mormon feminist issues; however, the Internet has the capacity to reach a much broader audience and facilitate activism through discussion lists, blogs and websites. Your blog, for instance, has received thousands of hits. That's mind boggling. It remains to be seen how or if such sites will have any effect on Church practice or policy.

7. What is your vision for the women of the Church? What advice would you give to a new generation of Mormon feminists?

After 30 years of activism, I'm feeling pretty tired and cynical. I was pleasantly surprised to learn about your blog since many of the younger feminists I know have left the Church. However, it also saddens me that, after 30 years, we're still talking about the same issues: How can women have a voice in a patriarchal institution? How do we combat sexual abuse in a Church where all men are seen as possessing a spiritual authority women don't have? How do we deal with the schizophrenic messages that tell us men ought to preside over their families but also see their wives as partners? How do we live with the disconnect between sharing equal status with male coworkers in the secular sphere and taking a back seat at Church? How do we justify remaining part of an institution that encourages women to participate in their own subordination? Where is God the Mother in all of this? Perhaps we're trying to reconcile the irreconcilable.

"IN SEARCH OF MORMON FEMINISM: A CONVERSATION WITH LAUREL THATCHER ULRICH" BY KRIS WRIGHT (MAY 16, 2005)

Laurel Thatcher Ulrich is the James Duncan Phillips Professor of Early American History at Harvard University. A graduate of the University of New Hampshire, where she taught for many years, she is the author of numerous articles and essays on early American history. She won the

Pulitzer Prize for History in 1991 for *A Midwife's Tale: The Life of Martha Ballard, Based on Her Diary, 1785–1812*.[40] During her tenure as a MacArthur Fellow, she assisted in the production of a documentary film based on *A Midwife's Tale* that aired on the PBS series *The American Experience*. Professor Ulrich's work is also featured on a prize-winning website dohistory.org. Her most recent book *The Age of Homespun: Objects and Stories in the Creation of an American Myth*[41] explores the production and consumption as well as the social meanings of textiles in pre-industrial New England.

Laurel Thatcher Ulrich is also one of the original members of a Boston collective who founded *Exponent II*. She has published many personal essays in "periodicals associated with the unsponsored sector of contemporary Mormonism." Several of these essays can also be found in *All God's Critters Got a Place in the Choir*,[42] which she co-authored with poet, Emma Lou Thayne. I am grateful to Sister Ulrich for taking time out of an extremely busy schedule to answer a few questions about feminism, history and Mormonism.

1. There are many people who think that Mormonism and feminism are incompatible and cannot coexist. Others say that Mormon feminism is dead. How do you respond? What is your personal definition of Mormon feminism?

Well, this blog would seem to answer your first and second questions. If there are women out there claiming to be "feminist Mormon housewives," then they must coexist. I am not sure I have a definition of "Mormon feminism" as a discrete entity. I am more interested in persons (male or female) who claim to be Mormons and feminists. Each of us has multiple identities. My Mormonism and my feminism intersect in a belief in the absolute equality of all of God's children and in a belief that we have a responsibility to make the world better.

2. How did you come to identify yourself as a feminist?

I probably began using the word around 1970 when the group of women who eventually founded *Exponent II* began meeting to talk about the implications of the new women's movement for our lives.

3. You are the author of several acclaimed women's history books. How has your work as a historian and feminist scholar affected your religious feminism?

This is a big question. Mostly it has taught me that the issues Latter-day Saint women face are part of much bigger problems. Being a historian gives me a perspective on how things change. It doesn't tell me what to do, but it broadens my experience of the world and of humankind. I sometimes say that I am an "evangelist for history." I really think it helps to take the "long view" of things. But the relationship between my profession and my faith goes both ways. My Mormonism constantly informs my scholarship, in ways that are no doubt too subtle to see. I'm quite sure that my sense of history came from what the church now calls "family history" and what we used to call "genealogy." I was fortunate in having parents and grandparents who told stories about "pioneer days." But it goes beyond that to a fundamental outlook on what matters. I think the small details of ordinary life matter. Seeing religion work (and not work) among people I know well enlarges my capacity to understand its power in the past as well. It doesn't tell me about the details or theology or replicate precise contexts, but it helps me sympathize in ways I might not be able to do if I had a purely secular outlook. Readers who want to know more about the relationship between my personal life and my scholarship might enjoy "A Pail of Cream," an issue published in *The Journal of American History* 89 (2002): 43–47.[43] I think it can be found online.

4. Some have questioned whether second-wave feminism has any relevance or appeal to today's young Mormon women? What are the accomplishments of second-wave Mormon feminists? What were the challenges? What do you think the legacy of *Exponent II* and the group of women who founded it is?

For the challenges read Claudia Bushman, "My Short Happy Life with *Exponent II*," in *Dialogue* Fall 2003.[44] I think somebody needs to do a serious study of the accomplishments. It is easy to remember the pain and suffering, the excommunications and the like, harder at this distance to list the achievements. I think there are many. At the top of my list (remember I am an evangelist for history) is the rich and still growing scholarship in Mormon women's history. Popular history in and outside the church hasn't even begun to absorb this marvelous work—but it is there and it will endure. A second obvious achievement is what feminist discourse has done for women's own lives. I see self-confident young women all around me who probably could not be doing what they are doing if it had not been for the pioneering work of their literal and figurative "mothers." Then there are some small things, like two-piece garments and changing platforms in ward buildings.[45] Believe it or not, those things didn't just happen!

5. What have been the issues facing Mormon feminists in the period after September 1993?

Discouragement. Backlash. The growing conservatism of the larger society and the Church. On a larger scale, I think the biggest challenge is in knowing what our responsibilities are in the larger world. War, the disruptions of the global economy, pornography, sex trafficking, poverty and growing inequality in the United States, lack of respect for mothering and the "helping professions" in general—like public school teaching, nursing, and social work. Plenty of challenges for Mormons who take their faith seriously.

6. Jan Shipps has said it is "dangerous" to do Mormon women's history because of the feminist theology that flows from it.[46] Is she correct

in this assertion and in concluding that Mormon women historians cannot be permitted any authority in interpreting Mormon women's history?

I am trying to remember exactly what she said. Since I haven't read her essay in a while, I'll just have to respond to your general question, whether it is "dangerous" for Mormon women to interpret their own history. I'd say that historians (male or female) who presume to define Mormon theology can get in big trouble institutionally if their ideas counter those of current General Authorities—but that isn't a problem confined to women. Because our faith is so bound up with our history, reinterpreting Mormon history can be threatening to some people. But here's where my broader orientation as a historian helps. Good history is almost always "dangerous." In the 1990s "history wars" broke out all over the United States—and in some places that continues. Think of the Thomas Jefferson/Sally Hemings debate, for example, or the argument over the Enola Gay exhibit at the Smithsonian (about the plane that dropped the atomic bomb on Hiroshima), or the arguments over slave reparations. Women's history was assaulted on many sides during this period. At one point, a congressman from the Midwest even attacked funding for the PBS documentary on my book *A Midwife's Tale*. Women's history is dangerous. That is why it is important. But if it is serious history—not slapdash research in the service of a cause, Mormon or otherwise—it can make a difference.

"CHRIST CENTERED MEETINGS" BY RACHAEL LAURITZEN (AUGUST 9, 2005)

I know that Joseph Smith was a prophet of God. I know tithing is a true principle. I know the pioneers went through a lot of difficult things, things I would definitely shrink from doing. I know we need to choose "good" friends who love us, uplift us, and inspire us. And I really do love my family and friends. Even a few neighbors and ward members.

But is this really what our church is all about?

I find myself growing increasingly dissatisfied with an absence of or, at best, a merely implied Christ-centered focus during church meetings. Maybe we all take it for granted that the Atonement of the Savior and our devotion to Him are truly the foundation of our church, gospel, and testimonies and that all other doctrines are merely appendages to it. However, I find it disturbing that my ward's "testimony" meetings rarely address this focus. It's especially evident in what the little kids generally say (because they are prompted to say it and/or they hear others say it, and it's the default, basic testimony format): "I know the church is true. I know Joseph Smith was a prophet and that Gordon B. Hinckley is a prophet today. I love my mom and dad and my brothers and sisters. I know the Book of Mormon is true. InthenameofJesusChristAmen." What really is the focus and what really is the appendage?

Now, I visited my parents' ward this last Fast & Testimony Sabbath and was delighted to hear much more Christ-centered messages than what I (cynically) expected to hear from my long conditioning. For me, this was obviously an exception. And testimony days are not the only offenders. How many talks on tithing and missionary work and pioneers and prophets and the word of wisdom and priesthood and the Book of Mormon have I heard with very little (if any) reference to the reason these doctrines actually mean anything to us? I mean, without the Savior, Jesus Christ, Redeemer, Son of God, and Mediator, then we might as well pack up the whole show and move on.

Why doesn't every talk or sermon given shape itself around and conclude with its relationship to Jesus Christ? Why do I pick up programs that have a quote by and picture of Ezra T. Benson and the name of the ward, but no mention of the Person whose church this is and whom we profess to worship? Why is it when I visit the tiny, local Baptist church, I hear more testimony of the Savior than I do in a month's worth of LDS meetings? Is it just my funny little corner of the Promised SLC[47] Valley that can't see the forest for the trees, or is this a church-wide trend? And how, oh how, do I persuade people to redirect their focus?

"FMHLISA'S ULTIMATE POLYGAMY POST" BY LISA PATTERSON BUTTERWORTH (OCTOBER 21, 2005)

It just occurred to me that I ought to put up some sort of disclaimer for non-Mormons who stumble upon this: This post will probably make absolutely no sense if you're not familiar with the Mormon view of the afterlife. And you'll probably think we're all a bunch of weirdos and you'd be correct.

I have very mixed feelings about polygamy.

On the one hand, in a detached sorta way, I like having ancestors strange and scandalous enough to be notorious. Polygamy makes for great reading, and just think of how yawn much of Mormon history would be without it. Really, how can you not take secret delight in the words, "My great-grandfather had 14 wives."

On the other hand, I'm a BIG fan of traditional monogamous pair bonds. They're so morally comfortable. They're so "in." Everyone is doing it.

On the (same) hand, all other considerations aside, I loathe the ultimate and inarguable imbalance of One Man, Many Women. I really hate that, it screams wrong to me deep in the pit of the stomach and on the back of my neck and in the curl of my toes. Wrong. Unbalanced. Servitudalamity. Bad. Yicky.

And the *our ways are not God's ways*, and *we can't really know how this will all look in the eternities* explanations . . . I'm not a big fan.

I can only understand what I can understand.

Which doesn't mean that my understanding, based on my 21st century morality system, is eternally right. But it is right for me, now. And I'm all I've got. And now is when I am. In my small brain.

I haven't the faintest notion what eternal marriage would, could, or should look like. Despite the way we talk sometimes, it can't just be about eternal procreation, because if that were the case couldn't the same thing be accomplished with heavenly lab assistants creating test-tube baby souls and planting them in spiritual uterine replicators for eternity? Silly I know, but my point is, procreation itself isn't the point, however that takes place, it isn't the point, it can't be, it's the relationships that matter. Husband/Wife, Parent/Child, God/Child, the relationships are the point.

Like I said, I don't know what eternal marriage looks like, but I do know that my earthly marriage is all about intimacy. I've shown my husband every dark corner of my soul, I've trusted him with every tender spot I have. And he still loves me, dark tender spots and all, and I trust that he always will. I give him those things, he gives them back. We are painfully vulnerable to each other. He could destroy me with a few misplaced words. But I trust that he won't.

It is my hope that this soul-soaked painfully exposed love is what eternal marriage is about. Because it is, in my opinion, the best feeling ever. Naked trust.

Sex is just sex. (I love sex!) I think I could live with my husband having sex with other women. If I knew his soul was still mine. (And he still had the energy to keep me satisfied, and let me tell you something, I have high standards.) Not saying I'd like it, I'm not sure it's even possible to separate the two, but in the end it's not the penis I care about, it's the heart, the soul, the brain, the essence of him that matters.

Polygyny, even in its presumably "ideal" form, assumes that I give my soul to him, Sister Wife Sarah gives her soul to him, Sister Wife Susan gives her soul to him, Sister Wife Sandy gives her soul to him, and yet, he's only got one soul to give back. He will have relationships with these women that are separate from me, from our bond, from our intimacy. Maybe it's possible in some plane removed from human weakness that this separate bond can be achieved without harming our intimacy, without secrets, without jealousy.

However, it would still be fundamentally unbalanced. I would have only him, and he would have all of us.

If this brand of "ideal" marriage really is possible, and if all involved really could be above jealousy, if love, soul-deep intimacy really could be shared in this way, then why should men have the opportunity to love so many and women be restricted to only one?

Honestly, I'm open to the idea that man plus woman (the bond my culture makes comfortable and attractive to me) may not be the only workable pattern, maybe not even the ideal. But I cannot fathom a reason why man plus women should be acceptable when other combinations are not. Why not woman plus men? Or other combinations?

The only explanation for this gender imbalance that makes any logical sense is one that I find very unappealing. Explanations tied to biological sex. Eggs are expensive, sperm is cheap. Collecting uteruses to spread your genetic material makes perfect sense. The opposite, not so much.

But despite the sordid facts of human history, women are not just uteruses to be collected. I know the world works this sexist way and probably always will. Because eggs will always be precious and sperm will always be cheap. But I don't believe the eternities work this way.

I do understand that we, Mormons, believe that gender, or sex rather (not the act, the characteristics, whatever those might be), is an eternal quality. I'm fine with that, I like being a woman, I like the idea of being a woman for eternity. But I can't imagine that eternity, that eternal relationships, would be defined by such base, terrestrial, biological constraints as gestation periods and uterine capacity and the ever manly concern that the child is really "his."

And racking my brain, I just can't think of any other reason for the inequality. If my husband can find eternal perfect love with a whole passel of women, and if this really is a great and wonderful thing, why can't I experience that same "joy"? If I am willing to share him, shouldn't he be willing to share me?

(And even saying that, I have to tell you, yicks me out more than a little. I'm really very fond of my cultural attachment to traditional pair bonds.)

Or am I completely wrong. Is it really about procreation? And the relationships are simply there to serve that sole purpose. Because if that is the case, it's not a heaven I even want to go to.

When women say "If I die, my husband better marry a woman I approve of" or "I would have to be Alpha Wife" I just know celestial glory can't really be like that. What would be "glorious" about a place full of strained unhappy unequal relationships?

This is where faith comes in for me, it will all work out. I can't quite make the (comfortable to me) pair-bond-for-everyone eternal marriage work out in my mind. I despise the inequitable implications of polygyny. And the eternal marriage free-for-all (debauchery-less, of course) lacks in appeal on many levels, although it seems the most likely to me. It certainly ties off more loose ends than the first two, you know the loose ends, the story of the woman whose first husband died on their honeymoon, and who raised ten kids with her second husband but couldn't be sealed to him. Those are the sort of loose ends that the free-for-all ties up nicely. Not to mention Joseph Smith's apparent proclivity for marrying women who already had husbands. Or Brigham Young's proclivity for marrying Joseph's widows.

Regardless, I'm serious when I say I'm not interested in polygyny in this world or the next. I simply can't imagine a circumstance under which it's anything but sexist, unequal, and tied to male-centric (terrestrial) reproductive concerns. If you've got a better imagination than mine, feel free to enlighten me.

Refrain from giving me Sunday school answers like: *"There will be more women than men in the CK."*[48]

Puh-lease, even if it is true, which I doubt, give Ebenezer 600 wives, there should still be 40 guys left over to be my husbands. Doh!

Or

"We just don't know the mind of God."

If that's all you've got, just keep your mouth shut. I'd love to hear some actual thoughts, holes in my thinking, leaps my imagination has not taken, or even your own opinion. But for that regurgitated tripe, just sit on your hands.

Or

"There is no imbalance, he has four thousand wives, but you get to be a MOTHER!"

If you say this, or any variation, I will find you, and I will slap you.

Or

"You are not humble enough to accept God's plan for you."

You don't know God's plan for me, so back off.

Or

"I'm righteous and you hurt my feelings."

My response is here.

Did I really stay up until 3AM to write this? My kids are going to tear me apart tomorrow.

"THE FELLOWSHIP OF THE PRIESTHOOD RING" BY EMILY SUMMERHAYS (OCTOBER 23, 2005)

I awakened today from my Sunday afternoon nap with the image in my mind of a circle of brethren blessing an infant. As I lay all snug in my blankets, I remembered how snug it felt to be inside just such a circle when I was confirmed, the world blocked out by so many suitcoats, the warm weight of so many large, steady hands balanced carefully on my bowed head. I thought about how comforting and powerful these circles seemed to me as a child, and how I would smile as groups of friends, cousins, uncles, and grandfathers would saunter up to the front of the room, clap each other on the shoulder, and close ranks around a tiny babe.

This image, brought no doubt to the front of my mind by having just read and reread J. Stapley's truly interesting posts on Women and the

Priesthood (found here and here—do read them[49]), is something I had not thought about in a long while (our ward doesn't get much action), and I found myself wondering what that tightly woven ring of woolen suit coats might feel like to a mother whose baby is cocooned inside of it, whose male family members form it, and who is essentially locked out of it. This circle is the first in a long line of blessings, ordinances, and ordinations—all of them milestones in the lives of her children, and all of them closed to her.

But why? Even leaving aside, for the moment, the question of women receiving ordination to the Priesthood, it would seem that there is no reason for women—right now, today—not to at least participate in these circles and join with their families in the laying on of hands, so long as a Priesthood holder does the talking. J. Stapley's most recent post quotes Joseph F. Smith on this matter:

> A wife does not hold the priesthood in connection with her husband, but she enjoys the benefits thereof with him; and if she is requested to lay hands on the sick with him, or with any other officer holding the Melchizedek priesthood, she may do so with perfect propriety. It is no uncommon thing for a man and wife unitedly to administer to their children, and the husband being mouth, he may properly say out of courtesy, "By authority of the holy priesthood in us vested."[50]

Granted, this quotation deals specifically with blessing the sick, but why could the concept not extend to things like baby blessings and confirmations, especially as they relate to mothers and children? Can there not be a middle ground that allows women participation in these sorts of events without compromising the male sphere of Priesthood holding (because I think we can all agree that the P-hood won't be given to women any time soon, if ever)?

I love these rings, and I count them among the more powerful images and experiences of my spiritual life. However, I can't help but wonder how much more powerful that ring image might be if it included the mothers, aunts, sisters, and grandmothers, too. How much more comforting might the weight of those hands be if it included the loving hands of a mother? How much stronger would the fabric of our membership be if we could witness not only the fellow-ship of these rings, but the intertwining love, strength, and faith of both sisters and brothers?

Or am I wrong? Is there something about the mere presence of women that would somehow undermine the power, authority, or mystique of the circle? Should there never be any middle ground, even if there could be?

"POWER MATTERS" BY JUDY CANNON (NOVEMBER 9, 2005)

This post was made to the Exponent II *Listserv Sept 21st of this year. It is reposted here with Judy's permission:*

I like the use of the concept of "soft power" and "hard power" in relation to women in the church. I think that it's true, on a day to day basis, many (if not most) women in the church feel perfectly fine about participation, treatment, and even exercise of power within a limited domain within the church. Most women are not treated as inferior by men, although there are certainly still cases in which chauvinism abounds. But I think the important thing to recognize is that whatever power women exercise in the church comes in the form of "soft power," or purely in the form of influence, rather than hard power, or decision making power.

As an example of this . . . a RS president can strongly influence the bishop on welfare issues regarding a woman and her family in the ward, which occurs frequently in our ward. But in the end, the RS pres. cannot say that welfare needs to be taken care of in a certain way in the ward. She cannot say give a food order to this family, or give monetary help to that family. She can suggest this to the bishop, but only the bishop can make that call. If the RS president disagrees, tough. The RS president can suggest names for the bishop to call to certain callings, but again, that is the bishop's call, he can agree to do it, or call someone else, she will accept whoever is called, even in the case of her own counselors.

Another arena of soft power that many women have access to is as mothers and wives. Women in the church such as mothers and wives of GAs and prophets can influence their way of seeing the world, raise future leaders in the church by giving them certain values, but in the end, only the men can make decisions and pronouncements that can govern the church. Thus, a wife and a mother can help her husband/son value care for the poor, anti-gay marriage values, etc., but in the end, only the priesthood holders can say as church policy that applies to each member of the church, women and men, that we should oppose gay marriage or support giving to the poor. Thus, women in the church can wield a lot of soft power, but no hard power. NONE.

So, within the church, it's nice that women are treated well, and thus, may feel very equal and "not need the priesthood." But realize that whatever influence women do hold depends SOLELY on a priesthood holder who ALLOWS her to influence him, and that he still possesses the right to reject any influence. Fortunately, we are now at the point where men are encouraged strongly to value the opinions of women within church hierarchy. But, in cases where men decide not to, there are no consequences. Until men decided that women can speak and pray in sacrament meeting, women could not do so. We depended on their enlightenment for our participation. This is why hard power differs from soft power. You can argue the importance of certain types of participation, but in the end, men decide how and in what form women participate (in all but ordinances), but certainly, it can change at any time as women have no access to change anything ourselves.

I contrast this to the feminist movement, in which women who may or may not have had soft power fought for hard power, through actual legislation that guaranteed rights and held penalties for abuses. There is much debate as to the positives and negatives of the feminist movement, but for me, the single crucial aspect of feminism that overrides all its negatives is that feminism recognized that "soft power" does not give women any real rights and feminism recognized the necessity of hard power, which forced society and men to guarantee rights for women whether they were inclined to or not.

I've had friends argue that women have had much "power" (soft) in the past but realize all the power was dependent on men to allow women to exercise that power. There may be many examples in history of women being educated, but these only occurred when men ALLOWED it. So, in cases where men didn't want women to be educated, they weren't. The women did not make these choices for themselves.

In the past, women may have been treated well in marriage, but in marriages where men abused wives, there was no penalty. It's easy to look back and, in our current progressive values of equality, many women don't feel the need for hard power. It seems like many of the legislated rights are not necessary or even important. But in the end, without the enforcement of any rights, there is always a chance they can be abused. For those who married non-abusive men, they may feel no need for legislation that punishes men for abuse, but wait until one woman gets abused, then it's clear that hard power is necessary.

This is the difference between some societies today, such as the regime under the Taliban, and our society. The Taliban can treat women well, but in the end, women have no recourse if men decide to turn on them. That is not true in the US. Without feminism, women were totally dependent on men to treat them well and to give them rights. This may have happened in some cases, but women could not ensure their own well-being. So, hard power means that women now have the right to self-determination.

Unfortunately, in the church, we women are still dependent on the goodwill of men, and thank heavens there is much of that goodwill amongst men in the church. But let's not deceive ourselves into now thinking that we actually hold any power. We don't. Thus, for me, women cannot be said to be equal within the church apparatus, regardless of how we might feel about it. Again, I'm not arguing that this is necessary for salvation, but the church organization as we know it on earth does not treat men and women equally.

According to the introduction to the Book of Mormon authored by Apostle Bruce R. McConkie in 1981, one of the groups in the book of scripture—the Lamanites—"are the principal ancestors of the American Indians." In October 2006, Church leaders revised this introductory statement to present the Lamanites as being "among the ancestors of the American Indians." In explanation of the change, a spokesperson for the Church said that the new word choice "takes into account details of Book of Mormon demography which are not known."[51] Many saw the language shift as a clear response to DNA research that cast doubt on the genetic connection between Native American peoples and their supposed Israelite ancestors.

The Church's complicated history with and relationship to polygamy was in the spotlight in 2006. In March, the HBO series *Big Love* premiered, telling the fictional story of a polygamist family living in Sandy, Utah. The show ran for six seasons and was met with critical acclaim, but The Church of Jesus Christ of Latter-day Saints responded with concerns. In an official statement, the Public Affairs Department criticized *Big Love* for how the series might minimize the seriousness of abuse in polygamous communities, "reinforce old and long-outdated stereotypes" about the mainstream Church's view of polygamy, and demonstrate "an unhealthy preoccupation with sex, coarse humor and foul language."[52] Later in 2006, real-life polygamist leader Warren Jeffs was arrested after being on the FBI's Most Wanted list for nearly four months. As the infamous president of the Fundamentalist Church of Jesus Christ of Latter-day Saints (FLDS), Jeffs was charged with committing a variety of sexual crimes in Arizona, Utah, and Texas and was eventually sentenced to life in prison.

Two new feminist-themed Mormon blogs arrived on the scene in 2006: Zelophehad's Daughters, started by a group of seven siblings (six sisters and one brother), and The Exponent blog, an extension of *Exponent II*, a printed periodical for Mormon women (founded in 1974). Both Zelophehad's Daughters and The Exponent blog would grow to have a clear voice and impact on the Mormon feminist community, amassing impressive archives on an endless variety of topics.

Feminist Mormon Housewives racked up some 375 posts in 2006, both from permabloggers (including new additions Janet and Nikki Matthews Hunter/Idahospud) and enthusiastic guest contributors. Several new series were initiated over the course of the year, including Dear FMH, featuring questions from blog readers, and Day in the Life, which invited active participants to write about a typical day in their lives in the comments section. The blog hosted discussions on *Women and Authority*,[53] early election speculation, negative temple experiences, and infertility, among other subjects, in this building year.

"KIDS, KID-GLOVES AND SELFISHNESS" BY PIPER ANDERSON/STARFOXY (JANUARY 22, 2006)

In my freshman high school English class we read a short story, which I cannot find or remember the name of.[54] In the story, a 19th century mother who had been wealthy as a child, but had been poor since she married, inherited a sum of money from a relative. Though her family was poor, they were not in debt, so the money was extra money.

The story begins as the mother arrives in the city planning to buy material to make new Sunday clothes for all of her children. As she enters the department store she sits down to take a rest and accidentally lays her hand on a pair of silk stockings. She remembers wearing them as a child and decides to buy a pair, thinking that she can get slightly less expensive material for her children. She continues in this fashion, until she has spent all of the money on an entirely new outfit for herself, including kid-gloves. With the little money left over she goes out for lunch, all the while remembering her childhood and the luxuries she once enjoyed.

As my class of infinitely wise (and fairly affluent) 15-year-olds discussed this, all of my classmates decided her behavior was reprehensible. I was the only one who claimed that most of us would have done the exact same thing. I particularly remember one boy saying, "How selfish could she be?"

Here's another story: It's 5:30 AM, and my husband of two years is sleeping soundly while our five-month-old baby is laying on the bed in between us fussing. The baby has been fed, burped, and diapered. He just wants to be awake and play with someone. My husband sleeps through the grunts and flailing fists hitting him in the face. I know I'm going to be at least partially awake from then on, even if I wake my husband to take the baby out of the room and play with him. I'm still really tired, and I think I'm starting to get sick. I could let the baby fuss and keep laying under the covers with my eyes closed, I could wake my husband and ask him to take the baby, or I could just get up and play with the baby. Either way someone isn't going to be completely happy, be it me, my husband, or the baby, and for some reason I have to decide who the unlucky person is going to be. This morning it was my husband.

The work required of mothers and housewives is unique in that it literally never stops. Dinner has to be provided every day. Dishes, clothes, floors and rooms are continuously dirtied. Kids need to be watched, and played with, and disciplined. My baby often gets in a mood where he demands to be carried around with me whenever he is awake. If I need to use the bathroom during this time, I put him down and he cries until I pick him up again.

The point is, whatever time or money a mother spends on herself could have been spent on her children or housework. One could even say that the time and money she spends on herself is time and money she is taking away from her children. So where does one draw the line? Obviously a mother has needs, and at least some of her wants should be met as well. When does it become selfishness though? When is the time I spend on myself time I not only *could* have spent with my kids, but time I *should* have spent with them? When does letting my baby cry because I'm not holding him amount to neglect of his needs, and when does holding the baby all day amount to neglect of my needs? Is a little selfishness really that bad? Couldn't you say that indulging yourself as a mother actually helps your children because as the old saying goes, "Ain't Mamma happy, ain't nobody happy"?

"ABE LINCOLN & YARDWORK" BY RACHAEL LAURITZEN (FEBRUARY 4, 2006)

One of my three callings in the ward is preparing the Sacrament meeting programs each week. I do my best to magnify this calling, making sure the printed program (at least) is Christ-centered and looks like some care and thought went into it. I always include a scriptural quote that's topic-related and Christ-centered. I also pick the hymns for Sacrament meeting (under the hat of my 2nd calling). So that I can shape the hymn choices and program around the topic du jour, as well as name the correct speakers for the week, I have requested that the bishopric provide me with a schedule of talk/meeting topics for a couple of weeks out or, if I'm lucky, a couple of months.

Last Thursday, I got the latest schedule. It's not complete, but it does go through April. As I was looking it over, I noticed that next week's talk topics are 1. Free Agency and 2. Abe Lincoln. Abe Lincoln? Well, he was a good guy, generally, and a faithful one I believe, but the gospel connection . . . ? I admit, I'm already a little frustrated with the lack of Christ-centered Sacrament meetings in my ward, but rambling on about home teaching or Girls' Camp at least has some relevance to our LDS-ness. But Abe Lincoln? And yes, I realize that Presidents' Day is coming up. But they're not talking about Groundhog's Day tomorrow, are they? Well . . . it IS Fast Sunday. I suppose somebody might.

I went on, turned over the page, and noticed that one of the topics in April was "Neat Yards Invite the Spirit." Huh. Weird topic, one that one of our neighbors would probably pick to target us because our backyard is a work in progress (but we have dogs . . .) and we don't mow the front yard as often as she would like. She likes it scalped, we do not. Ah well. Then I saw the date: April 16th. It occurred to me that April 16th this year is Easter Sunday. So our Easter Sunday worship service this year is going to be focusing on . . . yardwork? Yup. Yardwork.

Am I the only one who finds this disturbing? This—a non-observance of Easter—basically happened last year as well, both in my ward, my sister's ward, and my parents' ward, and we ended up discussing it over our family Easter dinner. We were all rather frustrated. My sister is convinced that "church headquarters"[55] doesn't realize this kind of thing is widespread (maybe just in Utah) and at one point was entertaining the idea of writing to them to "raise awareness." I also finally decided to call the bishop and respectfully tell him my concerns, which I did this morning. He seemed to take it well, but also seemed interested in changing the subject. He did mention that April 16th is High Council Sunday, so I gave him an easy out and said that maybe the stake had just overlooked that Easter was that day. (Never mind the fact that the stake is apparently "just overlooking" THE Most Important Holiday on the Christian calendar.) The bishop said he'd look into it. Maybe something will happen. Who knows?

But I'm still feeling deflated, frustrated, and a little depressed that my church, the one that claims to be Christ's authoritative church, gives so little attention to Easter. And generally has so little Christ focus during our weekly "worship" meetings. Even the missionary sacrament meeting last week focused on programs, not the Heart of the gospel, and believe me, the lack of Christ-centered meetings definitely deters me from inviting investigators to church. And even if I did, the meetings would just turn them off, so it doesn't help out either the church or the souls it's trying to save.

What happened to offering our oblations weekly unto the Most High? What happened to talking, rejoicing, preaching, and prophesying of Christ? What happened to Easter in the Church? And what can we do about it?

"LESSONS I LEARNED IN THE TEMPLE" BY CAROLINE KLINE (FEBRUARY 25, 2006)

Admin note: we understand that the temple is a very tender topic to many people and this post is going to be a challenging one to handle with civility. We ask that you respect Caroline and her experience for what it is, her experience. As per our commenting guidelines, we do not welcome comments that condemn Caroline for her belief, nor comments that call her righteousness into question. We also ask that you be very thoughtful in how and what you write about specific temple ceremonies, everyone has a different sacred/secret line and we will not hesitate to erase if you cross ours.

I wanted to like the temple. My fiancé hoped I would since, as a literature major, I would be able to appreciate all the deep symbolism. But while he knew I was a feminist, there was no way he really could have anticipated just how dark an experience I would have there.

Surprisingly, my meltdown in the temple didn't occur until the third time I did an endowment session. While I had not particularly enjoyed these two previous times and was bothered by the presentation of women's role in the temple, I had been sitting next to my new in-laws and had dealt with it. This third time, to put it lightly, I was unable to deal with it.

When I saw Eve forced to make the obedience covenant,[56] when I saw all the other women in the room promise to hearken unto their husbands, when I saw Eve silenced and pushed aside, I pondered the implications of this. And I lost it. Started sobbing my heart out and continued to sob the rest of the session. For me. For Eve. For all the women who had made this promise and wondered if they were somehow inferior to men. And this was not tame, silent crying. I was gasping, I could barely breathe. My wails filled the whole ordinance room and celestial room for the entire hour and a half. I had never in my life felt such overwhelming grief and darkness and despair. I felt as if I had been stabbed in the heart, because this was the place that I was supposed to feel closest to God. This is where ritual communicated eternal truth. I felt I had been stabbed not only in the heart but also in the back by a religion that I had given myself to. That I had invested my eternal future and my eternal marriage in. I felt utterly betrayed. For two years or so, the memory of that experience was so painful that I couldn't talk about it with anyone. The grief was too deep to be communicated.

But in the last couple of years I have begun to be able to acknowledge that moment as an instrumental part of my development as a person. I have found peace in not having to always hide this part of my spiritual makeup from others. As I am now able to less painfully reflect on the experience, I realize now that I should have gotten up and left the endowment room. I should not have continued to participate in something that hurt me so much. But I didn't know how to, didn't know it was even an option. Like a ride at Disneyland, I thought that I just had to endure it until it came to an end. And after four years, I have only just begun to understand that there were and are options to not participate in things that violate me and my spirit. While I am an active church-going Mormon who embraces the unique LDS vision of divine potential for all humans, I do not currently participate physically in temple rituals. And I am starting to be able to not participate emotionally and spiritually with what I see as mistaken conflations of a sexist culture with doctrine.

Four years ago, I allowed male leaders to tell me what a woman was, what a woman's essential qualities were, what I should be striving for in my female life. The things they were telling me often bothered me and hurt me, but I pretty much accepted it, because I was a Mormon and it was an all or nothing proposition. One didn't reject the statements of leaders who were the mouthpieces of God. Ironically, it was my experience in the temple, and the resultant soul-deep conviction that the women's obedience covenant is wrong, unjust, hurtful—a cultural remnant of a sexist past—that has liberated me. I have begun to realize that I can choose to not believe in ideas that violate me as a woman, that cut me down, that make me think less of myself and my potential.

And I have chosen. I am now on a spiritual journey that puts far less emphasis on church leaders, and much more emphasis on my conscience and my relationship with God. I will never again give anyone or anything the moral authority to hurt me the way the covenant in the temple did. While I intend to thoughtfully listen to Church leaders, I myself will ultimately decide my role in life. I won't let others define womanhood for me and then constrain me with the definition.

And after having felt anger at well-meaning but IMO[57] hopelessly wrong ideas of authorities, I am trying to more compassionately allow the leaders their journey, a journey which no doubt contains lots of mistakes and wrongheaded assumptions about women, but which also, hopefully, will contain moments of transcendence.

They are human. I am human. And in all my blundering, and outrage, and grief, I know that I will have moments of transcendence too.

"WHO WOULD WANT THE PRIESTHOOD?" BY EMILY SUMMERHAYS (MARCH 2, 2006)

I often hear Mormon women preface or end their remarks with phrases like "not that I want the Priesthood," or "not that I'm advocating ordaining women," etc. I'm absolutely certain that there are a great many women out there who truly don't want it, even if they'd like to see other institutional changes in the church. However, I think that there is a lot more to statements (disclaimers?) like this than a mere denial of desire. After all, as things currently stand, if a woman were to admit that she wanted the Priesthood (for herself or others), she would also be saying that she disagreed with a fundamental tenet of the gospel as we know it, and she would be opening herself to all sorts of speculation as to her loyalty, her testimony, her righteousness, and on and on. In some ways, saying that you'd like to see change indicates to others that you're willing to lobby for it, and I think that in many cases, whether we're conscious of it or not, using that little disclaimer is a way of saying: but please don't dismiss me or my ideas as heretical. Or, please don't leave me more alone than I already feel.

So I'd like to see if it's possible for the question "Do you want the Priesthood?" to exist in a kind of vacuum. That is, is it possible to want (or not want) the thing for its own sake?

Imagine, if you will, that the prophet has told us he's had a revelation that women now have the option to be ordained to the Priesthood. Moreover, imagine that people have had time to adjust to this pronouncement such that a woman who chooses to be ordained will suffer no cultural repercussions—no accusations of false pride, no insinuations of heresy, no sly remarks about her lack of femininity. And then, also, imagine that ordination is optional for men, too, and that the choice (in either sex) not to be a Priesthood holder is not met with assumptions about sin or other unworthiness. Since we're imagining, let us imagine that this system of choice and accountability works, for the most part, smoothly, that every family is covered by the Priesthood, and that men and women work in harmony. Couples bless their children together or by turns, and both women and men feel represented in administrative councils, and over the pulpit. Whoever feels the call to serve is free to answer it.

With all this held in this your imagination . . . who among you would want the Priesthood?[58]

"I am female and I WOULD want it" -- 35.6% (84)

"I am female and I WOULD NOT want it" -- 20.3% (48)

"I am male and I WOULD want it" -- 17.4% (41)

"I am female and I'm not sure" -- 14.4% (34)

"I am male and I'm not sure" -- 6.8% (16)

"I am male and I WOULD NOT want it" -- 5.5% (13)

Total votes: 236

"DIFFICULT QUESTIONS, UNCOMFORTABLE ANSWERS, AND SIMPLE FAITH" BY LISA PATTERSON BUTTERWORTH (MARCH 27, 2006)

A woman I just adore stopped me in church yesterday and asked me a really compelling question.

> I've been reading *Mormon Enigma*,[59] and it's not saying what I
> want to hear. I think it's accurate but it's making me cranky. Is
> it worth reading if it makes me feel this way?

First off, I can't answer that question as a blanket sort of statement. It depends so much on what a person needs in her own life.

On the one hand, I'm not a big fan of the bury your head in the sand method of strengthening-the-members. It's a very shallow sort of strengthening, if you ask me. But having said that, Life is Hard, and sometimes burying your head in the sand is an urgent matter of survival. If that's what you need to make it for the next five minutes, until tomorrow, until next week, then dig in. You have my blessing (I know that's just what you all have been waiting for!).

But as a general matter, I would have to say that Yes, Learning is Important. Yes, Feeling Uncomfortable Is Worth It. In fact, it may even be vital.

We all have a small little cushy space in which we feel comfortable. And I think it's all too easy for us (in our flawed human nature) to translate comfortable, easy, pleasant into GOOD.

But I think we are wrong when we shy away from things that make us uncomfortable without determining why. Sometimes things make us uncomfortable because they harm people, like say, pornography and genocide. But sometimes we are uncomfortable simply because things are unfamiliar and/or complex.

My space is inhabited by white middle-class Mormons. Just about everyone I know is a white middle-class Mormon and I'm very comfortable around white middle-class Mormons. And the sad truth of the matter is, you put me in a room full of poor black Baptists and I'm distinctly less comfortable. This doesn't mean that poor black Baptists are bad, it just means that I'm comfortable with things I already know. And I don't know a whole lot about interacting with poor black Baptists.

Likewise, I've learned a certain brand of history my whole life. I'm comfortable with a history in which Joseph Smith's "flaws" included being a tad too jovial and wrestling with his children in an undignified, un-prophet-like manner. The uncomfortable truth of the matter is, Smith's flaws were far more numerous and infinitely more serious.

I may never be comfortable with poor black Baptists (even given the opportunity, unlikely in the greater metropolitan Boise area) and I may never be comfortable with the truth of Joseph Smith's flaws.

But I refuse to believe that the mistake is in *learning* about Joseph Smith. The mistake is in our expectations that Answers should be comfortable, simple, or easy.

People are messy. History is messy. Doctrine is messy. Church is messy. It's a messy messy world.

Messy uncomfortable history doesn't make simple faith untrue or irrelevant. Irrational perhaps, or maybe superrational, er something . . . but faith isn't supposed to be about rationality. Faith is about being brave enough to believe.

Faith really is a leap, and you will never be able to make all the history, the science, the scriptures, the prophets, the manuals, answers-to-prayers line up neatly to justify your faith. If you insist on this outcome you must either not ask questions or you will end up lying to yourself.

We are perverse creatures. We want to believe and we want to be rational. Yet another messy paradox. Belief is irrational, and Rationality is hollow. Messy, messy, messy.

There is no simple solution. Faith without reason creates a frightening arbitrary ignorance. Reason without faith, a hopeless meaningless futility.

Embrace the mess. Escape your comfort zone. Allow yourself to ask difficult questions and face uncomfortable answers and unsolvable complexities. Seek. Learn. Grow. Allow yourself to believe irrationally. Hope.

"THOUGHTS ON EASTER AND THE CROSS" BY RACHAEL LAURITZEN (APRIL 17, 2006)

Well, we had "Easter" talks in church yesterday and an Easter performance by the choir. Most of it was underwhelming and hard to hear (the first speaker was an older, rambling gentleman who was too far from the mic). But it WAS on topic. Mostly.

But during the second (necessarily short) talk and in several subsequent family/friends-of-family conversations, I kept hearing people talk about how we LDS don't wear the cross,[60] display it, or put it on our churches because we have such a wonderful understanding of Christ's Resurrection.

Well, yes, I'd have to agree. Sort of. But (momentarily leaving aside the subcurrent sense of superiority I got from most of these comments) what I kept thinking about to myself is that it almost seemed like we, as a group, are not putting enough emphasis on Christ's suffering. As in, yes it happened, yes it was necessary, no we don't understand it but we try oh-so-hard to appreciate it, but ... let's get on with the uncomfortable stuff and just talk about the happy ending. The problem is, I think, that it's supremely important to grapple with the unpleasantness of the Suffering of The Lamb and give it its due attention when discussing or discoursing on the Atonement and Resurrection. It IS where the price for our sins was paid and those sins swept away. It WAS the very hardest, awfullest thing that God the Son ever had to do, so very awful and hard that He got to the point where He'd rather not do it, if at all possible. But He DID do it because of His Love and Mercy and Grace. And I think it's important to delve into those principles of our individual salvation and relationship with God.

So what I'm saying, then, is that I'm starting to think that it wouldn't be such a bad idea for us to "accept the Cross," whether by wearing it, talking (more) about it, or whatever. I suspect a lot of our collective rejection of it has at least as much to do with distancing or distinguishing ourselves from traditional Christianity as it does with our supposedly greater emphasis on the Resurrection—and I'm not sure that we really emphasize it more. Yes, we emphasize correctly that we are one of fewer religions who believe Jesus still has His body, but as far as I can tell, rejoicing in and emphasizing the joy and significance of the Resurrection is something that all Christians of whatever stripe do. Why can we not rejoice in the similarity of our worship and belief, while respecting and maintaining important doctrinal differences? Why must we culturally train ourselves to look down on the wearing or expression of the Cross? It doesn't make sense to me anymore.

"FEMINISM I CAN EMBRACE" BY TRACY MCKAY (AUGUST 9, 2006)

> There was a time that my angry Feminism got in the way
> of my even wanting to dress up and look like a woman.
> —Emma Thompson

Do you ever lie in bed at night, thinking about all the things you want to say and coming up with clever and creative ways to say them? Clever ways that utterly vanish when the real opportunity to express yourself actually presents? I've been doing that a lot lately, and while I want to blame it on lack of sleep and having three kids under 5, I honestly think this problem has plagued me my entire life. I am so glib, sharp and precise in my mind, and so often muddled, distracted and unclear in real life. Not fair. So lately I have been thinking about Feminism, and how I really feel about it.

The first time anyone asked me if I was a Feminist was at a natural foods store where I worked in Santa Cruz, California. I was 18. She was a co-worker of mine, and I was standing behind the bakery counter, making tea. Somewhat off-guard, I looked up and said that, no; I didn't consider myself a Feminist. The verbal beating that ensued was shocking; she berated me for my position, belittled my intelligence, and basically concluded that I was repressed and misinformed, and once I loosened the shackles of my bondage, I would see things as she did. How's that for a start? In a nutshell, this is, even today, my complaint about modern Feminism.

There was time, not too long after this incident, that I would have answered the above question very differently. Perhaps it is a rite of passage for many young women—I can and do only speak for myself. There was a period of years where the message of modern Feminism was very bright in my sky, and I subscribed to many of its popular ideals (and magazines and authors). But slowly, as I became more aware of my own heart and found the courage to look at how I really felt deep inside (rather than subscribing to a particular social movement's cannon), my point of view shifted. And when it shifted, I again found myself maligned and belittled by a movement I thought was there to embrace and empower me to do exactly what I was trying to do—make up my own mind. Herein lays the problem. Because the opinion I began to form was not in direct line with the party line (for lack of a better word), I was again labeled misinformed and repressed. And this made (still makes) me very angry.

Another big bone I have to pick with the mainstream Feminists is the bright and shiny banner of "The Right to Choose." Heads up—*this one is very personal to me*. Now, the right to choose implies someone actually choosing—having several options and making a well-informed and thoughtful decision. From personal experience, I know how slippery and sketchy this idea is in reality. When I was very young, I made some astoundingly poor choices and ended up pregnant. I want to make it perfectly clear that I am not blaming anyone for my own actions, but I also want to make it clear that vulnerable and frightened young women *can be* and *are* taken advantage of under the banner of "choice." When I went to the doctor, when I went to a family member, when I talked to a counselor, what was repeated over and over was how lucky I was that I lived in this age when a woman could have a safe and legal abortion. Repeatedly, I was told how simple and easy "it" was, how empowering this would be—yes, someone actually said that to me. NO one, not one counselor, doctor or friend said to me that I could make a choice other than the one they were offering—it was simply assumed I would terminate the pregnancy and was told I should be grateful for the ability to do so. I was also told that at 8 weeks "it" was not a child, but still just tissue. Now I know that was an outright lie. When I asked other questions, they were brushed aside. I also know that I am not the only single, frightened and alone young woman who was pushed through something she may not have really wanted in the name of "modern progress," "women's rights" and Feminism. Everyone was so careful to protect my "rights" as a modern woman; no one stopped and looked at the scared girl. "Choice" is not even a remote reality when all options are not presented fairly and accurately. Protecting women from the reality of what their "choice" actually entails is, in fact, treating them as half-persons, disregarding their intelligence and ability to discern for themselves the path they wish to take.

Which leads me to my real question? Is mainstream modern Feminism really serving women, real women with real lives, or is it merely serving its own agenda? Am I a Feminist? Not the kind I used to be. Do I believe that men and women are created equally? You better believe it. Are we the same, able to do all the same things on an equal and level playing field? Nope. We are inherently different, but neither is superior or better than the other—different but equal. My husband and I will never be an equal match in physical strength, nor will he ever be the artist I am. He is more spiritually sensitive; I'm more of a whirlwind. We each complement and compel the other, amplifying and lifting, where I am weak, he is stronger, where he struggles, I lift him up. We are Equal, but we are not, and never will be the Same.

The world is not perfect—I understand that there are women who really do need help. But to offer help and then expect or even demand that those women who benefited then fit into a proscribed political or world view is only a new kind of bondage. "Help" with the idea of freeing people to make up their own minds and hearts, even if the path they then choose doesn't fit with the very doctrine that freed them.

When Lisa asked me to guest post here for two weeks, my first reaction was "ME? Why??" because although I am a frequent reader and commenter, I truly hesitate to call myself a mainstream Feminist. For the life of me, I couldn't figure out how my voice would fit in, but I am beginning to see that there is room, is a need, for more than one voice that cries "I am Woman."

Reading and even occasionally contributing to sites like this and some of the other faith-based feminist sites has helped me realize I can care for women's issues and status without compromising my deeply wrought morals and personal viewpoint. I can disagree without being disagreeable, I'm not angry, and I don't have to embrace misandrist attitudes to be a feminist.

So I once again find myself re-evaluating how I feel about feminism, and my place on the line. Now that I have a daughter, I am keenly aware of the hurdles she might face, and I want to do everything I can to help her have any opportunity she wishes. But I am also the mother of sons, and I won't have any part of any movement that marginalizes or maligns men or the boys who will become men. What I am looking for is a place where all of my children can be lifted up and nourished without expense or detriment to the other. I am not interested in riding a pendulum that swings too far to the left or the right—I will stay right here with my own heart, kindly and thoughtfully making quiet decisions for my life. That is Feminism to me.

"I'M A SLUG" BY LISA PATTERSON BUTTERWORTH (SEPTEMBER 1, 2006)

It's officially time for my semi-annual housewife breakdown.

All three gallons of newly purchased milk in my fridge were funky this morning, I was out of bread, I had only two eggs, so my kids had leftover chocolate cake and whipped cream for breakfast. My floors are funky, my laundry is overflowing everywhere, the sink is full of dishes, my bathrooms smell like urine, stacks of stuff are overflowing their various receptacles, and I can't find a single *pair* of shoes for my children. It's almost lunch time and I haven't showered yet, I just used chocolate to bribe Brick[61] to pee in the toilet, and then gave him a popsicle which he is now eating while watching his third movie of the day, and it's only 11:30.

Add to that my nearly constant sense of pointless drifting isolation, and it's pretty much breakdown time. Again (sorry).

I just get so tired of the constant unceasing drudgery of keeping it all up, I let one thing slip, then another, then it all spirals (with lightning speed) into mass pandemonium. Want to read a book? Braw ha ha ha ha ha! Let go of vigilance for a single day, and pay for it with yogurt on the walls and missing toothbrushes and poop on the patio.

I'm not depressed exactly, but I am starting to fantasize, once again, about going to the hospital. All that forced inactivity and quiet. No monkeys using me as a jungle gym or demanding my attention every time I get the gumption to acquire myself a goal. The hospital sounds fabulous, just for a week or two.

I don't know if there is something unique about being mauled by small monsters all day that makes this "time-for-a-mental-breakdown" thing inevitable. But, I'm getting the hang of this housewife thing, starting to see the cycles, and most all the moms I know face this to one degree or another.

Perhaps everyone does (housewife or no), but I really don't think it's wrong to say that it is a more pronounced event for many housewives.

The obvious answer is that I need "me" time, I need to plan it and schedule it. But the reality of my life is that it's just not possible. I've already maxed out my baby swapping favors for doc appointments and whatnot. As hard as my husband tries, he just can't pick up my slack, he's maxed out already. Everyone who might help me is embroiled in their own trauma right now. And then there's the problem that I don't feel entitled to it. I'm a spoiled rotten housewife with every advantage that life has to offer and I cannot start using people who are also feeling maxed-out without giving back, and I can't give back right now.

I have to suck it up, and I think I can, I hope I can. I have to.
Now that I've got to thinking, here are some things I've decided:

First, mothers aren't allowed to have breakdowns, not really, and as an angry feminist I'm just going to come right on out and say it. This is sexist. Yup, that's what I said sister. SEXIST.

I will explain. Let's all rewatch that classic movie *It's a Wonderful Life* for a moment in our minds. Remember that part where George is yelling at his patient wife, Mary, his hair's all crazy, there's probably some spit flying, he's losing everything, EVERYTHING. (I love that movie). And then Mary, the perfect wife, is all, *George, shhh you're scaring the children.*

We all have a lot of sympathy for George, poor guy, he's losing everything, EVERYTHING!

Now rewind and watch it again, only switch the role, let Mary have the breakdown in front of the kids, she's losing everything, EVERYTHING (including her suicidal husband it seems), now let George be the one who says, *shhh you're scaring the children.*

I'm serious, close your eyes, play that scene in your mind. Watch Donna Reed screaming, her hair all crazy, probably some spit flying.

I'm the one making up this-here example, and even I recoil in horror at that image of Mary, in ways I did not recoil at George's behavior. I've been so programed to think that Mothers have to be superhuman and selfless, that I have an impossibly hard time allowing Mary to have a breakdown. She certainly deserves one more than I do.

Sexist, yup.

That said, I don't think it's in the best interests of children or society to be encouraging mothers to have screaming fits in front of their kids (and yeah, there are plenty of mothers who do), but on the flip side, I don't think it's in the best interests of anyone that we have so little sympathy for women's (selfish!?) needs. (While also allowing men much more slack if they, say, abandon their families to throw themselves in a river.)

My second thought on this whole matter is this: There just isn't any backup system for housewives. We don't have days off. Family vacations aren't a vacation for us. Help often isn't available and breakdowns aren't allowed.

So what I think we need to do is set up a system for safe breakdowns. First we must expect these breakdowns, encourage them even, to remove the stigma.

Second, we must allow house parents (and single parents) to individualize their own breakdown, some can let their houses go to pot and stop showering, others can lock themselves in a padded room, others can have time to scream and punch things and cry. Meanwhile the children will be taken care of by sweet nannies, grannies, and gay couples waiting for their adoption papers to clear. And of course this system will be implemented by our new national health care system (just after they end world hunger and create whirled peas).

Ah, good times.

"INFERTILITY: GROWING PAINS SUCK" BY JANET GARRARD-WILLIS (OCTOBER 16, 2006)

> Before the world was created, in heavenly councils the pattern and role of women were prescribed. You were elected by God to be wives and mothers in Zion. . . . Since the beginning, a woman's first and most important role has been ushering into mortality spirit sons and daughters of our Father in Heaven.
>
> —Ezra Taft Benson[62]
>
> The body and the spirit are the soul of man.
>
> —D&C 88:15[63]

When the prophets speak of the exalted place of motherhood, I do not growl. I agree. And then I grieve.

Many people have noted the problematic nature of the analogy which partners motherhood with priesthood as the respective female and male responsibilities in this life, usually by noting that fatherhood functions as the companion to motherhood. For me the crux of the problem lies with the fact that since 1978, all worthy men can hold the priesthood. All worthy women, however, cannot be mothers. Someday perhaps a social worker will bestow the title "Mama" upon me (at least I desperately, desperately hope so!), but my body won't be ushering any spirits into the world. Thus, President Benson's quotation causes me pain because it implies that, as a childless woman, I have failed my "first and most important role" in this terrestrial realm.

I have meant to write this post since Lisa first asked me to do a guest stint. I wanted to write something academic, something intellectually and spiritually stimulating. It turns out I can no more write about infertility in an intellectually detached fashion than I could stand naked in front of a room full of people while teaching an anatomy lesson. Of all the trials in my life, this is the only one which renders my soul naked.

I use the term "soul" for specific doctrinal—rather than dramatic—purposes. Quite obviously infertility creates a problem for women embedded in a culture which legitimizes femininity almost entirely through motherhood. In the time since my husband and I discovered that we would likely have no biological children, I've become the embodied locus of this cultural struggle. Some women apologize to me when they get pregnant; others avoid me altogether. Some offer charming opinions on what sins I may have committed such that God would rescind from me the blessings of motherhood. (For the record, these are usually the same folks who imply that adoption is a merely a consolation prize, that somehow my future adopted kids won't be "really" mine—so obviously I should ignore them entirely.) Some say this happened to me, and not to them, because I am "so much stronger." I'm sympathetic to their difficulties in placing people like me into a convenient cosmology. Certainly we could parse out these cultural tensions in any number of useful ways. Still, it is not my abundantly fecund culture which most troubles barren old me. It is the violent divorce of my soul.

LDS doctrine strays from the rest of Christianity with its renegade contention that the soul is composed of both spirit and body. One half of my soul, my spirit, desperately wants to fulfill the promise I made in the temple to multiply and replenish the earth—in fact, my spiritual desire to be a mommy has always run second only to my desire to know God. I am laughably, ridiculously, hyperbolically maternal. Yet the flesh and blood portion of my soul renders the desires of the spirit impossible. And while I'm grateful for medical advancement, the endless rounds of drugs—specifically intended to disconnect brain/ovarian body communication—

disrupt my ability to "read" my own body. The stirrups, the scans, the needles, the countless time spent staring at the tiles in the doctor's office all remind me that I control almost nothing. Should my body ever bear a child, the pregnancy will result from third and fourth party knowledge and manipulation of my body rather than from an act of love between me and my husband. I have ceded control of my corporeal self to a bunch of men in white coats. I learned a long time ago that my body is me, that Joseph Smith's prophetic utterance about the soul jived spot-on with my experiences. My blood carries the heat of my passions and my limbs carry out the choices I make in spirit, both working together to build whoever it is I am. I have a testimony of that doctrine—I even love it, and that's no small thing for a woman who suffers from several incurable autoimmune diseases.

But when it comes to infertility, my soul cannot work in concert. It remains bifurcated, and I am learning to hate half of my own soul. And when I don't feel hatred towards my bodily half, I don't feel that it is mine at all—then it's just a lab rat which brilliant scientists have taken from me in their sincere desire to mend what nature made wrong. Now, I believe Paul's words that "all things work together for good to them that love God"; I have to believe it in order to avoid becoming bitter towards a God whom I utterly adore. But I can't see how my soul will reconcile. I don't know how to "feel like a woman," not just because a prophet located the center of womanhood in a place I cannot go, but because the woman I am has been ripped in half. When we are broken, we are open to God. What grace will come to this cracked place where the two halves of my soul used to join? That is the question of my current life. That and whether or not I will ever hear a tiny little voice call me "mama."

"ON MOTHERHOOD AND BEING 'BROKEN'" BY EMILY SUMMERHAYS (OCTOBER 17, 2006)

On the heels of two very poignant posts by Eve[64] and Janet[65] on their experiences with infertility and the resultant scramble for meaning within themselves and their lives, I find myself needing to speak up for that small contingent of women (for I comfort myself that there must be more than just me out there) who struggle to find maternity within themselves, not physically, but spiritually—those of us who apparently just don't feel what we're "supposed to" feel. *Let me please be very clear from the outset that in the following I am in no way belittling others' struggles, heartaches, loves, desires, or choices. I'm just speaking for myself, and in fine FMH tradition hopefully giving voice to one of those things of which we rarely speak.*

I was recently in a doctor's office and was told that I need to further investigate the possibility that I might have a problem with my ovaries. I happened that same week to be reading a novel in which the protagonist is diagnosed with this particular ovarian problem and is rendered infertile. Instead of being horrified by the possibility that my ovaries might not work, and that I might never have children, I found myself instead horrified to realize that I was actually a little bit relieved. And (most horrifying of all), truth be known, a little bit . . . hopeful. Y'see, if I were *physically* "broken," I wouldn't ever again have to worry about being *spiritually* so. I have nothing but love and respect for Janet and Eve and everyone else who has experienced the heartache of infertility, but when I hear stories like theirs, part of me wants to say . . . yes . . . it is very hard to be an infertile woman in the Church, but as awful as it is, at least you're still occupying an approved space. That is, you do not have children only because you cannot. Your heart is in the "right" place. But me, well . . . as far as I know, I'm a fully functioning baby making machine, so if I don't want children, Church culture and doctrine clearly dictate that there must be something very seriously wrong with me.

I have never had any real desire to bear children. I can ooh and ah over other people's kids, but I have never felt that infamous biological clock. I never have dreams about babies. I've never once felt a yearning to conceive. In fact, the thought of myself as a mother terrifies and exhausts me. True, I have chronic health issues that terrify and exhaust me anyway, and I'm often sorely tempted to use my health as a "get out of being judged for not fulfilling my divine role free" card, but in reality, if I truly wanted babies, I think I could find a way to make it work. But I just . . . don't. Sure, I think I'd like to see what a child of mine and Z's might look like, what our children might do and be, but honestly the dread outweighs the curiosity, and if there's one thing I fear more than being a Mom, it's being a bad one (which I'm quite sure I would be).

I must admit that the expectation that I should have children, or if not have them, be breaking my heart to have them, makes me feel like I myself am just not enough. Sure, I'm a child of God, but as far as the Church is concerned, I'm only important in so far as I can create other children of God. This has never made sense to me. For, deep in my heart, I feel (and have always felt) that I *am* enough. To me [to flip around Eve's post (forgive me, Eve!)], *motherhood* has always been the secondary life. Because to me, *my* life is primary. Me. I *am* the end result. I can do and create so many things—why does one of those things have to be babies?

I am not without faith, and though I cannot say exactly from whence it comes, I have always felt that my life is important, not for what I can bring to the world *through a child* (who will then only be considered important in and of herself until she herself is qualified and expected to bear children), but for what I can bring to the world. Period.

But though I am square with myself and God, I know I'm not square with the Church or its people. A few commenters on Janet's thread mentioned hating teenage mothers for wasting/abusing their reproductive capabilities. Others mentioned how terrible it made them feel to know that others, not knowing of the infertility struggle, judged them as unrighteous (the implication being that of course they weren't unrighteous—they would bear children if they could—it's those who can but don't who are unrighteous). Believe me, I know these comments come from pain, but really, what of people like me?

I can have children (as far as I know). Does that make me the object of resentment and hatred? I fear so. Does it make me disobedient and selfish? I'm afraid most think that, too. But as always, I like to consider the letter of the law in relation to the spirit of it. The letter dictates that I ought to just get on with it and multiply, but what of the spirit? I believe that parenting is one of the most important and wonderful things women and men can do with their lives—*I* just don't believe it's the most important thing I can do with *mine*. And because I absolutely and fully realize how important it is to raise children in love and happiness, I don't want to bring children into the world unless or until I know they can be wanted as they should be wanted—as Janet wants them, or as any number of you want them. Not as an obligation, a duty, or a sacrifice of self, but as a cherished hope.

For now, my cherished hope is that sometime we can all look at each other and not hate, judge, or resent. We all have our measures of sorrow. We all have our measures of doubt. We all have our measures of fear. And we all have our measures of joy. I wish you all as much joy as you can find, where you can find it, whether it's in the cabbage patch, the adoption office, or not.

The worldwide membership of the LDS Church surpassed 13 million, and the Church announced that it had called its one millionth missionary. A PBS documentary titled *The Mormons*, which aired in April and May, examined the story of how members of the LDS Church progressed in the United States from social outcasts to mainstream citizens. The documentary featured interviews with Church leaders, including Church President Gordon B. Hinckley, and scholars, such as D. Michael Quinn and Margaret Toscano, who both spoke about their experiences with excommunication. Mitt Romney announced his candidacy for the President of the United States in February, which turned the American public's attention to the Church. Romney's Mormon faith became a recurring topic of discussion in the race; a Pew Research Center poll found that 24–27 percent of respondents would be less likely to vote for a presidential candidate who was Mormon. The study also found that 31 percent of respondents did not consider Mormons to be Christian.

In April, the Public Affairs Department published a lengthy interview with Elder Dallin H. Oaks and General Authority Lance B. Wickman on the Church's stance on homosexuality. Oaks stated that the LDS Church "must take a stand on doctrine and principle. This is more than a social issue—ultimately it may be a test of our most basic religious freedoms to teach what we know our Father in Heaven wants us to teach."[66] The Church released two further publications that reiterated the LDS Church's position on same-gender attraction, including the booklet *God Loveth His Children* and an *Ensign* and *Liahona* magazine article titled "Helping Those Who Struggle with Same-Gender Attraction" by Apostle Jeffrey R. Holland. All of these publications stressed the importance of keeping one's actions and behaviors consistent with the law of chastity, which restricts sexual relations to married heterosexual couples.

In October, newly called General Relief Society President Julie B. Beck delivered an address at the Church's semiannual General Conference titled "Mothers Who Know."[67] Beck's talk placed premium value on physically bearing children, nurturing, cooking, cleaning, limiting personal endeavors outside the home, and women building power and influence through raising their children to be faithful Latter-day Saints. The talk provoked instant criticism and conversation throughout the bloggernacle. On the FMH blog, Lisa Patterson Butterworth's initial post on Beck's talk received over 300 comments, and a number of other posts followed.

As the blog entered its fourth year, it was producing more content and generating a larger response than ever, with 462 new posts and two new bloggers: Quimby and ECS. The bloggers collaborated on Women's History Month posts in March and on a short series titled "How I Became a Mother," which spotlighted various individual encounters with fertility, birth, and parenting in ways both traditional and unexpected. Readers of the blog grew more connected to each other, organizing several get-togethers, known as "snackers," in locations across the United States.

FMH hit it big with a profile in the June issue of *Bust* magazine. The article was thorough and complimentary, focusing on Mormon feminists who elected to stay active in the Church. FMH blogger EmilyS hinted at the group's growing confidence to claim its voice:

> I feel that the blog is building a community of people who are aware of these questions and who are less and less afraid to ask them. And if at any point in time there is to be a change, I think enough people need to be asking the question that prompts the prophet or whoever is in charge to ask, 'What should I do with this?'[68]

"BLESSING SICK CHILDREN" BY LISA PATTERSON BUTTERWORTH (JANUARY 11, 2007)

As many of you know, in the early days of the church women gave blessings to the sick. I had always heard rumors to this effect, but prior to reading *In Sacred Loneliness*[69] I had assumed this was an exception for desperate circumstances, but instead I found that it was standard and expected practice.

I'm not entirely clear on the process by which women giving healing blessings and exercising other spiritual gifts became taboo, it's something I need study more. Anyway. . . .

Keeping that in mind, here is my (true) story.

My best friend's family all fell ill on Christmas Eve. And her youngest (2yo), having other complicating health factors, ended up in the hospital just as Santa was landing on rooftops around town. Her (very sick) dh[70] stayed home with the other (very sick) kids. Even with five on-call doctors being called in at 3am on Christmas morning, they couldn't get baby boy's breathing under control, and things got very scary, very fast.

As she sat in the Emergency Ward, praying desperately, watching doctors scramble, watching her son struggle for every shallow breath, she knew he needed a blessing. She couldn't call her dh, and she couldn't think of a single man in their new ward that she felt she could call at 3am on Christmas morning to rush to the hospital.

"You could do it," I told her at that point in the story, "women in the early church gave blessings all the time."

"I haven't told anyone this," she admitted, "but I did."

I cannot know what was in her heart and mind at that moment, I can't know what prompted her to give that blessing, I don't know the words she said, and I'm not clear on the power or authority she did or did not have to do so. But I'm glad she did.

All in all, though, the story makes me sad. Sad that she should feel so helpless and dependent on men, sad that something so precious has been lost to us, sad that she should feel embarrassed, even guilty for using the gifts of the spirit.

So . . . what would you have done?

"LIMINALITY, PART II: FOLK ON THE FRINGE" BY JANET GARRARD-WILLIS (FEBRUARY 19, 2007)

I started part I[71] with the story of the Samaritan woman who met Jesus at the well. If ever a person may have felt like a pariah walking into the back of a pre-fabbed chapel, it would be her. We don't deal well with divorce in our culture; we extend even less courtesy to adulterers. In her time she also belonged to an apostate sect AND had gender sitting in her demerits column. She could have touted any number of reasons for laying low and simply worshipping her Lord quietly from the sidelines.

But she spoke up. She launched right into evangelism central. Apparently people listened to her—Christ's apostles, who initially found the Samaritan path and her place in it particularly noxious, even felt compelled to feature her heroically in the gospels. Maybe the joy of conversion outweighed her anxiety, but considering that caste systems held more firmly in Jesus's time than in my own, I'm willing to bet that this woman entertained moments of concern. Likewise Alma the Younger, the Sons of Mosiah, and Paul all cavorted from one social pinhole to another, quelling whatever fears they felt and trusting that God and their love for Him outweighed all else. Of course, they also scampered out of Dodge to evangelize to Lamanites and gentiles—trading liminality in one locale for the other.

Let's face it—sometimes it might be psychologically easier to depart a current ward and don a black name-tag indefinitely. Sticking up for our faith amongst those who naughty-mouth it lends a dandy feeling of heroic martyrdom, whereas plunking down in the same pew each week to defend the integrity of our own doubts, struggles, penchant for dying our hair puce or voting to the left of Pat Buchanan can easily convince us that, even if we desperately want Mormon Community, it simply does not want us. Plus, angels have yet to knock me off my donkey in regards to, well, anything. Angels and conversations with the Lord might make speaking up a little easier.

Still—and I realize I'm an overtly friendly extrovert whose personality simplifies the equation—I believe we do a disservice to our community when we remain silent in our struggles. If we seek *communitas*—the shared space of transformation—in addition to the personal revelation also integral to our faith, we have to share. I'd hoped to construct a brilliant plan for how to help move ourselves and our congregations away from a segregation where "folks on the fringe" leave church wary and exhausted. I question lots of stuff and I hardly fit the "Utah Mormon mold" if there truly is such a thing (except, the horror, I do reallytrulyhonestly enjoy green jello with pears in it). Yet I rarely feel marginalized for more than a few moments. This is no doubt because I'm obnoxious and people really can't shut me up. With a stick. But when I have felt relegated to the "problem people, please abjure" category, it's hurt.

Since we're all so different, I gave up on formulating a brilliant plan in favor of a generalized reiteration not to hide your light under bushels of any variety—including bushels made of lace tablecloths and Franklin planners. If you've got a gift for teasing out multiple meanings for a scripture verse, eschew the tidiness of the tablecloth and make a nice little scriptural mess. It can lead to honest conversation. Those folks sitting next to you made a covenant at baptism to bear your burdens—and you did the same. How can we do that if we pretend our lives are light as a feather (and we act stiff as a board, which is to say veritably dead, when we're at church)?

Here's some stuff I've done, but that's just me. This is individual stuff, I know—we probably need concerted efforts as a group, but this is the only place I know to start. Contributions from non-extrovert freaks encouraged :).

1. My Woman at the Well obsession reveals the biggee: speak up, act, be a part of things. Don't let stereotypes define your ability to love God or others. Wear that Ani DiFranco t-shirt to the ward social and go ahead and sing the lyric to "sitting in the boardroom" if it makes you happy. Chances are someone else in the ice-cream line will like it, too.
2. Questions don't preclude service. Tell the bishop you're willing to serve. If you've got limitations, make 'em clear.
3. Questions don't preclude faith, either. Share what you believe and also what you HOPE to believe. Admit they aren't the same thing.
4. Cultivate the art of polite disagreement, involving concession. GD[72] disagreements seem to lead to open dialog rather than defensive harangue if you can find something about the speaker's original premise to start by agreeing with. At least sometimes.
5. Willingly entertain the possibility that you are wrong.

6. When someone engages honestly with the congregation—even if you aren't up to commenting in front of the group—thank them. Empathy offers a great foundation for *communitas*.

"RECIPROCITY IN A PATRIARCHAL, BUT EQUAL PARTNER, MARRIAGE" BY ECS (JULY 19, 2007)

I'm troubled by the concept of "presiding but equal partners" that we hear frequently from our Church leaders when they talk to us about the proper structure of a marriage relationship. In the August 2007 *Ensign*, Elder Bruce Hafen and Sister Marie Hafen have written an article titled "Crossing Thresholds and Becoming Equal Partners."[73] This article sheds some light on what presiding in a partnership of equals may look like.

First, there's also some excellent information in the article about how the Restoration clarifies Eve's role in the Fall (Mormons think Eve is awesome), and some potentially problematic definitional stuff about the man being a "ruler" over/with women (not sure I understand this part). But then the authors turn to one of my major concerns with the presiding/equal partnership paradigm—reciprocity in patriarchal marriage relationship. If the man presides in the marriage (as long as he is righteous), when does the man have an obligation to listen to and, if appropriate, defer to his wife?

Here's what the Hafens have to say about that:

> Spouses need not perform the same functions to be equal. The woman's innate spiritual instincts are like a moral magnet, pointing toward spiritual north—except when that magnet's particles are scrambled out of order. The man's presiding gift is the priesthood—except when he's not living the principles of righteousness.

Here's the good part:

> If the husband and wife are wise, their counseling will be reciprocal: he will listen to the promptings of her inner spiritual compass just as she will listen to his righteous counsel.

Nice! I'm going to show this article to my husband so he'll stop pretending he can't read my inner spiritual compass. Anyway, according to this quote from the article, women have "innate spiritual instincts" that act as a "moral magnet," while men are bestowed with the "presiding gift" of the priesthood. This article reflects LDS Church teachings about the superior spiritual instincts women possess naturally (e.g., nurturing). In fact, the article quotes Boyd K. Packer saying

> the virtues and attributes upon which perfection and exaltation depend come [more] naturally to a woman.[74]

This leads me to my question of what (if any) innate spiritual instincts do men have? Does the "presiding gift" of the priesthood bestow spiritual gifts onto men akin to the woman's naturally occurring spiritual gift of being a "moral magnet"?

I'm wondering if the spiritual gifts men and women possess, either naturally or through the gift of the priesthood, differ. And, of course, what happens when the naturally occurring woman's moral magnet points in a direction that contradicts the man's presiding gift of the priesthood? The authors don't say.

In the next paragraph, however, the authors discuss a true equal marriage partnership:

> And in an equal-partner marriage both also bring a spiritual maturity to their partnership, without regard to gender. Both have a conscience and the Holy Ghost to guide them. Both see family life as their most important work. Each also strives to become a fully-rounded disciple of Jesus Christ—a complete spiritual being.[75]

Good stuff. So after reading this article, I'm still left with questions about the concept of presiding. I don't understand why it's necessary, or even possible, to have someone presiding in a partnership of equals (particularly if their access to (and their substance of) spiritual gifts is identical). But I love the language in the last quote: Both men and women have the Holy Ghost and their individual consciences to guide them in loving and serving their family. That's the message that resonates with me, and so that's the one I'm going with for now.

"THE FEMINIST MORMON OXYMORON" BY LISA PATTERSON BUTTERWORTH (OCTOBER 19, 2007)

> Being a Mormon feminist is a bizarre space to occupy because Mormons see you as very radical, and secular feminists see you as brainwashed.
>
> —EmilyS (shamelessly flaunting her eloquence in BUST[76])

I've been thinking about this bizarre space quite a bit lately, really ever since President Beck's Conference Talk and the subsequent influx of feedback from the type who would call me (us) radical. A part of me finds the whole "radical" allegation silly. Me, radical? I spend most of my time with three-year-olds. I wipe a lot of door knobs and drive a station wagon and have been dutifully submitting to patriarchy for a good 33 years now. At the very least it seems like radical would be much more interesting than this.

On the flip side, brainwashed? Puh-lease. The scrub-brush-wielding patriarchs haven't been near this brain with soap & water in, like . . . ever. It's a mucky mess in here, and I littered it up with untidy faith all by my lonesome. (Well, maybe I had a little help from my friend Jesus.)

But then (funny as I am while being blithely dismissive) I have to wonder, is there any basis to these allegations?

What do they mean exactly by radical anyhow? And is radical always necessarily bad? I mean come on, Joseph Smith was nothing if not radical. And Jesus, seriously, radical dude. But from the tone of the "radical" accusations generally, I'm not catching the "dude" radical vibe. I think they mean something bad radical. And not like Michael-Jackson-"bad" either. Dude.

So what is this bad radical that I (Mormon feminist) embody? I'm not sure honestly. In my head I've guesstimated that 95% of the "bad radical" in those accusations is a mixture of misinformation, misunderstanding, hyperbole, spin, bloggernacle culture shock,[77] and convenient (yet lazy) fiery rhetoric. Feminazi, blah blah, man haters, blah blah, wanna be a man, blah blah, destroy families, blah blah, angry bitter, blah blah. (Boring, untrue, useless, fiery rhetoric) (blah blah). But I'm open to the idea that perhaps buried in me, in this blog, there are substantive ideas, genuine intelligent disagreements that a smart and orthodox Mormon person could thoughtfully classify as radical (in a bad way). Though I would probably prefer to label their substantive ideas as conventional (in a bad way).

I've just decided that what I have here is a semantic dilemma. For example, should your average Mormon desire to call me radical based on my belief that uttering the words "father" and "preside" together (in the same paragraph as "equal partners" no less) is an unfortunate illogical unnecessary sexist bad habit, well then color me radical with a smile on my face. But problematically the accusations of radical are usually paired with the man-hating family-destroying, (yawn) angry-bitter rhetorical foolishness. Thus making me feel less enthusiastic about embracing said problematic adjective.

Still, as adjectives go, I'd take radical over well-behaved any day. (Sadly, well-behaved probably suits me more.)

And speaking of adjectives, I'm sure no one's shocked that "brainwashed" isn't one of my favorites. (To be fair, I can only remember a couple feminists who have gone out of their way to imply that my stubborn Mormoniness must be brainwashy, meanwhile I get the "radical" reaction from the orthodox Mormons on a pur'dy regular basis). (Though come to think of it, I have far more general interactions with Mormons than I do with feminists.)

What do they mean by brainwashed anyhow? Do secular feminists really think I've been systematically programed, coerced even, into believe something that I didn't freely choose? I kinda doubt that's the case. Though I'm sure most secular feminists do view Mormon patriarchy as sexist and unhealthy and my willing submission to it (on any level, while claiming to be a feminist) as highly problematic. Can't say that I blame them, really. But while I, myself, see patriarchy as a flawed system and view my willing submission to it (on some levels) with a great deal of angst, I am also aware, as a secular outsider can never be, that as a practical truth, most of the women I know who willingly choose to submit to their presiding husbands (in ways that I find disturbing both as rhetoric and in practice) live mostly happy, healthy, fulfilling and attractive lives.

I do think that there is a tendency among the intellectual elite to assume that women of a traditional bent (nearly all of the women I know and love) have not thought their way through to a better (less Mormon) option. I guesstimate that 95% of this attitude is pure ignorant snobbery. Most of the (mostly conservative) Mormon women I know are smart and informed and capable of making intelligent non-brainwashy decisions about faith and feminism and politics. Their lot is neither to be pitied nor dismissed.

And yet ... there is veracity too in that we Mormons tend to hide, bury, or ignore uncomfortable truths. Using myself as an example of a (very) average seminary graduate, I only had the vaguest notion that Joseph Smith practiced polygamy (and no idea who Eliza R. Snow was). Further, even the mildest critique of our leaders or institutions, no matter how true, is automatically routinely labeled as complaining, as anti-Mormon, as non-sustaining, as heresy. No discussion allowed.

And in an atmosphere where exploring difficult facts is discouraged and asking uncomfortable questions is viewed as synonymous with unrighteousness we, Mormons, don't exactly deserve a reputation for unflinching intellectual honesty either.

However, it certainly doesn't follow that this flaw makes our faith wrong, nor does my stubbornly clinging to it make me brainwashed.

So what does it all mean? I have no idea, but I have to go do the dishes now.

No wait a sec, I think maybe it means something like, that the distrust that both sides, feminists and Mormons, have for each other, and in turn for me fence sitting in both worlds, while tossed around on largely baseless lazy "radical" "brainwashed" rhetoric, still has some basis in legitimate err ... concerns. Or something. Maybe.

"A WOMAN'S WORK IS NEVER MEASURED" BY LISA PATTERSON BUTTERWORTH (NOVEMBER 4, 2007)

A million years ago I had an assignment to interview a woman older than 50 and then write a paper about her experiences. I interviewed my Auntie M, she is an amazing woman, strong and brilliant and funny, she has raised six brilliant daughters. She has always been a housewife. A power housewife, volunteering for everything, a community leader. A powerful woman, truly. Though never paid, of course.

We were given a list of questions, most of them I have forgotten, and the answers too. But one, I think, was key to my future claiming of feminism. It had to do with work, and how her work was valued, and she answered with this story.

She had conceived, organized and completed a huge project to restore a historic building in her community. This was an enormous undertaking spanning years, involving raising millions of dollars and thousands of hours of labor and resulting in a hugely successful and valuable asset to the community. At the end of the project, as plaques were being made, and donors assigned "levels," it was decided that the lawyers and accountants (and men, basically) who donated their time would have their donations represented in a dollar amount corresponding to what their professional fee would have been for the services rendered. Seems fair.

Until it came time to assess the value of the time of women like Auntie M, and it was determined that her time had no value. Literally. None. Thousands of hours of work, work that utterly drove the project on every level, work that without which there would have been no plaques, no restored building, no donors to thank. Invisible, thankless, undocumented, unaccounted for. Her labor made everything else possible, but it disappeared into a haze of platitudes. *The work you do is so important.*

This made her sad. But saddest of all to me ... "Didn't you fight them?" I asked her, "Why didn't you fight them?"

Her reply: A hopeless little shrug, and a "I don't know how to value my time either."

(Go ahead, feel the rage, throw something.)

This happened probably 30 years ago.

In the 21st century, I like to hope that it is obvious to us all how grossly unfair this was.

Except. . . .

See, I sincerely doubt that anyone, even then, actually thought Auntie M's work was worthless (despite the evidence to the contrary). I'm sure that everyone involved was perfectly aware (on some level) that her labor was, in fact, indispensable. For some reason they could not see their way to giving her labor a monetary value. Perhaps it was a simple lack of imagination, but I think it was more than that.

You see, women do 70% of society's unpaid work (men 30%). Everyone is perfectly aware (on some level) that this work is INDISPENSABLE. That nurturing, volunteer work, laundry is indispensable. Without it, nothing else would happen. And yet no one can see their way to assigning it a monetary value. I'm not talking about paying us for it. I'm simply talking about measuring it. Acknowledging it.

The economy is driven by our labor, this unpaid labor that is done mostly by women. And yet, when the value of the labor performed by

Americans is calculated, when the suited men in government cubicles work their numbers, the vast majority of work done by women, the work upon which the whole system is based, is utterly ignored. Invisible, thankless, undocumented, unaccounted for. Our labor makes everything else possible, but it disappears into a haze of platitudes. *The work you do is so important.*

Grossly unfair, and not lost in the mist of history's misogyny. It is wrong to ignore one woman's work, and it is wrong to ignore millions of women's work. Perhaps it is a simple lack of imagination. But I think it is more than that.

The fact is, until we fundamentally change the way we think about the work women do, until we dispense with the idea that the only "counted" labor is paid labor (traditionally male labor), until we replace empty platitudes with real measurable acknowledged value, then mothering and nurturing and homemaking will continue to be ignored, marginalized, and dismissed.

I'm sure people will argue that it's just numbers, that not every important thing needs to be measured. But the sad fact remains that if we do not place a value on it, it slips easily from unmeasured into unvalued. Invisible. Auntie M.

If we truly want to value motherhood, then we must start by measuring and truly acknowledging that value.

"WOMEN WHO KNOW" BY EMILY SUMMERHAYS (NOVEMBER 15, 2007)

> In the Book of Mormon we read about 2,000 exemplary young men who were exceedingly valiant, courageous, and strong. 'Yea, they were men of truth and soberness, for they had been taught to keep the commandments of God and to walk uprightly before him' (Alma 53:21). These faithful young men paid tribute to their mothers. They said, 'Our mothers knew it' (Alma 56:48).**[78]

I would suspect that their sisters were taught much the same thing, and that these sisters also grew up to be exceedingly valiant, courageous, and strong. These women, like their mothers before them, grew to be Women Who Know—women who know who they are, and who God is; women with great power and influence for good.

Women who know see each other. They look beyond types and sizes and backgrounds and colors to the individuals beneath. They forgive each other hasty words and unkind acts. They give each other strength and the benefit of the doubt.

Women who know, know that they can do better. They recognize their own failings, and endeavor to shore up these weaknesses, but do not let failure keep them down. They are not ashamed to plead for help from

Heaven, they do not fear to reach out for assistance from friends and family, and they do not suffer in silence. Women who know, know that we all fail, that we are all imperfect, that we all need help. Women who know, mourn, and let others mourn with them.

Women who know understand that womanhood is not only and always equated with motherhood. They exist outside the categories of Maiden, Mother, and Crone. They recognize the many other facets of their lives that make them women, make them sisters, daughters, wives, friends, people. They know themselves to be wholly themselves, and precious in the sight of God for their own sakes. Women who are mothers may recognize motherhood to be the greatest of their gifts or responsibilities, but also know that there is much they bring to the world apart from their children. These mothers strive to teach their children of the individual importance of each spirit daughter and son of God, and endeavor to teach by example.

Women who know, know that counsel is just counsel—not decree. They know that in fact their greatest guide is God, and that their most important choices should be made, not on the say-so of well-meaning strangers, but in tandem with Heaven and, should they have one, their husband. These women recognize the wisdom of counsel, but remember their individual worth, and know that God has a Plan specifically for them. Women who know seek their Path by prayer, and also by faith.

Women who know, know that they don't know everything. They recognize the great wealth of knowledge to be gained from people from all walks of life, from all parts of the world, and from all religious backgrounds. Women who know reach out to their sisters and brothers throughout the world, striving to share knowledge even as they seek it, understanding that shared wisdom cultivates strength and compassion.

Women who know, know that strength and compassion are their twin inheritance—neither one without the other—for these are the gifts of Christ: Charity, that never faileth.

**This quotation lifted from the introduction to R.S. General President Beck's recent General Conference talk, Mothers Who Know[79] (as if you didn't know). This post is not intended so much as a response as a . . . variation on the theme.

So . . . what else do Women Who Know know?

"MY CHRISTMAS STORY" BY QUIMBY MASTERS (DECEMBER 8, 2007)

It is February. I am in Syria, in a Bedouin tent, surrounded by American friends and Bedouin strangers. They have served us tea; and while my friends urge me to drink it, so as not to appear rude, my Mormon faith in the Word of Wisdom compels me instead to pretend to drink while surreptitiously pouring mouthful-amounts on the ground. I hope Heavenly Father will forgive my dishonesty and my cowardice; I am sure my Seminary teacher would tell me to use it as a missionary opportunity, but I'm less sure that would be looked upon favourably. Our Bedouin host has also offered us flat bread and fermented goat cheese. The cheese is delicious; but I wonder if it is safe to eat, having been told that it sat all day in the hot sun; so I politely dip my bread in it, but only occasionally. (Later, I learn it was a wise decision; while my friends spent the night trekking to the toilet to throw up, I slumbered on undisturbed.)

All around Syria, the sky is lit up with fireworks; people are feasting; children are opening their presents; and there is a sense of gaiety. It is the end of Ramadan, and we are on a week-long break from our studies. For some reason Ramadan ended a day earlier in Egypt. The day before, my friend and I gingerly picked our way through the blood-stained mosaic tiles in the foyer of her apartment building in an upscale suburb of Cairo; another family in the complex had killed their Ramadan lamb that afternoon. Here in this tent, there is just this—a meagre meal of fermented goat cheese and bread, some tea, and stilted conversation. I try to memorise the details. The tent is roughly divided in two rooms. I imagine it is much the same as their ancestors' tents looked 1000 years ago, but with some modifications. The walls are covered in kilm and Persian rugs, but through the gaps, I see black tarp. Our host is cooking over an open fire in the centre of this, the living room; but there is an old pickup truck outside, which the men use in their shepherding. My friend pulls out her chapstick. Fascinated, the woman asks to try some. We all pull out our tubes of chapstick and pass them around. We insist they keep them.

Most shepherds in the Middle East are Bedouin; that is as it has always been. The fields outside of Bethlehem, a predominantly Arab settlement at the time of Christ's birth, have long been a popular feeding ground for local tribes of Bedouins. We have no way of knowing for sure; but I like to think that the angels appeared to the Bedouins with their tidings of joy.

I imagine the Bedouins, who are being told to go to Bethlehem to pay tribute to a Jewish baby. The Bedouins, while not as hated as the Kurds, are at times only tolerated in the Middle East; they are not quite considered Arab, and often those Arabs who live in the towns and cities will look down their nose at them because of their poverty and nomadic lifestyle. And of course, the Jews at the time of Christ's birth were not the most inclusive of people; they were known to avoid even other Jews, and had as few dealings as possible with non-Jews. What did they think, these Bedouin shepherds? Were they fearful of rejection? Did they come bearing gifts? Perhaps they chose a fat lamb—an exorbitant gift, surely. Perhaps they offered tea, flat bread, and fermented goat cheese. Perhaps they offered only their awe and wonder.

I also imagine Mary and Joseph, set upon in an intimate moment by a herd of Bedouin shepherds. Were they welcoming? Were they fearful? After all, if you are raised to not interact with a group of people, it must be threatening to suddenly have them appear in droves at your front door. Perhaps, if they brought tea and food, Mary accepted it gratefully, exhausted after her labor. I am sure she welcomed their awe and wonder; what mother doesn't?

I am walking along a street in Melbourne. It is early December, unusually hot and sticky. The aromatherapy shop is displaying seasonal greetings and advertising for sale Frankincense and Myrrh. I wander in, intrigued at the prospect of such a fitting scent for the home. The owner of the shop explains to me that one originated in China, and the other in Ethiopia. Both are sold in their resin form. She shows me how to burn them, and I leave with a bag of each and a roll of charcoal.

I've never actually found any proof that one of the resins came from as far away as China; most sources claim they are both from Ethiopia or the Arab peninsula. But it is a bit of folklore I hope is true, because it adds to my enjoyment of the season. (The annual burning of Frankincense and Myrrh, however, does not. Five years on, and after I have shared the resin with family, friends, and complete strangers, I still have plenty; they are not pleasant scents.)

At any rate, it is probably safe to assume that few of the Wise Men were Jewish. There is a large Jewish population in Ethiopia; folklore there claims that the Queen of Sheba was Ethiopian. So it is possible. But certainly, if there was a Chinese Wise Man, he would not be; and if there was a Wise Man from the Arabian peninsula, he would probably not be, either.

I like to think that those first worshippers of Jesus Christ were Bedouin, Chinese, Ethiopian, Arabic—a rainbow of diversity, symbolic of the Atoning sacrifice, which is for all of us. Christ, this infant boy from a culture that was as insular and isolated as any culture ever has been, made His first effort to reach beyond His community when He was not yet old enough to speak.

Unless you believe the story from the Koran. It is one of my favorites. As Mary proudly displayed her infant son to her family, they scorned and scoffed at her for her promiscuity. Then the Christ child, still a babe in arms, opened his mouth and quieted them: My mother is a virgin, and I am to be a mighty prophet.

All of the known world was united in worshipping and welcoming the Christ child. Europe played a role, too: Palestine was at the time an occupied country; the Jews an occupied people. Mary and Joseph were in Bethlehem to pay their tribute to the Roman government. Surely it is possible that some of the visitors, that first Christmas in Bethlehem, were Roman?

I like to imagine it is so, because the inclusion of a Roman would mean that all of the classes were represented too: king and peasant, occupier and occupied.

Each year, as I put out the pieces of my Nativity, I despair that the faces aren't more widely representative of the ethnicities I like to imagine were there. There is a Wise Man who is darker than the rest; but his features are not terribly African, and he could be merely an Italian with a good tan. The rest of the characters are unmistakably European. It is a beautiful set; but I long to someday find one that is the rainbow of diversity I imagine. The Christmas story is not for us alone; the mission of Jesus Christ was to redeem all of us, rich and poor, from every corner of the Earth. Over the centuries, we have lost the exact details of who was there; but I believe the purpose of the story is to remind us that we are not so unique in receiving the benefits of the Atoning sacrifice of Jesus Christ. All of us are beneficiaries.

It is a day later. We have left Palmyra, and we are now in a small church in Aramaic Syria. The priest tells us this is the oldest Christian church in the world; he claims the wood in the ceiling beams has been carbon-dated back some 2000 years. He proudly shows us a small gorge where Christ is meant to have walked. And then he gives me the greatest gift of all—he sings the Lord's Prayer, melodic and reverent, in its original Aramaic. The language of Christ, now almost dead; but Christ Himself lives on. He speaks only halting English, this ancient Orthodox Priest in his cassock robes and flowing white beard, and I speak no Aramaic. Many of our central doctrines are different. But as I stand there, listening to their song, I know we are united in Christ, drawn together irrevocably by an infant born into mortality some 2000 years ago.

"CALLING OUT" BY PAULA JENSEN GOODFELLOW (DECEMBER 10, 2007)

When I was a freshman at USU,[80] I discovered *Dialogue: A Journal of Mormon Thought* and used to go read the back issues in the library, when I should have been studying. That was where I first discovered Juanita Brooks and read an essay by her called "Riding Herd." In it, she said,

> One day Dad said to me, "My girl, if you follow this tendency to criticize, I'm afraid you will talk yourself out of the Church. I'd hate to see you do that. I'm a cowboy and I've learned that if I ride in the herd, I am lost. . . . One who rides counter to it is trampled and killed. One who only trails behind means little because he leaves all responsibility to others. It is the cowboy who rides the edge of the herd, who sings and calls and makes himself heard, who helps direct the course. So don't lose yourself, and don't ride away and desert the outfit. Ride the edge of the herd and be alert, and know your directions and call out loud and clear. Chances are you won't make any difference, but on the other hand, you just might."[81]

Although I'm deeply Mormon, even then I was troubled by several aspects of LDS practice, culture and doctrine. Brooks's story appealed to me as a reason to stay in the church. Thirty years later, I'm not sure that I've been very good at influencing the herd; in fact, in many ways the herd has run the opposite way than I would have liked. Raising kids, working for pay at times, and schooling has taken a lot of my time, and I've not made many concerted efforts to call out to the herd. I've mostly sat in the corner and felt like the sheep who has wandered from the fold (but not all who wander are lost). A lot of the things that bothered me when I was 20 still bother me now. I tend to put them on the shelf, or just keep quiet, or just read a book and ignore stuff, but for some reason, something in me snapped in October when I heard Relief Society President Julie Beck's talk in General Conference, about "Mothers Who Know,"[82] and I got tired of just being quiet. I spent a while trying to write my own response, which I planned to post at theculturalhall.com, but could never come up with anything that I thought was positive enough. For me, the talk was deeply disappointing, for many reasons. I won't list them here. (Maybe I will later in another post.) I didn't ever put up the blog post, but then a group of women I've known for the last decade or so began drafting a response to the talk which ended up being called "What Women Know."[83] I decided to join in as one way to ride on the edge of the herd, calling out.

In this post, I'd like to ask the question of how do we "call out loud and clear" using the example of the response to President Beck's speech. First, I'd like to make it clear that I'm not speaking for anyone else in the group who drafted the response. However, many of the people who signed would share at least some of these feelings. (And, I'd like to mention here that our group never considered it to be a "rebuttal." That's a term that's been attached to it by bloggers and the *Salt Lake Tribune*. It's intended to be a response only, not an attack, rebuttal, manifesto, or proclamation.)

One criticism of What Women Know is that it was a public response to President Beck's talk. But her talk was a public speech—why not a public response? Several people suggested that we should have written private letters—well, how do you know that we haven't? For me, it just seemed time, after many years of being too afraid to speak out, to actually say what I thought, in public, to let people know where I stood. Just having a voice was one goal for me. And the slim chance that some positive change might come as a result of speaking out was another motivation.

Let's consider some other options for responding to the talk that have been suggested to us:

1. Discuss it privately with friends. That might make us feel better but probably won't do much to change anything, unless we happen to be well-connected in the church. Only talking to our friends is an approach that keeps us from having a true voice. And if we're discussing things that make us unhappy—then we're accused of murmuring.

2. Write personal letters to Julie Beck. If we write quiet letters to Salt Lake City, nobody else knows we're suggesting there's a problem. This leaves most everyone else in isolation, including ourselves.

One great thing about the emails we've received has been the response from many women—and men—saying that they're glad that someone spoke out and that they're not alone. One sad response from someone who has left the church said, "Where were you women when I was considering leaving the church?"

3. Talk about it in Relief Society. Hmm, are we serious, here? I suppose that in some wards there might be some honest discussion of how this talk made many women feel. But my guess is that in most wards, even mildly critical discussion would be stomped down quickly. And would any of that conversation be passed along higher up?

4. Talk to our local leaders. Not a bad idea, and it might possibly work to bring about change on a local level, for a time, but realistically we still might be accused of murmuring, and our local leaders are not likely to have a lot of power to pass on our opinions to those in higher positions.

5. So we made this choice, as phrased by a member of our group: "We're talking out loud. Not murmuring. Not expecting anything to change. Just asserting our right to be grownups, to talk out loud."

So, any experiences with riding on the herd and calling out loud and clear? And if so, how'd it go? What approach did you take?

2008

Church President Gordon B. Hinckley passed away at the age of 97, and senior apostle Thomas S. Monson replaced him. Church leaders also called Elaine S. Dalton as the President of the Young Women's organization. Later that year, Dalton and her counselors, Mary N. Cook and Ann M. Dibb, sent a letter to priesthood leaders announcing their decision to add a new value, virtue, to the Young Women theme. This emphasis on virtue, equated with sexual purity, became a theme of Dalton's presidency.

In April, law enforcement raided a Fundamentalist Latter-day Saint (FLDS) compound near Eldorado, Texas, and an investigation into child abuse allegations and custody rights soon followed. The LDS Church commissioned a survey of 1,000 people in late May and found that 36 percent thought the Texas compound was part of the LDS Church; another 6 percent thought they were partly related, and 29 percent were not sure. These findings prompted a new campaign on the Church's website to clarify the disavowal of polygamy by mainstream Mormons.

The LDS Church offered clear and repeated support of Proposition 8 in California, in partnership with the Protect Marriage Coalition. The proposition sought to add an amendment to the state constitution that would define marriage as exclusively available to opposite-sex couples. The First Presidency sent a letter to congregations throughout California in June asking Church members to support the measure. Many contributed funds, volunteered time to canvas in their areas, and participated in phone campaigns.

Proposition 8 passed in November. In the days following, a *New York Times* headline read "Mormons Tipped Scale in Ban on Gay Marriage."[84] Throughout the bloggernacle, authors and readers tried to parse out conflicting feelings of belief in Church teachings, desire to follow the prophet, support for gay and lesbian couples, and objection to the Church's role in the political campaign.

FMH published a large number of posts on the subject of Proposition 8 and the Church's involvement, leading to many heated and heartfelt discussions. Overall, the blog added 520 new posts to its archives during 2008 and three new permabloggers: mfranti, Serenity Valley, and Shelah. The blog, which had always been home to intensely personal writing, took on an even more vulnerable tone in this year as a result of tender losses and pains. Lisa Butterworth began to document her father's failing health. He passed away in May, leaving her to process her grief and complex feelings about the passing of her family's patriarch. Rachel Lauritzen also mourned the death of a loved one, a child still in utero. The loss of baby Grace was met with love and sympathy on the blog as readers responded to requests for prayers and for donations to Heifer International to serve the needs of hungry children around the world in honor of Grace. Permablogger Janet, who had celebrated the chance to be sealed to her adopted son earlier in the year, announced in October that an anticipated second adoption had failed. All these occurrences and the ways in which they were received by the FMH writing and reading community highlighted the ways in which the blog inspired real relationships and connection.

"CHOSEN?" BY REBECCA MCLAVERTY HEAD (JANUARY 12, 2008)

Every week I teach the Gospel Principles[85] class. Though the manual is in serious need of updating, I enjoy teaching the basics of the gospel to a small class of investigators.

Every now and then I find something that I just feel uncomfortable teaching. Usually something I'm not sure I believe or something I don't think is doctrine, just opinion/culture. In this situation I usually just leave it out, yet I sometimes feel maybe I shouldn't—I have an important job to educate investigators/new members into the ins and outs of the church, and although I may not like some things, they are part of the church's teachings.

This week's lesson is on the Heavenly Family (premortal us and the fact we have Heavenly parents).

> He has chosen the time and place for each of us to be born so
> we can learn the lessons we personally need and do the most
> good with our individual talents and personalities.[86]

Sitting in my comfy, 21st century, Western home of course I can say this and believe it entirely. But I have a really hard time believing that God chose for a child to be born with AIDS in famine-ridden Africa. I have a problem believing that someone's "lesson" is being sold into child prostitution and repeatedly assaulted on a daily basis. I have a problem believing that God says John can go to a rich family and have the best education money can buy, but Peter over there can live in poverty and never get and education—he'll need to leave school early to earn money for his family.

Firstly, does anyone know of any quotes by prophets saying the same kind of thing as the quote from the lesson? (Is it really doctrine?)

Secondly, is there a possible way to reconcile the horror of some people's lives with this statement?

"MOTHERING WITH DISABILITIES: THE PERSONAL OF THE POLITICAL" BY JANET GARRARD-WILLIS (FEBRUARY 29, 2008)

I am a disabled mother.

One could easily argue that all mothers of very young children qualify for the term in a loose sense—if you think I'm absolutely batty, then you haven't recently run the gauntlet of an icy supermarket parking lot while toting a baby, the capacious innards of a diaper bag (only slightly smaller than the luggage I took to Europe for a month), and your fan-damily's weekly edibles while keeping eyes alert for cavalier drivers incapable of using a turn signal. Doing anything with munchkins presents oft-daunting challenges, even as it presents the endless pseudo-springtime of seeing the world renewed through baby eyes: Look! An avocado! What is that thing? Fascinating: I must eat it. Look, dog poo! Same reaction. Rather more scary for mama and possibly papa.

But no, I am extra disabled. My bladder disease enervates nearly every aspect of my life. Despite the United Nations' 2006 proclamation which secures me the right of employment regardless of disease,[87] I cannot currently hold a job in good conscience. What sort of college professor vacates classes three times an hour to go pee? I had to stop presenting papers at hoity toity academic conferences for fear that midway through my own diatribe I'd have to curl up on the floor like an agonized pill bug. I cannot finish my dissertation—ever tried to sustain an academic argument in 15-minute bursts accompanied by pain? I'll have to figure out how, but so far I suck at it. I cannot take road trips in non-urban areas (God bless heavily forested roads), cannot camp without freezing the hineys of my tent-mates by unzipping the flap a zillion times, and cannot sleep for longer than 30 minutes—which means every night consists of a series of catnaps. I cannot go longer than 6–7 months without surgery. I cannot have sex with my husband without expecting charley horses to gallop through my innards for the next 5 hours and require, quite possibly and no kidding, opium and valium. (And yes, before someone asks, they are slight compensation for the agony which requires them. Heh.) On a less druggy note but still five-alarm freaky to my own mother, I cannot get through a normal day without low-dose narcotics every 4–6 hours.

I also cannot expect to ever get better. Though, luckily, there is hope and I'm pursuing it with Obama-like fury, for I do not want to accept the present as my future king.

But tralalalala, this mostly has not bothered me. Why? Because my life is BEAUTIFUL. I love my family and they love me. DH and I live in a character-filled (heh, pun) 106-year-old house perched on the cusp of a gorgeous canyon, and we can walk to the Salt Lake temple in 15 minutes.

Friends fill my extroverted cornucopia with laughter and happiness like a Thanksgiving tableau. I have theological questions which keep my mind and soul zinging about, but instead of angst (well, mostly) my relationship with God has me singing extemporaneous ditties in the car because the sunset is pretty and I like chatting with Him about it. I've got a decent mind and a decent heart. And most of all, after 11 years of marriage and enough tears to re-sink Kate and Leonardo, I have a baby. And he is beautiful.[88]

He is also the reason disability tires and angers me now, rather than merely annoying me. No United Nations proclamation, surgery, pill, or quantity of logic can explain to a 9-month-old baby why Mommy could fit that week's groceries into the bags under her eyes or why she cannot venture out on the 5-mile hike in an un-treed area he would so like to explore. My Muffin, he's a busy boy. He just wants to play on the grass and cavort through life joyfully accompanying my ditties ("mamapapapalalababBAHBOO!") with me holding his hands and keeping him from face-planting on the sidewalk. He cannot and should not have to understand why I am ... less than I should be. What I mostly am, physically, is tired and quite uncomfortable.

Selfish, self-pitying, self-absorbed post. Yes yes. I've had the general topic on my roster for months, fully intending to research and write something a bit more political and poignant—but see "inability to sustain academic argument" above. Nonetheless, and as pathetically self-pitying as this may be, it is nonetheless a FEMINIST topic.

It is not a sexy one. It lacks the flash, polemic, and poster board of Roe v. Wade or glass ceilings. Nonetheless, it is heavily imbricated with those things, and connecting the dots does not take long, though I'm not focusing on those two things right here. But I tentatively suggest that The Biggee for feminism and disabled mamas is this: mothers most frequently bear the brunt of child care as well as other domestic labor. Because a domicile lacks the camaraderie and colleagues of paid employment, disabled mothers bear this brunt largely alone. Feminist movements have been rightly criticized in the past for occluding the struggles of "the common woman"—blue collar workers, single moms, queer women and mothers, the poor, stay-at-home mothers, and basically anyone removed from the abortion debate or academia. Such criticism has happily been instrumental in compelling a more inclusive movement. But SAHMs[89] remain the most ghettoized of women in the feminist movement (and they sit in "no-man's land—another pun—of the Mommy Wars as well) for they lack the sort of clout that gets the poster boards a'waving. Disabled moms face an additional challenge: not only do they labor alone and largely invisible, they often lack the energy necessary to organize and make their voices heard and their causes examined. Disabled men in the workforce (and women, for that matter) have it rough, but they also have organized resources, unions, and other recompense to help weather the rough spots. SAHMs, not so much. And we cannot explain this to small children, who suffer as do we.

And if other mamas are at all like me, they also suffer from pride and do not want to ask for the help they need, of either a government or a congregation. But we're a numerous lot. If I just consider the bloggernacle, I quickly run out of fingers and toes to count disabled mamas upon. We are many, and we are mostly silent.

I am unsure what to do about that. Hopefully I'll get to more in-depth political analysis with Part II, but right now I'm starting with a blog post.

"BABIES, CAREERS AND POWER STRUGGLES" BY SHELAH MASTNY MINER (APRIL 17, 2008)

Over the last year, I've asked my DH the same question over and over. He always gives me the same answer. I ask again and again (and again), hoping, I guess, that I'll wear him down if I ask enough. If you know me, you know the question, you know the answer, and you, like my DH, probably think I should just get over it (for those of you who don't know me, the question is, "Can we have another baby?").

I realize that lobbying for yet another baby to keep me at home and tied down probably doesn't seem like the most feminist of positions. But I've realized recently that it's precisely my feminism, and not just my hormones, that keeps the discussion at the forefront of my mind.

When we got married eleven years ago, we had two common goals that we wanted to accomplish over the next decade. We were going to have four kids and we were going to get him through his medical training. We originally thought he'd probably become a radiologist. It seemed like the perfect combination of science, family time and earning potential. But during his fourth year of medical school, he decided that radiologists were doctors who reported to other doctors and basically weren't in the driver's seat when it came to patient care (my DH is the world's worst backseat driver, so I can see how this would have been a hard thing for him). He had also fallen in love with cardiology—where he would get lots of patient contact, lots of autonomy, lots of intellectual challenge, and generous earning potential. The sacrifice? Family time. We talked about the decision a lot, and eventually decided that he should make the career move that would provide him the most long-term satisfaction, even if it meant less family time in the short term. Recently, he opted to extend his fellowship by another year, again so he'd have more career satisfaction, even though the extra year would not earn him any more money and would probably mean more phone calls in the middle of the night to do emergency procedures at the hospital. Again, we weighed the pros and cons, and he, with my support, did what he wanted.

So here's where things get tricky. I think we both feel that although both of our opinions count when it comes to his career (especially when it pertains to the family), he gets the ultimate say. As a married couple, we make our big family decisions together. I agree with making decisions together. For most of our marriage, it has served us very well. We rarely disagree—except this time. So where does that leave me? Since he's not home much, virtually all of the day-to-day decisions about the family are mine. I decide what to buy and eat, where and when we vacation, whether or not to put the kids in swimming lessons, how to keep the house, what the kids read and when they do their homework, and a hundred other small decisions every day. I'm dang good at it too. So yeah, any small-to-mid-level decision in the family falls to me, and I guess it rankles that while he has final say about his own career, we have to come to an agreement about big decisions in what has become, at least temporarily, my career.

As any smart married person knows, when one partner in the couple doesn't want a baby, there should be no baby. He says, "Four kids was our original agreement." But why should an agreement made more than ten years ago still carry so much weight? It almost seems like the (totally stupid) criticisms of Mitt Romney's flip-flopping. While I might not agree with Romney's increasingly conservative positions, I had no problem with him changing his mind on issues as a result of his experiences (if experience, and not pandering, was what made him change his mind). Ten years ago I thought I'd be overwhelmed by four kids and wouldn't be able to handle more. But experience has shown me that heck, what's one more when you've already got a house full?

I've finally decided it's not even about the baby. If I'm really honest with myself, I'm pretty sure I could either take or leave having another one. But it's hard for me to finish a phase of my life that I've loved. And it's harder to give up absolute control in making a decision that I think should be (at least mostly) mine to make.

"Traditional Marriage Is Dead (and It's a Good Thing Too)" by Laurie Burk (June 26, 2008)

The bloggernacle is awash with posts on same-sex marriage, the First Presidency's upcoming letter[90] and the demise of traditional marriage. Over and over I read comments about how "traditional marriage" is under attack. How gays and lesbians marrying will "destroy marriage." How we have to fight to defend "traditional marriage" and the family from, variously, the homosexual agenda, the evils of the world, the forces of Satan, etc. etc. etc. But the sad (glad) news is that traditional marriage is dying or dead in much of the world and has been for a long time. And its demise has nothing to do with gays or lesbians. It was us women who killed it, forced its reinvention and started us down this "slippery slope" to where we are today.

What we call marriage in this country is a very recent invention. Throughout the millennia marriage has been not about two people who love each other and want to share a life together, but rather about power, property and paternity. About male control of women's work, women's lives and women's fertility. The importance of virginity, the stigma of bastardy, the "head of the household" status, coverture,[91] and in some cultures arranged marriages, bride price, dowries, honor killings, and the right of husbands but not wives to divorce at will—all of this was (or shamefully still is) part of the effects of traditional marriage.

These basic underpinnings of traditional marriage cross cultural boundaries. Yes, the monogamous found the polygamous found the polyandrous to be barbaric and uncivilized and just plain wrong. Not too much tolerance there. Nevertheless, things like monogamy vs. polygamy were differences of degree, not type. Traditional marriage began its decline the day women became autonomous people. The day our status became human, not property.

So we (our culture and our religion) had to redefine marriage to be relevant to 21st century life. We now talk about love and sharing our lives and being equal partners and mutual respect. Because of this, the world and the church have had to reinvent marriage. Society has reinvented it through laws. Many decry no-fault divorce, but once marriage became a joining of two loving, devoted and equal partners, it's hard to force one to stay when he or she no longer wants to. Others decry same-sex marriage, but once society redefined marriage from a chattel arrangement to one between equals, you need more reasons than unshared religious values or the "ick" factor to prevent people from marrying the one they love.

The church has also reinvented marriage, most recently in the Proclamation on the Family. But as grand or inspired or annoying or frightening as you might find that document, it doesn't reflect the reality of what marriage in the church was 100 or 50 or even 20 year ago. Re-read the polygamy parts of D&C 132, or ask someone who took her marriage vows before 1990 what she covenanted: it was a kind of marriage quite foreign to the one described in the Proclamation on the Family.

The LDS church has already reinvented marriage to conform to our ideas of morality and modern culture. Others have too. The battle now isn't over whether "traditional marriage" will survive but rather over who gets to have their redefinition accepted by the rest of society.

"A Sad Little Quiet Spot" by Rachael Lauritzen (July 27, 2008)

I buried my little daughter this week. It was not easy. But we've been praying for peace and we have found some. I've actually smiled this week, teased people, helped cranky toddlers calm down, and done lots of normal things. I've had outbursts of grief, where the ache of missing my baby took over my heart. I want her back so very badly.

But mostly I've had this quiet spot of sadness in my heart. People ask me how I'm doing, often people I don't know well, and what am I supposed to say? So I tell them that I've been better, but we're doing okay. And sometimes my mouth smiles, but my eyes don't.

And sometimes I forget, just a little. It seems like an eternity since last Saturday, when she was born. And since we buried her, a terrifying normality has started to creep back into our lives. Terrifying because she was here so briefly and I fear losing connection with her, emotional and spiritual. The physical connection is fading fast. My breasts made milk for the baby they expected, but no baby was there to suck. I gave birth to a small, small child, so the stress on my body was also small, relative to a full-term birth. And there is so little tangible evidence that she was ever here.

We lingered at her grave today. Marigold[92] pulled drooping flowers out of funeral sprays, and we sang to her. I have larkspurs from the graveside service that I want to press inside my scriptures, once I decide which verse I want them next to. And I think about the songs and poems we chose for the service.

I think also about the vast swelling of love and kindness we've received from every corner, including the funeral home and the cemetery, and including so many family and friends, some of whom I've never met. Grace's ark fund[93] is over $3,000 now and I get teary with gladness that her short little life will affect so many for good, will help other little children to have happier, healthier, more comfortable lives.

And I think of how my faith in Christ and the promise of Christ's atonement has become so much more tender for having loved and lost, and offered, again, the gift of regaining my loss. Grace may have been denied a long, happy life on this earth, but she has been welcomed back to God, pure and innocent, never having known sorrow or suffering. And that, too, is a gift from God, just as my little Grace was to me.

So I have a sad little quiet spot in my heart. But I have a quietly glad and peaceful spot too. I look forward to death, after my (I hope) long, healthy, and happy life. And I hold to the hope that I can stay close enough to God to rejoin my perfect little baby.

"MORMONS FOR MARRIAGE" BY LAURA COMPTON/HERA (AUGUST 21, 2008)

Why Mormons for Marriage?[94]

I was driving through southeastern Idaho on my way home from a family vacation when I received the text message on my cell phone: "CA Supreme Court just legalized gay marriage." We started flipping through radio channels, looking for a news station so we could hear the full story. Why is there never a news station when you need one?

We'd been waiting for this ruling for years, and I was joyous for my dear friends who were sure to take advantage of the ruling. When the Knight Initiative, Prop. 22, passed in California eight years ago, its constitutionality was immediately questioned. Although 61% of voters had supported the statutory change that defined marriage as between one man and one woman, voter turnout for that particular Primary election was low—only 7.5 million people, not even one-third of California's 21.2 million registered voters, even showed up at the polls that day. (There were 4.6 million people who voted for the proposition and 2.9 million who voted against it.)

The Church was quite involved in the campaign process supporting Proposition 22. In my ward and stake, members were organized to walk precincts and call voters. This electioneering was incorporated into our mid-week youth and Relief Society activities. People were called in to bishops' offices and asked to donate to the campaign, messages were read from the pulpit and signs supporting the proposition were passed out from the Cultural Hall[95] after church meetings. At first, it was not quite clear whether the church's involvement was coming from regional leaders or from Salt Lake City. By the time the election rolled around, though, nobody wondered any longer. We were told the direction was coming from the prophet himself.

While all this electioneering was happening, people were starting to squirm—was it legal for the church to be involved in political matters, even if they called the matters moral ones? Were bishops really asking members to donate to political campaigns? Were financial goals or assessments being made to various wards or stakes? Was there room for gay people in the church at all? Did they really threaten our homes, families and religion?

Sadly, some people, in their self-justified "calls to repentance" and in the sure knowledge of the righteousness and correctness of their position, took their zeal for all things good one step too far. Souls—and lives—were being lost. As the election came and went, those of us left behind had the task to clean up what was left of the mess. We needed to repair bridges with the community and we needed to convince non-members that we were not homophobic bigots, but mostly we needed to heal our own flocks. People felt unwelcome at church and unloved by God because of what they experienced during that election process.

Fast-forward not quite a decade, and we are re-visiting this issue once again. This time, though, the stakes are higher. This time we are amending the constitution—a document that is primarily for limiting governmental actions and defining citizens' rights. Instead of preventing marriages, we will be ending marriages. And because of California's domestic partnership laws, and broad adoption rights, children are found in many of these newlywed homes.

There are also more GLBT people, friends and family, LDS and not, who have come out to share their experiences.

Why me? Why now? I believe there is room for everyone in the church, and somebody needs to stand up and point out the spaces, even for those who don't support the proposition at hand. The church says, in its document about the Divine Institution of Marriage, that members will "decide their own appropriate level of involvement in protecting marriage between a man and a woman."

In order for people to decide what to do, they need information. LDS people are probably not going to go searching the web for sites like EqualityCA because there's no "faithful" LDS tie-in. If they find signingforsomething, they'll read the bitterness and see the pain and be able to take a stand, but they won't be linked up to personal stories about homosexuals and the Church. That's where Mormons for Marriage steps in.

The goal of Mormons for Marriage is to provide a place of support and issues education. It is not a place for heated debate or discussion. It is a place to provide community for members who might feel isolated in their ambivalence or opposition to Prop. 8.

My personal experience has been that as I have stepped forward to speak truth from my heart and soul on this and other issues, that others have joined me, either publicly or privately. It is incumbent upon those of us who have the ability to voice our opinions to do so in a loving manner that we may show by our examples that the Church—and the Gospel—is for everyone.

I know far too many people who have sacrificed too much at the altar of the LDS church's stance on homosexuality. Too many marriages have been ruined, too many spouses, husbands and fathers who have lost each other, their children and their lives. Too many of my friends have died at their own hands or severely injured themselves trying. Too many of my friends have been beaten, shamed, driven away from home. Too many live in fear that their secrets will be known to the wrong people, and too many children of God grow up learning to hate themselves because they go to church and hear the message that people like them are abominations. Too many of my friends and family members have been cut off from the church they once loved (and often continue to appreciate) because their local bishops and stake presidents did not have the ability to understand them. Their pain is my pain.

After much prayer and consideration, I feel at peace with my Lord and Savior by following this path of love. Surely His grace is sufficient to cover me, and He accepts my best efforts as much as He accepts the widow's mite. After all, it is all that I can give. It is all that I can do.

"RECONCILING MORMON FEMINISM WITH PATRIARCHY" BY LISA PATTERSON BUTTERWORTH (SEPTEMBER 17, 2008)

The following reader question is worded rather tactlessly, but if you can look past that, it really does get to the heart of what probably confuses a lot of non-Mormons about women (and feminists) in our Church. So I thought I'd make a good-willed effort to answer it honestly.

Ruby asks:

> This is what has confused me since I've discovered this site. If you are really feminist agents of change what have you changed in your church to share power? I don't read anything about being on committees debating resolutions for women to take their equal place in the hierarchy. The priesthood for example is debated endlessly in the catholic church. There are female rabbis. Women are working within their religious institutions and making some progress. Otherwise why would a woman stay in an abusive institution?

I think the way each of us reconciles our relationship with the Church is different. There are really two questions here: first how we reconcile on the inside of ourselves, and then how we reconcile in our interactions with the institution (or be agents of change).

For me, on the personal level, it comes down to recognizing that life and people and institutions are complicated and messy. And to accept that faith (like love) is not always logical, but still a positive force in my life. Of course it would be lovely if the (earthly) Church was perfect, as it would be nice if all my friends, family, and auxiliaries were perfect, but it's a human world and we have to accept that the good and lovely will come with a dose of the miserable. And love each other anyway. Because we are messy and noble like that.

I have faith in (and love for) (a lot of) Mormon "doctrine" (insofar as Mormons have such a thing). I am comfortable and happy in (for the most part) Mormon culture. Sure there are plenty of things that don't make sense, that drive me bonkers, that seem blatantly illogical and/or unfair. Sure it seems like I should work to change those things.

However, Mormonism isn't really set up that way.

The thing you have to understand is that the organization of the Church is based on Divine Authority and Revelation (which is in and of itself a messy and complicated thing). We believe that our Prophet (and no one else) has divine authority to receive revelation and speak to and for the Church. We also believe that everyone has a right to personal revelation for ourselves, but not for anyone else, nor for the Church as a whole.

Which (obviously) sets up an interesting tension. *Because* I believe that the Prophet speaks for the Church, I do not feel like I can make a "committee or resolution" to demand that priesthood be extended to women. But while I do have faith in the Prophet, I don't have faith in a sex-exclusive priesthood/hierarchy. Nor can I see any reason but sexism and imbalance and unfairness in patriarchy (but this is not true for most women in the Church).

There are at least several dozen lame excuses and reasons given for this imbalance, but I find them all full of pure hogwash. I figure God gave me the ability to logic for a reason, I figure I should use it. And yes, logically the Church is a sexist organization. And logically sexism is wrong.

But despite the fact that I can and do acknowledge this, I do not feel comfortable labeling it an abusive institution. Yes, abuse situations do occasionally arise, and yes, examples of sexism, both petty and profound, are a dime a dozen (as they are in most institutions), but most Mormons (including the hierarchy/patriarchs) are making deeply good-hearted efforts to live lives that are fair to women as they understand it and according to their own faith. And most women in the Church are happy and thriving—living rich, fulfilling, even empowered lives.

How do I reconcile these opposing beliefs?

I don't.

I could give up my faith in the Prophet, or try to, but then I'd be cutting out an important part of my heart and happiness and joy in the world. I could turn my back on my belief in equality, or try to, or I could ignore basic logic (as many do IMO) and twist my beliefs about equality until it becomes something that doesn't look much like equality anymore at all. But then I'd be making myself into someone else entirely. And I like me. So instead I just accept that (much like quantum physics) it makes no sense to me. Perhaps it will someday, perhaps the Church will change (it changes all the time), perhaps my understanding will change (changes all the time), perhaps it will someday makes sense, perhaps it never will. But somehow, I am at peace with that. Most of the time.

So that's how I (don't really) reconcile it. I'd be very interested in other Mormon feminist views.

"RAGE AND SORROW" BY SARA BURLINGAME (NOVEMBER 6, 2008)

This is crazywomancreek's[96] final guest post. Please do not read if you object to strong language.

Trying to craft something concise and comprehensive, but my thoughts run wild. Never once did it cross my mind that prop 8 would pass. I had prepared myself for a McCain/Palin presidency, but the idea that my home state would pass prop 8 was so beyond imaginable that all of my thoughts were centered on how best to win the hearts and minds of our opponents once it was defeated.

So part of my total loss for words, this wild scrambling anger that grips at my heart, is purely the result of how utterly, utterly off guard this catches me. Of course I knew that my friends here at FMH were funding the Yes on 8 campaign by tithing, but since it was going to fail, why kvetch? It seemed ungenerous.

The Obama presidency is a wondrous thing. I think we will hear more in the coming weeks about what it means to people—because literate and given to expansive prose as my people are, we are almost universally struck dumb at this overwhelming achievement. Having said that, there is a real cognitive dissonance for myself and others; to jive this global celebration of our country's munificence, this gorgeous, distinctively American spirit of equality and independence with its polar opposite, the revocation of rights, the invasion of families. How to process that the hand that gives also strikes down?

For me there is such bitterness in the concept of my rights being put to a vote. Let me be clear, my partner is a man, but I speak of my rights in this because they are. If history has not taught us the truth of that statement it is only because we have not paid attention. I am not in the habit of asking to have rights given to me, I demand them, I take them, I claim them, because they are not yours to give me. Except that they are. We have chosen to live together as a society, so my rights are subject to your good will.

There was a lot of anger over the "nasty ads" that highlighted the Church's role in the Yes on 8 campaign. This may change and become more temperate over time but today, Thursday the 6th, all I can think is the ad went nowhere far enough. Had they shown your families sending money to the Church, that money funding television ads that play in a family's home, their fear being sparked by that ad that maybe gay people weren't like them and didn't deserve the same rights, that person checking yes on their ballot and then, if you could capture it on film, the anguish of thousands of people being turned away from the bedside of their loved ones as they lay suffering, the reality of every gay married and unmarried person that your neighbors, at best, consider you "separate but equal," and if your neighbors happen to be Mormon, the cold knowledge that they made this possible with their monetary contributions to the church, whether they believe it is fair or not, that would only begin to go far enough. Missionaries muddling through underwear drawers and ripping up a marriage document? And you're worried about how you're portrayed?

I believe that history will judge us. Even as a child when I heard the story of Rosa Parks, the question sprang to my mind, who were those white people taking her seat? Every person on that bus seemed not just complicit to me but oblivious to the fact that they were being given a rare opportunity to not only do the right thing, refuse to accept her second class status, but to make history. As a young Bahai girl filled with images of religious persecution, martyrdom, and conviction, it is fair to say I envied them their place in history and could not imagine why they ceded that post to others. How will we tell our children that we stood by, even gave money so that our brothers and sisters could be relegated to second class citizens?

I think I know how and it disgusts me. We will rewrite history. We will say we were headed in the right direction. It took time. But we will be riding on the coattails of others, those who risked real persecution, those who did the actual work of standing before their leaders and saying, I cannot support this and you will not do it in my name. And when the war is over and the battle is won, even though we stood on the sidelines we will claim the victory as though it were our own.

And today I feel like if you are paying money to create this outrage, we are not on the same side. This just tears me apart. There is, as Ray said, something sacramental to laying yourself bare before others, to taking that which is ugly and raw and turning away from every instinct of self-preservation, the desire to gloss, make pretty or make "nice" and to instead say, this is my blood, these are my scars. It is easy to say this is a virtual forum, most of us don't and won't ever know each other in real life, are we making too much, creating drama where there should only be a measured exchange of ideas?

That may be true for you, but it just isn't for me. I am fucked up beyond all recognition over this. It makes me sick and my guts ache. I rely on this community of strong Mormon women. You have been a ballast and a shelter for me, a place that has expanded and improved my thoughts and feelings. It is no small thing. I do not as a rule dismiss my feelings or belittle my attachments.

I spent the day yesterday reading Walt Whitman and MLK's Letter from Birmingham Jail, crying, holding my baby and trying to put on a face to "meet the faces that you meet"; smiling when people congratulated me on Obama's win, looking serious but professional when I talked to the banker, but underneath it all was this ponderous heaviness, this weight on my heart that would not lift.

Spiritual or secular, we read, I hope, not just for comfort but for edification. In the fifth paragraph of Letter from Birmingham Jail, Dr. King reminds us of the four steps of a nonviolent campaign: 1) collection of facts to determine whether injustices are alive, 2) negotiation, 3) self-purification, and 4) direct action.

Before we take direct action we are commanded to self-purify, rid ourselves of acrimony and hatred, realize that our enemy is not our enemy but our sister. I am not there yet. I want to get there. I know that when change comes it will be because the women and men who come here will be the ones who made it happen. I hope to return to FMH someday with something better to offer you than the sorrow and rage that I have now. Thank you for listening to me.

"OUR CHILDREN" BY QUIMBY MASTERS (DECEMBER 17, 2008)

I am six days away from welcoming a new child into the world. This Christmas miracle—the littlest Angel—is making his arrival on Christmas Eve. I tell my two-year-old that Santa is bringing us a baby this year. I think she would rather have a monkey.

I am overwhelmed.

I am not overwhelmed by the season—knowing that this baby would arrive on Christmas Eve at the latest, I prepared early. The presents are wrapped and labelled and hidden away; my husband knows the location so that, if I go into labor (which is not expected—as of yesterday the baby's head was still not engaged), he will be able to find them and put them under the tree. Nor am I overwhelmed by the arrival of a baby—the nursery is ready; I have washed the clothes and folded them in their basket; all is ready to welcome this precious child.

Physical preparations are easy. No; I am overwhelmed by something else entirely: I am humbled at the thought that our Heavenly Parents would think to entrust me with another one of their special spirits. Surely a spirit as perfect and pure as this deserves a better mother!

I look at my two-year-old, so sweet and good and tender, and I am amazed that They trust me with her. I am too scared to trust anyone with her! A place recently opened in occasional day care, and although I know the day care workers are accredited, licensed, and fully vetted, and although I know it is only for a few hours a week, and although we signed up for the waiting list, when we were asked if we wanted the place, I said no. I wasn't ready to let her go yet. I wasn't ready to send her into the world, even into the safe cocooned world of a small local day care facility.

How do our Heavenly Parents do it? How do they find it in themselves to trust us—imperfect, flawed, faulty as we are—with their most wonderful creation?

I am not a bad mother. I would never hurt a child; I very rarely raise my voice with my daughter; all of her needs are met. We read together, we play together, we cook and go for walks and chase the chickens and feed the lambs and cuddle ducklings and collect rocks and sticks and leaves. There are other mothers out there who are far, far worse than me. But rather than assuage my guilt, this multiplies it: If by the standards of wider society I am a good mother (or at least not a bad one)—with all of my shortcomings—isn't that all the more reason for our Heavenly Parents to keep their children close to them? What sort of courage it must take to send these spirits out into the world, knowing that some will be hurt, knowing that some will be deeply hurt and in turn hurt others!

"Our children are the sum of us," Harry says in a line that always brings tears to my eyes.[97] They are a conglomerate of our strengths and weaknesses. But we, too, are the sum of our children: In the 30 months I have known my daughter, I have become a better person—more patient, more selfless, more open to the world. And so I welcome the lessons I will learn from this new person. And at the same time, I tremble to know that there will be times when I will fail to be the mother I ought to be.

I put my hand on my belly and feel the hard knob of a foot and think: soon you will not be mine alone. And this knowledge is bittersweet. So long as this child is inside of me, I can protect him, I can keep him from the harms of the world. But once he has entered this world, how do I protect him, not only from the world but from my own faults and flaws and imperfections? How do I best nurture these perfect, pure spirits, and return them safely to our Heavenly Parents?

Surely this is the flaw in the Great Plan—to entrust such perfection to such imperfect people!

"THE PROBLEM WITH SILENCE" BY LISA JENKINS (DECEMBER 22, 2008)

First, I want to state my love and admiration for President Hinckley. Please take this in the spirit it is mentioned and intended. This is not a personal attack on him but the ideals he speaks of. It is through an interview he had with Larry King[98] from which I base today's post.

> Larry King: Are people ever thrown out of your church?
> Gordon B. Hinckley: Yes.
> Larry King: For?
> Gordon B. Hinckley: Doing what they shouldn't do, preaching false doctrine, speaking out publicly. They can carry all the opinion they wish within their heads, so to speak, but if they begin to try to persuade others, then they may be called in to a disciplinary council. We don't excommunicate many, but *we do some*. [emphasis added]

I've struggled with my faith for about four or five years now. It wasn't until Prop 8 and this idea of keeping silent came to my attention when I felt compelled to express myself publicly. For the first time I found I did not agree with the church's stance.

I remained quiet at first, keeping my opinions between my husband and myself, but to help me make the right decision I needed to talk about it. Under the weight of my dissenting opinion, I finally conversed with some online friends and later the few who read my new blog. Then I dared let some family know through either my writing or during conversation. While my husband warned me of the reactions likely to come, I was never prepared.

People online told me to rip up my recommend. One friend, someone who introduced me to the church and whom I've known for nearly a decade, told me she no longer wished to read about what I thought, that she hoped I'd come to terms with my issues—but I wasn't to talk about them. She'd have no part of that.

To say her response shocked me would be inadequate. It broke my heart: *You feel I'm having issues and the best you can do is ignore it and tell me we can keep our conversation to husbands and children?* (yes she said that)

Seriously?

My ex-roommate told me when the prophet speaks we don't need to pray. Not if we sustain him as Prophet.

Another close friend of mine looked at me like I'd suddenly grown another head or perhaps a few horns atop the one I already have. My husband said his father regarded him in the same manner. They couldn't or didn't want to believe that we could have received a different answer than the prophets.

My friends and family who know avoid the topic now. It's as if they hope my doubts will somehow magically disappear. Pretend they don't exist. Ignore them and they will go away. She's sneezing, you might catch cold.

These reactions only made my questions harder to ignore, all the more determined to be answered. I never looked to "go against the church." I didn't want to disagree with the prophet, I never had, but how do I deny that peace in my heart, even when it *does* go against the church? I know from experience you can ignore it, but it always comes back. Always.

Elder Dallin H. Oaks has said it's never okay to criticize our leaders—even when the criticism is justified.[99] I get the reasoning behind this. It's not good to spend all our time criticizing anyone. We need to focus on the good, count our blessings, that sort of thing. But where do people go when they have doubts and questions, when they can't reconcile certain things? Bishops and stake presidents, general conference talks and *Ensign* articles would have us pour ourselves into the scriptures, in prayer, to get a blessing. To "have faith." A former bishop responded to my tearful admission of a crumbling testimony by telling me to watch BYU-TV.[100]

It seems to me that we as a church do not enjoy speaking of such things. In my experience we *don't* talk about it, and I have to ask: does this kind of willful ignorance help? Hardly.

Doubts and questions do not silence themselves. Scriptures and prayer don't always give me peace I need, no matter how long or hard I try with the best of intentions. This is deeper than that. People seem to think it's easy to question. I assure you it is petrifying.

We like to find rational explanations for our commandments. "We are told to tithe because it is a matter of sacrifice to the Lord, to help us pay for our temples and buildings. Look how it kept our church out of debt!" While a matter of faith, we are also driven by reason. Fair enough?

So what of times when I can find no rationale? You might say this is a time for blind faith—and I might agree, except I received an answer contrary the First Presidency's letter.[101] Would you say I must heed the answers to my prayers, or would you insinuate the prophet had said my prayers for me too? Some may suggest pride, a hard heart, etc. no matter what I say. I think these reactions are made from fear as we've been told it cannot happen, that our answers will always reflect that of the church and if they don't, then we're wrong.

I understand this sort of reaction if a person went out and told people the church was fundamentally and wholly false—but this isn't about that. I don't think a genuine search for truth, even unseemly truth, is a good basis from which to ex someone, or even six someones, such as with the September Six.[102]

The idea that one could inadvertently learn things that don't add up, discuss them, and then be told to stop, *just stop or I'll call you to the disciplinary council*, raises about a million red flags in my heart. It's potentially faith shattering, worse than any embarrassing fact I could ever discover. And I wish it wasn't.

We talk about the power in strong, unyielding testimonies, but I ask what is a testimony if it isn't challenged? Will silencing otherwise faithful dissenters really do the church good? I know we fear modern day Korihors,[103] but I don't think that's what we're dealing with. We're dealing with good, well-intentioned people who disagree in some instances, and discussion should not only be allowed but encouraged. If our souls find strength in opposition, then so should our testimonies. If the church is true it will withstand the storms. Truth always prevails.

I would like to be able to discuss my doubts without fear of excommunication. Yes we get enough negative advertising, but for us to pretend the problems don't exist or are all unfounded is foolish at best. It will come back to bite us, either on an individual or general level. I'm confident about that.

In July, the Pew Research Center released an in-depth report titled "A Portrait of Mormons in the U.S."[104] The study demonstrated Mormons' high weekly Church attendance, exceptional commitment to their faith, and belief in the LDS Church's claim to be the one true church. The report noted that Mormons were more likely than members of other religious traditions to be Republicans.

The Mormon Women's Oral History Project at Claremont Graduate University launched in May. Headed by Claudia Bushman and her students, the project seeks to add the voices of ordinary Mormon women to the historical record. Brigham Young University announced that it would be discontinuing its Women's Research Institute as part of efforts to streamline and reorganize the Women's Studies minor.

Jessica Oberan Steed organized the first annual Sophia Gathering in California in May, adding to a handful of recurring Mormon feminist spiritual retreats. The Mormon Women's Forum honored Lisa Butterworth for her work with FMH by giving her the Eve Award for 2009. In receiving this honor, she joined Mormon feminist luminaries like writers Carol Lynn Pearson, Janice Allred, and Lorie Winder Stromberg.

The Bloggernacle received an important addition this year. Tamu Smith and Zandra Vranes started the blog Sistas in Zion, which later became a radio show. Later, the pair published a book, *Diary of Two Mad Black Mormons: Finding the Lord's Lessons in Everyday Life*.[105] Smith and Vranes offered commentary that pushed back against the whiteness of Mormonism, including Mormon feminism. The Sistas do not identify as feminists, but their work has influenced Mormon feminists.

FMH permabloggers and guest posters authored more than 350 posts in 2009 and added two permabloggers: Tresa Brown Edmunds/Reese Dixon and Derek. In January, the blog created a new series titled Manuary, which featured a variety of guest posts from male readers, covering such topics as vasectomies, temple preparation, and what it is like to be a gay Mormon.

Toward the end of the year, two posts generated significant response and helped to define the views of the online Mormon feminist community. "So What's Your Beef (Mormon) Ladies?"[106] asked readers to "compile a comprehensive list of feminist concerns with the church." The post received nearly 500 comments lamenting such items as the patriarchal leadership structure, inequitable temple covenants, disparities between budgets for male and female youth programs, and scarcity of female role models in scripture. "On the Other Hand . . ."[107] asked readers to weigh in with their reasons for maintaining some degree of faith or activity in the LDS Church, despite many problems and difficulties. Readers responded with more than 220 comments, citing such motivations as personal witnesses from the Holy Ghost, faith that injustices would be rectified through the power of the Atonement, good relationships with local church members, and belief in the power of covenants to seal families together eternally.

"CAN THE CHURCH BE A HOSTILE PLACE?" BY JONATHAN DAVIES (JANUARY 30, 2009)

Scott Peck, in his book *A World Waiting to be Born*,[108] states,

> The experience of their home life tends to shape children's visions of the world. If they grow up in a warm, nurturing home, they tend to envision the world as a warm, nurturing place. . . . Children raised in cold, hostile homes, however, tend to see the world as a cold hostile place.

I found this helpful in interpreting my experience, not so much with family, but with my upbringing in the church. My home had a degree of hostility and repressed emotion and that has surely influenced my and my siblings' understanding of the world. But unfailing love and support in spite of our familial dysfunction has seen us through some difficult experiences and has left us, if not with a rosy view of the world, with a belief that it is possible to pursue a good life.

But I wonder how I would see the world if my family had been unflinching in upholding the doctrines of the church. While the church is a warm and nurturing place in appearance, it can be hostile to people whose experience opposes its teachings. My experience with being gay is one such experience and is, indeed, a common one. My family was forced to deal with the fact that I am gay and with the fact that the hostilities of my upbringing brought with them damage that could not be worked out in the framework of the gospel. The church itself, meanwhile, was, and remains, reluctant to confront this squarely.

For most of my adolescence I failed to sense warmth and nurturance in my church experience. The issue of worthiness would have come into play around baptism, and beyond that there were always interviews to determine worthiness for priesthood or temple recommends or dance cards.[109] And there was more and more uncomfortable discussion over homosexuality, the most pointed of which appeared in a pamphlet called "To Young Men Only," which was distributed in priesthood when I would have been in high school, though never discussed because, I assume, it was too sensitive. It began with lighter issues such as keeping the Sabbath and

Word of Wisdom and seemed to climax at Chastity, where it was stated harshly that no one is consigned to such a dreadful experience as homosexuality and anyone who says otherwise is a terrible liar intent on destroying vulnerable people like myself.[110] This message, delivered without room for question or discussion, was for me one of coldness and hostility.

The community of Affirmation: LGBT Mormons, Family & Friends[111] is an important testament to the gay Mormon experience and to the need within our community to recreate a worldview that is not hostile. Affirmation has helped me to reconcile my being gay and having grown up Mormon with the prospect of being a well-adjusted person. And as I reconcile what were once such conflicting issues, I begin to find the fact that I am gay less and less worthy of obsession. Meanwhile, I am concerned that the church, with its recent drive to stop "Proposition 8,"[112] is finding the issue of homosexuality increasingly interesting and worthy of desperate measures to keep it out of mainstream acceptance and tucked discreetly in youth pamphlets to be read secretly and sometimes painfully.

Coming back to Scott Peck's work, I also note his comments on resistance to change:

> Because resistance is such a barrier to organizational health and growth, some of the most advanced business corporations in very recent years have initiated a program of routinely scheduled periods of self-examination. ... They have found it valuable ... at regular intervals to look formally at whether the aims of the business have fallen out of sync with its mission statement, whether these aims need to be brought back into line, or whether the statement itself needs to be rewritten to reflect current realities.[113]

The church has, on numerous occasion, revised outdated practices. But when it shirks on issues that trouble it, it ends up causing unnecessary harm. I feel fortunate that my family was willing to re-examine its own priorities because their support has been vital. But I worry that, at least in the community I grew up in, it is the exception to the rule for families whose experience does not fall in step with the church to rethink ideas that the church has so firmly upheld.

"FAITHFUL DISSIDENTS: BEING THE CHANGE YOU DESIRE" BY CLAUDIA FOX REPPEN/THE FAITHFUL DISSIDENT (FEBRUARY 12, 2009)[114]

I'm all for peaceful activism, but we all know that The Church of Jesus Christ of Latter-day Saints is not a church of activists. At least not in the traditional sense.

I've been thinking about the role of "faithful dissidents" in the Church and whether being one is, in fact, a form of activism—the only kind that will ever possibly result in the change you desire.

I call myself *The Faithful Dissident*[115] because I'm basically still a "faithful" Mormon in most ways, at least on the outside. I still go to church, pay a full tithe, keep the Word of Wisdom, though many could ask why. My "dissent" is very much on the inside: in my thoughts, feelings, and spirit. It's also a virtually silent dissent—unless you count blogging. I've only discussed my true thoughts on the subject with half a handful of people face-to-face.

A common struggle that I've observed with other Mormons who think and feel like I do is the feeling that any faithful perseverance in the Church will simply be in vain; that things never change and we'll always be wrong on everything. Such feelings inevitably give way to apathy, anger, and, in some cases, even bitterness.

But are faithful dissidents underestimating the impact that they have on the Church? Even the angriest and most apathetic of dissidents have to admit that things have changed and do change in the Church, even if it can sometimes seem to come at a snail's pace. And even the most puritan and orthodox of members have to admit that although God may be the same "yesterday, today, and forever,"[116] that's not the case with the Church. Change *does* come and it comes from *within*, not from without.

I think about my mother's generation and those before her, where stay-at-home mothers were the norm (at least in the Church). I'm grateful that my mom was always home with us, but I'm more grateful that she chose to be at home with us. (At least I think she did). I think that those who chose to have a career had to endure a lot of guilt from fellow Church members. Now it seems that the majority of RS sisters (at least in the areas where I have been) work outside of the home. Some do it out of financial necessity, while many do it for personal fulfillment. Some mothers find that they have to get out of the house in order to maintain their sanity. And although I think it's a stretch to say that LDS women are able to have a guilt-free career today, I think that leaders have softened their words on the subject over the years and my generation of LDS women has a slightly greater sense of freedom than our mothers' generation.

If faithful LDS women had accepted that birth control was such an evil abomination, as earlier prophets proclaimed, would it be such an acceptable "personal decision" today among Mormon couples? Does God really look at birth control differently now than he did 50 years ago? I doubt it. But the Church sure does. (See *Bored in Vernal's* very interesting "Evolution of Birth Control in the Mormon Church."[117])

Most of you have probably read descriptions of the earliest garments that covered most of the body. Today, our garments are probably less than

97

half of what early Mormons wore. What we wear today—even with our garments on—would have been considered immodest back then. Did God lower his standards on modesty, or did the Church learn to accept a more liberal clothing style among its members that changed with the times?

I often think of earlier black members who had to endure some pretty demeaning teachings about why they were who they were. Amazingly, some still joined the Church. As we see when we look back at history, not even something as powerful and revolutionary as the American Black Civil Rights Movement was enough to bring change to the Church's policy on race. It appears that the most powerful catalyst to change in the Church came from within: blacks defying the odds by joining a "white church" and wanting to attend the temple. Were it not for the dilemma of all the Brazilian members who were ineligible to attend the temple that was to be built in their own country simply because of the African blood flowing through their veins, would the priesthood ban have been lifted? Probably not—at least not then.

If homosexuals had never challenged the sentiment that they were choosing to be gay, or the fact that even just having a same-sex attraction was at one time grounds for excommunication (see an excellent LDS gay history timeline on Dichotomy[118]), would we see any openly-gay Mormons today, let alone those who attend the temple regularly?

Are all these changes truly founded in revelation? Are they simply coincidence? Or did they come about because of faithful dissidents who remained true to the Gospel, yet weren't afraid to think outside of the box and even push the envelope a bit?

A commenter on my blog, Papa D, said something after one of my recent posts that really struck a chord with me. He said:

> When I lived in the Deep South, invariably a black investigator would join the Church, face intense pressure from family and friends for joining a "white church," stay active for about 3–6 months then fade into inactivity—sometimes citing the fact that no other black people were joining the Church. Just as invariably, about 3–6 months later another black investigator would be baptized—and the cycle would repeat exactly. After a few years, if those black members would have stayed active, there would have been a thriving black membership in the Church in that area. I'm NOT blaming them for leaving. I actually understand how difficult it is to remain active in an organization when you feel like a token member—especially when you feel like the others in the organization don't really understand you. For many reasons, I get that completely. All I'm saying is that when someone leaves they automatically contribute to the stereotyped self-

fulfilling prophecy against which they complain. They also reinforce, unfortunately, the stereotyped view of those who are unlike them—that black members, or liberal members, or gay members, or feminist members ad infinitum never make lifelong members. Being a pioneer or Christlike rebel is hard, but leaving only exacerbates the problem at both ends. "Be the change you desire" is great advice, as long as that desire doesn't include bitterness and harsh confrontation and self-righteousness. It's a tricky balance sometimes, and it requires serious humility and meekness, but it's worth it in the end for those who can do it.

I've been thinking about this a lot lately, particularly about how it applies to my good friend Cody (aka Gayldsactor[119]), who is likely facing excommunication in the near future after holding a commitment ceremony with his partner. Cody is active and very much a believer. He holds no malice towards the Church or the laws it has to uphold. He may soon no longer be a Mormon on record, but he will always be one in his heart and intends on living as such in every way that he can—even if he is excommunicated.

I think that the Church needs more people like Cody. I have no idea what's in store for gay members of the Church in the future. It would seem foolish of me to make any optimistic predictions about any future acceptance of homosexual relationships within the Church. But at the same time, I often have this feeling that something's got to give. The "homosexuality question," I believe, is the issue of my generation in the Church, and the story is not over. Members like Cody will be "sacrificed" along the way, but it will not be in vain. Just like all the early black members of the Church who lived and died without being able to hold the priesthood, enter the temple, or receive any of its ordinances, perhaps without having any family members to do their temple work, a way must be paved for all those who remain as faithful as they can if God is truly fair and just.

But the way will not be paved until enough faithful dissidents are committed to paving it. And it requires faith, patience, sacrifice, and—perhaps the most difficult—a whole lot of humility.

"THOUGHTS AND QUESTIONS DURING SUNDAY SCHOOL" BY REBECCA MCLAVERTY-HEAD (FEBRUARY 22, 2009)

Today in Sunday School, we had a lesson on priesthood. Our teacher often takes lots of comments and doesn't get through most of the lesson. The discussion on the role and blessings of the priesthood (we barely touched on the restoration) was interesting and had me wanting to ask several questions in relation to women and the priesthood. I didn't want to derail his lesson, so kept quiet and wrote down the questions I thought of. Maybe you can share your answers/thoughts/ideas with me. . . .

We talked quite a lot about what the blessings of the priesthood were. The first few comments were all experiences related to healing blessings. They were good examples, but I did think—you don't need the priesthood to heal someone, right? Healing is a gift of the spirit (see I Cor. 12:9, Moroni 10:11, and D&C 46:20), which means it's available to everyone—man and woman. So why does it seem necessary in current church practice that the priesthood is used to heal, and it be unacceptable for a woman to heal?

My mind then wandered to stories I've read in the early church where women were set apart to heal. They were given the authority to anoint and lay hands on others and give healing blessings. What authority did they use if not the priesthood?

A little later while still discussing blessings of the priesthood, it was mentioned that the temple is the place where we are richly blessed by the priesthood. I agree. My mind wandered again, thinking back to some specific times I've visited the temple. In the temple, women temple workers give the signs of the priesthood to other women. How can this be done without the person giving the sign having the priesthood? Also, in the temple we wear the robes of the priesthood. I've wondered for a long time the significance of this, and again wondered how someone who doesn't hold the priesthood is allowed to wear the robes of it.

These are really just some random thoughts I had during Sunday School and hope they make sense! I would love to hear your thoughts on any of the above questions.

If you talk about the temple, please do so in an appropriate way or I will delete your comments.

"MORMON UNDER PROTEST" BY ECS (JUNE 29, 2009)

In today's *New York Times*, a woman shares her account[120] of how she worships as a Catholic despite her deep disagreements with the Catholic Church's doctrine, practices, and politics. She calls herself a "Catholic under protest" because, as she describes it, she is "simultaneously outraged by and in love with the Church." This piece resonated with me because in it I heard echoes of conversations I've had with many Mormons (both online and in real life). This quote from the article may be especially relevant to a faithful, practicing Mormon who finds him or herself in conflict with Church policies:

> I recognize it is my obligation as a conscious, conscientious
> Catholic to discern—to know that the church no more

belongs to the Vatican than it does to me. Once I accepted that being Roman Catholic did not require that I be a papist—once I understood that it was possible to be simultaneously outraged by and in love with the Church—I saw the obstacles to being a practicing Catholic in a new way.

I've heard this sentiment expressed quite often—that the Mormon Church is my church, too—regardless of any disagreement I might have with the Mormon Church's political positions or current doctrinal interpretations. It turns out, however, that it's much easier for a Catholic to simultaneously love the Catholic Church and be outraged by its practices than it is for a Mormon. And it's much easier to express this outrage as a Catholic than as a Mormon. First, the author (Michele Madigan Somerville) states:

> I love the radical Catholic Church. I love that there are Roman Catholic bishops sticking their necks out to ordain women. That Catholic doctrine places mighty emphasis on the role of conscience in worship and creates fertile ground for conscientious dissent. I support dramatic change as energetically as I can.[121]

There is no "radical" element in modern Mormonism. No Mormon bishop (or General Authority—sort of the equivalent of a Catholic Bishop) publicly advocates for the ordination of women (can you imagine?!). There is, however, Mormon doctrine that places a "mighty emphasis" on developing a personal relationship with God and receiving direct revelation from Him. This doctrine, found in the book of James, led to Joseph Smith's First Vision, yet it has not created a safe space for faithful dissent within the Mormon Church.

Somerville next mentions a speech she heard during an interfaith gay pride celebration held in a Roman Catholic Church. The speech was given by a former Catholic nun who continues to worship as a Catholic even though she is a lesbian and lives with her partner of 25 years.

> That night, her address was filled with surprises, but only one aspect of her speech shocked me: her fervent recommendation that progressive Catholics remain in the Church—so as to be in a position to create change. She still worships in a Roman Catholic Church.

Likewise, progressive Mormons are frequently encouraged to stay and work within the Church to effectuate change. After reading the article, however, I realized how much easier it is to be a faithful, practicing Catholic under protest than a faithful, practicing Mormon under protest, because a Catholic under protest may join any number of organizations working within the Catholic Church that publicly advocate alternative worship and Church practices. For example, instead of paying her tithing to the Catholic bishops, Somerville pays it to the Women's Ordination Network and to a fund for survivors of abuse suffered at the hands of Catholic priests. I Googled the Women's Ordination Network and I was amazed. This group is a well-funded organization established in 1974 that publicly advocates for the ordination of women in the face of clear authority stating that God does not want women to be ordained. Yet the outspoken, radical members of the Women's Ordination Network co-exist alongside traditional Catholics. I've heard that because Mormonism is a young religion, it has not yet matured to the point where it can tolerate faithful dissent (Catholics had this problem, too—the Spanish Inquisition, anyone?). And the Catholicism practiced by a feminist writer living in Brooklyn, N.Y. is no doubt very different from the Catholicism practiced somewhere in Italy or South America. Yet a feminist writer who is "outraged" by the Catholic Church finds a space to voice her dissent and in so doing can still see herself as a faithful Catholic.

I wonder whether it is merely a matter of time before Mormons can tolerate a Mormon version of the Women's Ordination Group (or a similar group), or whether there is something unique about Mormonism that would prevent such groups from thriving.

"WITH YOU" BY NIKKI MATTHEWS HUNTER (JULY 30, 2009)

It began last week with some very hole-y garments.

I found my recommend to take to Beehive Clothing.[122] Could it be true that I last used it four years ago? I knew it had been a while, but I had closed off that tender part of my heart that rebruised with each endowment or sealing session I had forced myself to go to, and the time had passed regardless. Driving through the gates of the Boise temple grounds to the doors of Beehive Clothing, I cautiously opened a peephole into the heart-cloister:

Is it time to try again?

Over the following three days, a rapid-fire series of "coincidences" led me to the unmistakable conclusion that God, seeing an opportunity, was not nudging but pushing me toward following through that question with a Yes, and as soon as possible. I renewed the recommend that Sunday and was in the temple Wednesday night.

The endowment session was almost completely full of headed-home missionaries from the Idaho Boise Mission. A marked contrast with the typical silver-haired, long-married, and sometimes sleepy patrons, these young sisters and elders sat alert and silent, and for some reason the sight of their smooth and ringless left hands drew my attention as we made our covenants.

When I passed through the veil into the Celestial Room, I noticed that the missionaries had formed a line along the edge of the room; as each sister or elder was led through the veil, she or he was greeted by every member of the line before taking a place at the end to wait for the next missionary to arrive and repeat the process.

Sisters squeezed one another wordlessly as their smiles beamed a greeting; I watched elders hug each other in the two-slaps-to-the-shoulder embrace that men are wont to do, and then chastely shake hands with the sisters when they came upon them as the procession of solidarity continued. Tears flowed freely among both elders and sisters; their smiles and faces read *Our missions are complete; it's good to be here with you.* I couldn't stop staring.

I thought about what we had all done in the previous hour— performing a microcosm of the progression and destiny of both the individual soul as well as the collective condition of God's entire race of children. These missionaries had completed two years or eighteen months of precisely the same thing; as with my own struggles being led through the process that is an endowment session, each elder or sister labored not only for the souls they sought to save but also for his or her own—sometimes faltering—sense of self in relation to God's will. And now, here we were together in the same Place, despite whatever worldly or personal weights preceded our gathering: *It's good to be here with you.*

As the glimpse faded and the fresh bruises insisted on my attention, a few sisters came one by one to sit a moment and put an arm around my shaking shoulders. My tears and bowed head prevented my eyes meeting theirs, but I accepted tissues from ringless left hands. A new kind of wordless solidarity had formed, and my gratitude outweighed my embarrassment at being the center of it. From whatever part of the world each of these sisters had gathered, they created a Place for me in that moment that spoke again: *It's good to be here with you.*

"THE GLENN BECK CONUNDRUM" BY TRESA BROWN EDMUNDS (AUGUST 28, 2009)

I know I'm not alone when I say this, but I really, really, really hate Glenn Beck. But here's where I may be on my own: I feel a little guilty for that.

I do my best to avoid his program, I really don't need more stress in my life, but he's kind of hard to avoid. He has a knack for saying the most outrageous, offensive, off-the-wall garbage that infects all the rest of the media I actually do seek out. Here's a little taste after about a two minute google search:

He called Katrina survivors scumbags[123] and said that he hated the 9/11 families.

While on a different network, and with Bush in the White House, he spoke out about the need for healthcare reform, and then reversed his position once on Fox News, complete with alarmist ranting.

He basically cheered[124] while homes (and a military base, by the way) burned (full disclosure: a natural disaster) I (and my house, thank heavens) lived through.

Repeatedly warns that our country is marching to socialism, and not just socialism, but fascism![125]

Threatened Muslims with concentration camps (and bonus at the link, also asked a Muslim congressperson to prove they weren't working for "the enemy").

And then, most recently, gave this little gem[126] out on a talk show:

This president has exposed himself as a guy over and over and over again who has a deep-seated hatred for white people. . . . This guy is, I believe, a racist.

So, he's repellent, and whether he actually believes this stuff or just says what will garner him ratings, I just can't see a case made where this is at all morally sound.

On the other hand, he is, by all accounts, a devout Mormon and has repeatedly shared his conversion story[127] with whatever outlet would listen in a manner that comes across as tender and sincere. Plus it automatically tugs at my heart when he talks about the conversion being spurred by his daughter with Cerebral Palsy. I'm a sucker. He even credits God and his participation in the church with his media success, recounting how the day after he was baptized, jobless and without prospects, he got a call from some important media guy that led to where he is today.

My instinct is to write this guy off and accord him all the hate in my heart. To apologize to anyone I see and make sure they understand that he is not a representative of the faith. To wonder where his local leadership is and how no one sees a problem with him being honest with his fellow men. To question how his conversion, particularly a conversion motivated by the desire for Zion, could in any way be sincere when he sows such ugliness in the world.

But I have been participating in FMH for long enough to see commenters level every one of those accusations at every single poster here. There are loads of people in the world, heck, even the bloggernacle, who think that trying to be a Mormon and a feminist, or a Mormon and a democrat, or whatever, is just as irreconcilable as I see Beck's political preachings and Mormonism to be. I have seen time and time again as some driveby so-and-so has asked one of the permas why they haven't been ex'ed for supporting a group counter to the work of the church, or how they have to apologize to everyone they see to make sure no one mistakes one of us as a representative of the church.

In general I tend to be a proponent of "Big Tent" Mormonism. I'm in favor of individual journeys of faith, and I know that my practice of religion is not how other people need to experience it and vice versa. But is there a line beyond the member/non-member divide? Should there be if we are striving for Zion? If I want to be accepted as a Mormon Feminist, does that mean I need to extend that same privilege to Glenn Beck? Or can I just say, "He doesn't count"?

"A FEMINIST MORMON ON YOM KIPPUR" BY JOANNA BROOKS (SEPTEMBER 28, 2009)

I am a feminist Mormon married to a Buddhist Jew. Tonight, on Erev Yom Kippur, we will stand side-by-side in a Southern California synagogue, prayer books heavy in our arms, and ask to be forgiven, as we have done together on this same autumn night every year for the last decade. Yom Kippur means "Day of Atonement." It is the most solemn holiday on the Jewish calendar, a day when even marginally observant Jews find their way to their local shul, or synagogue, to stand together and recite the words of the Kol Nidre prayer for forgiveness:

> All solemn vows, all promises of abstinence and formulas of prohibition, and declarations of austerity, and oaths which bear a name of God, whatever we might have sworn and then forgotten, whatever earnest, well-intentioned vows we might have taken up but not upheld, whatever punishment or harm we might unwittingly have called down on ourselves, from the last Day of Atonement to this Day of Atonement, from all of them, we now request release: Let their burden be dissolved, and lifted off, and cancelled, and made null and void, bearing no force and no reality.
>
> And there shall be atonement for the whole community of Israel, and the stranger dwelling in their midst—indeed, for an entire people that has gone astray. (Numbers 15:26)

Tonight, as on every Erev Yom Kippur for the last decade, I will cry fat hot tears when the Kol Nidre is read. All dry eyes around the sanctuary, but me: the stranger dwelling in their midst, the Mormon feminist in synagogue on Yom Kippur.

And as it has happened every Yom Kippur for the last decade, tonight, I will reach into my vintage carpet-bag purse and find that *once again* I have forgotten the Kleenex, so instead I will take out my oversized black Jackie O. shades and put them on to give my tears a measure of privacy.

I cry because this Kol Nidre prayer for mercy, release, and reconciliation, for the lifting of the burden of promises I have failed to keep, how can this prayer not resonate for me too?

As I do every year, I will ask to be forgiven all of my regular, everyday failings, my mean streak, my untruths, and my impatience. I will also ask (as I do every year) to be released from the weight of the worry and disappointment I cause my orthodox Mormon family because I am an unorthodox Mormon, a Mormon feminist, and I married outside the Church. I will ask to be released from the great silences that freight our conversations. I will ask to be forgiven all the times I kept my mouth closed when I wanted to tell them: I am not lost, I am not confused, and I have not forgotten; I am the person you raised me to be; I am a person of faith, and I have made difficult decisions.

This was an especially difficult year to be a Mormon feminist, so I will have new broken vows to account for: my failure to obey the Church leaders who asked me to support Proposition 8, my failure to understand why my Church and its members committed themselves so expensively to the Yes on 8 cause, my anger at Mormon parents who forsake their gay children. And as I do every night before I go to bed, I will pray for all Mormon people: I will ask that all of us be released from the intense feelings of fear, hurt, suspicion, aggression, pride, and resentment we all experienced during the Proposition 8 campaign, feelings that still ricochet around my wardhouse and my Relief Society room one year later.

Tonight, as I do every year, on Erev Yom Kippur, I will lean my head into my husband's shoulder, breathe in the warm, familiar scent of his wool suit, and feel blessed to have married a man who is not ashamed of my tears or my struggles or my shortcomings, a man who stands side-by-side with me as we ask forgiveness from God. God is merciful. *God is merciful.* Tonight, if just for tonight, I am released from the bondage of my disappointments, my outlaw faith, my straits, my narrows.

"DEAR FMH: THE WIDOWS' PLIGHT" BY ANONYMOUS (SEPTEMBER 29, 2009)

My great-grandmother was married twice. Her first husband was killed in WWII, after one child and only a few years of marriage. Although she supposedly never truly got over him, she remarried and was with her second husband for many decades, up until they both passed away a few years ago.

The temple work has been done for her, and she has been sealed to both men. But everything I've read leads me to believe that she will have to choose who she wants to spend eternity with. This seems horribly sad and unfair to me. I know without a doubt that God is a loving heavenly father, and that eternity will be joyful for us. But how can I reconcile that with the idea that my great-grandmother, and women in the same situation, will be forced to make such a difficult decision? I cannot wrap my head around the notion that widowers have the opportunity to live happily with all their wives in heaven, but women cannot do the same with the men they've loved.

"Indoctrinating My Babies: Primary Songs and Gender Roles" by Shelah Mastny Miner (October 29, 2009)

Our ward had its Primary program a few weeks ago. Our family was spared any major embarrassment—all of my kids delivered their lines without incident (my five-year-old proclaimed, "In our family, my mom is responsible for taking care of the kids"), and none of them grabbed the standing microphone, Sinatra-style, and crooned into it at the top of their lungs (although that did happen). Since then, the kids have had Primary songs on the brain, this verse of "The Family is of God"[128] in particular:

> A mother's purpose is to care, prepare, to nurture and to strengthen all her children. / She teaches children to obey, to pray, to love and serve in the fam'ly.

I don't know why it rankles when I hear my son's sweet little voice singing this song. I expect that when I send my kids to Primary on Sunday, they'll learn about stories from the Bible and the Book of Mormon, and they will also learn about things like the Family Proclamation. In short, I don't expect them to learn anything different from what they are learning, it just surprises me how much the lyrics make my skin crawl.

Our Primary Presidency really did a great job corralling the masses, getting them to sing, and making things move smoothly (and on time!). They also infused humor into the kids' talks. One of the kids in my son's class said that his dad "is responsible for going to work and changing light bulbs." It's true that I'm responsible for taking care of the kids, at least 95% of the time, but my negative reaction to his statement shows that I'm a little bit resentful about that too. It just sounds like I don't have anything else interesting going on in my life when he puts it that way, and I think I'm afraid that it's true. Would I prefer that he says that his mom is responsible for "meeting her kids' most basic needs and spending lots of time on the computer?" That would be true too, and a heck of a lot more likely to earn him a laugh.

I guess I like to think that I'm a stay-at-home mom because we decided as a couple that it would be the best thing for our family's particular needs, not that I'm doing it because of cultural pressure and expectations (even though, at the time, we were so young and naive that I don't think we seriously considered that any alternatives could work for us). As I looked around while the song was being sung, I saw the physician mom sitting across the row from me, and the working mom behind me, sitting next to her non-LDS husband, and kept thinking, "If I'm having this reaction, I wonder what they're thinking."

Last year's hot button Primary program song may have been "Home."[129] We've been singing "Home" at our house for years because it was written by my husband's grandma Caroline Eyring Miner. The lyrics go like this:

Home is where the heart is/ And warmth and love abound./ Home is where warm circling arms/ Go all the way around.

Home is where there's father/ With strength and wisdom true./ Home is where there's mother/ And all the children too./ Home is where our Father,/ Who dwells in heav'n above,/ Guides us in the way we live/ And lets us feel his love.

When I actually started thinking about the lyrics, I wondered whose family she was writing about. This one sounds so traditional and so idyllic, and while Caroline had eight kids, she was a working mom (in the thirties, forties, fifties, and sixties—if you went to Highland High School, she may have been your teacher), a published author and award-winning poet, and a world traveler who did as she pleased. I know the line about being a mother is only five words long in the song, but I worry that we might see our roles as reductive, as closely circumscribed as those five words, when those are the lines our kids get in their heads and put on repeat play.

So how do I get out of this funk? Play some Laurie Berkner to get the song out of my kid's head? Apply to grad school? Or just, somehow, make peace with my current lot in life? How?

"Shutting Down BYU's Women's Research Institute" by Elisa Koler (November 4, 2009)

My name is Elisa. I am a senior at Brigham Young University in Provo, Utah, a famously conservative university owned and operated by the Church of Jesus Christ of Latter-day Saints, or Mormons. 98% of the student body subscribes to the LDS faith, but we are nevertheless an extremely diverse group of students, ideologically speaking. Of the approximate 30,000 students at BYU, 48% are female, and 2,691 students are enrolled in the Women's Studies minor, almost 10 percent of the entire student population. At such a (let's face it) conservative school, the fact that we even have a Women's Studies minor is a pretty big deal, and the BYU Women's Research Institute has contributed enormously to the university community since its founding in 1978. From 2006 to 2008 alone, the WRI funded 132 faculty research publications relating to women. Some of the brightest and most promising students at BYU are involved with this program.

However, on October 29th the BYU Administration issued a press release (that's what it's called, but in fact it's nowhere to be found on the

BYU website or in the school newspaper) saying that the WRI is being shut down come January 2010. The Administration claims that they are "streamlining and strengthening" the program but what they're really doing is removing all funding WRI used to receive and consolidating it into one faculty research grant and a token amount of funding available for students. Most BYU students found out about this through blogs or other outside media sources rather than through the university itself, and to put it lightly, most of us are infuriated.

There's a reason why this is being kept hush-hush. All major universities have a Women's Studies Program, and shutting down ours is more than just a bad idea, it's a disaster waiting to happen. Money is not the issue: BYU receives generous donations from LDS alumni even in this economy. Additionally, 52% of the WRI budget came from outside, non-BYU sources. This is, in short, another attempt by an overtly conservative administration to shut down any "feminist" activities—because a lack of education makes many people at this institution think feminism is a dirty word.

I believe in the importance of scholarly research devoted to women, and my friends and I are making as much of a fuss as we can. But this needs to get out. It's an ESPECIALLY bad PR move for BYU, and by extension for the LDS Church, to shut down this program, and the more people know about this and express their disapproval, the better.

This is what I am telling those I write to who are not of our faith: Just because the choices LDS women make based on our faith are considered old-fashioned doesn't mean that we aren't strong, intelligent women who believe in gender equality and everything else feminism stands for. I am proud to consider myself a feminist, and so do many other men and women at this university. We desperately want for this program to not go the way of several other important programs at this university (such as our International Development minor, another magnet for more liberal and therefore supposedly more dangerous students, which was eliminated recently), and it's possible that if enough people outside of our community stand up for the WRI, maybe the higher-ups will change their minds.

One more thing: I may be a convert, a democrat, a feminist, and I may have a swearing problem that I still haven't licked, but this is my church too. I'm not going anywhere, but it's things like this that make it so hard to be a BYU student. This is not an issue of faith. Most of the students at BYU are faithful adherents to the LDS faith and are not being oppressed or silenced by the Church itself. Rather, it is the bureaucracy at the university level that is the source of the problem for myself and all other like-minded students here. I have found that my faith is one of the greatest sources of my personal empowerment as a woman, and that my religious beliefs and my social beliefs complement rather than contradict each other. For BYU students, the solution is not to abandon our faith, but rather to find ways to reconcile the beliefs of another generation to the ideals we uphold with as much fervor as we do our religion. Shutting down our Women's Research Institute would be a step in the entirely wrong direction.

For more information, here is the official "press release."[130]

Most of us found out because of this article,[131] from an independent publication run by Mormons, which is unaffiliated with the Church or BYU officially.

The Facebook group working to prevent this.

I'm not sure if the BYU student newspaper accepts letters from non-students, but here is a link to submit a letter to the editor.

More information about BYU in general.

A couple of blog entries with some other students' reactions.[132]

"THE GHOST OF RELIEF SOCIETY PRESENT" BY MEL SELCHO/SISTER BUTTERFLY (DECEMBER 10, 2009)

I just attended this year's Christmas Relief Society meeting. Our ward was split recently, and the table I was sitting at was evenly divided between old ward and new ward. We started introducing ourselves, and I was last. As we went around the table, each of the women offered nothing besides her name when it came to identifying her individually. Instead, each said what her husband's calling was, how old her children were, what her husband's job was, what her children liked to do, etc., etc. By the time it got to me I was so speechless I just said, "I'm Sister Butterfly." Something in me couldn't bear to introduce myself as the person to whom I am married and the children to whom I mother, and yet some part of me feared there wasn't anything else to tell.

Maybe it's been a while since I've been fully engulfed in full Mormondom (quarterly Relief Society meetings have eluded me much of this year), but when did we give up our entire identities to our families? In Primary on Sunday even the children introduced themselves by their name and their favorite thing to do, not by their parents and siblings.

I have no expectations that I wouldn't want to know about the important people in the lives of my Relief Society sisters. I belong to two other small groups of women outside of Relief Society, and it is wonderful to meet their loved ones and hear stories about them. But getting to know these women involves the story of their whole lives, the things they love, the places they wish to travel, how they feel about local politics, and the funny things that happen to them. Family definitely plays a part in that, but it does not define the whole with these friends, even in the introductory stage of our getting acquainted.

Yet I sat at an impeccably dressed table in an elaborately decorated LDS Cultural Hall talking to these women who I know I must have a lot in common with because we all attend the same church, and no one could join me in any real conversation outside their children and husbands. I felt like we were all invisible to each other, that we had so lost who we were that we had nothing left to share. Truly, I would have preferred celebrity gossip, home decor how-to, or even weight loss techniques to this. Well, upon second thought, maybe not. But are these the only choices??

In all fairness, I am a bit sensitive to the whole meaning of motherhood right now. I savored this part of my life when the kids were little, and I spent time with them in ways that were meaningful just like I would with a friend: taking them places we would both enjoy, introducing them to things I love, experiencing life together. But now that they are older my SAHM job is mostly to facilitate the rest of my family's interests and work. I pack lunches for them to eat at school and work. I take them to classes and practices where I never touch a ball or dance a step. I make them food to take to parties I don't attend. I go to lunch with other mothers to talk about what I'm buying them for Christmas.

And now, I go to Relief Society, and instead of providing relief to my soul with weightier matters of spirit or to my psyche with lighter matters of hair color and good books, I am left wondering if I'm the only one seeing my own ghost.

2010

In a leadership meeting, President Thomas S. Monson confirmed that the number of LDS Church members on record had exceeded 14 million the previous July. The launch of a revamped Mormon.org signaled the Church's mounting interest in refining its public image. The website's new version featured slick design and a diverse offering of profiles from Mormons around the world. Some Mormons questioned the authenticity of the personas that Mormon.org tried to promote, asserting that the diversity of backgrounds, worldviews, family structures, and personal choices presented on the website would not necessarily be common or welcome in an average ward.

In August, a federal judge struck down Proposition 8, which had been approved by a majority of California voters two years previous. Elder Marlin K. Jensen, serving as Church Historian, visited the Oakland California Stake and participated in a meeting where a number of gay and straight Mormons shared their experiences of personal pain resulting from the Church's involvement in Prop 8. Jensen offered tears of his own and a simple apology:

> To the full extent of my capacity, I say that I am sorry. I
> know that many very good people have been deeply hurt, and
> I know that the Lord expects better of us.[133]

Mormon feminist scholar Joanna Brooks, writing for the Religion Dispatches blog, noted that

> it was *not* . . . an apology for Proposition 8 itself. It was not a
> renunciation of Mormon doctrine on homosexuality. But it
> was a significant acknowledgment of the experience of gay
> Mormons and their allies, an instance of dialogue between
> Church leadership and membership.[134]

At the next General Conference in October, senior apostle Boyd K. Packer delivered a talk which many saw as a discouraging development in the ongoing story of how the Church addresses homosexuality, in which Packer suggested that God would not create gay people.

The Mormon Women Project, launched in January by editor Neylan McBaine, was a noteworthy and popular addition to the online world of Mormon women. The website started as a collection of transcribed interviews with LDS women around the world. Those interviewed reflected the experiences of women from a variety of ages, races, languages, marital statuses, sexual orientations, and cultural backgrounds. It resonated with a

Mormon feminist audience without alienating those with more conservative views. In September, a group of Mormon women, including FMH bloggers Tresa Brown Edmunds and ECS, announced a new project—LDS Women Advocating for Voice and Equality, or LDS WAVE. The organization published Calls to Action on its website, asking interested parties to join in various efforts such as forming local book clubs to discuss faith and feminism, starting podcasts, or writing letters to women leaders of the Church.

FMH brought on several new bloggers, including nat kelly, Stephanie, Sara Burlingame/crazywomancreek, Kimberly, and Lindsay Hansen Park/Winterbuzz. Some favorite posts included a series of book-club-style discussions on Maxine Hanks's *Women and Authority: Re-emerging Mormon Feminism*,[135] a classic collection of essays, and on Simone de Beauvoir's *The Second Sex*,[136] the book of feminist philosophy credited with instigating second-wave feminism. The question of activism was weighing on the minds of FMH writers and readers more than it had in previous years, thanks in part to the founding of LDS WAVE and the flurry of concerns that impacted Mormon feminists in mounting ways. Objections to the Church's treatment of gay people, its overwhelming emphasis on modest clothing for young women and girls, and its tradition of male-only priesthood were regular topics of conversation on the blog, and increasingly, people were beginning to ask about how to create change in the Church. This question would rise to the surface more and more in the years to come, both at FMH and in the wider Mormon feminist community.

"THE WRONG TROUSERS" BY RACHAEL LAURITZEN (FEBRUARY 17, 2010)

A couple of weeks ago I went in to the bishop's office to get my temple recommend. He's our new bishop, formerly the 1st counselor in the bishopric, and the one we invited over to our home when we gave Marigold her baby blessing. He's a good man, I like him, and I'm looking forward to, erm, a new administration. (There's an old post about yardwork and Easter Sunday, if you're curious.[137]) He also shaved off his decades-old mustache when he became bishop; my understanding is that he did it at the urging of the stake president.

He gave me my recommend—and, no, I didn't lie to get it; the questions don't directly involve my doctrinal concerns, nor do they ask if I like the temple (you don't have to like it to be worthy, you know). He did ask a little about whether I go frequently and I told him no, but that I was planning to go soon for a family member's endowment. He didn't press.

Then, at the end, he said, "I notice you've been wearing . . . trousers . . . to church."

I don't remember the exact play-by-play of the conversation, so what follows is the gist of the conversation, not the quotes. He wanted to know why, and I told him that, honestly and truly, I was tired of being cold in church. I tend to be cold in general, winter makes it worse, and church is absolutely the coldest place I regularly go. I also feel (but didn't tell him) that skirts and nylons are supremely inappropriate wear for Utah winters, both cold-wise and safety-wise. He brought up some things about "you know how the church feels about that" and how he'd seen some picture of people going to another church who were wearing jeans—essentially, shabby or casual clothes that didn't fit the church's emphasis on dressing nicely.

He also mentioned that since I've been wearing trousers, another sister has started to wear them too. (See, my bad influence is spreading!) I then ventured my other reason (though not the reason that drove me to wearing dress pants), which was that my understanding is that what we wear needs to be culturally appropriate and respectful. I even threw out that I knew that in other countries women wear pants to church because it's culturally acceptable. Which, I know, was a little bit of grasping because I think that the church encourages female members in other countries to wear skirts and dresses as well as in the U.S., but hey, he was giving vague, stereotyped examples, so why not? We were both trying to have a very nice, very polite "interview" about an issue we disagreed on. Seems bound to happen. Anyway. . . .

I finished with telling him that I tried to make sure that when I did wear "trousers," they were of equivalent formality as is typically worn, and I indicated his business suit. He finished with telling me that he wasn't telling me I _had_ to wear a skirt; but that he, as my bishop (under the title of his stewardship) was _encouraging_ me to wear a skirt.

All in all, I thought the conversation went well. DH was a bit more taken aback than I had been—he converted LDS and is still not used to (or happy with) the notion of a church dress code[138]—but I had been expecting it would come up sooner or later. However, the conversation did make me mentally sift through the issue again, and I think that I still think what I thought before. I think dress slacks or professional women's wear are perfectly suitable church wear, and I would enjoy some more church-culture latitude on the issue.

Shortly afterward, I was walking up to the temple with my brother in the evening and complaining about how unsuitable skirts are in the winter, and he suggested that I wear pants to the temple. Incredulous, I asked him what he thought they would do to me at the front desk if I were to do such a thing. He shrugged and said that the church is coming around on such things. I agreed, but I told him I thought their speed with it was on a geologic frame and he laughed.

So, last Sunday I was teaching the Primary and didn't want to push the envelope. Plus it was Valentine's Day, and I have this great red skirt that DH loves. I wore the skirt to church.

"My Mother the Beggar" by Natalie Hamilton Kelly (April 25, 2010)

One night on a Philadelphia street, I met a woman who changed my life in a 45-second interaction.

An interesting thing about living in big cities like Philly is that it's hard to ignore the world's problems. When you walk outside and see amputees and mentally ill people begging for food, you can't just ignore them and think you live in a perfect world. Often, in coming up with an explanation for the problems we see, we like to create a difference between ourselves and a person in need. I am housed, fed, and warm. You are homeless, hungry, and cold. It's comforting to think that this is because I am good and made wise decisions and you are somehow deficient and made poor decisions.

It's unnerving when one brief moment can shatter those comfortable explanations and force us out of our sheltered perspective.

My mother is a drug addict.

As a child, I remember feeling confused at my mother's sporadic absences. When I was 8, she moved to a different town for 3 months "to get better." When I was 13, my uncle came to pick her up. As she angrily left with him, my aunt softly spoke to me in the other room, explaining that I and my younger siblings would be living with them for a few months. By the time I was in high school, I knew the signs for myself, and I didn't need an adult around me to let me know when it was time for my mom to be absent again for a while.

The last 20 years of my mother's life are a tale of alternating tragedy and triumph. Married as a naive girl to a controlling, bipolar husband, her marriage was in an almost constant state of crisis. Pregnant right away, with 6 more following after, leaving was always a deeply complicated issue. My childhood journal is littered with the sentence *"My parents are getting divorced again."* Despite the horrible situation, she didn't know how to get herself completely out. She didn't want to turn against God by abandoning her covenants, and she was weighed down by a constant guilt about not properly hearkening unto her priesthood-holding tyrant. She also suffered from chronic migraines. And my father was a dentist, with boundless supplies of narcotics under the power of his signature.

And so my mother's addiction began. The constant migraines were the beginning of it. She needed to take care of her kids, and she just couldn't function with the debilitating pain, so she medicated more and more. But, she told me once, she distinctly remembers the first pill she took for *emotional* pain. Her dependency became severe. Because of it, she feared that she would lose custody of her kids (the only thing in life she cared about) if she left my father. When the addiction started to interfere greatly with her functioning, my father sent her to a rehab center to recover. She came back strong, empowered, and clean.

Four years later, after a hellish divorce from a now schizophrenic and abusive husband, her relapse was incapacitating. I was still too young and defensive of my mother to really understand what was "wrong" with her when she didn't leave her room for hours during the day. But after another painful separation, she returned like dynamite, tackling the challenges facing her as a single mother head on, fighting for her family's life with all the energy of her soul.

We were flourishing. She got us all up for school every day. She went to work. She came home and made dinner for us every single night.
And then her headaches came back, but this time they were different. Her face felt numb.

She had a brain tumor.

After the surgery, the narcotics came back.

Right at the beginning of my junior year, my mother went in for her brain surgery; by the following summer, I was living in what is, so far, the most hellish period of my life. Her relapse was overwhelming for me as a teenager finally old enough to see it fully.

I remember coming home often to find her slumped over the kitchen counter, attempting to make a PB&J. The can of peanut butter had been placed in the garbage can. Its lid was placed on the jar of jam. My mother was using the butter knife as a hairbrush. I got used to coming home, always as late as possible, to find her, totally stoned, wandering around the house in some state of confusion. I got used to putting her to bed each night, searching through her drawers until I found the pills, and flushing the cocktail collection I found down the toilet. Her loving, patient, prankster personality was gradually taken over by the drugs, and she became angry, accusatory, and paranoid. It was hard for me to look at her. Her eyes were shriveled. They were shrunken in her face, with unbearably deep wrinkles all around them, heavy lids only partly opened.

By the beginning of my senior year, it reached a breaking point. I moved out. My younger brother and sister, whom I had partly raised and felt terribly attached to, moved to another part of the state with an older sibling. My mother went again, against her will this time, to yet another rehab. She got out, cleaned up, and once again, things are moving forward.

There are a few patterns I've seen from my mother's story of drug abuse and sobriety. But there is one for which I am particularly grateful.

We always had support.

Anytime things went south, we had a network of people to pick up the shattered pieces. My wealthy, generous, loving relatives opened their homes to us indefinitely. My mother's well-off siblings and parents ensured that she went to expensive, well-staffed, excellent rehab facilities where she could take the time to heal, learn, and find herself again; this was a lot gentler than the cold jail cells she could have ended up in. The church, with its ample and effective welfare system, supplemented our meager welfare checks and any other economic shortfalls, guaranteeing that our cupboards were never empty and that I could afford to pay for all my little AP tests.

This brings me up to Philadelphia.

Late one night, I stopped into a Boston Market and got a hot dinner, not having the energy to cook for myself. A few blocks further on, as I was walking home to my dorm room, a woman approached me with a pitiful, familiar plea: "Change for food? Change for food?"

I muttered my pathetic, familiar response, "No sorry, I don't have any," and continued on my way.

About 10 steps later, thinking about how terribly skinny the woman had appeared, it occurred to me that I maybe didn't have change on hand, but I had a big bag full of nice, hot food. I turned around and caught her after another person turned her away.

Imagine me, heart bursting with goodness, sweet angelic smile, so happy with myself for my own noble generosity: "I don't have any change, but you can have my dinner!"

The woman took one handle of my bag, looked inside, and said weakly, "No that's okay. . . . Do you have any change?"

Two reactions were immediate: I was insulted that she was presumptuous enough to turn down my wonderful offer [ack, I still cringe at myself], and my mind filled up with the accusation that she was just a crack-head looking for her next fix.

And then I really looked at this woman.

She was African American, impossibly thin, and prancing a little nervously while she wrung her hands. The care in her face made it impossible to guess her age. I was riveted by her eyes.

They were shriveled. Shrunken in her face, with unbearably deep wrinkles all around them, heavy lids only partly opened.

I was looking at my mother.

It hit me with immediate, oppressive force that the differences between this beggar and my mother were almost nothing. And, at the same time, everything.

My mother, faced with some horrific experiences, made some terrible survival choices, repeatedly. Regardless of how much she was to blame, each time she fell, there was a net below her. Our family remained (barely) intact. She had wealthy relatives and a middle-class neighborhood. This woman, black and poor in a big city and racist society, had none of that structural back-up. I realized, without a doubt, that under a different set of circumstances, my mother would have been the one scrambling around outside in the cold, begging strangers. This woman didn't have wealthy brothers-in-law and generous bishops. So she was here, asking me for her next fix.

Where were her daughters right now? Probably not traipsing obliviously around an Ivy League campus, nobly bestowing their bounty on the less fortunate. My own close calls with homelessness suddenly felt a lot closer.

The space between us, simultaneously so wide and so startlingly narrow, swallowed me up. I fled home with a sob in my throat, hit in the face with a reality I'd theorized about before (with all my noble liberal goodness) but had never had to digest so personally. It was suffocating.

The structure is more powerful than the individual. I hadn't really "earned" any of the things I enjoyed, not in the romantic American sense of the term. That this woman should be reduced to rags because she was poor and black while my mother was given the chance to turn failure back into blossoming success because she was white and came from a middle-class background was fundamentally unjust.

Life shouldn't suck like this. I don't want to live in a world like this.

Something changed in me forever the night I left my mother begging for a fix on the streets of Philadelphia.

"OUR BLUE-EYED SAVIOR" BY NATALIE HAMILTON KELLY (JULY 27, 2010)

Recently, our up and coming blogger,[139] Petunia, daughter of mfranti, asked this question:

> So, out of curiosity, why is Jesus ALWAYS depicted as white? He was born in Israel and anyone who comes from Israel now or then does not usually come to be of a lighter complexion. Or is He depicted as white because He wasn't born from His mother and father's genetics but from the Lord's? The more I come across photos of the Lord, the more it provokes me to wonder, why is He depicted this way?

I have to say, I was not that precocious as a 16-year old. I lived in a mostly white world, and it never occurred to me that there was something wildly disingenuous about a blue-eyed Jesus or a blonde-haired woman at the well.

I really never thought about the cultural meaning behind pictures of Jesus until I was directly prompted to do so while teaching a seminary class a couple of years ago. The class I was teaching was probably about 65% African, 20% African-American, and 10% white. I was teaching in our RS room about some topic from the New Testament, when one young man, a visitor to our class and a West African immigrant, raised his hand to ask a completely unrelated question.

"See that picture of Jesus behind you? Well, sometimes I see pictures of Jesus and he's Black. Why does he look different in his different pictures?"

Taken a little by surprise, I muttered a quick reply:

"Well, Jesus was actually Jewish, so he probably looked just . . . Jewish. [embarrassed pause] Anyway, that's not what we're talking about right now."

Utter teaching fail, I know.

Anyway, later that very week, I happened to be introduced to this video, a lecture at the Harvard Divinity School by James H. Cone.[140] Cone is the father of Black Liberation Theology in America, a movement inspired by the liberation theology movement in Latin America.

Liberation theology is, quite possibly, the worldview that most closely matches my own of all that I have ever come across. It is an argument that God is not neutral in history—God is on the side of the poor and the oppressed, against the wealthy, powerful oppressors. In order to be *with* God, and to build up his/her kingdom, you must also be with the poor. Zion cannot exist without justice and equality.

There are many different branches of liberation theology now, including feminist (!) and queer liberation theology. But the one introduced to me the week after I blew off a student's question is the one that I have found most compelling so far: Black liberation theology.

Cone describes how Jesus was downtrodden and oppressed during his mortal ministry. He details how Christ was persecuted, misunderstood, and hunted, until finally his oppressors tortured him and hung him to a tree.

And then he talks about the lynching tree in America.

And how Black Americans could be hunted down and caught for any perceived offense. And how their oppressors, while filled with righteous indignation and claiming God as their backer, would burn them at the stake, or string them up in a tree.

But Jesus is not with the people doing the lynching. He is up, in the tree, being hung.

Jesus is Black.

I went to my seminary class the following week, hoping the same young man would be visiting so that I could amend my answer. Sadly, he was not there, so I just reminded the class of his question, said that I had been thinking about it all week and that it was really important, and offered my new answer (amidst much incredulous eye-raising from my much more orthodox co-teacher), which basically followed what I roughly outlined above.

Since then, I've read a book by James H. Cone called *God of the Oppressed*.[141] He talks about a few different manifestations of Jesus.

There's the historical Jesus, or who he was. There's the present-day, resurrected and exalted Jesus, or who he is. And there's the future Jesus, coming in glory to bring liberation to all, or who he *will be.*

Historically, Jesus was Jewish. And, as Cone argues, that was no accident. Members of the kingdom of Israel were oppressed and/or enslaved for centuries. They were subject to foreign rule. That the liberator of humanity would be born to these people, desperately seeking their own liberation, is a beautiful lesson of history.

Now, as then, there are innumerable groups of oppressed peoples. There are innumerable people fighting in solidarity to end that oppression and bring about the Kingdom of God. And in an American context, few groups can claim the mantle of Christlike persecution as those of African descent.

I have struggled with the culture of the church, insofar as it is a culture of achievement. I struggle with the portrayal of wealthy, privileged, powerful people as the truest followers of Christ. The Jesus I know is poor and ragged. He is long-suffering and humble. He is powerful, but his power comes from love, from his commitment to putting his body with those who suffer.

In our popular cultural representations of Jesus today, he is often portrayed as white, muscular, and somewhat handsome. The Jesus in these pictures came to atone for your sins and to sit on the board of Wal-Mart. His clothing is nice. His hair is combed. His cheekbones are chiseled. These pictures do more than pay homage to divinity—they reinforce cultural mores. More troubling, they take a symbol as powerful as Jesus and co-opt it to look and act like European/Western ideas of nobility and power. The ubiquity of a blue-eyed Jesus is condemnatory evidence of our widespread cultural imperialism. Jesus is not one of the powerful and the privileged.

Who is Jesus today?

He doesn't understand our suffering just because he underwent it in history, but because he is going through it with us NOW. That means Jesus is Queer. He is disabled. Divorced. Homeless.

Jesus today is Black.

"PROPOSITION 8 AND DAVID, TIM AND TODD" BY ECS (AUGUST 5, 2010)

I haven't posted for a while (have you missed me?) because I've been having fun this summer with my real-life friends and family instead of blogging. A few of the highlights have been trail running in Millcreek Canyon with Shelah and chatting one afternoon with Mel (thanks again for the ride to the airport, Mel!).

Something else happened this summer. Yesterday, in fact. A federal judge ruled[142] that Proposition 8 violated the 14th Amendment of the Constitution and struck down Proposition 8's provisions that deny same-sex couples the right to marry. As you know, the Mormon Church encouraged its members to donate millions of dollars and to spend countless hours to pass Proposition 8, and the Church responded to this news here.[143]

The Mormon Church, however, did not respond when three LDS gay men committed suicide this summer. The big Mormon blogs in the bloggernacle didn't either.

While there is some disagreement about the motivations for these suicides,[144] there's no question that the LDS Church fosters a community of intolerance and bigotry towards gays and lesbians. (Don't make me start pulling out the G.A.[145] quotes, because I totally will). The Church's aggressive political activity supporting Proposition 8 is only one manifestation of this intolerance.

And while I'm pleased that Judge Walker struck down Proposition 8 yesterday, I'm saddened that the LDS Church continues to preach that gays and lesbians are defective and irretrievably broken human beings. Even though David Standley, Tim Tilley and Todd Ransom did not implicate the LDS Church in their suicides, it's difficult to see how anyone could grow up in the LDS Church and miss the very clear message that if you're gay, you're uniquely broken and confused and unacceptable to Heavenly Father. And if you're already prone to depression and melancholy, you would no doubt internalize this message as indicative of your failure as a human being and continue to suffer at the hands of your neighbors and family members who—as co-religionists—should offer you comfort and solace instead of hurtful religious doctrine decrying homosexuals.

As we (some of us) celebrate the Proposition 8 ruling, we need to recognize that nothing much has changed. We need to work to make our religious community a welcoming place for people like David, Tim and Todd, or more people will die because of our active intolerance or our uncomfortable silence.

"MARTYR NO MORE" BY SHELAH MASTNY MINER (SEPTEMBER 2, 2010)

A few weeks ago, I did an interview for a soon-to-be published piece for the Mormon Women Project.[146] The interviewee talked about growing up in the 1950s in a household with eight kids where her mother worked and was also involved in lots of church and civic projects. Her daughter said, "She was not a martyr at all. I think that's a great gift for children. If your mother is free then you are free."

I've spent the last ten years being a martyr to some degree or another. I've grumbled as I made the beds they left unmade, complained to myself as I emptied cups from the dishwasher and swept crumbs from the floor, and rolled my eyes at the piles of dirty clothes my husband left on the floor.

Last week, I started school again. It's going to be hard for the next two years, for them and all of me. My heart breaks a little bit every morning when my three-year-old cries about going to preschool ("But I want to stay home with you!" she says, and who wouldn't, after all, want to sit around the house with a steady stream of grape juice, Nick Jr, and Mommy love?). So my husband has been dropping her off.

Before I started school, I would have sent him off to work, figuring that taking my crying child to preschool fell under the domain of "my responsibility," but honestly, he can do it. It doesn't make him feel guilty the same way it does to me (he has, after all, been leaving for work without guilt for the last decade). Similarly, I'm not home to stew and stomp my feet if beds aren't made and dishwashers aren't unloaded. No, my house isn't perfect anymore, but from 50 miles away at school, I don't care either.

I've thought a lot about killing the martyr inside me since that interview. I've recognized that I have been a martyr, and I wonder if it's an easier role for SAHMs to fall into than it is for women in other situations? I also wonder if martyrdom is more of a female characteristic than a male one? (And honestly, I'm not sure about the answer to that one.) But I figure that even if I learn nothing more from going to school for the next two years than getting over the "woe-is-me" attitude I've sort of unknowingly adopted, that will be an education in and of itself. Have you had to kill your inner martyr? How did you go about it?

"Mormon Feminism in Action" by Meghan Raynes Matthews (September 7, 2010)

Mormon feminism has had a big year. After being pronounced all but dead, it has been thrilling to see this renaissance take place in such a short period of time. The year started with the rebirth of the feminist literary tradition; the Our Visions, Our Voices[147] tour put on by the Mormon Women Writers was amazing. And, of course, *Exponent II* magazine is back with a bang.

Then there were the *Patheos* and *The Guardian*[148] articles written by FMH's Tresa Brown Edmunds, proudly proselytizing our cause.

I am not alone in recognizing a groundswell in the movement. The same publication that asked only six years ago where all the Mormon feminists had gone[149] now declares that Mormon feminism is back. One of the most exciting developments has been the creation of the Mormon feminist activist organization, Women Advocating for Voice and Equality (WAVE).

This organization seeks to put action to all of the words, hope, and pain that have been shared over the years by Mormon feminists on and off the internet. On our newly redesigned website[150] there is a place to share your experience as an LDS woman, participate in social justice causes worldwide, access words of wisdom by LDS women to include in your lessons and talks, and a resource and support section to answer questions about feminism in general and Mormon feminism specifically. Each month there will be a call to action, an opportunity to participate in something that will improve the experience Mormon women and men have in the church. This month's action is a call for quotes by and about women for an LDS Women's Quote Book.

There are some who believe that this new Mormon feminism will fail. They are wrong. Mormon feminism has already won. Despite the very public beating feminism took twenty years ago, the fruits of our foremothers' labor can be seen every week at church. Women can give talks and prayers, they are invited to council meetings, changing tables are available in both women's and men's restrooms, Heavenly Mother's name can be invoked without an automatic discipline meeting with the bishop.

There is absolutely more to be done, and this time around it isn't just a small number of intellectuals in Salt Lake City talking about women's issues at Sunstone. It's the young women of the Save the WRI movement, it's Claudia Bushman and her Mormon Women's Experience project [the Mormon Women's Oral History Project at Claremont Graduate University], it's WAVE, it's the bloggers and commenters at Exponent, FMH, and Zelophehad's Daughters. The new Mormon feminism includes faithful women all over the world, of all ages and life situations, gathering on the internet, going to retreats and conferences and then going forth into their wards and branches and being the change they so desperately want.

Undoubtedly, there will be some who throw about the old and tired accusation of apostasy. I can say from experience that nothing is further from the truth. When we first created WAVE, all of us had powerful personal revelation, a message from God that spurred us to action. Those of us who are participating in this movement are not out to destroy the church; rather we seek to strengthen it by aiding in the church's retention of women. We love our daughters and know that they deserve so much more than crumbs from the table.

All that we desire are the good gifts that Christ promised God has for all of Their children (Matt. 7:11). With a desire like this, the new Mormon feminism cannot fail.

"FAITHFUL AND FEMINIST: TOWARD BALANCE" BY LISA PATTERSON BUTTERWORTH (OCTOBER 5, 2010)

My heart hurts.

I have been very sad about all the hostility toward President Packer. His talk hurt me deeply,[151] but at the same time, he is much like my dear father, and he is my brother in Christ, and he is a prophet of the Church I love. It's one thing if I complain about him, and quite another to hear it from someone outside the family.

I know I chose this path, I chose to live with the cognitive dissonance of trying to embrace both my faith in the Gospel and to be true to my feminist beliefs. And to do so openly and publicly. It pulls me in both directions, hurts me from both directions. Sometimes I wish I could just choose one, and live comfortably there, with lots of moral certainty and very few shades of gray. I have been there before and it is a very cozy place to be. It just is.

But I am what I am, sometimes I think this path chose me. I can't figure out how to stop caring about equality, and my attempts to stop believing in the Gospel were roundly rejected by the Lord. And I can't seem to stop blogging about it when I know it helps so many who struggle like I do.

But being a feminist Mormon is at times lonely and scary and frustrating and full of unresolvable conflicts that must be balanced ever so carefully. We work very deliberately toward that delicate balance, but it's never easy, this is not a cozy blog.

If you want to be comfortable and have people agree with you, you are in the wrong place. You can go to Sunday School for that. You can go to a secular feminist blog for that. They both serve important purposes. But we can't be that here. If you are full of certainty, you are in the wrong place.

But having said that, this *is* a community. A real community full of people who love each other, and who care, and who want to understand and help each other. Even when we disagree.

And because it is a community, and because we care about each other, we have to have rules, manners to live by, to help us work through these really uncomfortable moments when those last bits of our cozy certainties blow apart in the winds of harsh reality. We have to be gentle with each other here, the topics themselves are hard enough, tender enough without adding vitriol and petty meanness and sarcasm and anger into the mix.

And even that can't be said with certainty, because as we know, a huge part of the feminist dilemma is the unwritten code that tells us to be silent, the code that tells us our anger is unfeminine and unattractive, the code that tells us we are being bossy and pushy when the men doing the same things are being nobly assertive. See? No easy answers.

How to create that space that allows those tender open wounds to heal and allows those full of anger and pain to express themselves openly? Can it even be done? Maybe it can, if we use love as our guide, if we temper ourselves and really listen to each other.

And for the most part, we have managed to do that beautifully. I've been continually astonished at the quality of the people who come to comment here. Heartened by the patient kindness, the gentle disagreements, and the building of real relationships that transcend the blog space we are in.

Sure I have always received feedback (constructive and otherwise) from people on both sides of the aisle, people who insist that by defending and submitting to the patriarchy I defile everything that feminism stands for, and people who insist that by defending and advocating feminism I defile everything the gospel stands for. And I suppose being right in the center of that divide is where we must stand.

I've been running this blog for a long time and thus I have seen the pendulum swing back and forth many times (a little more feminist over here, a little more faithful over there, a little too nice over here, a little too mean over there), and for the most part the corrections occur on their own (with a little nudge from us bloggers on occasion). But we have slowly been coming to the consensus over the last few months that our pendulum has gotten a little stuck. And this post is an attempt to get us moving back to the center.

Over the last while the tone of comments has shifted as such that it is no longer a safe place for people with more conservative, traditional, or less classically feminist points of view. I say this with some reluctance, and after letting this go on far too long because I do so enjoy and admire most everyone who comments here. And also because I fully understand the desire to push back against so many of the "Sunday School" approaches that just don't work for me.

But that said, this really needs to be a place where people can come with their questions, their own brands of faith, their testimonies firm and strong or bruised and shaken, full up to the eyeballs of Sunday School answers, some that work for them better than others, and receive help to put themselves back together again *as works best for them and their own relationship with God.* And that may mean that some people continue to accept ideas that make me want to tear my hair out by the root. My job is not to convince them that their testimony should look exactly like mine.

We cannot be a community based around a single creed, I believe there are nearly endless good ways to live one's life, many pathways to righteous living, lots of lovely ways to be a faithful Mormon and/or a committed feminist. Yet I have seen a disturbing tendency of late to create an us vs. them, insiders vs. outsiders, women who know vs. them that don't atmosphere here. It's an easy stance to take (one I'm sure I've been guilty of myself) and an instinctive defensive one, no doubt, because we do feel so much pressure of this very nature in the culture of the Church itself. (We're under siege, this value is too important for compromise, dismiss those unrighteous/illogical people, they aren't like us.) But we must try to rise above it here, we must try to see people, listen to people, love people, rather than expect obedience to values and ideals we hold very dear.

I know this can be painful, near to impossible when an idea is central/momentous/vital/urgent to us, when we see so much harm and pain as a result. But the trick is, the ideas will never change, the ideas can't even be addressed, if we don't touch each other and respect and love each other as people first and foremost and always. And that most decidedly includes Boyd K. Packer and my dear father, and the 90% of our grandparents who would agree with them.

Sure there are times and places to be uncompromising, to be angry, to be loud and proud and in your face. But this blog isn't that place. Not for the feminists. Not for the faithful.

So . . . a few things come to mind.

- Ask questions instead of making assumptions.
- Assume good intentions. (As N.O. always says, cluelessness is often indistinguishable from malice.)
- Be Kind. Not *nice* necessarily, but do actively consider the impact of your words as though you are talking to a person with feelings that matter. Would you say this to someone sitting on your couch?
- Look for common ground. We all have lots of it.
- Disagree respectfully. Never resort to name calling. Avoid labeling.
- Consider an apology. If you made a mistake or weren't careful about tone. (Though it is not necessary to apologize for your beliefs nor for disagreeing nor for just existing.)
- Take time to listen, actively listen, reread in a different tone, consider what they probably meant to say (we aren't all brilliant communicators).
- Resist the dogpile, sure it's easy to surround someone and beat them to a pulp, but would Jesus like it?
- Ignore Trolls, they ruin it for the rest of us.

and my two favorites:

- Do not question someone's righteous.
- Do not undermine, undervalue, mock or disparage someone's faith.
- Anything you want to add? (I'm running out of time, kids'll be home in ten minutes)

And in conclusion, please be patient with us. We are human, with big ol' flaws and tempers and distractions. We all have lives that are engrossing and crap we have to do (though we'd rather be blogging than cleaning toilets, but toilets make their demands, darnit). And if you don't agree with us about how we envision our feminist and faithful blog, our purpose or our hopes, I guess you're a bit out of luck. This is our home, we provide the jello and funeral potatoes and non-alcoholic beverages and graciously allow you all to visit us whenever you like, please only spend your time here if you can respect our home and values.

"ME, THE MISSIONARIES, AND HEAVENLY MOTHER" BY SARA BURLINGAME (NOVEMBER 1, 2010)

I always thought my missionaries would be women. I've been an active participant on FMH and involved with LDS culture for the last three years or so, but there are still gaps in my knowledge, and I thought meeting with the missionaries would help with that. When I imagined how this would happen I just assumed it would be women who would teach me but guess what? There just aren't that many. So when some missionaries were tracting my neighborhood last spring and I was struggling to fit Noodle's[152] stroller in the trunk it seemed . . . right.

Before Elder Edwards and Elder Cruz even had time to give me their spiel, I'd laid out my bargain: they would not be getting a convert out of this conversation—if they wanted to invest their resources in a more spiritually profitable relationship, I totally understood and no hard feelings. However, in return I would feed them well and I could almost guarantee that they would have the best stories to tell—I think discussions with a queer, atheist, feminist who is sincerely interested in the church is the trump card when RMs play "Who had the craziest investigator?" And for good measure, my girlfriend Rose was home applying for grad school and said she'd take the discussions with me.

They were very nice boys. Super nice and terribly devout. Did I mention they were nice? I was particularly impressed with Elder Edwards in the first discussion relating the story of Joseph Smith praying in the grove. The young missionary practically trembled with the Spirit as he told it. It is a rare thing to see a man just barely out of puberty willing to be emotionally expressive about anything—much less faith, much less in front of strangers.

But (you knew there was a "but" coming, right?) it was downright weird how little they knew or cared about basic doctrine. Who was Eve? Was she duped or was she noble? Is there a hell? Who goes there? Who is our Heavenly Mother? Is she Powerful or is she Weak? It didn't seem to bother them at all, they had object lessons aplenty and funny anecdotes to spare, but no actual answers and no curiosity about the lack of those answers.

Nonetheless, I think our time was productive, I learned some things that I hadn't known, enjoyed getting to know them and held up my end to feed them well and give them good stories. I was also very clear about my intentions going in, namely that earnest questions on my part were acceptable but that I would never be provocative for its own sake.

Our 6th and final discussion entailed going to church (it was Elder Cruz's final week and he was giving his farewell talk), which was its own kind of nightmare—and I am not being hyperbolic. I've been to that ward heaps—I first went 5 years ago to see my friend's baby blessed, and I've been 7 or 8 times since, but I've never had a Perfect Storm of Church Badness experience like the one we had that day. Which is another post. Anyway, church was bad and the final discussion which included the quorum president was ... weird. Not intentionally weird, but one adult male and two adolescent males lecturing two adult women on the Law of Chastity is never going to be normal. So after causing a ruckus in Sunday School, Relief Society AND my final discussions, I rather thought I was blackballed; there would be no follow up visits to convince me to enter Zion.

So, I was genuinely surprised when the doorbell rang two days ago and the fresh faced missionaries introduced themselves. Remember how polite and deferential I was my first go around? Well, you can blame it on Zelophehad's Daughters, I certainly do. Lynette's recent post on "Why I do want to believe in Heavenly Mother"[153] and James Olsen's excellent post on Times and Seasons, "In Praise of Heavenly Mother,"[154] had me all het up about the disparity between what the Church professes about HM (reverence and godhead status) and what the Church practices (neglect and sloppy answers.) So I really wanted to know, "Who in your life do you claim to revere but in practice ignore?" How am I, a non-member, meant to take your claim that I will be welcomed into a plan of eternal salvation that includes a Goddess that I hope to emulate but know nothing about—seriously?

As I wrestled with the theological implications of having a female divinity who is nearly invisible, two ideas kept presenting themselves to me: one, how sincerely SWK prayed for answers to the priesthood ban and two, how much pressure there was for him to provide some kind of answer. To clarify, when I say "pressure," I am mainly referring to faithful pressure—that is, earnest people looking to their shepherd for answers. (I feel like I know enough of how the Church works in response to hostile pressure to not advocate that route.)

So I guess my question is, what would that look like and do you believe it could be successful? On a local level, could men and women ask their leaders to pray for more light and knowledge about their Heavenly Mother? What about sharing personal visions of her in F&T meeting? Do you think the church would gain or lose converts if there was new revelation re: HM? What is a practical and effective way of bringing Heavenly Mother out of the dark and into the light?

"Some Easy, Non-Doctrinal Changes" by Natalie Hamilton Kelly (November 6, 2010)

In our pining for greater gender equality in the church, we feminists are often told that we cannot change the doctrine, that God's will cannot bend to the whims and wishes of His children, and that our understanding is too small and dim to understand the lofty things of eternity, so we should probably just accept it on faith and move on.

And blast it, maybe those critics are all spot on.

So here, friends, are some changes that could be made with no doctrinal ramifications:

1. Equalize funds and funding sources for YW and YM programs.
2. Allow women access to all callings that do not require the Priesthood, such as ward clerk and Sunday School President, and allow women to have oversight of a ward's finances.
3. Allow women to give opening and closing prayers in sacrament meetings everywhere, and to pray from the pulpit in General Conference.
4. Include more women's voices in lesson materials, church publications, and General Conference addresses.
5. Find a way to incorporate the General Women's conference as a fully recognized session of General Conference, at the same level of importance as the Priesthood Session.
6. Give women stewardship over women's sexuality. (See Article 13.)[155]
7. Eradicate teachings that men are incapable of controlling their own sexuality and that women are responsible for reining in the sexual temptations of both men and women.
8. Allow married women in every ward to file tithing under their own name, regardless of their husband's membership or level of activity.
9. Allow every person facing a disciplinary council, male or female, to have a representative of their choosing present with them in all meetings.
10. Make the Church Handbook of Instructions[156] available to all members.
11. Standardize mission requirements for men and women—same length of service and same age eligibility.
12. Use women's honorific titles with the same regularity that we use men's. If we insist on "President" Packer, we should insist on "President" Beck.
13. Incorporate inclusive language. Instead of singing "God will force no man to heaven," we can sing "God will force no one to heaven." (See Hymn #240.) Instead of talking about mankind, we

can talk about humankind. Help your fellow men and women instead of just your fellow men. Easy fixes.

14. Make sure every meetinghouse has baby changing stations in all restrooms and adequate facilities for nursing mothers.

15. Ensure that male and female leaders are present in every meeting that will affect the entire ward.[157]

Look, I didn't even bring up the temple or Heavenly Mother. Totally circumspect, no? I'm pretty proud of my heresy avoidance here.

For even an orthodox member, these changes are not threatening. And neglecting these things is causing tangible harm to many men and women. What other non-threatening changes would you like to see made? Leaving doctrine (loosely defined) completely intact, what could change to improve the LDS experience for many women? What do we have to do to make this happen?

"IT JUST MAKES SENSE." BY NATALIE HAMILTON KELLY (NOVEMBER 22, 2010)

I've recently gone all conservative[158] on you folks. So I thought I'd straighten up any misconceptions.

I favor the ordination and full incorporation of women into the priesthood.

See? Still a crazy radical. I just couldn't bear to disappoint y'all with so much moderation.

I've been reading different things lately—about the women's movement, about the abolition of slavery, and other Mormon women stuff. I read Chapter 15 of *Women and Authority* and liked a lot of what Edwin Brown Firmage had to say.[159] I didn't agree with all of it, but one thing really just hit me:

> Once I thought about it in a searching way, without simply accepting the prohibition as if it were the natural order of things, I was shocked to conclude that no reason—not one solitary reason which is not on its face absurd—exists why women should not be ordained.

Upon reflection, I feel the same way. I just don't see the problem with it. Really. I can't think of a single reason that bears close scrutiny as to why women can't hold the Priesthood.

Are we just waiting for a revelation about it? I'm not so sure that's the right approach. We don't need God to tell us everything that is right or wrong. Sometimes, you should just do something because it is smart and shows greater love for God's children. Did we really need a prophetic revelation to tell us that Black members of the church should be fully fellowshipped? Really? We couldn't figure that one out on our own?

The question of women and the priesthood is, to me, equally self-evident.

Let's look at the words of Frederick Douglass from 1848, which were written in regards to women's suffrage:

> In respect to political rights, we hold woman to be justly entitled to all we claim for men. We go further, and express our conviction that all political rights which it is expedient for man to exercise, it is equally so for woman. All that distinguishes man as an intelligent and accountable being, is equally true of woman, and if that government is only just which governs by the free consent of the governed, there can be no reason in the world for denying to woman the exercise of the elective franchise, or a hand in making and administering the law of the land.[160]

So much of this can be applied to the question of women and the priesthood. All the benefits that flow to men from holding the priesthood are also needed by women. All the qualifications that men have for leading the church are found equally in women. All the challenges that confront men in filling these callings would be as challenging and as enriching for women. And the servants of the Lord, called to serve all of God's children, cannot fully serve those whose voices they are not allowing themselves to hear.

Many women in the church are searching for a way to make their voice heard, to feel like they have power in themselves, to find meaning in their eternal progression besides being the supportive appendage of the righteous male they've attached themselves to. These yearnings have led many women to think that a separate structure is what is needed—that the current structure of the Priesthood is irrevocably male, and instead of trying to change it from within, we should erect our own structure, based on our own voices, which we know will not be co-opted by the same patriarchs we'd like to acknowledge us as equals.

I'm open to such arguments. Really I am. I'm excited to discuss them below. But so far, I still think we need to just share the power that already exists.

Setting up a separate but equal hierarchy, while tempting, does not really appeal to me. Our current system invests the final word always, always, in the First Presidency. They have veto power over everything in the entire church. I have a hard time imagining a women's organization that would not be subject to that same veto power.

Additionally, I think that setting up separate leadership organizations for men and women will only reinforce the pernicious notion that men and women are eternally different and justify different authority, treatment, roles and power based on those supposed differences. I like what Firmage had to say about this in *Women and Authority*. Men and women are fundamentally *the same*. Sure, we're a little different. Maybe. But our commonality, rooted in our shared heritage as children of the divine, is so overwhelming as to drown out the differences. And like Audre Lorde says:

> Difference must not be merely tolerated, but seen as a fund of necessary polarities between which our creativity can spark like a dialectic.[161]

What differences we might have, if they are significant, can only be a source of strength. If we want our mortal organization to become as divine as possible, shouldn't we maximize the various sources of goodness, wisdom, courage, leadership, and strength that are found in God's children? Our differences can cause sparks of enlightenment and advancement. What did that 13th Article of Faith[162] say again?

But, if we're so similar, you might ask, why do women need to be in the leadership? Won't the men, if they're so much like the women, take care of all those needs? Unfortunately, the very exclusion of women *creates* difference between us. That manufactured difference is often then pointed to as the reason we have separate roles. Men are leaders with influence and authority. Women are voiceless supporters in the background. How could these separate roles not engender the development of separate character traits and behavior?

This is not a grab for power. I am not eager to control my ward. It has nothing to do with my desire, or lack of desire, for any given calling. Really, I *don't* want to be bishop. Really.

I just don't understand how womanhood disqualifies me and all of my sisters from being a part of our lay clergy. I'm not sure what it is about womanhood that our leaders think is ill-fitted for leadership and the performance of ritual. You know what womanhood means for me? It's not being inherently spiritual; it's not being emotional and intuitive; it's not being curvy and liking boys; it's not pretty and pink and shiny; it's not being a great cheerleader for the boys in charge; it's none of those things that I'm told womanhood is.

It's experience. I feel like being a woman means something because being a woman means that I am going to have all these experiences in common with other women. We all experience, or could experience, the same sufferings and the same joys. Not every woman is a mother and/or housewife, or wants to be a mother and/or housewife; but most women know what it's like to be given stewardship over children, to be left in charge of keeping a house clean, to be the source of succor and comfort for people that come to her. We know the pain of monthly menstruation, and the layers of meaning behind that pain, or its absence. Not every woman is sexually assaulted; but every woman can feel that deep shudder of horror when the mere thought of it thought crosses her mind, and the utter revulsion that creeps into her soul when she hears of the depravity suffered by her sisters. When I hear of women being stoned for being raped, or being cut to take away their sexual stimulation, or being forced to hide who they are and how they look because their mere existence is regarded as a dangerous nuisance for the *real* members of society: that is when I feel like a woman—because I know that it could be me. Because this has been the lot of my people in so many instances.

Being a woman, to me, isn't about femininity. It's about experience, and the shared experience that I have in common with women from all times and all places. We've all existed and lived and loved and suffered under the same system that takes away our voices. And we all have the wisdom and smarts gained from that experience to offer our community. But our community needs to accept our voices for that to happen.

What I want is not a big important calling. What I want is for my community to never be the source or supporter of the vile system that has hurt my foremothers, and *is* hurting my sisters, since time immemorial. What I want is for the Gospel of my youth to align with my vision of Zion. What I want is to be trusted and valued.

We're not valuable because we're women. We're not valuable because we're soft and pink and humble. We're not valuable because we're uber-spiritual and naturally good.

We're valuable because we're human. We have insights because we live and work and play in this world, right alongside the men. There's no reason that we can't live and work and play and worship right alongside the men.

So yeah. I guess I'm officially counted as a "radical feminist," seeing as I want to revolutionize the way the church is run and end millennia of patriarchal rule in spiritual matters. I don't know how much faith I have that these changes are likely or even possible in our current institution. But, dang it, I'm stuck in this community, and I want it to be worthwhile.

I dunno. Maybe I should just try to go find a local Quaker congregation; they seem to have some stuff figured out.

"POWER IN IMPERFECTION" BY LINDSAY HANSEN PARK (DECEMBER 30, 2010)

You might not have to submit to your husbands, but you'll have to submit to the dark machinations of my brain, and occasionally a Lady Gaga reference, for the next two weeks (insert evil laugh here) since I've been asked to be a guest poster. Suckers. You don't know what you're in for.

How do I start without sounding narcissistic???? I'm the perfect Mormon Housewife.

(Narcissism be dam*ed!)

I've read the article that spoke of a woman first realizing her sexual power here. Good read, and it made me think of my own sense of false power. I don't remember exactly when I realized my power in the church, but I know that I learned that being a domestic goddess gave one status and power in the church. Maybe the seedling of my feminism yearning for equality where there was none started it, or maybe my compulsion as a people pleaser was the culprit. Maybe my own vanity. Who knows. . . . Either way, I followed in step, learning how to cook, clean, craft, create, plan, and serve with the best of 'em.

When I became a "grown up," my house was a blank canvas awaiting the talents of my convictions. Vinyl machines and paint stores could nary a keep up with my whims. I wanted my house having my visiting teachers both impressed and intimidated. When I served a meal for my neighbors, I relished the husband's comments of "I wish my wife could cook like this." Oh how wickedly evil of me, yet like every evil scheme, it gave me power. In my community I was respected, revered and trusted. Not because of my ideas necessarily, but how well I executed a ward activity and how clever my handouts were.

Secretly, my mind was writing checks that my body couldn't cash. I was suffering from a horrible
eating disorder.[163] Bulimia if you want the dirty deets. I gave every appearance of Mormon perfection (as I saw it) and had the esophagus to prove it. I know I'm not alone in this. The eating disorder stats for Mormon women are crazy high (so says my therapist), and I know you're out there reading this, ED folks.

I'm sorry if my admission makes you uncomfortable while reading, but after living such a life of dangerous secrecy, I'm all about transparency now. I am not ashamed of my life or what the experience gave me. Uncomfortable revelations—thy name is Winterbuzz. I remember hearing an ad about drug addiction in Provo. The woman in the ad talked about the taboo of drugs there. She said, "Secrecy is killing our kids." Hollah! I hear it. Secrecy was killing me. All 90 lbs. of me.

Through my supportive husband and friends, as well as a great therapist, I was able to rein in the raging beast that consumed my life. Temptation is always piping, but I won't dance. Sometimes I tap my feet and sometimes my mean old brain wants me to hop on that scale for a beat down. Yet I soldier on, day by day. The greatest obstacle I had to overcome, which my behavior was directly linked to, was the idea that I had to have this perception of perfection. I held onto it like a dear child.

It just isn't real. Perfection in Mormondom doesn't exist in real time. If you think your neighbor or friend has got it down, here's the news: They don't. We all suffer, struggle and screw up.

Coming to terms with myself and becoming my own authentic self is my new goal. And what might seem like TMI to some of you, Ms. Mabbity Mab once pointed out, has become my life's nuanced theme: Being truthful.

While I am familiar with the limits and purpose of TMI, I was hurt because of secrets and I won't have my secrets hurt someone else. (What I would have given in college to know of other Mormon women's struggles with food. . . .)

Now, I'm a Utah Mormon so I don't know what you East Coast hippies decorate your homes with (hemp and communal friendship?). My BFF from Montana (I'm looking at you Mabbity Mab) commented on the strange phenomenon of vinyl signs and faux walls that she saw often in Utah homes. Sure, her home is nice where she lives, and she indulges in HGTV from time to time, but this craft race was strange to her.

She's a little right. I'm not sure why women feel the need to make their home the cutest one on the block. Not that there's anything wrong with it necessarily, it's a fun hobby and lots of women are very talented in it. I know why I did. I did it for power, purpose and a place among my peers. That's me no longer. I put beautiful things in my home that make me happy, sure, but I'm no longer concerned with creating or perpetuating a false atmosphere.

My husband, an eternal angel and saint, said to me once that I was part of the problem in the whole "Utah Mormon" stereotype. I was perpetuating the pressure and competition that I was already the victim of. I refuse to do that now.

I'm in search of my true and authentic self. That's the kind of feminist I am, the kind that doesn't tell a woman what she should be, but one that lets her be what she is and wants to be. No guilt involved. So as far as domestic goddesses go, let's go for truth:

My house is a disaster right now. I have Hot Pockets in the freezer. I feed my family more frozen pizzas than my conscience is okay with. I can't sew to save my life. I pretend to like football for my husband's sake, but I can't fool him, I'm lost on Monday nights. I sometimes talk on the phone when I should be playing with my kiddos or cleaning. I don't do regular FHE.[164] I'd rather sleep in than do morning family prayer. Oh, and I occasionally hire a cleaning lady when I feel too far behind. I'm opinionated, a little too passionate, I don't curse very often—but I want to. I am a dedicated feminist, but sometimes a lazy one. I don't always recycle, and I rely on spell check constantly since I can't spell "rhyme" or anything with an ie or ei. Yep, that's me. The imperfect Mormon housewife full of contradictions and problems and occasional silliness. Love me or not, it's okay, I love myself. I've found myself a certain amount of daily peace that keeps me going.

More than that, I've finally found my power. True power of self that comes from within. My visiting teachers might be a little less impressed with my feminist ideals and the uneven vacuum lines in my carpet, but their validation is not currency I spend anymore.

(Now here's my obligatory PSA: If you are struggling with a darkness, you're not alone. There are lots of us out there. God loves us, and He loves you and is aware of your pain. Be kind to yourself. Try to be positive and happy. You will survive. Find out the things you like about yourself and hold onto those things with all your might. Sometimes "enduring to the end"[165] means enduring our own hearts and brains no matter how taxing they might be.)

There is power in imperfection. There is power in truth. Here's to hoping you can all find a lil' bit of it yourselves!

"No question the Church of Jesus Christ of Latter-day Saints is 'having a moment,'"[166] proclaimed Walter Kirn of *Newsweek* in a June 2011 issue.

> Not only is Romney running again—this time, he's likely to be competing against his distant Mormon cousin Jon Huntsman Jr. The Senate, meanwhile, is led by Mormon Harry Reid. Beyond the Beltway, the *Twilight*[167] vampire novels of Mormon Stephenie Meyer sell tens of millions of copies, Mormon convert Glenn Beck inspires daily devotion and outrage with his radio show, and HBO generated lots of attention with the *Big Love* finale. Even Broadway has gotten in on the act, giving us *The Book of Mormon,* a big-budget musical about Mormon missionaries.[168]

In the wake of this Mormon Moment, the LDS Church launched the "I'm a Mormon" campaign to improve its public image and gave a measured response to the satirical musical *The Book of Mormon*. Michael Otterson, head of Public Affairs for the Church, issued a statement that affirmed the value of the Book of Mormon as a work of scripture that has the ability to impact people's lives. Administrators at BYU amended the honor code to allow students to be open about their homosexual identities and continue at the university, even if gay relationships and sexual activity remained violations. Students and community members at BYU started an organization called Understanding Same-Gender Attraction, which met on campus to discuss the issues surrounding being gay in the Church. A survey from the Pew Foundation noted that Mormons identified as Christians, even though a third of American adults did not see Mormons as Christians.[169]

BYU Studies published an article by David L. Paulsen and Martin Pulido that surveyed the references to Heavenly Mother by LDS Church leaders from the 1840s to the present.[170] Paulsen and Pulido engaged in the project to counter the popular idea of a required "sacred silence" on the subject of Heavenly Mother. Jonathan A. Stapley and Kristine Wright authored an influential article for *Journal of Mormon History* on women's ritual healing in Mormonism.[171]

LDS WAVE published a booklet, titled *Words of Wisdom: A Collection of Quotes for LDS Women*. The collection of quotes on women and women's issues by LDS Church leaders was organized by topic. The booklet included statements on subjects such as Heavenly Parents, partnership in marriage, and the value of education. The first Mormon feminist podcast, *Daughters of Mormonism*, launched this year. It ran for 50 episodes and included the personal stories of the host, Sybil, and the panelists, as well as discussions of Mormon women's spirituality. All of the voices on the podcast identified themselves by first name or pseudonym only. Mormon feminist Jana Riess published *Flunking Sainthood*,[172] where she recounted her adventures in experimenting with spiritual practices from several different religious traditions.

The FMH blog launched a closed group on Facebook, titled Feminist Mormon Housewives Society. At this point, many bloggers were still using pseudonyms, but Facebook required that people identify themselves with their real names. This allowed bloggers and readers to participate more directly in Mormon feminist conversations, away from the view of more traditional friends, family, and ward members. Blogs allowed for bloggers to start conversations about particular topics, but the format of closed Facebook groups allowed any member of the group to initiate discussions and ask questions.

"AGITATING FAITHFULLY" BY DANE LAVERTY (JANUARY 25, 2011)

> David Ransom: At present women are not allowed to be priests in your Church. . . . Is it possible that the rules could change in the future as the rules are on Blacks?
> Gordon B. Hinckley: He could change them yes. If He were to change them that's the only way it would happen.
> David Ransom: So you'd have to get a revelation?
> Gordon B. Hinckley: Yes. But there's no agitation for that. We don't find it. Our women are happy. They're satisfied.

Wait, Pres. Hinckley, can you say that one more time?[173]

"He could change them yes. . . . But there's no agitation for that."

So it's not carved in eternal stone that women will never hold the priesthood in the church? It's possible that God would change the rules?

"He could change them yes."

But you'd need a revelation, right?

"Yes. But there's no agitation for that."

So what you're saying, if I'm hearing you correctly, is that there's a link between agitation and revelation. In other words, when the church members ask for something, it's possible that God will actually grant it to them? (Is that so crazy?)

Now this is an important point. I was recently asked, "If it is God who decides whether women are [allowed] to hold the priesthood, why is 'agitation' a consideration?" I think this is a common sentiment in the church—that since we have a prophet who speaks for God, our job is just to sit and wait passively for instructions. But is that how God's pattern works anywhere else in our lives? When we seek blessings, do we just wait for them to conveniently arrive, or do we actively seek them? When we seek revelation, we pray. When we seek knowledge, we study. In the words of the Lord, "He that is compelled in all things . . . receiveth no reward." Or, in the less-divine-but-perhaps-just-as-useful words of quotationsbook.com, "The man who waits for a roast duck to fly into his mouth must wait a very, very long time."

So personal revelation comes in response to personal action. Does that mean church revelation comes in response to church action?

"So you'd have to get a revelation?"

"Yes. But there's no agitation for that."

That sounds like a "yes" to me.

Feminism and gender issues have not always been on my radar. I was comfortable in anti-feminism and traditional gender roles for most of my life. I brushed off claims of inequality as the ungrounded, faithless complaints of bitter women.

Reading the experiences shared by many of you here at FMH caused me to consider that perhaps these complaints were actually grounded in valid concerns. This was a transition of several years for me. It culminated a few months ago when my oldest daughter, five years old, asked why women can't have the priesthood. I could find no reasonable or scripturally based answer to give her, and I could not stand to say, "That's just the way things are."

I recalled Jeffrey R. Holland's words,

> Bear your testimony. Don't just assume your children will somehow get the drift of your beliefs on their own.[174]

I realized that if I want my children to know that God desires to bless His daughters just as much as His sons, I would need to find some way to communicate it to them. I wanted to do more than just say it occasionally at Family Home Evenings. I wanted them to know that gender equality is not a shameful belief, that it's not something that must be spoken quietly, only in the walls of one's home, and never in the hearing of other church members.

So, doing my best to take President Hinckley at his word, and with a hope and a prayer in my heart, I've built a website where faithful members can "agitate" for gender equality in the church: Agitating Faithfully.[175] (Okay, so it's not the most creative name ever. Sue me.)

Agitating Faithfully is a place where church members can publicly stand in supporting gender equality. Just go to the site and add your name to the list. It takes about 45 seconds. If you take a look now, you'll see that there are over 100 names signed to the list already.

The list of names isn't a petition, at least not in the traditional sense. I'm not going to submit it to church leaders and "demand" that they change church policy. I don't think that's how God operates, and I know it's not how I operate.

Instead of a petition, the list is a public statement of belief—a testimony. It's not for the church leaders, it's for the church members. It's about creating an atmosphere in the church that encourages and supports members in expressing minority opinions.

It's about reaching out to those members in the church who feel alone in their "crazy" belief that women and men might actually be equal and deserve equal blessings, and letting them know that they are not alone.

It's about reaching out to our friends, both inside and outside the church, who believe that Mormons all think the same way, and helping them see that faithful members of the church can, in fact, hold a diversity of opinions.

And it's about reaching out to God, in hope that He will hear and answer our works and our prayers.

So I invite you to come visit Agitating Faithfully. If you agree with the site's mission, please add your name to the list. If you don't agree with the site's mission, feel free to come by and check it out anyway. There's a Q&A section where you can publicly ask and answer questions. We've also got a Facebook site where I post updates and where you can connect with other faithful agitators. Also, you can hear more about how the site came to be at the Mormon Stories podcast.[176]

I'm amazed at the support I've seen so far. The atmosphere has been almost entirely positive, and I hope we can keep it that way. It's wonderful to be here at a time when we can be heard. And whether or not the church policy ever changes, I am and will be grateful for the friendships and connections I make with each of you in doing this. Thank you all for being awesome!

"ASK MORMON GIRL: HOW DO YOU RAISE DAUGHTERS IN THE CHURCH?" BY JOANNA BROOKS (MARCH 28, 2011)

Dear AMG:[177]

What's your experience raising daughters and with the Mormon Church? How do you do it? I have a 13-month-old daughter. I am struggling with what I will teach her and model for her. Where do you draw the line? How do you say listen to this, not that (when talking about talks given by people in the church)? I am a convert, so I don't know what is being taught in Young Women. I guess I'm just generally not sure how I will convey to her the good things about the Church, but still teach her important things like what feminism promotes.

—KB

Well, KB, since my daughters are only 5 and 7 years old, I want to start by professing a big dose of humility with this parenting business. There are wise women and men reading this right now who have years and years more parenting experience. In fact, I want to just hurry up and finish the column so I can scroll down and read their comments right now. I still have a lot of learning to do.

In many respects, I think the Church provides a more favorable environment than the non-LDS mainstream for young women's development because Mormonism strongly mitigates against the sexualization of young people and prioritizes their spiritual and intellectual development. (After getting letters here at AMG from young women under 18 who've felt bruised and battered by their first forays into sexual activity, I'm more convinced than ever that it's a terrific idea to delay as long as possible. But ECS made a great point here[178] about the dangers of portraying young women's sexuality as a threat to young men.) Mormonism also taught me to take myself seriously as a reader and a thinker, and it taught me the strength that comes from making difficult but good choices.

In other respects, I do worry about the impacts on my daughters of being raised in an institutional environment where almost all positions of visible congregational authority are reserved to men and where men are designated presiders and providers simply by virtue of having been born male.

Funny thing is, so far, my daughters seem not to notice the whole patriarchy business. One day on our way home from church, I was telling my daughters (in a very even-handed way) about how at times conservative Mormons have promoted the idea that women belong in the home rather than in positions of public leadership. And my then six-year-old said, "Are they crazy? Don't they see that women run everything at church?" And she started naming all her Primary teachers and leaders. "They're not just staying at home," she said. "They're in charge!" That's when I realized that from her perspective as a kid in Primary, women did run the church.

My daughter saw her Primary class that way in part because she is being raised by a Mormon feminist mom and a Jewish pro-feminist dad in an egalitarian marriage. What we model at home really matters. And especially because I was not a regular church attender for the earliest years of their lives, I have always felt that the responsibility for my daughters' spiritual education rested primarily with me.

So there has never been a time in my daughters' lives when they have not heard God consistently characterized by both me and my husband as a He and a She, a Mother and a Father. I have also shared with them at home as much Mormon feminist knowledge and outlook as possible to give them resources they may not get in more traditional Mormon settings.

I have tried to talk openly and compassionately about differences among Mormons. This lesson came home to them very early because as pro-LGBT equality Mormons in California, Proposition 8 had a huge impact on our lives. My daughters know that there are conservative Mormons and liberal Mormons, that some of us rooted for Proposition 8 (like Grandma) and some of us rooted against it (like Mommy), but that we are all still Mormons and that we definitely still love Grandma even though we may disagree with her on some things. It is often considered taboo to talk about differences among Mormons, but I am hoping that by modeling an open and respectful attitude towards difference my daughters will understand that they have the support from me they need as they shape their own standpoints and perspectives, as well as the right to find a path in Mormonism that works for them.

Finally, I have emphasized prayer and the process of seeking spiritual knowledge, because no Mormon teaching has been more pivotal or revolutionary for me than the belief that each of us can ask God directly and individually for help and direction in any circumstance.

I hope this helps, but I'm ready to shut up and listen. Readers, what wisdom can you add? What else should KB bear in mind as she raises her baby girl, and me as I raise mine?

Send your queries to askmormongirl@gmail.com, or follow askmormongirl on Twitter.

"'WOMAN, WHY WEEPEST THOU? WHOM SEEKEST THOU?'" BY LINDSAY HANSEN PARK (APRIL 24, 2011)

Jesus loves me. Wanna know how I know? Because today, of all days, He answered my prayer and used a little piece of His atoning sacrifice to bring healing to my heart.

For the past several months, I've been angry at the church.

My heart has been broken, absolutely shattered, chipped away bit by bit over the church's involvement in Prop 8, and since October conference, I've been looking for excuses not to attend. My spirit has been nursing this wound but since it was Easter, I didn't have an excuse not to go, you know? So, I got my little family all dressed and ready to go and was determined to feel my Savior's love and not let anything else bother me.

I was a little skeptical and anxious because my ward is very orthodox as a whole and very family oriented (which to them means anti-gay). They are wonderful folks, whom I love and who I know love me, but this one particular stance/doctrine/idea of homosexuality-being-a-sin silently divides us.

142

Anyway, as I sat down for Sacrament Meeting, my focus was more on getting my two boys to behave than anything else. Two young men sat next to me, and I thought, "Oh no, the Bishop has sent the missionaries to sit by me."

The gentlemen had no tags but did have their scriptures and sang the Easter hymns with fervency and were very good and patient with my kiddos.

The speaker quoted John 20:5: "Jesus saith unto her, Woman, why weepest thou? Whom seekest thou?"

And I internalized my struggle to the Lord.

"Lord, I weep because my heart is hurting. Lord, I seek Thee but sometimes I don't think I can find You here."

And then the strangest thing happened. Our ward choir sang the most beautiful song about everyone coming to Christ (I'd never heard it before). The music swelled, and the lyrics burst forth about Christ's love for everyone, and I looked at the two gentlemen sitting next to me and they were holding hands and weeping too.

The three of us sat quietly weeping in the back of the church while the choir sang, and I knew that this wonderful couple was an answer to the prayers of my heart. And for a small moment I knew, truly, that politics and doctrine and opinions aside, the Savior of the World drew the aching hearts of God's children nearer to Him in absolute and glorious redeeming love and light.

It was truly a miracle! (Maybe not water to wine, but if you knew the area I lived in, you'd see the absolute remarkableness of it all.)

It might seem like a silly (or blasphemous) anecdote to some, but today the Lord showed me what hope looks like. He showed me courage from the gay couple who could look past their hurt to come and celebrate the mission of Jesus Christ.

As the closing prayer ended, I noticed the stranger next to me whispered "He is risen!" and he and his partner folded up their chairs and left the building, leaving me with a renewed faith in what our Savior's love truly feels like.

"THE CHURCH IS LOSING US . . . HOW CAN THEY KEEP US?" BY LINDSAY HANSEN PARK (MAY 2, 2011)

In the wise words of TV's greatest master teacher and philosopher, Dr. Phil:

"You can't change what you don't acknowledge."

So I was happy to see reported in the SL Tribune[179] that the recent reasons for eliminating Student Wards and shifting to Young Single Adult congregations, as well as a few other recent changes in LDS missions, etc. were a result of the LDS Church's response to losing members, mostly in the 18–30 age group. (Although this loss is happening to all religions, the LDS Church continues to suffer from this same decline, and our leaders are finally starting to acknowledge this).

Other trends (taken from Ldschurchgrowth.blogspot.com and Cumorah.com):

- The drop-out rate/retention rate among RMs is disturbingly high.
- This year, the Church experienced its first Stake Shutdown, or First Stake Consolidation in Australia.
- The number of actual convert baptisms has decreased almost steadily since the 80s. This is based on the annual statistical report delivered in Gen. Conference.
- Most of the growth of "The Church" continues to be natural growth, through births rather than conversions. However, baptisms of children-of-record are declining too.
- Growth of Mormonism in North America and Europe is virtually flat and is actually declining in some countries (prompting the shift from European missions to South American ones).
- With the exception of new "minority" wards being created in some inner cities, Mormonism is dying off in urban centers, even in SLC.
- Most conversions to Mormonism are in the Third World, and the drop-out rate in those countries is very high. Surveys done in Mexico, Chile, and Brazil indicate that less than 20% of the "members" claimed by "The Church" self-identify as Mormons.

Us LDS folk frequently appeal to our religion's growth rate as an evidence of our gospel's truthfulness, so it's no surprise that we're a little shy to brag about our membership tank.

Mormon author David G. Stewart, Jr. writes:[180]

> The rapid growth of the Church of Jesus Christ of Latter-day Saints has been a frequent and recurring theme in the secular media. The claim that the Church of Jesus Christ is the "world's fastest growing church" has been repeated in the *Los Angeles Times*, *Salt Lake Tribune*, *Guardian*, and other media outlets, while sources claiming that the LDS Church is the "fastest growing in the United States" are too numerous to chronicle. Sociologist Rodney Stark's 1984 projection has been widely cited: "A 50 percent per decade growth rate, which is actually lower than the rate each decade since World War II, will result in over 265 million members of the Church by 2080." In Mormons in America, Claudia and Richard Bushman claimed, "Mormonism, one of the world's fastest-growing Christian religions, doubles its membership every 15 years.

Latter-day Saint media have also lauded rapid church growth. The LDS Church News has described international LDS growth with a litany of superlatives, including "astronomic," "dynamic," "miraculous," and "spectacular." The claim that the LDS Church is the "fastest growing church in the United States" has been repeated in the *Ensign* and *LDS Church News*. In a recent General Conference, the Church of Jesus Christ was described not only as being prolific, but also as retaining and keeping active "a higher percentage of our members" than any other major church of which the speaker was aware.

A closer examination of growth and retention data demonstrates that LDS growth trends have been widely overstated. Annual LDS growth has progressively declined from over 5 percent in the late 1980s to less than 3 percent from 2000 to 2005. Since 1990, LDS missionaries have been challenged to double the number of baptisms, but instead the number of baptisms per missionary has halved. During this same period, other international missionary-oriented faiths have reported accelerating growth, including the Seventh-Day Adventists, Southern Baptists, Assemblies of God, and Evangelical (5.6 percent annual growth) and Pentecostal churches (7.3 percent annual growth). For 2004, 241,239 LDS convert baptisms were reported, the lowest number of converts since 1987. The number of convert baptisms increased to 272,845 in 2006, but both missionary productivity and the total number of baptisms remained well below the levels of the early 1990s. Even more cause for concern is the fact that little of the growth that occurs is real: while nearly 80 percent of LDS convert baptisms occur outside of the United States, barely one in four international converts becomes an active or participating member of the Church. Natural LDS growth has also fallen as the LDS birth rate has progressively declined. LDS church membership has continued to increase, but the rate of growth has slowed considerably.

I could go on and on about numbers and graphs and charts for membership growth and decline. I've seen Mormon YouTube propaganda touting our church's enormous success at bringing sheep to the fold. Even our manuals still brag about our great latter-day expansion, calling it a challenge to keep up with such "tremendous growth."

On the flip side, there are loads of stats from a variety of sources (from anti-mo to distinguished news outlets) that paint a bleak picture of church activity.

Either way, the bottom line is this—the church may be growing here and there, but it isn't growing as much as everyone in it would like, and the leaders are starting to notice. And worse, church members are not being retained like they should be. (I read some estimates that anywhere from 2 to 5 million of the 14-ish million were actually active members but couldn't seem to find anything conclusive. Anyone have numbers on this?)

The *Salt Lake Tribune* article quotes Elder Ballard as trying to tempt young saints with promises of power and leadership as incentive to stay in the church:

> We want you to see yourselves as bishops, Relief Society presidents. . . . [even] seated on the stand as an apostle... We need you to be prepared.

I'm not sure this is the right approach. Changing and integrating wards is a step, but I think the church has much larger issues to deal with if they want to retain members, especially the rising generation.

Instead of blasting off my opinions, I'd love to hear yours.

In your responses, I'd love to see two things (and maybe it might even help out the spying eye of lurking GA who might get some good ideas? Yeah, probably not):

1. First, what immediate changes would you like to see that would benefit your life and make church going easier for you?
2. What do you think the church needs to do as a whole in order to stop this trend of decline?

"LOSING YOUR ETERNAL FAMILY, A LESBIAN SISTER'S STORY" BY MARS VASQUEZ (MAY 28, 2011)

I grew up in a Mormon family. My father was the 9th member to be baptized in Honduras, Central America. My mother was a Catholic, but soon after marrying my father she converted to Mormonism. I am the youngest of 5 children, and up until I was about 17, I was a devout and faithful member of the Mormon church. I served as the president of the Laurels,[181] often spoke in Sacrament Meeting and was recognized as a strong leader amongst my church peers. I loved the church. I loved what it did for my family. My family has always been my number one, so for me, the promise of families being forever was the most appealing aspect of the religion.

I identified with an attraction toward members of the same sex at the age of 8. I hid that secret for many years, praying to God to help me be "normal." I self-loathed for many years but found comfort by being in the service of others. I've always put myself last, because, well, I, my very being was a contradiction to everything I believed and once loved so dearly. But you can only deny yourself for so long, and so at age 18, I came out to my family and friends. I'll spare you the details of what it's like coming out to a

Mormon/Latin family. To feel like you disappointed and insulted your whole family by choosing to do nothing more than finally putting yourself first is a horrible feeling. I would never wish being gay on anyone. However, I am gay, and I stopped apologizing for it many years ago. I am 33 years old now and my relationship with my family has evolved into something quite amazing. As a child my mother was never very affectionate, and very rarely, if ever, did I hear the words "I love you." I'm not saying that I wasn't loved by my parents because I truly was. My parents showed us love by providing and sacrificing for us. We were always clean, well fed and always had a roof over our head. When we migrated to the United States, my parents worked multiple jobs and constantly put their needs last so that they could give the best of what they had to us. I grew up having no doubt whatsoever that I was adored by my parents. All of that love was put to the test when I came out of the closet. Although we struggled for a couple of years following my bombshell confession, we recovered well.

My mother is now more affectionate; she tells me she loves me all of the time, and so does my father. My sisters show it more as well. I hear "I love you" so often nowadays, and although I appreciate it and revel in it, I also know why they do it and I struggle with the reasons. There is a certain sadness in my mother's eyes every time she grabs my face, kisses me and tells me that she loves me. It almost feels like every time she does it, she's saying goodbye to me. She's getting in as much love as she can because she knows, according to her beliefs, that after this life—she won't have me anymore. She's sad for me. She loves me so much and she shows it so much because I know that in her mind, the time on this earth is all the time she'll ever have with me. I'm angry that she can't just love me because I'm me. I'm angry that all that beautiful love has to be tainted with a hint of sadness. My mother is sad for me. Well, I . . . I am sad for my mother. I resent God, but I do so mostly because I don't understand him. I don't understand a God that can promise my beautiful and faithful mother everlasting happiness in a celestial kingdom while her daughter sits in some Tele-whatever kingdom. If our familial bonds are to extend into the next life, how can my mother be happy without me? What switch will God flip to make her forget about me? I don't understand a loving God that would send someone into hell simply because they loved. Today, I do not fully believe in a Christian God, and the more I've come to realize that, the more melancholy I feel, the more confused I become. I believe in him less and less each day and there is very, very little left of him in my heart. I am searching for something, I want to believe in something, but in my rational mind, I'm finding that I believe less in God, and find myself believing more in science. I believe that when I die, my anatomical functions will slowly shut down and the energy that currently resides in me will be released and freely dissipate across millions of particles, and when I embrace that . . . I don't feel as sad for my mother. How did I get here? And why do I cry as I write these words? Why does it hurt to feel like I've lost everything I grew up believing and yet at the same time, I feel free and happy to know that for the first time in my life, I am confident in who I am and in the good I bring to this world? I am a loving person, I constantly go out of my way for others, I love life and take pleasure in the little things it offers. I love people and I love my family. I am so passionate about my family that when I'm away from them for an extended period of time, I feel I might just shrivel up to pieces and die. I believe in humanity and in the power of the human capacity to make life amazing, to make dreams come true and to make life better for those around us by simply smiling and giving more. I am a phenomenal human being. My family believes in a God that feels I am not worthy of spending eternity with them. There is no part of me that accepts a God like that. Not because that God doesn't justify my means. But simply, because at my core, I cannot believe that the same loving God I grew up serving and adoring would judge me based on who I sleep with rather than by all the good I strive to bring and give to the world each and every day. My name is Mars, and I am currently mourning, evolving and searching.

"SOMETIMES IT'S HARD TO BE A GOOD MORMON" BY BRITTANY MORIN-MEZZADRI/LADYMO (JUNE 30, 2011)

This week at church I sobbed my eyes out to the point that my head was dizzy, my fingertips tingled, and I had a hard time catching my breath. It was at the same time a faith shattering and faith affirming experience today. I simultaneously hated and loved the church. I knew that it was both a place I never wanted to be again and a place I needed to be for the rest of my life.

Here's what happened:

My friend came to church with me today, and I prayed that it would be a good experience for her and that she could learn something that would help her find her path (she's holding tightly to Proverbs 3:6). I tend to arrive early and almost always have enough time to do a little reading before sacrament meeting. Today, I was reading Luke 6:27–38. I sat for a while thinking that this is actually a lot easier than I might think. It's easy to love your enemies when you don't think you have any. It's way easy to bless those who curse you when there are none who are, I think.

I spent some extra time with verses 37–38. I will be measured with the same stick I use to measure someone else; forgive and I can also be forgiven. Thinking about those verses, I realized that I'm not very good at that. I am way too quick to judge and far too hard hearted to forgive. If someone insults me or hurts my feelings, I send death daggers from my eyes to the back of their skull. If I perceive injustice, I tend to get far too angry and want retribution. I know this about myself . . . I don't like this about myself. I know I need to change this.

Sacrament talks were lovely. I learned a lot. Sunday School as well. Things were smooth sailing and by the time I got to Relief Society I had just about forgotten my mini-lesson during my downtime. The lesson was on Elder Maynes's talk "Establishing a Christ-Centered Home."[182] Of course, this led to discussion of family, both heavenly and earthly. We discussed the various ways our Heavenly Father has blessed us and what specific blessings come from families. When the teacher asked, "What are some different ways the adversary tries to keep us from the blessings of our families?" my heart cringed. I knew where this was going, and I sat and silently begged, "Please no New York. Please no Prop 8. Please please please, no no no."

A woman in the back raised her hand and said, "New York recently passed a bill allowing same-sex marriage and they say that 8 other states are about to follow. Our duty as Saints is to take a stand and prevent this from happening. It's disgusting, destroying the family, and it must be stopped." Mind you, I was sitting at the front of the room with the other interpreter and my friend just saw my face fall. I sat there for about 15 more seconds. I thought I could tough past that and ignore it, but I could just feel my insides burning and tears about ready to explode. I felt so unloved, so hated, so betrayed, and so disappointed.

I grabbed my things and left the building. I didn't stop to talk to anyone. I just left the building and sat in the shade under a tree and sobbed and sobbed. This isn't the first time I've encountered someone, inside or outside of the church, saying something to this effect. I tend to be able to respond appropriately (read: not firing death glares at them so ferociously) and can engage in a respectful discussion about human rights and "this is my family, back off." I have a hard time engaging in that conversation at church. When I'm there, I feel vulnerable and raw and like I'm sitting there with my heart open as if to say, "This is yours. Do with this whatever you need." I also understand that church is not the venue for political discussions, and that if they do arise, I must refrain from participating. This doesn't leave me with much. First, my heart is trampled on and I have nothing with which to defend myself, it seems. The only response I have is to leave and cry and be all hurt and angry and send death dagger thoughts to the person who served such an injustice. So not WWJD. (Oh, did I mention, I'm a little dramatic sometimes.)

Anyway, I sat outside and just kept thinking, "Why am I part of this church? I don't belong here. They're all a bunch of fools who hate my family and nothing I do is going to stop that. I can't be a good Mormon and still be faithful to my family. If I have to choose, the Mos gotz to go."

If it weren't for the fact that my roommate was still in the building, and that I was her ride, I probably would have just left and stewed in hate and hurt for the rest of the day. So instead, I sat as far away from the building as I could.

The Relief Society President, Sister S, came out and found me sobbing like a 3-year-old under a tree. I am so grateful for that woman and her family. We sat and talked for a bit, and she reminded me that sometimes people say really stupid things. Sometimes it's hard for people to divorce doctrine from culture. Sometimes, even the best people with the kindest hearts say the most distasteful, hurtful, un-Christ-like things. I reminded her that sometimes I'm that person, too. She let me sit there and emotionally vomit my frustrations with how people talk about homosexuality or gay marriage. She let me forcefully defend my family and my right to love them and their right to be treated like human beings. She sat there and just loved me the whole time.

At one point, she said, "The point of the lesson today was to know that every one of us is a child of God. He created us and He loves us no matter who we are or where we come from or what circumstances we find ourselves in. It doesn't matter if you're gay, straight, blue, purple, in the church, out of the church, good or bad. I sound like Lady Gaga, but she's right!"

She said, "I have a question for you. Can you forgive her?" I knew what all of that meant. My whole mini-lesson prior to sacrament meeting was exactly leading up to this question. Could I forgive this woman? Could I forgive her, could I forgive the culture of the church knowing how strongly she/it protests against the rights of my family? For a quick moment, I thought, "I have absolutely said and done some stupid and thoughtless things in my life, and I have for sure caused someone to hurt this badly because of those stupid and thoughtless actions or words. I need to forgive if I'm ever to be forgiven."

In that conversation, Sister S made me feel so loved and so aware of the fact that I am a child of God. She helped me understand the Atonement of Jesus Christ and what Luke 6:37–38 actually meant. She comforted me with so much love and support and understanding that I started crying because of that, and I knew that this was exactly where I needed to be.

I recently read a talk from President Uchtdorf, "The Love of God."[183] Love that man, right? Here's what he has to say:

> Because love is the great commandment, it ought to be at the center of all and everything we do in our own family, in our Church callings, and in our livelihood. Love is the healing balm that repairs rifts in personal and family relationships. It is the bond that unites families, communities, and nations. Love is the power that initiates friendship, tolerance, civility,

and respect. It is the source that overcomes divisiveness and hate. Love is the fire that warms our lives with unparalleled joy and divine hope. Love should be our walk and our talk.

In another talk, "You Are My Hands,"[184]

I hope that we welcome and love all of God's children, including those who might dress, look, speak, or just do things differently. It is not good to make others feel as though they are deficient. Let us lift those around us. Let us extend a welcoming hand. Let us bestow upon our brothers and sisters in the Church a special measure of humanity, compassion, and charity so that they feel, at long last, they have finally found home.

When we are tempted to judge, let us think of the Savior, who "loveth the world, even that he layeth down his own life that he may draw all men unto him. . . .

"[And] he saith: Come unto me all ye ends of the earth, . . . [for] all men are privileged the one like unto the other, and none are forbidden." (2 Nephi 26:25–28)

He's talking to me, who needs to understand the two-way street of tolerance, civility, and respect. He's talking to the sister in Relief Society, who, while probably unintentionally, made me feel like I was deficient. He's talking to Sister S, who lifted me up and showed me a special measure of humanity, compassion, and charity.

So, that was my day at church. I have a lot to learn and a long way to go and will likely have a lot of practice with forgiving and being forgiven. While sometimes it feels like it's one blow from crashing to the ground, I do have a testimony of the church. I know that I am a child of God and that I will make mistakes and that if I can learn to forgive, I too will be forgiven.

"THE FOUNTAIN OF YOUTH" BY KIMBERLY FITZPATRICK LEWIS (JULY 8, 2011)

I was at the hairdresser for my usual cut—which I stretch out to every 8 or so weeks, because I'm kinda cheap that way. All of a sudden, my hairdresser gasped and said, "Oh no! Grays! Time to color it, immediately, if not sooner!" I don't think that had the effect he intended because I burst out into peals of laughter. He was seriously annoyed with me. He separated out the 3 betraying white hairs and held them up as proof positive that we had a true emergency on our hands. I informed him that it didn't bother me in the slightest—that I was aware of them and I was glad that they were stark white because I think white hair is quite striking.

Wrong answer. The conversation that ensued:

"Striking? Looking old?"

"Yes, my friend S has white hair that she keeps in a trendy style and she looks great."

(With doubtful expression and raised eyebrows) "I'm not trying to sell you on dying it, but you will eventually beg me to color it."

"No, I believe in aging gracefully, I have no problem with doing so or with looking like I am the middle-aged person I actually am."

(Now he's laughing at me and half-sneering.) "When you have lunch with your girlfriends and they all look better than you, you will come running for a good color."

(Cracking up again.) "They already look better than me, now that I think about it. I'm okay with that."

Anyhow, I left there, shaking my head at what I considered the ridiculousness of it all. Honestly. But as time elapsed, I started to get seriously annoyed. I realized that it mattered more to me that it was a middle-aged man telling me I shouldn't look like a middle-aged woman. I also know him well enough to know that he's having difficulty with aging himself—he had told me that he had placed his hands on either side of his jowls (which he exaggerates) and pulled the slackened skin backwards, so that he could recognize the 20-year-old in himself again. "Why?" I sincerely queried. "Do you not like the 50-year-old you have become?" "No," he said, emphatically. "Oh, that's too bad, because you are a very nice-looking man and you are aging very well," I complimented. "No one ages well," he returned.

So, he has issues and he is in the business of making people look their best. And we all know that looking one's best is relative to the proportion of how much younger you look than you actually are. People pay a lot of money to fool themselves that we don't have an expiration date—because that's what is underlying this culture of youth ... fear of death and the desire to escape the reality of it.

I met cancer years and years ago. One of its legacies for me is that I no longer fear dying because it stared me in the face. Each year I live is on borrowed time and I know it. I've made my peace with it. My profession as a nurse has further emphasized the limited capacity we have to stave off the inevitable. But boy, do we try hard ... sometimes using interventions that simply make the entire process even worse. (That's another post.)

I have taken care of a lot of people whose cosmetic surgery has gone awry—sometimes to the point of death. Up front, I have an issue with risking one's life for the sake of looking younger (notice I did not say "better" because that isn't necessarily the outcome either). But I am sympathetic to reconstructive surgeries and am glad for the availability of it to people who are actually disfigured or have lost a functional ability due to injury or birth defect. I'm one of those ... a veteran of 3 plastic surgeries to restore half the side of my face and lip—I couldn't hold liquids in my mouth (also couldn't use a straw) after my face was torn in a bicycle accident. I'm grateful I'm not disfigured and glad I can drink water. I understand a breast cancer survivor wanting prosthetic breasts—even if I probably wouldn't do that part of it myself ... mostly because I would compare how they no longer had any functional use other than making it necessary to continue purchasing bras. To a point, I understand wanting to restore what was there or is damaged or is missing—or wanting to remove excess skin after mega weight loss. But it must be considered very carefully.

I believe in maintaining optimal health—eating well, exercising, and nurturing the soul as it grows nearer to meeting our Maker. But I do get tired of the pressure put on people to "fix" signs of aging. The pressure is harder on women, but it's catching up on men too. I realize that generations growing up under this pressure have a very real belief in this maintenance of youth deal and that the appearance of aging has become a true issue they feel obligated to correct. Also, I'm not denying that there is very real loss involved in the aging process—just that it is a stage of development we are supposed to face—are intended to come to grips with ... not avoid. There are benefits in learning how to sincerely grieve our youth and embrace the later stages of life. There is value in winding down and preparing for our deaths.

But I'm not playing and I'm not agreeing that it's okay to do this to people. Go ahead and put personal energy in fighting this losing battle, but recognize it for what it is—emotional blackmail marketing. I know a lot of women and men who feel so much better having done procedures and that's fine—as long as it's 100% understood that you are undergoing major surgery and you may not be satisfied with the results. In comparison, dying the hair is no big deal, truly. But it's all part of the same issue—beating off death with dye.

How are you handling growing older?

In March, the LDS Church opened City Creek Center, a large outdoor shopping mall located in Salt Lake City, Utah. In a *Bloomberg* article on how the Church makes its money, Mormon excommunicant D. Michael Quinn noted, "In the Mormon [leadership's] worldview, it's as spiritual to give alms to the poor . . . as it is to make a million dollars."[185] President Thomas S. Monson announced a new, lowered missionary age in October's General Conference, stating that men could serve at age 18 and women at 19. On November 6, Mitt Romney lost the US presidential election to incumbent Barack Obama.

The group Understanding Same-Gender Attraction (USGA) at BYU released an It Gets Better video in April. This was part of an international movement of LGBT adults to give hope and comfort to struggling LGBT teens. Although the movement created tens of thousands of videos, the BYU video grabbed national attention. In December, Church leaders told USGA representatives that the organization could no longer meet on BYU's campus. The Boy Scouts changed their policy to allow gay scouts to participate, and the LDS Church accepted the change. Mormon LGBT people and allies formed Mormons Building Bridges, a support and advocacy organization, and marched in Salt Lake City's Gay Pride Parade in June. Participants inspired LDS people to do the same in other Pride events around the country. The Church released the website mormonsandgays.org, which was an attempt to help gay Mormons, friends, and family members struggling with homosexuality. The language of the website stopped short of full acceptance, reading, "Even though individuals do not choose to have such attractions, they do choose how to respond to them."

Mormon historian Matthew Bowman published the influential book *The Mormon People: The Making of an American Faith*,[186] which looked at the relationship between Mormonism and American culture. Hokulani Aikau released a landmark study on the intersection of race, religion, and culture in *A Chosen People, a Promised Land: Mormonism and Race in Hawai'i*.[187] Mormon feminist Terry Tempest Williams, best known for her writing about the environment of the American West, published *When Women Were Birds*.[188] FMH blogger Joanna Brooks authored *The Book of Mormon Girl: A Memoir of an American Faith*[189] and was a guest on the popular TV show *The Daily Show with Jon Stewart* in August.

FMH launched a podcast in June, which was hosted by Lindsay Hansen Park. It was one of thirteen progressive Mormon podcasts started in 2012. Two months later, Mormon womanist Gina Colvin created her own podcast, *A Thoughtful Faith*. Both became important educational tools for countering dominant narratives about history and culture within Mormonism.

Hannah Wheelwright started the Young Mormon Feminists blog in July with the tagline "Not in Primary Anymore." The What Women Know organization created and disseminated a petition titled "All Are Alike unto God." The document called on LDS Church leaders to make numerous changes to the way they treated women and girls, stopping short of a call for women's ordination. Bloggers and commenters at FMH discussed the inconsistencies in how temple volunteers handled menstruation and youth temple baptisms, prompting a large-scale information gathering campaign. This resulted in an official clarification of temple policy, allowing menstruating women and girls to participate in baptisms for the dead at all temples. In December, the Mormon feminist group All Enlisted, led by Stephanie Lauritzen, organized Wear Pants to Church Day. The group encouraged Mormon women to wear pants to church to raise awareness of gender inequalities in Mormonism. In a *New York Times* article about the event, Joanna Brooks called it "the largest concerted Mormon feminist effort in history."[190]

"HOPES OF A FEMINIST HUSBAND OR WHY I WANT MY WIFE TO HAVE THE PRIESTHOOD" BY RYAN HAMMOND/RAH (JANUARY 21, 2012)

I want my wife to have the priesthood. I really, really, really do.

I want to stand in a circle in front of friends and family, my hand on my wife's shoulder and our fingers intertwined, to hold and gently bounce our newborn while giving her a name and blessing. I want my wife to feel that exhilarating and utterly terrifying moment when you pause, then plunge blindly on with faith—hoping that your words might be inspired or at the very least pleasing to God. I need her to understand with the understanding that only comes through the doing how these blessings are one part one's own deepest desires, and maybe one part inspiration, and how you hardly ever know which is which. I want her to experience that moment when you think that your will just might intersect with the divine and the cosmic satisfaction when what you have crafted, however awkward or stumbling, feels deeply right. I imagine us each giving our child separate blessings, our personalities and faith blending, complementing and filling in the nooks and crannies left by the other. Would there be a more beautiful symbol that this new life is not only a beautiful amalgam of our physical traits, but also destined to be the spiritual fusion of our perspectives, faith, and beliefs?

I hear our children each vacillating, changing their minds—Mom to baptize, Papa to give the gift. No, Papa's arms are strong, I want HIM to baptize me. No wait Mom's arms are strong too, but her blessings are always better. Then I see my wife standing there, waist deep in the clear blue water, dressed in white, her arm raised to the square with our beautiful daughter, her miniature mirror-image clinging to her. The familiar words ring out strong and clear. A woman's voice. My partner's voice.

Now I stand with my wife and lay hands on a sick friend and feel her faith meld with mine. I anoint with consecrated oil and then wait with anticipation to hear the blessing that falls from her lips, glad to share the responsibility. I long to hear her speak with "the power of the holy priesthood," unabashedly and with full legitimacy in the eyes of God and our fellow Saints.

I cannot imagine a sweeter experience than asking my betrothed, the one person who understands me better than my own self, for a blessing when I am struggling. What blessings could she call down on me from the heavens that no home teacher could?

I am sitting in ward council where I watch my wife preside with grace and humility. I am proud to be known as the bishop's husband, to see her on the stand waving at our kids. It has meant some lonely, busy nights taking on extra childcare and more of the household responsibilities than I used to. But it is worth it. My daughters and sons know that Mom is special, capable, important, and that everyone in the ward respects her. I know she looks down on the ward seeing the secret sorrows and triumphs that only a bishop sees, and I love her for it all the more. I hope that if someday I am called to do the same, she will share the wisdom she has gained.

Do these sound like unrighteous desires? Wouldn't our marriages, our families, our wards, our church benefit immeasurably simply from instantly doubling the priesthood available to us? Wouldn't the world? Wouldn't we as a people be strengthened by increasing women's authoritative and revelatory voices among us?

I know some will say that many of these things can happen under the status quo. My wife can pray for me and my children. The Spirit can help her feel connected to a child's blessing. But as a man, as a priesthood holder who has had these experiences, can I say they are qualitatively the same? I have been the recipient of priesthood blessings and the giver. Sweet experiences all, but edifying in unique ways. I have prayed in faith for the sick, for a child, for my spouse. Praying for a blessing isn't the same as performing one with authority. If it is, then what is the priesthood? I know women are respected for the callings they so ably fill, but they can only gain from filling a wider set of roles. We can only gain from having women as our ecclesiastical leaders.

These are just hopes. But vain hopes? A heretic's hopes? Maybe. Heavenly hopes? I desire to believe.

For those who cannot imagine these scenarios, I say that until we can imagine them, open our minds and hearts to them, God cannot reveal them. So I dream.

"P-P-P-POLYGAMY MEGA POST!" BY LINDSAY HANSEN PARK (FEBRUARY 2, 2012)

Yes, we're talking about it again. Yes, we're talking about it still.

Some of you will say, *"Can we please talk about something else?"* Yes, yes you can. Just not on this post. According to Joanna Brooks, we don't talk about polygamy enough.[191] And she's right, it's an icky thing to many Mormons, especially those who fail to realize the deep significance and weight the theology once carried, or maybe especially for those who do.

Gloria Steinem said, "The truth will set you free, but first it will piss you off."

Yep, that about sums it up for most of us. Since starting the Forgotten Women series,[192] I have been able to be involved with many FABULOUS discussions about this topic with people all across the faith spectrum and all over Mormonism. I've heard so many amazing stories and feel so blessed that this series is important to so many of you. Often, my motives are questioned. Some ask what is it I'm *really* trying to do? Before we start up with the Forgotten Women series again this upcoming Tuesday, I thought I'd answer those questions for you.

What am I really trying to do?

I'm trying to talk about polygamy. For many women in the church, the looming possibility of having to share their husbands is so painful to them, they can't even discuss it. How many of you feel that you can openly chat about this in Relief Society? How many of you can talk about becoming a polygamous wife as a reward for your righteous living, in the Celestial Kingdom without feeling deep fear and pain? I'm going to guess not many of you. Not many of the women I know are or have ever been okay with it. I have a faithful SIL who can't even say the word aloud. I am tired of women being so hurt by the very word "polygamy" without even understanding why it was instituted and how it is lived.

So, that's what I'm doing. I'm putting the info out there and letting people make up their minds on how they feel about it. Does Joseph's lived practice of it make you feel better about it or worse? That's what you get to decide, not me.

Before my study, polygamy always wounded my heart and made me fear for heaven. It wasn't until I researched it to hell-and-back-again that I let myself calm down. I see it as something Joseph tried, and it didn't work out. I don't think God has it in store for us. And if Mormon heaven is a hell to most women, what's the point? (My ward members will say that I'll feel differently about it in the afterlife. That would be so super cool if our agency dissolved so magically.)

I always say half-jokingly that if we find out someday that Warren Jeffs has it right, I'd rather have tawdry talks with Oscar Wilde in hell for all eternity than have sex with Warren Jeffs, even once. I'm good, thank you very much.

So for me, airing this stuff has healed my heart. I no longer fear it, and I no longer believe God believes in it. That's for me to choose, and not one of you has to go down the same path. It's painful to learn it, but not so much worse than the looming threat of it. And after you know of it, *you* get to decide what you believe. You.

Where are my biases?

This brings me to where I stand. Everyone approaches history with a bias, you just can't escape your own lens. Mine is that I think polygamy is hurtful to women. Mostly because it functions under a patriarchy. When a woman's sexual, physical, and spiritual logistics are placed in the hands of a man, I just don't think it's healthy. Now, that doesn't mean I disagree with those who practice it. I'm trying to be open minded to my fundamentalist friends who believe it a sacred order of God. My ancestors believed it was a sacred pattern of heaven. There needs to be weight put to that. Because I have this bias, I try to not filter the entire story as polygamy being "wrong." I desperately try to put the story out there without letting that position color the history. Sometimes it slips in, but since I'm putting it out there— you can know when you read the posts that this is my bias and use your own filter accordingly. And to the fundamentalists who practice it, I realize this viewpoint isn't fair to you, but I tell you so you can factor it in. I do, however, love the idea of eternal ties of Heaven. A sort of Oneida standpoint that we're all married in heaven. That spiritual or celestial relationships are so intimate, that we're all tied together. But that's a topic for another time and requires the patriarchy to stop functioning as we understand it doctrinally.

Why do you have to talk about something so negative?

I get accused of focusing on the negative aspects of history quite a bit. My answer to that is, there are a hundred and one women of faith blogs you can check out if you don't want to read anything but faith promoting stories. Go check them out! Go to church! Go to the Relief Society birthday party. If you want the history, warts and all, come here. Like Tresa Brown Edmunds so famously told me once, "If people don't like what they read, that's on Joseph, not on you."

I told this to my church historian friends—if the history gives me a positive story about polygamy, I'll publish it. Unfortunately, there's not a lot of that. There's a lot of heartbreak, sacrifice, confusion and pain. There's also some pretty cool faith, strength and sisterhood to be discovered too. Truth is hard and sometimes it's ugly. It's dimensional. It's complicated and complex, and these women deserve to have those complexities come to light. They lived it and we get to celebrate it and appreciate it and admire it and cry from it and learn from it. Life is hard and it is real and we all know this and these histories are no different. We have this in common with them—a faith and a religion that has forever shaped our lives, no matter the end result, and I think that's pretty amazing! We're big kids. We know what heartache and problems are—we can handle it, if only allowed to.

What are my sources?

I've spoken to some brilliant LDS employed church historians about this series. I thought they were going to be critical, but they were far from it. We've had some wonderful discussions about the Nauvoo era, and I thank them for those talks. That said, they have pointed out that every source has its flaws. I try to help you understand that without engaging in apologetics. When John C. Bennett quotes Joseph, we need to keep in mind he had an ax to grind with a good friend-turned-enemy. When McClellan writes, we need to keep in mind his primary purpose in the later 1800s was to convince Joseph Smith III that his father practiced polygamy. When we quote the stories of the wives themselves, we need to keep in mind that many of the reminiscences were written many years after the events took place. However, please also know that I take these sources VERY seriously. I know how suspicious us LDS folk are taught to be of "outside sources." I only choose the most credible, especially from an LDS standpoint. The bottom line is, don't take my word for it. Polygamy is well documented and you can find family and personal histories online, pdf documents, and more just from your computer. And if that still isn't good enough for you or you're left reeling, sometimes Mormon apologists can be helpful. FairMormon is a group of faithful Mormons who try to give explanations for uncomfortable things in history. Their explanations might help you. They are far from perfect, and many find them more problematic than useful. That's for you to decide.

Where do we go from here?

Because this series was started to honor these women and help alleviate the pain their stories bring, I recognize that the stories have caused a new sort of pain within the readership. The pain of cold, hard truth. I'm resentful when I express my pain and people say, *"Oh, that's so cute. Someday you'll understand these things like I do, and it will all be better."* Don't accept that garbage. Pain is real and it serves a purpose. Take your pain seriously. It's important to work through. Don't let anyone, me or anyone else here or in your real life, tell you how you should feel about this. Polygamy is a tricky issue with many interpretations to be had. You get to own yours. Pray to Heavenly Parents about it. Study the issues deeply, if that helps (it did me).

Pick up Compton's *In Sacred Loneliness*[193] (and a hundred other recommendations I can give you). Learn everything you can about Joseph. Polygamy was just one aspect of his life and ministry. Context always heals my wounds and to get context on these things, you need to study and dig and dig and study. I'm still doing it. Talk about it. Talk about it some more. Come here and vent. As Sisters in Zion, we're all in this together, past and present, and I'm grateful to this gospel for that.

"Blood in the Water" by Layne Huff (February 9, 2012)

I am an advisor in our ward's Young Women program. Last night we took the girls to the temple to do baptisms and were treated to a bizarre demonstration of what felt to me like passive-aggressive unrighteous dominion, but I may be overreacting. We waited over an hour after our appointment time to start, while one of the confirmation rooms sat empty and the men in the font stood around waiting for people to baptize, and the towel lady behind the desk chewed me out when I asked for more towels because we had given our towels ("They were already GIVEN towels. They only GET ONE TOWEL!") to the people whose appointment was a half hour after ours and yet were all confirmed and baptized before our girls started. But the strangest exchange happened right when we got there. The woman at the desk asked if we had any girls who were only being confirmed, and we confusedly answered no. She asked again, more loudly, I guess in case we didn't speak English, and we said no again. Then she explained to our Young Women's leader that girls who were menstruating were not allowed into the font and could therefore only be confirmed. So Terri asked the girls if any of them were on their periods, and two scarlet-faced Mia Maids admitted that they were, but both had brought tampons. No, said the woman, they would still not be allowed to be baptized. When Terri asked why, the woman answered, "Well, if you think about it. . . ."

If you think about what? If you think about the miniscule amount of blood that might get past the tampon? An amount that would not mar the white jumpsuit that they were required to wear for confirmation, but would apparently render an entire baptismal font's worth of highly chlorinated water unusable? If you think about how dirty blood is, and therefore how dirty women are because they bleed once a month? If you think about the good old days of Leviticus, when women were considered unclean while menstruating and postpartum?

I have never encountered this policy before (because I'm pretty sure it's policy being treated as doctrine) and wondered if others had. In asking around, I found a few women who have experienced it, and one who thought it was no big deal. Internet-anecdotally it actually seems fairly common. I am flummoxed. It's not a laundry issue, or they wouldn't have them suit up for confirmation. Are we really depriving these young women—many of whom are desperately in need of positive experiences tied to the temple and the Gospel—of the opportunity to perform saving ordinances because they might drip blood in the water? For the sake of ick?

If so, that is not just ridiculous, but reprehensible.

"Call to Action: Addressing the Temple 'Issue,' Period." by Elizabeth Hammond/Elisothel (February 12, 2012)

Layne (at FMH)[194] and Rebecca J (on BCC)[195] have recently discussed online the apparent policy in some temples where women having their periods are excluded from participation in baptisms for the dead. After hearing all the stories, we are calling on the power of She-Ra and FMH to help solve the issue through a little grassroots effort.

The spirit of this call to action is one of cheerful Mormon helpfulness to ensure that the temple experiences of young women, new female converts, or any woman who wishes to participate in the sacred ordinances—especially baptism for the dead—are smooth and positive. Otherwise, the extant possible embarrassment of being unpredictably excluded from ordinances because it's "that time of the month" may continue to publicly embarrass and unnecessarily shame many a worthy woman.

Defining the Problem and What We Have Learned about "The Policy"

1. Women in some temples are being told or asked not to perform baptisms if they are having their period. We have confirmed through the recent experience of many readers at FMH and BCC that this practice is still being enforced, if sporadically, within the temples.

2. The sporadic nature of this enforcement is causing particular problems when youth or other groups go to the temple since it is catching many leaders and parents unaware, leading to situations that often embarrass young women.

3. The underlying logic and reasoning behind these actions is unclear. There still appears to be an active folk doctrine of "ritual uncleanliness" or even "impurity," where a bleeding woman may somehow render the temple defiled. The origin is unclear—this may have been taught by temple workers, leaders, or at very least inferred by some based on their experience with the practice.

We have not been able to track down, to this point, a history of where this "policy" originated. However, we have verified two accounts from current or recently-released temple presidents reporting that *there is no centralized, church-wide policy* which recommends or requires the exclusion of menstruating women from baptisms.

Such decisions appear to be left to individual temple presidencies to regulate. This helps explain why there seems to be so much variation in past and current experiences for temple patrons. Based on the comments and experiences unearthed on these posts, it appears likely that such a policy was widespread in the past.

What You Can Do!

The first and most powerful thing we in the bloggernacle can do is to systematically collect information about the policies and practices of each of the active temples.

Here is a link to a public Google Doc,[196] prepared by Cynthia L.

You will see there are two tabs within this spreadsheet.

The first, "Temple Policy," helpfully lists every active temple along with its contact information. What we are asking you to do is to call your local temple this coming week and ask specifically what the temple policy is. Fill out the designated space on the Doc based on your conversation with the temple baptistery worker/coordinator/temple leader etc.

We would like multiple, different informants for each temple. However, we don't want to overwhelm any given temple. Before you call your temple, please open the spreadsheet, and if you see more than 10 responses for your temple, consider calling another temple. We encourage you to stick to temples to which you have a specific connection. When you call please identify your connection to the temple and reason for asking. For example, if you are a youth leader or parent of a YW, RS president, work on a church temple committee etc. it is good to let them know this. We don't want anyone to feel like they are being "attacked" by an outside group/persons with no local interest in the response. This is neither our intent nor within the spirit of what we are trying to achieve.

There is also a second tab in the spreadsheet entitled "Recent Experience." If within the last 6 months, you have personally witnessed a situation where a policy excludes or discourages menstruating women from participating in temple ordinances, please record your experience here. (We have mostly discussed exclusion from baptism, but if you have witnessed exclusion from initiatories, endowments, or other ordinances please let us know!) We are focusing only on recent incidents rather than historical ones.

The idea behind this sheet is to provide usable information so that we can inform a temple either 1) if their policy allowing baptisms to all women has not been clearly communicated and acted upon by its workers or 2) help demonstrate to a temple which still officially holds this policy the negative experiences it might be causing. Temples, especially big temples, face a difficult challenge in training and monitoring large numbers of consistently shifting volunteer staff. We can help by providing them timely feedback to identify where problems are occurring so they can deal with them positively and proactively.

Technical Note: In both these spreadsheets, if you are reporting on a temple which has a previous entry simply "insert a new row," copy down the temple name, and then fill in the rest of the fields. You can do this by right clicking on an existing row with the temple you wish to report on and choosing "insert below." Let's try to keep all responses for a given temple grouped together.

Let's Do This!

Systematically collecting this information will give us a chance to see the extent of the problem. After enough information is collected, we will report out the results and use this data to discuss how best to proceed. Hopefully we will find this a minority policy and mostly an issue of simply better educating volunteers to comply with current policy. Simply repeatedly asking the question of each temple will probably lead to a number of productive conversations. It will put us in a good position to help temples that hold this minority practice understand that it is unnecessary. We can put together a positive plan for addressing areas of concern and may even try and find a way to give the data to the appropriate individuals in the COB, YW presidency, or local temple presidencies along with an explanation.

The temple should be a safe place for all women, period! Let's make it happen!

"Feminist and Faithful: There's a Lot That We Just Don't Know" by Alice Fisher Roberts/Alliegator (February 27, 2012)

I'd Like to Bear My Testimony. . . .

Several years ago, my Mister's cousin was putting together a book of family pictures and testimonies to present to their grandparents as a Christmas present. I copied a recent family picture and contemplated what I could possibly write that would be both honest and appropriate.

I was raised by somewhat unorthodox parents, but I had a typical experience growing up in Utah in the church. I remember a young woman leader at girl's camp complimenting me on my strong testimony. I loved the gospel and was so proud to be a part of something so powerful, and so beautiful.

Enter Prop 8. I had been a budding feminist for most of my life, although it took a while for me to get over the built-in fear of "anything different" before I became a regular at FMH. Prop 8 was the last straw for many, and in a way, it was the last straw for me too. I will never be able to go back to the easy faith I had before, nor would I want to. My testimony was deeply shaken. When you don't know anyone who is gay, it's easy to imagine that they're "the others," but when you know people, and love people, you can't do that. You shouldn't be able to do that.

At a temple recommend interview, when asked if I supported any groups whose teachings were not in harmony with the gospel, I answered honestly, "I don't know." A friend had asked me to donate to Equality California, to support the fight against Prop 8. I donated. I donated to do what I could to counteract the fear and misinformation swirling around me. The poor Second Counselor didn't quite know what to do with me. He saw my pain over the issue and signed my recommend, telling me he'd talk with the bishop about it, and if the bishop had any concerns, he'd call me.

Then we got sick. We didn't make it in to see the Stake President for several weeks, during which time, my bishop became concerned and called me in for a visit. I was relieved to discover I wasn't in trouble. I laid out all of my pain and concerns to this sweet man, and he told me a story that I will never forget. One that I cling to in times of struggle. . . . I won't share it all since it is not my story, but it concerned the church's teachings on suicide and a very personal experience that drew that teaching into question. . . . My bishop's point in telling the story was that there are SO MANY THINGS WE DON'T FULLY UNDERSTAND. Sometimes we think we do understand, only to find out later we were wrong.

We're all doing the best we can to do what our Heavenly Parents want us to do, but all of us, prophets included, receive inspiration in a language we can understand, and interpret it through the lens of our own life experience. This means we make a lot of mistakes.

I had prayed and fasted for resolution for my pain over Prop 8, and didn't get an answer, until I gave up. I admitted to Heavenly Father that I might be wrong, and that I needed guidance. It was then that I received, not an answer to fix anything, but a clear assurance that God loved me, and that whatever happened, it would be okay.

I have since come to view challenges in the church in a softer way. Everything that causes me concern (because those things haven't just disappeared and are unlikely to anytime in the near future) is viewed through a new filter of life experience. Sometimes things are painful, and sometimes things don't make sense, but it's okay, because God loves me, and eventually things will be okay. If a teaching doesn't make sense, maybe it's the best we know right now, but maybe there's something about it we don't really understand.

I can be honest with myself, and be loyal to a gospel which I love. I do love the gospel. I love that it's a gospel of love, of hope, and of joy! I love that we can make mistakes, but learn from them, and grow, and work to become better people. I've learned that good people make mistakes, and we need to be gentle with each other. I love that families are so important, and that we can be united together forever.

I have had several very strong impressions throughout my life that this is the place for me, this is my home, where I belong. I speak up (in loving ways) in Sunday School and Relief Society. I try not to shock people (too often), but I share my perspective, because this is my church too, and it's not fair to let anyone think that one side on social and political issues is the "true" way. I'm grateful for a Savior who wraps me in arms of love during my deepest darkest times to let me know that it will be okay.

I'm grateful for Cub Scouts, (formerly) the most awful calling in the church, because it makes me grow and pushes me to serve in areas I would never seek out on my own, and I've grown to love it.

I love this church, warts and all. I look forward to a time when my concerns are answered, and painful sacrament meeting talks or Sunday School lessons are done away with, and the things we don't understand are made clear, but until then, I know God loves me, and it will be okay.

(I'd also like to tell my family that I love them, and all that.)

"FACING FEAR AS MORMON FEMINISTS: A CALL FOR ELDERWOMEN" BY JOANNA BROOKS (FEBRUARY 27, 2012)

I've been thinking about fear and Mormon feminist community. When the Church excommunicated Sonia,[197] fear broke in among us. When the Strengthening the Members committee kept files on Mormon feminists, fear broke in among us. When our feminist elders were excommunicated, disciplined, stigmatized, shamed, and fired two decades ago, fear broke in among us, and it has stayed with us, and now girls who were babies when the September Six were tried are afraid still.

The excommunications threatened to repress and disable a generation of Mormon feminists, leaving women of my generation and younger without Mormon feminist elderwomen. And despite it all, many of our Mormon feminist elderwomen have hung on. I can say their names: Nadine, Lorie, Paula, Margaret[198] . . . many others. They are with us here, on this site, and in digital and real life Mormon feminist gatherings all around. But we need more Mormon feminist elderwomen who can speak up when fear breaks out.

We are not alone in being afraid. Feminist women from so many communities have faced fear. And their words can be a strength to us whenever we must face our own.

Here, for example, is a great poem, "The Low Road," by the Jewish feminist Marge Piercy.[199]

When I am afraid, I pray. And I read this Marge Piercy poem.

And I watch this "Poem to Get Rid of Fear"[200] by the Mvskoke (Creek) poet Joy Harjo.

And then I watch spoken word artist StaceyAnn Chin perform "Not My Fault."[201]

And I remember what sister Audre Lorde, a self-described "Black lesbian mother poet warrior," said to her fellow feminists: "We can learn to work through fear the same way we can learn to work when we are tired."[202]

We need more Mormon feminist elderwomen who know how to work when they are afraid and tired. Women who can say, I know the best and the worst of my people, and I will not be moved. Women who have studied their own minds, and women who have studied the world they move in: women who have their wits about them when it comes to surviving. We need women who wear their scars as boldly as tattoos they designed and inked on themselves. We need women who have done marriage, divorce, sex, birth, death—menarche to menopause and beyond. We need women who have blessed and cursed, women with long memories, memories that remind us that Mormon feminists have faced fear and repression before. We need women who can say, I will not run. This is my house. I know who I am. I know what you can take from me, and I know what you cannot take from me. Women who can say, when fear comes—as it will—it will come—I can guide and support my community.

Women who can say, yes, I've seen this before, and I am ready to look it in the eye, state the facts, and stand my ground with Spirit-assured confidence. I will stand though my very legs are shaking. Shaking like they were when I squatted and gave birth to my daughter.

Yes.

We need more Mormon feminist elderwomen.

We need you.

"DRUMROLL PLEASE: TEMPLE 'ISSUE' REPORT" BY ELIZABETH HAMMOND AND RYAN HAMMOND (MARCH 7, 2012)

Here is the exciting conclusion of the temple baptism project, in two parts: First, the overview by Elizabeth Hammond, then the details by Ryan Hammond. Enjoy!

Squishy Reflections *by* Elizabeth Hammond:

Check out the post explaining the Temple "Issue" Project[203] and coverage on it by the *Salt Lake Tribune*.

This project was perceived by many to be a form of activism, and that translated to touchdown dances for some and penalty flags for others. Those who perceived threat saw us as some kind of stealth feminists building pits for our temple-working neighbors, perpetuating folk doctrines to embarrass the Church in a politically sensitive situation, and making mountains from molehills. Others saw it as championing a cause, doing something real, and flexing our lady 'ceps. Which was it, and what can we learn from what unfolded?

To start, it's not like the FMH permas were sitting around ruminating on the injustices of baptismal coordinators—the project was conceived when such huge reactions to the FMH post[204] and the BCC post[205] indicated a far-reaching interest in the topic (the molehill mountain was there way before we decided to climb it).

People had a concern. People didn't agree on its source. People testified of their personal experiences. People put their own theories/assumptions out there. There was so much variation that we asked for clarification. The Temple "Issue" Project was information gathering—recon—not a sting operation. And we brought to light that the ideal policy we wanted (no restrictions on menstruating women) was the actual policy already in place. Nefarious motivations were also debunked (that is, in reality, hygiene isn't an issue, and workers are universally trying to PROTECT people's feelings).

This experience was fascinating in retrospect, and I have a few takeaways:

- Trying to help the Church can be perceived as threatening. Apparently collectively asking questions can be perceived as agitation.
- While righteous indignation is a positive force that causes growth, churning in it can be dangerous because it propagates negativity to a point that ignores reality. We were mad, for good reason, but not the reason we thought.
- Activism is complicated: for the first 40 years of the Restoration, Mormonism and feminism were seamless, but for the last 40, they've been at odds. We modern Mo-Fems are still getting our footing here.
- People still seem to think women's questions are not worth considering—just read the *Salt Lake Tribune* comments for some bitter smackdown dismissal (not recommended actually).
- Doing something can work. This was an interesting case study of Mo-Fems helping the Church. I don't know that the Church would see it that way? But if it can happen, that means it can happen again!

Yay FMH!

Brass Tacks *by* Ryan Hammond:

First the facts: 29 individuals from the FMH community directly called 68 temples and asked for each temple's policy regarding menstruating women and baptisms. This represented the majority of English-speaking temples around the world plus Germany and Spain.

Individuals recorded the position of the temple worker who provided an answer. Often, it was the operator who answered the phone. In many cases it was directly from the temple matron or the baptistery coordinator. Sometimes the operator went to directly check with these individuals.

- 6 of the 68 temples contacted were closed for cleaning or renovation.
- 14 of these 62 temples reported the practice in which menstruating women were asked to do confirmations instead of baptisms.
- 5 additional temples discouraged menstruating women from doing baptisms but allowed it if a woman really wanted to.
- The remaining 43 temples put no restrictions at all on baptisms.

Almost one quarter of the temples contacted (22.5%) claimed some version of excluding women. If you add the temples where it was actively discouraged this rises to 30%. We were careful to err on the side of undercounting exclusion and generally credited a temple with a positive response when they were vague or unsure but ultimately said they would allow it.

Based on our own calls (my wife and I personally called half the temples) and the reports of others, here are some of the more qualitative patterns we saw:

- First, the majority of temples not only had inclusionary policies but were very clear and strong about it. Many times temples expressed surprise that *anyone* would think a temple would exclude a woman on her period, and often they explained how they went out of their way to try and make any nervous girls feel welcome and comfortable.
- However, even among the temples with official inclusionary policies it was still clear that someone could run into resistance or untrained temple workers, etc. This helps explain why there is such a variation in people's experiences. Many women have never run into a problem while others' experiences have been in temples where exclusion was the norm.
- Our general interpretation is that we should be happy that 2 out of 3 temples turned out to be aware of and generally following the Church's official inclusionary policy. However, that 1 out of 3 temples were out of step with the official policy is an unfortunate surprise.

- Women and men of the blog should know that if they run into resistance in their temple, they are in a strong position to politely push back. It would still be a good idea to call ahead if you are taking a youth group just so there are no unpleasant surprises.

Now a couple of quick notes regarding the *Salt Lake Tribune* article. We want to clarify two points.

First, in our discussion with temple matrons and workers, not once was there any indication that women were perceived as being "ritually unclean" or excluded for any other doctrinal reasons. What Liz was talking about when she wrote the quote was that, based on the discussion between FMH and BCC readers, it was clear that many women had struggled with their exclusion from baptisms and tried to identify a reason for the practice. Theories were offered, and it was clear that some inferred the temple perceived them as unclean, or at least that was the message they got when they experienced exclusion. This is not a far leap since ritual uncleanliness as a result of menstruation has scriptural roots (Leviticus 15). Menstrual uncleanliness, paired with "we want the baptistery to remain clean," implies that a menstruating woman can make the water unclean or "defile" it. This whole thing is an example of how people are trying to figure out their mystifying experiences and the misunderstandings that can take place when such things are not openly discussed. We have no evidence or belief that anyone is actively teaching that women are ritually unclean. Uncleanliness was the message women got, but in our discussions with temple workers the justification given for exclusionary practices was almost always related to hygiene and public health, or to helping women avoid embarrassing situations. The message women got was unintentional. This whole thing, in essence, was a blind spot . . . and we made people look.

Second, there was no active effort by those who called the temples to criticize or change any temple's policy. We were only gathering information and updated FMH for our community's awareness. We were not trying to gain attention in the media; the *Salt Lake Tribune* picked up the story on their own. The *Salt Lake Tribune* was kind enough to contact us to check details, but due to insane busyness on our part we didn't get a chance to clarify before it was posted. We had intended to share our findings with a few receptive temple presidents so the information could be distributed that way. We never intended to embarrass the Church. However, now that the Church has clarified its policy, hopefully those that run the temples will make them as inclusionary as possible.

Thanks to all here who contributed to the project—the thing unfolded in unexpected ways but has had a very positive impact! It will be interesting to hear of your baptismal experiences going forward!

"'I Don't Like Other Women'" by Melissa Mayhew/Rune (March 23, 2012)

"I don't like other women." "I just don't get along with other girls."

I'm guilty. I've said those words.

I'm plenty repentant now, in no small part because of the message that might have sent to other girls and women who might have overheard me. I don't remember exactly who might have, or where. My sisters? Ward members? Who might I have insulted and alienated with those phrases?

Granted, sometimes I was in a setting where there were a few other women around who I *thought* would know what I meant. Others who echoed the same sentiment. Among us, the words softened slightly. "I tend not to get along with other women." Making room, making exception for each other. And boy, did we feel special! Look at our little klatch! We were unique, we were actual people with actual interests and selves, not like those shallow, silly, boy-crazy creatures that were *other women*.

I'm also repentant because of the boys and men that overheard such comments as well, because those kinds of comments powerfully reinforce the unfortunate attitudes that spawn them. And there is only one word that adequately describes those attitudes, whether they are held by men, or women who "don't get along with other women."

Misogyny.

I was propping up misogyny. Now, I do give myself some credit. I *thought* I was bucking stereotypes, being rebellious, being an example of independent thought. And, really, I was taking my first, stumbling, clumsy little baby-steps into a bigger world of self-realization and a feminist awakening. But, to quote Gloria Steinem: "The first problem for all of us, men and women, is not to learn, but to unlearn."[206] And what I needed to unlearn was misogyny. In ways that I didn't comprehend then, I was steeped in it, surrounded by it, and had internalized a great deal of it. Negative, harmful, and limiting stereotypes of womanhood permeated the air I breathed. They were on TV, in movies, exuded in common and flippant jokes, vocalized from the pulpit. Women were shallow, silly, had no sense of direction, couldn't drive, were easily confused, used their bodies and "wiles" to manipulate men, were villainous if they did, were valueless if they couldn't, and so many other myriad messages both explicit and implied.

So, of course, my reaction was, "But that's not me!" And there were other kinds of messages that reinforced my reaction, since my world was, of course, not entirely misogynistic. Women could be and do anything, feminism was a thing that had happened, we were equal. I'd heard it, the same way I'd heard of paradise. So, I came to the conclusion of a budding feminist, entirely immature in the beginning of her journey. Those stereotypes weren't me, weren't what I wanted to be, so I must not be like those *other women*. I was in reaction mode, defending myself knee-jerk and wholesale against the stereotypes. It hadn't even occurred to me yet to challenge the misogyny as a whole. I couldn't begin to see how deep the cultural dislike of women and womanhood in general was planted in me, to the point that I hated seeing in almost all other women something that I feared to acknowledge in myself. After all, I was a woman, and to really own that would make me a target for all that ugliness, wouldn't it? So I convinced myself I wasn't *that* kind of woman.

But a reactionary identity is not a whole identity, and defining oneself by the exclusion of others is a bitter and lonely way to live. Insisting that you are the exception to a generally held belief reinforces that the generally held belief is valid. If a woman awakening to feminist concerns wants to really grow past the barriers of misogyny, eventually she has to grow past casting herself, by defensive reflex, by accident, as the exception that proves the rule.

But that brings me around to something beautiful, because when I finally did come around more fully in my journey, in my growth and awakening, I discovered something. I discovered that *I loved you*. You wonderful women, you whole and varied and beautiful human beings, when I became a feminist, I learned to know you and to love you. As, step by step, piece by piece, I began to shake off and shake out the internalized misogyny I was so desperate should not apply to me, I figured out that it shouldn't apply to you, either. That you weren't stereotypes either. That I didn't have to shut you out because of the way you laughed, or if you really liked boys or baking or crafts. That I didn't have to worry about being "guilty by association" of being girly and bringing the full weight of the misogyny of the world down. That I didn't need to set myself against you, either in theory or in practice, in order to win a game I didn't need to be playing in the first place.

And I am *so much happier*. It comes back around in wonderful ways. In learning to love you, I learn to love myself better, to understand myself better, to forgive myself, to let myself be. To swing on in an upward spiral and find the health and the good that lies on the other side of overcoming harmful cultural attitudes. Of course it's not all perfect and easy and rainbows. Cultural attitudes are something we all still have to live with and navigate, and they carry a lot of inertia. Rooting out all personal blind-spots is more work than one lifetime can contain. But now I'm in a place of action, instead of reaction, and in a place of love instead of fear.

Maybe for my daughters, for my sisters, for my friends, I can take what I've learned and help make a world for them where no girl, no woman, feels like she has to differentiate herself from a misogynistic view by creating a negative identity and shunning "other women." Where the love is easier from the beginning, and where sisterhood comes as a matter of course.

Now, wouldn't that be paradise.

"ASK MORMON GIRL: WHY DON'T WE TALK ABOUT HEAVENLY MOTHER?" BY JOANNA BROOKS (JUNE 19, 2012)

Two—count 'em—two questions about Heavenly Mother materialized in my mailbox this week. And I realized with a start that in more than two years of *Ask Mormon Girl* columns, I had never written about this unique and inspiring aspect of Mormon doctrine here.

So here's question number one:

> I have a question for you about Heavenly Mother and why we don't talk about her. Do you think that the church really does it to "keep women in their place"? Why can't we pray to her? Why isn't she worshipped like our heavenly Father. This has been something that I have been wondering for a long time and if you have any ideas on reading or anything like that I would love to hear!! Thanks!
>
> —Stacey

And number two:

> As a lifelong, 52-year-old member of the LDS Church, I surprised myself yesterday by having a rather basic question occur to me for the first time. It occurred to me that perhaps part of the reason that we talk little of our Heavenly Mother in the church is that she is one of many. That is, perhaps God the Father has polygamous (read polygynous) relationships. Maybe my heavenly mother is not your heavenly mother. What do you think, and what do you think church leaders think? Are there some sources on this subject, or must we simply speculate?
>
> —Wendy

Yes, world, it is Mormon doctrine that God is not only a Heavenly Father but a Heavenly Father and Heavenly Mother. The idea proceeds very logically from Doctrine & Covenants 132:19–20, which teaches that marriage in an LDS temple is a requirement for attaining the highest levels of heaven, or "exaltation." Those who do, the scripture states, "shall be gods."

If doctrine holds that only the married are exalted to godhood, then it follows quite rationally that God is a married couple. This beautiful, symmetrical idea found an early articulation by the LDS leader Eliza R. Snow in her hymn, "O My Father:"[207]

In the heavens, are parents single? / No, the thought makes reason stare. / Truth is reason, truth eternal, / Tells me I've a mother there.

This hymn is in the official LDS hymnbook and is regularly sung in Mormon congregations around the world. And the 1995 "Proclamation on the Family" refers to our "Heavenly Parents." Clearly, our Mother is no secret.

But she sure feels like a secret. You could listen in on a year's worth of Mormon meetings and scarcely hear her named. What gives?

The silence around Heavenly Mother is not doctrinal. A far-reaching study published in the journal *BYU Studies* last year located more than six hundred references to Heavenly Mother in the writings and speeches of LDS Church leaders. It's really an important read—please download it for free here[208]—and the authors find that there is *absolutely no doctrinal basis for the prohibition of discussion of Heavenly Mother.* And that's the journal *BYU Studies,* for crying out loud.

The silence around Heavenly Mother, then, is cultural. It's just a human tradition—a habit that fell into place and has become difficult to dislodge. We don't find her as the object of discussion or even mention in General Conference speeches. Little inquiry is made into her attributes, character, or contributions, as if such concerns were marginal or even fringe. And thus for many decades there was a virtual vacuum of substantive reflection on Heavenly Mother.

Just as folk doctrine—some of it quite cruel—crept in to rationalize Mormonism's century-plus ban on Black priesthood ordination, a good deal of folk doctrine has also crept in to rationalize our lack of discussion about our Mother. I grew up in the 1980s hearing from my seminary teacher that Heavenly Father himself prohibits discussion of our Mother because he wants to protect her from the abuse of the world—from regular mortals taking her name in vain, and the like—a story that always sounded utterly preposterous to me. As if *God Herself* were too fragile!

One sometimes also hears in Mormon circles the hushed speculation that we don't talk about Heavenly Mother because there are in fact plural Heavenly Mothers. This is a bit of theological speculation we can trace to the nineteenth-century LDS theologian Orson Pratt's *The Seer,*[209] which was in its own day disclaimed by LDS authorities as a speculative rather than a doctrinal text. I have also met contemporary polygamous Mormon fundamentalist women who do believe that Heavenly Father has many exalted wives—many Heavenly Mothers for the whole human family. (I spent a memorable evening a few years ago, gathered around the dining room table—and they were utterly scandalized by the fact that talking about Heavenly Mother was so scandalized in the mainstream LDS Church.) The residual speculative idea that there are plural Heavenly Mothers is substantiated in some mainstream Mormon minds by the polygamous facets of D&C 132, plus current LDS temple sealing policies that permit living husbands to be sealed to more than one wife for the eternities (but not wives to husbands), as well as an ultra-literal projection of human procreation onto Heavenly Parents. Yes, it's true that some LDS people today imagine that our Parents in Heaven create the spirits of humankind in a manner similar to the means through which the bodies of humankind are created on earth. That's a lot of spiritual procreation, the story goes, hence the need for so many Heavenly Mothers. Again, none of this is doctrine, but it is the kind of storytelling we hear in the absence of doctrine. And just for the record, I'll say it again, I know plenty of women who would firmly disagree that eternal pregnancy in the company of a gaggle of eternally pregnant wives is heaven.

But again, these are non-doctrinal, folkloric reasons assigned for the lack of official discourse on Heavenly Mother. *There is no doctrinal reason for not talking about Her.*

And there was a moment two decades ago when our Mother was once again making a resurgence in Mormon talk and thought, thanks to Mormon feminists like Carol Lynn Pearson, whose marvelous play *Mother Wove the Morning*[210] has given us some of our best imaging of her power and presence. Then, in 1991, President Gordon B. Hinckley gave a talk[211] instructing LDS Church members that it was inappropriate to pray to Heavenly Mother. And Mormon feminist theologian Janice Allred, whose best-known work is a book entitled *God the Mother*,[212] was excommunicated. And in 1996, Professor Gail Houston was fired from Brigham Young University[213] for publicly describing her personal relationship with her Mother in Heaven, including her use of "meditation" and "visualization" to deepen that relationship. All of these events, I think, led to a renewed stigma around even talking about our Mother. On a day-to-day basis, she is bracketed in speech, again and again and again.

Who is responsible for perpetuating the silence? And who is responsible for the improper value attached to that silence—as if refusing to acknowledge Her or perpetuating some spooky sense of mystery about Her were a sublimely virtuous act. Who is responsible? We are.

A few weeks ago, I was in a group of LDS women, when one of the women related a story of a friend who had given a talk on Heavenly Mother on Mother's Day in his LDS congregation in the western U.S. He was extremely cautious, crafting his talk only from on-the-record statements by high-ranking LDS leaders. Why not, after all, talk about Heavenly Mother on Mother's Day? But as soon as he finished his talk, he was followed at the pulpit by his bishop, who denounced the talk and shamed the man. Within a few weeks, his Stake Presidency issued a statement asserting that talk of Heavenly Mother was prohibited.

"That was wrong," I said to the women in the group. "That's not doctrinal."

"How do you know?" the woman looked at me with big fearful eyes, stunned.

"Because I know," I said. It's not a mystery. The official statements are available for everyone to study. We need to take responsibility for knowing our own religion, right?

It's a refusal to know and act on our own doctrine that keeps Heavenly Mother in silence. And that refusal is rooted in culture. Gender-conservative Mormon culture often privileges polite demurral and passivity in women over intellectual curiosity and authority. Perhaps the quiescence we assign to Heavenly Mother is a reflection of what Mormon culture at its most conservative values in women.

I certainly don't think LDS Church leaders are plotting to keep Heavenly Mother out of the conversation. Not at all. I think they're preoccupied with the many challenges of running a worldwide church, and Mother in Heaven simply doesn't occur to them except as a fringe theological speculation. So it may be up to those of us for whom she is not a fringe concern—*perhaps because she looks like us or someone we love*—to take responsibility for knowing the doctrine.

And don't blame God for the silence. After all, why would God prohibit discussion of the truth that women are partners in Godhood, that God looks not only like the husbands, brothers, and sons we cherish but also like *us, our sisters, and our daughters*? That she has parts and passions like ours, as Mormon doctrine teaches. We live in a world where women's bodies are exploited, shamed, abused and distorted beyond recognition in popular culture, with serious spiritual consequences for men, women, boys, and girls. So many women—including (especially?) Mormon women—have issues with food, size, and embodiment that are tremendously costly to our spiritual lives and the lives of our families. Understanding the embodiment of God in female form calls us to emancipation from distorted and distorting relationships to our bodies.

I appreciate all the Mormon women and men who are making an effort to bring Heavenly Mother steadily and politely back into everyday speech and thought. (And readers, if you'd like to see some truly beautiful art and writing on Motherhood—including divine motherhood—do yourself a favor and get the latest issue of *Sunstone* magazine, a special issue dedicated entirely to the subject.)

I'll get back into my silence now, and turn the space over to you, readers. How do you experience the silence around Heavenly Mother, and are you ready to end it for yourself?

Send your query to askmormongirl@gmail.com, or follow @askmormongirl on Twitter.

"THE PARABLE OF THE TEN VIRGINS" BY LISA PATTERSON BUTTERWORTH (JULY 15, 2012)

One of the speakers today in sacrament meeting retold the Parable of the Ten Virgins. And as she spoke I went through an exercise that has been *very* useful to me of late in my spiritual journey. And I think I got a tiny moment of insight I thought I'd share.

But first, some background. I try to apply every story to myself. But not in the sense of putting myself in the shoes of one of the virgins (either prepared or unprepared), but me as all ten of them and me as the lamps, and me as the oil, and me as the bridegroom too. Me as everything, as everyone.

The approach occurred to me sometime this last year, as I sat through yet one more lesson in Sunday School about the evil world out there, and how great we are and not like them, and how we need to separate ourselves from "them" by covering our shoulders and hanging church art in our homes and making our kids watch terrible Book of Mormon cartoons. And of course praying more and reading the scriptures. And then the teacher brought in three pine tree limbs, a beautiful fresh limb, a fake limb, and a dead dry limb, and he proceeded to tell us about how we the Mormons are the lovely green living limb, and all "them" are fake and/or dead. And my soul cried NO!

What our Heavenly Parents must think of that particular object lesson, could I imagine them looking down upon their children, the children they love and cherish, every one made in their image, full of divine nature, and labeling a small percentage of them as "lovely and living" and the vast majority as "dead and fake." No! I could not imagine it. But then I realized, *I* was all three, I certainly have vital good sides of me that are lovely and living, and there are parts of me that I neglect and let turn brown and brittle, and there are parts of me coated in plastic and stored up for the summer. We are each of us all three, none of us is pure, lovely and vital in every aspect of our lives, we all have brown brittle bits and plastic fake bits. I wished I would have thought of that, and said so, before the lesson ended. Alas no.

And from then on, every time the lesson took a meandering journey through "us vs. them" land, a favorite theme in my particular ward, I would try to reapply that lesson internally, find the "us" in me, fine the "them" in me. And it was never hard at all. This approach made so much more sense to me if religion is the framework upon which I am to grow spiritually, and it is through Sunday School lessons that I must learn to become the best person I can be, what sense does it make for me to be looking for flaws in "them" or putting up barriers to protect myself from "them," isn't the growth supposed to be about me, aren't I working out my own salvation, aren't the lessons supposed to be about me and how I can make a better me?

And I felt guided line upon line, as the things I needed to know came to me as gifts from my friends. I learned from my dear friend Nikki (Idaho Spud) a whole new thing that had never interested me before, but which has deep deep roots in my Mormon soil, dream interpretation. The thing is, I'm not much into that new agey, touchy feely, symbolism stuff. It all seemed too weird and not-scientific and illogical, and full of weird. But I LOVE Spud, and I respect her, so I listened to something that seemed silly and frivolous before, and it fit perfectly with this insight that had helped me so much. You see, Jung says everything in our dreams is symbolic of us, every person, every landscape, every building represent aspects of ourselves. I still don't really understand it, the symbols still escape me, and my cynical logical voice still dismisses so much of it as phooey. But there's a deeper voice, something down in my gut that says yes, follow this, this will teach you things you need to know.

And so now every bible story, every Sunday School lesson, every dream, every parable, it is all me.

And as the speaker this morning told the story of The Ten Virgins (setting aside for now the horrifying custom of valuing and labeling women based upon their sexual experience!), if the wise women were me, and the foolish women were me, foolish, neglected, unprepared "me" in an hour of need may turn to the wise "me," but I am unable to loan light/energy/nourishment to those parts of me that I have not developed or prepared. What would it mean if I am a binary of wisdom and foolishness? What are these halves? If I only prepare half of myself, then I will have to leave parts of me behind, I will not be whole when the time comes. (For what? Not so sure on that point, second coming, celebration of a joining, a new phase in life, death?) So I reflected on the binary parts of me, the parts that might become separated. Body and Spirit. Heart and Mind. And what came to mind are the two decision-making parts of my brain, one emotional, and one logical. Heart and Mind. Body and Spirit. There has been a long tradition in Western thought (hello Plato) that if we all listened to our logical selves, ignored emotion, became very Vulcan-ish, all the world's problems would be solved. We often use "emotional" as an insult. Women are too emotional.

But it turns out that when people are perfectly logical, when their emotional centers turn off (usually through some sort of accident/illness), they lose their ability to make the most mundane decisions, crippled by the choice between cheerios and chex. And the reverse is also true, people whose logical centers turn off (again generally through accident/illness) lose their ability to plan for the future or control the most basic of impulses.

I have been told that the lesson of the virgins is to be prepared, to have enough oil ready so that when the bridegroom comes I can be a wise virgin and go to the wedding. My first instinct has been to think, how rude for the "wise" women not to share their oil, how can they not share, isn't Christianity all about sharing? But if I am all the virgins, what does this lack of sharing mean? Why can't I loan oil to my other half and drag my unprepared parts along behind me? But as the speaker this morning repeated again and again, "you cannot live on borrowed light," she was referring to testimony and why we must build our own. I think this is true, but if I apply it internally, I have learned that I cannot borrow light from my emotions to enlighten my logic, nor vice versa. I cannot logic my way to emotional truths, and I cannot emotion my way to logical truths. They are lamps that create very different types of light, and both are deeply crippled without the other, and both need oil, time, energy, nourishment.

For the first 17 years of my life, I knew the church was true. I had all the answers and they were simple, good/bad, us/them, white/black, I knew it deep in my gut, good, us, white. And then came the crisis, the simple answers did not stand up to logic. I spent many years of my life trying to "logic" my way back to a testimony, I wanted desperately to believe, but found myself unable to make myself believe something I didn't believe. And conversely, when something happened, something that felt very external, something that felt like the voice of God, the love of God, when that belief filled me, my logic immediately wanted to discount it, but the emotions, the feelings, core sense of knowing, it was all very very real in an utterly illogical way.

When my early testimony ruled I knew I was the superior owner of simple truth, and when logic took control, I felt like the superior owner of complex meaninglessness. But when my emotions and my logic attempt to balance each other, I find myself (mostly) freed from my natural state as self-righteous know-it-all. If I forget to nourish all parts of me, then when the time comes to move forward into the next big thing, a joining, a celebration, then parts of myself, essential parts of myself may not be ready for the feast.

"ASK MORMON GIRL: HOW DARE YOU MENTION ORDINATION ON TELEVISION??! (OR, BEHIND THE SCENES NBC ROCK CENTER EDITION.)" BY JOANNA BROOKS (AUGUST 26, 2012)

"Did God discriminate against men when he gave women vaginas? Why can't men have babies? So why can't your daughter pass the sacrament? Or be a prophet? I guess that too must be oppression of the woman right?"

178

We could call this installment of Ask Mormon Girl the "Inside NBC Rock Center" edition.[214] Because questions like these are the ones I've gotten aplenty after my three-soundbite appearance in the *Mormons in America* special.

The behind the scenes scoop—well, there's plenty of it. All throughout the process, I found the producers very kind and gracious and sincerely interested in humanizing our faith. I will say that I wish they hadn't shown garments on television, or given quite so much time to Abby Huntsman, as beautiful as she is to watch. I wish they had included the footage they took of my family praying at our dinner table. And I wish that the three soundbites they used from the two hour interview they did with me had drawn more broadly from my description of the joys of growing up Mormon, the experience of interfaith families, and the broad-ranging concerns of Mormon feminists and not just focused in on the question of ordination and the threat of excommunication. It's too often that Mormon feminism gets put in the ordination-excommunication box. And it's not a comfortable box in which to live.

I worried that might happen. My gut told me so before the program aired. I even reached out to my friend Mitch Mayne, an active and out gay LDS man who also appeared on the program, to see if he was feeling okay. We were nervous nellies. And when I saw that out of the two-hour interview, the three soundbites focused on ordination, my nervousness compounded ten-fold. And then my inbox started filling up with aggressive and grouchy email from people lecturing me about how "God gave women vaginas" and therefore not priesthood. Some folks on Twitter even called for my excommunication. Just because I observed that ordination is important to some Mormon feminists. Which is factually true.

The lesson I take from my experience this week is that just raising the question of ordination brings out incredible anxiety and defensiveness and even meanness in LDS people, even though it is an honest question that women of Judeo-Christian faiths have been asking for centuries. And it is a question our boys and girls, young men and women, will come to naturally as they develop and grow and learn more about our faith tradition. My six-year-old and eight-year-old ask me this question. I refuse to make them feel that it is wrong to ask.

I've searched myself, and I will say that women's ordination in the LDS Church isn't really a driving question for me. It doesn't cause me personal pain or struggle. I can't remember a time when it has.

But there are many LDS women I've met who have told me plainly, "Yes, I think women should be ordained." They've done so with a simple sense of conviction that has stunned me. Most of the women who have told me ordination matters to them are temple-attending and fully active.

They've been Primary Presidents and Young Women's Presidents. This question is important to women I care about and love.

That's why when *Rock Center* asked me to characterize Mormon feminism, I wasn't about to leave those women out. I told them, yes, ordination is important for some of us Mormon feminists, and that for some of us questions of decision-making and institutional participation and visibility take priority.

I find myself more in the latter camp. I can't recommend highly enough this recent article[215] by the *Salt Lake Tribune's* Peggy Fletcher Stack, in which she interviewed a spectrum of Mormon feminist activists who made an eloquent case for advancing the status of LDS women in ways that don't center on ordination. The article even presents a list of suggestions[216] for advancing the visibility of women in the Church without doctrinal change, including having more women speak at General Conference, appointing women presidents of Church-owned universities, allowing women to serve as Sunday School presidents, ward clerks, and in other leadership positions that bear no priesthood keys, allowing women to serve as witnesses at the baptisms of their children, lowering young women's mission age to 19, and even including Relief Society or Young Women's Presidents in personal interviews with young women—which personally seems like a smart idea to me.

Stack's article also included quotes from Pulitzer-Prize winning historian and Mormon feminist Laurel Thatcher Ulrich, who observed that the women of the LDS Church today are nowhere near as visible and active in leadership as our pioneer and early 20th century foremothers. Before correlation put most church programs and functions under an office of the priesthood, Mormon women developed their own curriculum and managed their own budgets for Relief Society. They practiced the gift of healing by laying on of hands. They led hospital building drives. They led suffrage campaigns. By comparison, Thatcher concludes, our era is "The Great Disappearance." When I read that, my stomach hurt.

I think we can do better. In fact, I think Mormonism is capable of providing some uniquely powerful answers to that question of women and priesthood. Gender has a uniquely powerful symbolic role in our faith tradition, and a complicated one. It's not an issue of black and white, "vaginas" vs. priesthood. I do think LDS women hold and exercise a form of priesthood in our temples. And I think that Mormon history provides us plenty of evidence that the "men have priesthood, women have motherhood" rationale is not even faithful to our own doctrine. It's not even correct. Last night, when I was reading my copy of *The Beginning of Better Days*[217]—a Deseret Book-published collection of minutes from the first meetings of the LDS Relief Society in 1842; please buy yourself a copy and study it—I about dropped my book when I saw how and how much the Prophet Joseph talked to these early women about priesthood. He told them that the Relief Society "should move according to the ancient Priesthood," and, yes, he "turned the keys" to them to govern their own Society. And I cheered when Emma Smith declared that Relief Society would "expect extraordinary occasions and pressing calls"—that "when a boat is stuck on the rapids with a multitude of Mormons on board we shall consider that a loud call for relief." Her boldness was instructive and exemplary. Nowhere, nowhere, nowhere in these sermons did Joseph Smith tell the Relief Society that their capacity to gestate and bear children was the equivalent of a male-only priesthood. So I don't think that simple answer reflects doctrinal truth, and I won't be using that explanation with my own daughters.

I think of Emma Smith's grand sense of the Relief Society's purpose— her bold "ain't no mountain high enough, ain't no river wide enough" attitude—and I do believe that as Laurel Thatcher Ulrich observes LDS women today are operating in an constricted sphere of activity. In his sermon to the Relief Society, Joseph Smith himself noted that women tend to be "contracted in their views" and should be more "liberal in [their] feelings." I wonder if in our post-Proclamation on the Family LDS world there has been a contracted overemphasis on narrowly-defined gender roles, an emphasis that doesn't fit the reality of many women's lives and can in fact distract us from the "extraordinary occasions and pressing calls"—as Emma Smith put it—of our lives and times.

So starting today, I have a new definition of Mormon feminism. *A Mormon feminist is a person who thinks that all people should have the opportunity to love and serve God with all their might, mind, and strength—regardless of gender, race, or sexuality.*

That means that women and girls around the world and regardless of faith tradition will have access to the basic rights and resources (including freedom from abuse and access to contraception and education) they need in order to exercise agency and stewardship in their own lives and the lives of their families. This means that women and girls around the world and regardless of faith tradition will be able to use the full range of their skills and abilities—not just their reproductive systems—to advance the work of God on earth. And this means that men and boys, women and girls will be supported when they ask the very basic questions about God and gender that people have been asking for millennia—the questions that allow us all to disentangle human culture and philosophy from the workings of God. At the very least, no one will get shamed, or isolated, or subjected to excommunication—real, virtual, or imaginary—just for asking honest questions and making factual observations.

My experience this week tells me that we're not there yet.

"Women's Conference (or Do Your Wifely Duty to Protect Your Husband from Sin)" by Cate (September 6, 2012)

I heard that my ward was having a "Women's Conference" on an upcoming Sunday and that the Bishop would be speaking to the women for Relief Society and then also for an hour after church for those who wanted to stay. The Bishop's "lessons" (I put that in quotes because they are more like lectures than lessons; him talking the entire time, sharing his PowerPoint presentations, allowing little or no time for any feedback) in the past have been ... interesting, and I'd heard that he had something "special" planned and didn't want to miss it.

I feel like despite our differences, I've always given the guy the benefit of the doubt. We have had long conversations about my eternal welfare and my beliefs/non-beliefs, and it is no secret that we don't agree on a large number of very important issues. Actually, in the past I have even commended him for being "gutsy" enough to talk about controversial subjects in church, even though in large part I disagree with the WAY he talks about them. "At least he is trying," I've thought. "At least he has good intentions." These are the things I've said to myself as I've sat through his various combined 5th Sunday lessons.

About a year ago, the bishop gave a lesson during Relief Society to all the women in the ward. There had even been a cutesy little mailer that had been sent out to all the women a few weeks before hand preparing them to "Come and Learn the Key to a Happy Marriage." The men took over all the women's duties for the 3rd hour, and we were shoved into the Relief Society room to hear his inspired message. I was hopeful. After all, I am married. I love my husband. Things were good, but I didn't want to miss the opportunity to gain some new "secret knowledge" that could make things even better. And even though I didn't always see eye to eye with the bishop, I still held on to the idea that he was being "inspired by God" and was leading the ward accordingly. So, yeah, I was probably cautiously optimistic sitting there on the blue upholstered folding chair, staring up at a big screen and the smiling bishop, waiting for his "special presentation."

The room quieted down, and he began. First with the disclaimer: "I've thought and prayed a lot about this and debated whether I was going to give this lesson or not for quite some time. . . ." "After much consideration I decided it needs to be done, and I do this only out of love, concern, and inspiration. . . ." Up pops the first slide in his PowerPoint presentation. "Happiness in Marriage: The Very Key." After a few minutes of explanation and a quote or two from a G.A. he throws up the next slide:

"Understanding the Male Sex Drive."

(You can already probably see where this is going. . . .)

Red flags pop up in my mind left and right. I can't help but mesh those first two slides together to form "Happiness in Marriage: The Very Key [Is] Understanding the Male Sex Drive." I'd been duped. This is NOT the "secret knowledge" I had hoped for. What ensued was an hour long presentation that I can basically sum up in one sentence.

Good Mormon women have regular sex with their husbands in order to keep their marriages "happy" and keep their husbands from sin.

I was hurting and I couldn't place why. I felt sick to my stomach and was upset at myself for being so upset. Obviously I must not be a "good Mormon woman" if I was experiencing this very negative knee jerk reaction to the lesson that had just been given. He ended with passing out books (*And They Were Not Ashamed* by Laura Brotherson[218]) to all the women (complete with Buckees sacks to hide them from our children until we got home and could find a secret place to stash them). I walked zombie like to the car, my mind racing. My husband loaded the kids into the car and shut the door. He looked at me and asked, "How was the meeting?" I just started bawling! I tried to explain what had made me so upset, but the words were unintelligible. Later when I'd calmed down I thought back through the lesson and tried to pinpoint the issues that were causing me such distress. There were several. I'll get to them more specifically in a minute.

A year has gone by, and I've learned that there had been some controversy surrounding the bishop's "Sex Talk" (as it had properly been renamed). Several women in surrounding wards had heard of his presentation and were curious. Also, there had been many new families who had moved into the ward who heard through the grapevine about the lesson. A few weeks ago, I received an email from the Relief Society stating that due to so much interest in this lesson, the bishop would be giving an "encore presentation" on a coming Sunday for any of those who would either like to hear it again or who hadn't heard it the first time. They called it "Women's Conference." The bishop was to give a lesson to all the women for 3rd hour and then was going to be giving the infamous "Sex Talk" directly after church for anyone who'd like to stay. There was going to be a lunch and we were encouraged to invite friends if they were interested.

Upon receiving this email, I decided to email the bishop with some of my thoughts and suggestions for his "encore presentation." I politely told him that I respected his courage and candidness but that some of the things he presented in the last talk could be worded differently to be less damaging to some of the sisters. I sent him several links to podcasts about female sexuality with Mormon therapists Jennifer Finlayson-Fife and Natasha Helfer Parker. I also attached some articles that I thought he might want to take a look at to help broaden his perspective. I was hopeful that he would be open to some constructive criticism and suggestions, especially if his motives were truly to love and support the women's best interests.

I went to the conference, preparing to take copious notes so that I could be sure to relay the lessons back to my husband and feminist friends as accurately as possible. Unfortunately, a year's time had passed and with it a year's worth of sitting through lessons by the bishop so THIS time, I must say, I wasn't nearly as optimistic. But, there was still this glimmer, this last thread in the back of my mind, that sincerely hoped that I would leave being able to cling to some uplifting message, some nugget of truth.

Sitting through the First Session (or 3rd hour lesson) of "Women's Conference" quickly became excruciating. Any hopes I had of having a decent experience were extinguished by the bishop's anti-feminist, fear inducing words. Maybe that will have to be a post for another day. It was appalling. And I was devastated. And I hadn't even gotten to the "Sex Talk" yet! My positivity was waning.

After a bathroom break, a long drink of water, and an internal motivational speech to myself, I made my way back into the room for the grand finale. The "encore presentation." My mother-in-law had met me to listen to this lesson since she is from a neighboring stake and had heard about it and was curious. We sat at the table, lunch was placed before me. I was too sick to my stomach to really eat. I got to a fresh page in my notebook, took a deep breath, put my pen to my paper, and it began.

I hoped that he had revised his lesson after receiving feedback from the women. It was obvious to me he had not. I mean, I'm sure a few things were taken out, and definitely several things were added, but still the message was clear: Good Mormon women have regular sex with their husbands in order to keep their marriages "happy" and keep their husbands from sin.

The only thing keeping me in my seat was my determination to write down every word and copy every slide. I didn't get EVERY word, but I did my best to paraphrase accurately. I did type up ALL of my notes and some of my thoughts about them to share with my online feminist friends, but for this post, I will only go through a few of the points in his lesson:

**Point 1: Understanding the Male Sex Drive

(Understanding Why Men NEED Sex and Women Don't)

- Why do you need to understand the male sex drive? Knowledge is power. The glory of God is intelligence. He explains that ignorance leads to misery, particularly in sexual matters.
- New slide and in bold: Male sex drive is…
- from God
- biologically planted from our Heavenly Father
- it is constant and recurrent

- it is instinctive

He gives a couple Packer quotes, one about how

> men were given their sexual desires to continue the creative power [I'm completely paraphrasing]. It is strong and constant in order to create a binding tie to their families so their families can be provided for and sustained.[219]

(So basically, God made men's sex drives strong so that they'd need to keep coming back for more from their wives. This way, the irresponsible men will be inclined to stick around and provide for their kids.???!!!)

**Point 2: Good Men Still Need Sex

(Good Mormon Men are TRAINED but Still Want Sex)

Next he puts up this big picture of a line of German shepherds at a police academy. In front of this line of dogs walks this little cat, and it is obvious that all the dogs want to do is pounce on the poor thing. Everyone giggles at what this picture is suggesting, and he continues on with his message. "This is a stupid cat. Luckily these dogs are so well trained that they can fight against even their deepest genetic desires and stay in line. But," he said, "just because they are keeping formation doesn't mean they don't REALLY want that cat. Trained dogs STILL look at cats."

(So men, you are dogs. And if you are trained well enough, you will stay in line. But you still won't be able to help wanting that cat. And women, your men, even trained men, still want other cats. Now does everyone feel nice and good about themselves? Great. Let's push on then.)

Since it is becoming clear that this is the main message of this lesson, he continues to reiterate this point time and time again throughout the remaining slides. "Most men don't resist these urges at the level that your husbands do. They're doing their best to restrain," he tells us. "The cat is temptation."

**Point 3: Mormon Men vs. Men of the World

(Your Husbands Only Get YOU When the Men of the World Get MORE)

Next slide.

This is probably my favorite one. *Note sarcasm.*)

Three numbers appear:

- 20,000
- 12,000
- 3,000

"Does anyone know what these numbers represent?" he asks the class. Heads shake "no" and he continues. "The 20,000 is the number of women that Wilt Chamberlain claimed to have had sex with in his lifetime. 12,000 is the number of women Warren Beatty had sex with. 3,000 are the number Gene Simmons is purported to have slept with." Disbelief and dismay goes through the room in a wave.

(What the HECK is your point guy?!)

He goes on, "Men want sex. Good men restrain themselves, but they still want sex. They strive to bridle their passions, but they can only control, not eliminate this desire."

**Point 3: Don't Take Offense

(Wise Women Understand They Need to Put Out ... or Someone Else Will)

He lists a ton of scriptures stating that God wants married couples to have good, frequent sex and that this is a power for good to bring couples together. He then reminds us that "there are women who WILL take your husbands," and Solomon says, "Be ravished with your wife."[220] He goes on to add that if you won't be ravished with him, a stranger will.

(I'm so exhausted by this point; the angry in me is turning into more of a begging-to-stop.)

He makes sure we understand that "wise women will understand this fact and not take offense."

("No offense" is probably one of the most ridiculous types of manipulation. Like, here, let me say something to you that is completely meant to be offensive, but you can't get mad about it because I said, "No offense.")

**Point 4: Young Men Look Forward to Sex with Their Wives

(Willing Wives Are Young Men's Reward for Good Behavior)

He tells the women that all through young men's lives there is a drumbeat going on in their heads that says: "When I get married I can have sex . . . when I get married I can have sex . . . when I get married I can have sex . . ." "I just need to hold on until a beautiful wife lets me."

(O. . .K. . .)

He tells us how often times the deprived spouse is loathing the thought of eternity with his wife. The deprived spouse takes the sexual rejection as a personal rejection and becomes resentful. And the deprived spouse is more tempted when he is deprived.

He reiterates again that "Mormon men look forward to marriage and having sex."

He tells a story about a sex starved husband who feels duped because his wife was loving and affectionate before marriage but after marriage she "pulled a bait and switch." He gives another Kimball quote on divorces happening in large part because of sexual problems.[221]

**Point 5: The Spouse with the Need Trumps the Spouse without It

(Seriously . . . that was the title of this slide. No snarky interpretation needed on this one.)

The bishop states, "The person who has the need TRUMPS the person who doesn't."

The bishop plays audio clips from a radio show hosted by marriage therapists: (paraphrasing) "Should a woman fake it? Hmmm. Well the very best thing is when SHE desires him, when she initiates sex. Second best, and a very close second, is when she gives a good reception to his initiation. The point is THE DEED GETS DONE. Don't worry about WANTING to. Just BEGIN. Get over the inertia. . . ." Then the talk show hosts give several (terrible) analogies about work ("No one wants to go to work, but once they get there they feel better and they can be proud that they got the job done" blah blah blah) and exercising (same thing, no one wants to start but the benefits outweigh the costs. . . .).

Then the bishop feels he needs to add his own analogy (terrible) and tells us all to imagine that our husbands were diagnosed with kidney disease and that the only way to save them was to drive them to dialysis two or three times a week. Wouldn't we do it? To save his life, of course we would. It is the same with sex.

He also gives another analogy (terrible) about a woman who doesn't necessarily like to eat (crazy lady!) but she became a master chef. When asked why she cooked so much she replied, "Well, my husband likes to eat good food. And I don't want him going anywhere else to get it."

(Once again reiterating that if women don't put out, their husbands will find it somewhere else.)

Back to the audio: "What about women who have a stronger sex drive than their husbands? Hmmm. Well this is tricky. Common, but tricky. Because now you are asking the man to eat AND cook. You need to find a way for your husband to satisfy you. What gets him going? What pumps up his testosterone? Conflict? Then start a fight! Do what you can to get him in the mood."

(Of course, it's still a woman's job even when she's the horny one, but for him, it's never his job really. Why would it be?)

**Point 6: The Temptation Is Great

(Women Aren't Responsible for Their Husbands' Sins . . . Oh Wait . . . They Kinda Are)

He ends his presentation by stating, "The world through their gigolos and whores have hijacked sex. We need to take it back." He also adds that as far as porn use and addiction and infidelity goes, he doesn't want to "pin" that all on the wives or make them feel responsible (Oh really? Huh.), but he points out, "Don't you want to be able to say, 'My hands are clean' if ever something like that happens to your marriage?"

(As if to say, do all you can to prevent your husbands from being dogs and THEN you won't be blamed for it. But only if you had sex with them at least 3 times a week. If you missed a day, then yeah, it's your fault.)

He wraps up his comments by reiterating, "All he wants is you. And all he can ever have is you. Don't resent that he wants you."

(Way to end on a high note bish.)

***

There was so much more to this lesson, but I tried to choose his main points for this post. To his credit, he DID talk a little bit about changing the way we talk about sex to our young women (i.e. no more smashed cupcake lessons[222]). He also quickly ran through the "Good Girl Syndrome" and advised the women to seek counseling through books or with a therapist if they had this problem (the problem of feeling like sex is too dirty to participate in). I wish I could say that most of his lesson was good, insightful messages like that. But unfortunately it was not.

Needless to say, I left feeling torn up inside once again. I was so disappointed that the lesson was not redirected toward the deeper issues with marital sexuality. I felt like speaking to the women like this was like putting a Band-Aid on someone else's scraped knee when you have a missing limb. There is such a need to address sexual issues in our culture, but this talk did not at all address the deeper needs of the relationships nor the deeper needs of these women themselves. Men may get more duty sex after this talk, but no marriage will have more intimacy, more love, or more joy. All I feel he wants from us is to fix the men's boo-boos and deal with the rest on our own and without complaint. Talk about egocentric.

I agree that women should have fulfilling sexual relationships with their spouses. I agree that sex should never be used as a weapon or a manipulation tool on the woman's or man's part. I LOVE sex! I hope everyone can get to a place where they LOVE sex. But this lesson was not a catalyst for healthy sexual change and growth. It was damaging, degrading, and preyed on the insecurities of these "good Mormon women." I am upset. I am upset by this lesson and the unlimited number of lessons like this that have been, are being, and will be given to women all around the church throughout their lives. I am upset about the way I feel the bishop abused his spiritual power to propagate his anti-feminist agenda, throughout the "Sex Talk" and the lesson given before it. But most of all, I'm upset by the head nods, the "so trues" and the internal "amen"-ing that streamed through the majority of the women in the room. I'm upset that they have internalized these damaging messages, and there's no helping those who don't want to be helped.

So, what are some of your experiences with the Church and female sexuality? How can we approach this topic with our women, old and young, that will be healthy for them spiritually and mentally? Should bishops or other church leaders be giving lessons like this at all? What can we do if we disagree with the messages that are being shared in a church environment?

"THE MORMON THERAPIST ON 'DOING YOUR WIFELY DUTY'" BY NATASHA HELFER PARKER (SEPTEMBER 10, 2012)

I've been asked by Lisa Butterworth to give my two cents worth on the previous post regarding a certain bishop's sexual education approach.[223]

I've purposefully not read the comments section, so I won't be swayed by all your fabulous brain power—and then you can send me through the ringer and let me know where I have room for improvement, attitude adjustment or more up-to-date information. I also need to make clear that I did not attend the meeting in question—therefore, I am only able to comment on what was reported by the original poster.

I'll start with giving the bishop the benefit of the doubt and point out possible positives while simultaneously sharing concerns with the approach taken. Bear with me please.

I want to take into account that many of our sexual views are cultural and generational. In other words, those of us in our 20s and 30s have grown up with widely different sexual norms and education than those of us in our 60s and 70s. An entire sexual revolution has occurred in the last 45 years alone. It is a fairly recent phenomenon that women are being taught they have a right to not only claim their sexual selves but find sex enjoyable to boot (both within and out of Mormon culture).

However, in this day and age, I am still surprised by the amount of LDS women who come through my office saying things like: "If I don't want to have sex in my marriage, my husband should be OK with that. He needs to control his passions." "I have no need for sex—my husband just has to get over it." "Sex is not necessary for marital happiness." I see many, many marriages which would be considered sexless (having sex less than 10 times a year), and this is not an arrangement both spouses are usually satisfied with. Stereotypically, the low-libido partner is female and driving this frequency. (Please don't throw me under the table yet—I will complicate this further as I go—there are many other, legitimate scenarios to consider). So, I'm assuming this bishop has received many complaints from women who have husbands who are requesting more sex, complaints from men who are not getting enough sex, and also seeing many people with pornography viewing behavior (which is easy to incorrectly correlate to non-satisfactory marital intimacy under one overarching umbrella). If he's not hearing from women who are viewing pornography or women with higher libido—this can usually be attributed to the fact that women in these scenarios, especially in a culture such as ours, think of themselves as weird and alone in their problem. Therefore, in my experience, they just don't speak to their bishop about these issues. Taking all this into account, I do think it is positive to normalize sexual drive, to understand how biology plays a role no one is at fault for, and to use whatever sex-positive Mormon doctrine and/or scripture we can get our hands on to give credence to the positive effects of healthy sexuality within marriage. Where the presentation fell strikingly short is that it only normalized the male drive and ignored the female drive altogether.

As far as the quotes he used from Packer—this stuff is based in evolutionary theory (ironic, no?). And evolutionary theory is fascinating in the context of understanding primary instincts, urges and behavioral patterns of the human race as a whole. Monogamy and marriage based on romantic love are fairly new and primarily Western concepts. At the same time, even though I may be programmed to hunker down with my babies to the point of murdering anything that risks harming them, while my husband is programmed to insert sperm in as many women as possible as well as killing children I've acquired from sperm other than his; both in an effort to increase our chances of promulgating our DNA—I think we would all agree most of us live in a time and culture with higher standards for accountability than our primal instincts. Yet our instincts and physiological differences still remain. There is research which shows men and women's brains react differently to visual stimulation. There is research which shows heterosexual men and women are attracted to traits within the opposite sex that are prime for making healthy babies (i.e. wide hips in females, broad shoulders in males, etc.). There is research which shows that a woman's psychological state plays a larger role in her ability to feel sexually aroused than a man's. There is research to support that both men and women have sensual thoughts throughout any given day—men usually report more frequency of these than women. There is research to show how different hormones such as testosterone and estrogen affect libido. I could go on. These can be helpful things to know—especially if they normalize our individualized experiences. However, these research findings do not apply to all—and stating "this is the way it is" isolates those who do not fit the mold, potentially and unintentionally damaging many within the sound of such sermons. And to challenge the bishop slightly: many of us have lustful or sensual thoughts we don't act on and would never dream of acting on—Mormon or not. This is called fantasy. Also, as Mormons, we unfortunately are not dramatically different in our statistics from the population at large when it comes to problems such as divorce, infidelity, pornography usage, etc.

There is truth in saying that when people are sexually unsatisfied within their relationship, this can cause deeper problems affecting other areas of marital intimacy. These problems can, in time, play a role in eroding the foundation of the relationship. As part of coping with these relational issues, people turn to all types of different behaviors (some healthy—some not): overeating, exercise, infidelity, gaming, pornography use, shopping, going out with friends, reading books, etc., etc. However, the problem with how this was presented is that it ignored that this dynamic can go the other way too: when people are emotionally, spiritually or intellectually unsatisfied in their relationships, deep problems within the realm of physical intimacy can occur. You can "put out" all you want—but if you make each other miserable, the sex isn't necessarily going to help. It might for a while—but not long term. Now, just because I agree that sexual dissatisfaction can lead to bad coping mechanisms, does not mean I think infidelity or other non-agreed-upon sexual behavior such as pornography use is justified or should be blamed on the spouse with the lower libido. Last time I checked, we are not held responsible for Adam's transgression (see Article of Faith 2[224])—nor Bob's, James's, Pablo's, etc.

It is important to recognize that negative sexual behaviors are usually indicators or symptoms of deeper seated issues. And these can either stem from relational problems (like unsatisfactory marital intimacy) or just as likely, if not even more than likely, individual issues the person has brought with them into the marriage (i.e. shame, trauma/abuse, habits, poor sexual education, communication styles, conflict-resolution styles, etc. etc.). I've come across statistics which show that as many as 90% of people who can be legitimately considered "sex addicts" (related to diagnostic criteria) have a history of sexual abuse in their background. 80% come from what are considered "rigid" family backgrounds which offer little flexibility when it comes to exploration which goes beyond the family's "rules." And believe me, there are plenty of unspoken "family rules" about sexuality within family dynamics. It doesn't matter how much sex a spouse offers this type of person—it will not solve the problem because the problem has nothing to do with the spouse. In fact many of these couples are having satisfying and frequent sexual encounters. If this type of couple is not educated on what they are truly facing, they will buy into the lie that their problem is each other. It sounds like this extremely important scenario was not even brought up as a possibility in this discussion—harmful for sure. And if the spouse begins an inappropriate self-blaming dialogue, you can see how easy it is to develop other mental health problems such as depression and anxiety.

As far as who "wins"—the lower libido partner or the higher libido partner? It is true that in relatively respectful relationships, the lower libido spouse often trumps—meaning they get their way. Making the assumption in this case that the lower libido partner is the female, I find that "good" Mormon husbands have also been taught they should control their passions at some level and are, therefore, willing to sell themselves short because that is the good husbandy type thing to do. Unfortunately, resentment builds along the way, consciously or not. However, this is not necessarily true in relationships where there is a negative power differential such as domestic violence or dated patriarchal dynamics where "the husband decides." Rape happens within marriages. Often a lower libido partner in this scenario will "give in" due to a sense of duty or gender role. In my opinion, any time there is a discussion of who is "winning," both are losing. More on managing different libidos later.

There is truth in that women's anatomy usually takes longer to work up to sexual desire than men. And often, if women are willing to engage in sexual play within a healthy relationship, even though they may not feel "horny" when they begin, desire builds in the process—or it can. This, of course, can be true for men as well. But if my numbers are right, men can become sexually excited in as little as 3 to 5 minutes while women usually take about 15–30. If you engage in sex out of duty only—the chances of warming up at all are slim. There needs to be some authenticity in the desire to desire. And as a woman, if you're not physically excited, you're not becoming lubricated or physically prepared to enjoy sexual advance—this can lead to painful or uncomfortable intercourse, so forget orgasm at this point—and if this has been a general pattern, why would you desire to desire?

It is best when we desire each other—but being realistic, in a long-term monogamous relationship there are going to be libido ups and downs affected by all kinds of factors: age, childbirth, childcare, stress, hormones, etc. It is best when both partners either naturally or purposefully take turns initiating. It is important for both partners to feel desired and wanted in a sexual way. If this isn't happening, reasons can be explored. Here is one example of how I try and help couples work through libido differences: a scenario I run into often is when childbirth and/or breastfeeding dramatically lower a woman's libido. If biology is agreed upon by the couple as the culprit, the husband can be reassured that the issue is not that he is not desired or special to his wife—her biology legitimately doesn't feel like having sex. They can agree that for an allotted period of time in their marriage he will be the main initiator—taking the pressure off her to perform in a certain way and taking the pressure off him that he no longer matters. When he does initiate, she can decide what type of sexual play she can offer at that particular time. (The range can be as far on one spectrum as encouraging him to go masturbate in the shower as he thinks of their pre-baby sex life to the other side of the spectrum where they have vaginal intercourse. There is much in between to choose from, such as oral sex, hand jobs, rubbing up against your partner, masturbating next to each other, massage, leaving it to another day, etc.) These are the types of options I try and help couples explore so neither one is feeling like they are holding their sexual relationship hostage. And both can feel good that their partner's needs are being met without having to sacrifice their own. It's about being authentic and caring.

I find Laura Brotherson's book[225] useful and a good place to start understanding one's sexuality from a religious positive perspective—especially for those who may hold more conservative views on sexuality. Just not sure those books needed to go home in a paper bag. It's good for our kids to see we take this topic seriously.

Now for the full-out problem areas:

I reject the notion that the key to marital happiness is how we manage sexual drive. Keys to marital happiness deal with communication and conflict-resolution styles. They deal with trust, validation, compromise and good listening skills. They deal with the ability to attach well to one another and the sense of mutual safety. They deal with feeling like one's spouse has your back and you've got theirs. John Gottman and Sue Johnson do great research and writing on marital dynamics and success, and I recommend their work. Sex can be affected by the keys—but it's not the key itself.

Healthy decisions as to why to have sex with your partner should not include being a gatekeeper to your partner's propensity for sin. Taking the needs of your partner into account is useful as touched on earlier—at the same time, if sexual decisions preside primarily on managing another's needs, this becomes a very unauthentic way to approach your own needs and feelings, which are equally important.

The slide showing the "numbers" is problematic for me on a number of levels—gossip being primary. I don't think we need to make our points at other people's expense—even sexually infamous people. It also heightens the drama, feeding on the frenzy of the anxiety this subject produces, forming a superficial bond—us against them. And how useful is it to have an "us" and "them" when we are all sinners in different ways to begin with?

If a spouse heads elsewhere for sexual gratification—regardless of the underlying reasons—it's ok to take offense. Sexual boundaries need to be agreed upon within each marriage. They may look different for different couples—they may need to be reworked as you figure out life together and what both your needs are—but for relational health to be optimal, these should be consensual. And if your spouse acts in nonconsensual ways, eroding the trust between you, you have a right to be angry.

If you need to start a fight to have good sex, then I highly suggest marital therapy.

I saw no discussion on how mental or physical health issues can affect sexual desire for either partner. These are legitimate problems spouses need to consider when it comes to realistic expectations and sexual health.

I saw no discussion on what it means to have a "successful" sexual encounter. Many believe that erection, lubrication and orgasm are the only ways to have success. To take the detail further, many have the expectation that orgasm through vaginal intercourse (which only happens for about 35% of women) happening for both partners simultaneously in missionary position is what should happen. I beg to differ. Anything from massage to intercourse to holding hands and snuggling on the couch while watching TV can be considered successful sexuality if framed correctly. And it doesn't matter who reaches orgasm first as long as the couple has a way to continue the play for the other person if wanted. This is where vibrators/dildos can be highly useful.

Bottom line:

It is both the husband and the wife's responsibility to authentically communicate their needs (sexual or otherwise), to recognize their spouse will not be able to meet all their needs, to be willing to compromise, to have empathy for the other's position and libido, and to have marriage-friendly ways of getting their needs met. Pitting one gender against the other is just not useful.

I know I have not been able to touch on every single scenario which would apply to every marriage. I hope my examples do not offend—they are not meant to pigeonhole people into different labels or situations. Sexuality is complex and highly individualized to each person's situation. I see a need for more sexual education and believe it can be done in a helpful way. It saddens me that this bishop's good intentions translated into some deep discomfort and damage for the original poster and others present. It is difficult to address this topic without having personal biases and experiences as well as cultural framework play huge roles in its communication. Please feel free to disagree with me or share your own experiences which were not addressed. Open dialogue can be so healthy when it comes to respectfully challenging preconceived sexual notions. Have at it. . . .

"MORMON MODESTY: WE HAVE TO DO BETTER" BY LISA PATTERSON BUTTERWORTH (SEPTEMBER 24, 2012)

My mom was a very good Mormon mother. And growing up in a small southern-Utah town, all the kids I played with were also raised by good Mormon mothers. So I know from personal experience that back in the 80s it was common for good Mormon mothers to dress their daughters in sun dresses without sleeves. And tank tops and short shorts. We played like this day after day without judgement or self-consciousness. With the innocence of children, you could say. Even in the conservative heart of the Mormon corridor, this just wasn't an issue.

So why is it such an issue today? Why is the church adding sleeves onto images of adorable (and perfectly modest) young girls[226] and classical (and perfectly modest) angels? Why is *modesty*, a topic I remember coming up occasionally as a teen girl, suddenly starting to feel like the center of everything? Every time I turn around my Mormon world is all modesty all the time. (Two articles in the *New Era* and one in *The Friend* this month alone.) And not only for teens who are struggling through puberty and all its adjacent *issues*, but for children,[227] innocent adorable children?

I have a theory. When I was a little girl in the 1980s Strawberry Shortcake was an adorable full-cheeked yarn-haired little girl.

And things have changed. . . .

Today's she is thinner, more sophisticated, more wardrobe!, with long luxurious hair and ever so slightly . . . shall we say "sexy."

This same slightly sexy makeover has happened to everything from Minnie Mouse to My Little Pony. Which is to say nothing of the blatantly sexy toys targeted at the 3–10 y/o market from the scantily clad Bratz and to the new phenom I just found out about, Monster High (think Bratz meets Twilight!)

Every sexy cue is present and accounted for, big eyes, pouty lips, high heels, short skirts, heavy makeup, tiny waist, large bust, impossible (literally) height-to-weight ratio, head-hips-legs all cocked at a come hither angle. All our "sexualized" cues tied up in a bow and marketed to sweet little girls.

Is it any wonder then, that a recent study shows that girls as young as SIX (6!!!!!!!) are sexualizing *themselves*?[228] That's right, six-year-old girls are smart enough to look around them, see that the girls in the skimpy clothes with the big breasts get all the social power, friends, boys, fame, popularity, and all they have to do is be perfect, skinny, polished, and on display for the enjoyment of others. We have all seen it, and not just on the Disney Channel, my kid's school is full of eight-year-olds with highlights, skinny jeans, and wedges.

So it makes perfect sense to me that good Mormon mothers (myself included) would look around at what is happening in "the world" and freak the heck out! (Tons of not-Mormon moms are freaking out too!) It's crazy and it's sick and wrong and it's everywhere. It really makes a ton of sense that some good Mormon mother watched an episode of *Monster High* and said to herself, "I sure am glad *The Friend* talked about modesty again this month."

This is a real problem and Mormons (and everyone) should fight back against this hijacking of childhood innocence. The problem is, that the way we are going about it . . . the Mormon approach is not fixing the problem. In fact our approach . . . well, Mormons are making it worse.

Did you catch that? Maybe I should add some caps: MORMONS ARE MAKING IT WORSE! In fact I think it may be important enough for some clarification and its very own line.
MORMONS ARE CONTRIBUTING TO THE SEXUALIZATION OF YOUNGER AND YOUNGER GIRLS.

Ouch. Right.

But it's true. It's not on purpose, we didn't mean to. And it's from the best of intentions, we only want to protect the joy and innocence of childhood. We only want our girls shielded from this ugly thing that is happening everywhere we look.

But that doesn't change the fact that when "the world" tells our girls that the way to be popular and important is to be pretty and sexy and perfect, then we teach our girls that the way to be good and important is to be pretty and modest and perfect. We aren't countering the sexy argument, we are competing with it. Sexy is hottest, no modest is hottest. It's still about attracting men, it's still about our bodies being on display. It's still putting the power and focus and worth of a whole and complex Divine child of God in the untidy imperfect package of flesh.

We aren't teaching something deeper about how our bodies are temples, a vital part of our very souls (and as Mormons it's a terrible waste of beautiful doctrine that we do not), nor how to love our bodies and how to treat them with respect. We are teaching that our bodies are dangerous and shameful, always the potential to be "walking pornography,"[229] and we must cover them (with stricter and stricter rules, more and more taboos, and longer and longer checklists of modesty judgement) so as not to force those around us to think bad thoughts.

Most of all we are training our girls and our boys to be thinking about their bodies and the bodies of others constantly as objects to be covered. Every good Mormon child I know is almost obsessed with whose shoulders and knees are showing. We have trained our children to look at all the bodies around them, all the time, and make judgements, sexualized judgements about them. Which is not to say that choosing to cover your child's shoulders automatically sexualizes them, it doesn't, it's a totally valid choice. But teaching your children that uncovered shoulders are immodest, disrespectful, or sexual does sexualize them and make them hyper-self-conscious and other-conscious about specific (not inherently sexual) body parts. This is not the natural state of children.[230] And that is 100% on us. Our fault.

We are facing a serious problem, the sexualization of young girls is not only mainstream, it's almost expected. And if we as Mormons are serious about combating this problem, then we need to stop and take a serious look at ourselves. We have to rethink the way we define modesty,[231] the way we view modesty,[232] the way we teach modesty,[233] the way we live modesty.[234]

I do believe we as a people will be held accountable for clinging to the comfortable and easy and false idea that by telling our girls to cover themselves we are combating rather than exacerbating this epidemic. It's so much easier to say, "Cover up because your body is so tempting," than to teach the deeper principals and truths that will truly empower us to break free from the body obsessed sex obsessed shallow cultural forces that we are now feeding rather than fighting.

My daughter just turned 12 and is starting the Young Women program and I'm sick at heart that all the work I have put into teaching her to love her body, to treat her body with love and respect, are about to be bombarded with messages that there is something shameful and potentially harmful to others in her body. She shouldn't have to think about things like that at all, she is still so young and innocent. I want the church to be my ally in this fight, but right now, tragically, I feel the church I love with all my heart is my adversary. And it breaks my heart.

"POLICY TO THEOLOGY: LET'S GET THIS RIGHT" BY ELIZABETH HAMMOND (OCTOBER 8, 2012)

Sister missionaries hold a special place in my life, since they taught me as an investigator and ministered to my needs as a young woman searching for the meaning of existence. And they succeeded.

My initial reaction to the announcement Saturday was not as ecstatic as many people's because I thought that it was a simple policy change, not a change in any female theology. I am a Mormon feminist from the perspective of an anticipated "restoration" of power and an anticipated "further light and knowledge" to come concerning women. That is, there are huge precedents for female liturgical and theological identity in the gospel, and there is the potential to develop exciting female-oriented doctrine about woman's relationship to deity and her destiny in the eternities. I don't see Mormon feminism as trying to change the church per se, but as a vehicle to keep hope alive until those developments finally come.

Lowering the missionary age doesn't directly serve these ambitions, and on my cynical side I decided that all the past decade's rhetoric to young men, imploring then to live up to their privileges and stop being so darned worldly and to prepare to be husbands and missionaries yadda yadda yadda, had failed. "They've been squeezing the young men, those young men must not have delivered, and now the Church is desperate enough to recruit the sisters." I also thought it was a manipulation to keep young women devoted to the Church—some of us who have observed all the marriage rhetoric have speculated that encouraging youth to get married is a great way to keep them active, since families stay more devoted than single members. These knee jerk responses mirrored my first reaction to *Daughters in My Kingdom*,[235] which I saw as trying to write women OUT of church history under the drumbeat of priesthood authority as opposed to trying to write women INTO church history. These first reactions were pretty cynical.

But . . . I have to admit there are signs that the Church is starting to take women's needs seriously. I don't think we're leaning toward equality any time soon, but I do think that this hour in history opens opportunities that we can capitalize upon, and that we can leverage what looks like a simple policy change into a significant future for women in the Church.

1. Let the Church Change

If we want to see progress then we need to be graceful about any progress we see. A change like this could certainly shift the YW rhetoric from   Modesty/Marriage/Motherhood   to Modesty/Mission/Marriage/Motherhood. (Maybe Mission will even replace modesty because we can sell "missionary dress" to the girls instead of making dress a sexual issue.) Some feminists may not necessarily see this policy change as a "victory" or get too excited about something so small, but neither should we focus our energies on begrudging the age-of-service or length-of-service policies. No need to bludgeon the Church for not always having been perfect. We can focus on the positive without being too satisfied with it.

2. Divided We Fall

We learned from the Women's Movement that when you offer new options to a traditionally-defined group, people will start to get passionate about which option is most valid. Enter the Mommy Wars: women get to have careers AND be mothers, so the SAHM and the career moms suddenly jump into the ring over how to be the "best" kind of mother. We Mormons obsess about being perfect anyway, and we'll be prone to discuss which option is "best": marriage, college, or mission (especially once we have girls who could marry or could attend school but feel called to serve). It will be our responsibility to build a church culture where ALL the options (get married/go to college/go on a mission) are EQUALLY VALID for any girl. That is, I could imagine groups of Mormons who believe that opening options is a litmus test for faith: REAL Mormon girls go on missions, or REAL Mormon girls get married. Let's not do this to ourselves. And I don't just mean a nice "you can do either!" sugar line. I mean PREPARING young women for all options.

At the Q&A following the announcement,[236] Holland and Nelson seemed to say there would not be new materials developed as a result of this policy change . . . so young women's leaders (not many of whom have gone on missions) will be left alone to create curriculum to prepare young women for missions, college, AND motherhood. We're pretty good at preparing young women for motherhood, and we now have a significant number of educated leaders to help prepare young women for college (AND we have a Perpetual Education Fund to follow through on that preparation). But how will we now prepare young women for missions? If we are using the same materials as the boys, that's fine, but there will have to emerge a whole new identity for missionaries who don't have the priesthood. Sure, we've had sister missionaries, but now their presence will be significant. What does that look like, what is the Sister Missionary of the new generation? We, as leaders, get to make it up apparently! I think this is actually a good thing, it means we can be creative and empower the young women to think of themselves in different ways than how our church raised us. What a fantastic challenge for us—a new era of identity building left in our hands and not in a correlated manual. Let's seize this!

3. A Generation Rising

It has become obvious to me that the female mission experience is unique in that it is the only time a woman gets to feel like "clergy." A woman gets to teach men! A woman is dedicated to God in a way that focuses on her service and faith, not on her identity as female. I assume this announcement will cause an influx of young women into the mission field, which means that in 20 years we'll have a significant number of female leaders who have served missions and obtained spiritual identities outside of the wife/mother "roles." More sisters serving may lead to the conversion of more women, in effect "feminizing" the church. I definitely feel that the role of the "mission president's wife" (we'll really need a new more respectful moniker for her—any suggestions?) will drastically increase in its responsibility and impact on the church. And not to be underestimated, in 20 years we'll have a significant cadre of male priesthood leaders who have clocked significant experience working with women as their ecclesiastical peers.

Indeed, a person like me who awaits a restoration of female power could easily read this as a churchwide change preparatory to further light and knowledge. I sincerely doubt that the church will adopt an "every young woman a missionary" stance like they did with the young men, but I DO think that by getting women the closest to "clergy" they can be, we can show the church what it's been missing. Pretty soon they'll wonder how they ever got along without us in official service. And maybe, just maybe, that will creep upwards.

4. Constant Vigilance!

In Maxine Hanks's book *Women and Authority*,[237] there is an essay describing how, when women enter a profession that is classically dominated by men, that profession decreases in status. Whether or not this phenomenon is "right" is beside the question—it is observable fact. I could see the service of a mission losing its romantic luster as it becomes so much more commonplace. I could imagine a situation where a division of labor evolves in the mission field, where women do one kind of service and men do another kind (with the men's brand of course requiring priesthood and thereby retaining its more exclusive prominence). It will benefit us all to be very aware of this likelihood, and to start thinking about how to train our young women who may serve missions to advocate for themselves to do the "hard" work in the field and not just gravitate (or more likely, be pushed) towards office work, only doing service instead of proselytizing, working more with children, or mostly teaching English classes. We need women to watch this, on a worldwide and ward level, and contribute to nurturing the concept of "Sister Missionary-hood" so that skewed forms of service don't arise. I think we need a watchgroup to do this, honestly, and do it publicly.

5. Today Is Tomorrow's Church History

The reason we know so much about early church history is not just because we have official documents, but because we have journals of the early saints. Men's journals outnumber women's journals by at least 10 to 1, and more likely, in the proportion of 40 to 1. The reason we have so many men's diaries is because a man was commissioned to keep a diary as part of his missionary service, like the writers of the *Book of Mormon* saw their recordkeeping as a religious duty. These accounts of missions were to serve as records of the power of God working through his people. For many men these days, the ONLY time they keep a journal is when they are on their mission.

Sisters, Brothers, *imagine* what Church History would look like if the women had kept journals. We KNOW it would be different. In my past year of reading the 1870s *Woman's Exponent*, composed for and by women, I have viscerally witnessed a very different kind of spiritual experience, and a very different version of Church History, than what exists in correlated accounts. Female spirituality has so much to add to our church, but it will always have only limited impact unless IT IS RECORDED into the ledgers of heaven. Suddenly, we have an opportunity to not only send out a bunch of women who will have a new kind of spiritual experience, but we have a chance to document female spiritual experience on a massive scale. In another 2–3 generations, when church leaders look back and see God working through the sisters (outside the home), they will not be able to see women through any form of narrow lens.

I implore any who will listen that we ensure female missionaries are commissioned to keep journals, and that somehow, these journals can be submitted, collected, and retained in a central place so they will be preserved. This is not just a nicety: instructing a woman that her life is important enough to write down, that it is critical enough to be preserved in professional archives, that her spirituality is necessary for future generations, is a huge alteration to female church identity. What greater way to enforce a person's inner power than to tell them their spiritual lives are so valid, so real, and so important, that they must be recorded in heaven? Like Jesus coming to the Nephites and asking why they didn't write the words of Samuel, maybe we should be asking, where are the words of the sisters? Here's a chance to institutionalize women's spirituality.

My strongest desire in relation to this policy change is that we will get women's voices into the spiritual history of the church—and show forth how God works through women so that the opportunities and theology of women will be forced to evolve to keep up with us.

I have to admit, this announcement makes me look at my daughters in a new way. If it changed even me, a feminist, to see their potential brighten with a new sheen, imagine what more is possible!

"Mormon Feminists in Whoville and Why You Should Wear Pants to Church this Sunday" by Sandra Ford (December 11, 2012)

One of my favorite stories as a kid was Dr. Seuss's *Horton Hears a Who*.[238] Like any kid, I loved underdogs almost as much as I loved silly rhymes. You know the story. Horton the Elephant is lounging around one fine spring day, when he suddenly hears voices coming from a tiny speck of dust. At first it seems like Horton is insane, but then the speck of dust turns out to be a tiny world called Whoville, home to a community of even tinier beings called Whos. The Whos extract a promise from Horton to protect them, and he agrees because he understands that "even though you can't see or hear them at all, a person's a person, no matter how small." I don't recall exactly how it comes to this, but by some turn of events, Horton's animal compatriots discover what Horton is up to and threaten to destroy Whoville. After all, as far as they're concerned, Whoville is just a dust speck, and Horton is a nut job. The task falls to the Whos to make themselves heard, so they can prove to their detractors that they exist. The Whos jump to action.

> The mayor grabbed a tom-tom. He started to smack it. And, all over Who-ville, they whooped up a racket. They rattled tin kettles! They beat on brass pans, on garbage pail tops and old cranberry cans! They blew on bazookas and blasted great toots on clarinets, oompahs and boom-pahs and flutes!" They also used their voices. If you've seen the animated retelling of the story, you probably remember their refrain: "We are here! We are here! We are here! We are here!

Sometimes, being a Mormon Feminist is a lot like being a Who. Some of us go years and years, thinking we are the only one. We feel like dust specks, invisible to the larger community of Latter-Day Saints. When we're lucky enough to realize that we're not alone, that there are lots of Mormon Feminists, fighting the good fight for gender equality in families and congregations everywhere, it feels like a miracle. There are enough of us that we've formed our own little Whovilles in more liberal cities and here on the internet. Among ourselves, we talk about Mormonism as we understand it, as a gospel of love, acceptance, and forgiveness. We envision a world where we can participate fully in our religion, where we are afforded the same opportunities as our fathers, husbands, brothers, and sons: a place where programs for girls receive funding on par with programs for boys; a place where young women are encouraged to serve missions on the same terms as young men; a place where women can finish their schooling without being criticized for putting off marriage and pursue careers without being condemned for abandoning the home; a place where mothers can bless their sick children and preside alongside their husbands in the home; a place where our spiritual progress is based on our worth as individuals, rather than on our relationships to the men around us.

I'm sure I don't need to tell you, Whoville can be an incredible place to be a Mormon. The problem is that it's still a dust speck. We are invisible to our religious community and to our religious leaders. In some ways, this makes life easier. We can attend church on Sunday, and fulfill our callings, and pretend that all is well, and nobody calls us to repentance, or accuses us of being apostate, or shames us for not getting with the Mormon program. But in other ways, living in Whoville is dangerous. When our religious community doesn't realize that we exist, they inadvertently say and do things that threaten the very existence of Mormon feminists. They make snide comments about the female investigator who wears pants to church. They openly criticize mothers who work to support their families. They ignore single women and women in part-member families and women without kids. Our leaders continue to publish manuals and write articles and give talks that alienate increasingly larger swaths of women. Faithful women who fail to conform to the traditional gender norms espoused by LDS church culture and doctrine, sometimes in spite of their best efforts, find that they can no longer call Mormonism their spiritual home.

Last week, Stephanie of The Mormon Child Bride[239] wrote that she was tired of seeing her sisters "die a slow spiritual death." She published a blog post inviting Mormon Feminists to whoop up our own racket and started a group called All Enlisted for folks interested in joining the cause. All Enlisted is intended to be a place of action—to inspire LDS men and women to engage in acts of peaceful resistance to gender inequality in the larger institution. We draw our inspiration from suffragettes and civil right leaders as we seek to build Zion, a place where women and men truly "all are alike unto God."

For our first event, we organized Wear Pants to Church Day. It is exactly what it sounds like. This Sunday, December 16, 2012, Mormon Feminists the world over will be wearing pants to church. Not jeans, or sweats, or yoga pants, but dress pants. Tailored suits and flowing shalwars and holiday-appropriate black velvet. Pants that are modest, elegant, and feminine, and not at all out of place in a church house. (Not that we think you need to be any of those things to worship God!) The purpose of this event is to give voice to and express support for women who don't conform to traditional gender roles and those who seek gender equality in the LDS church.

When this event was in the planning stages, less than a week ago, wearing pants to church didn't seem like enough. As feminists we want real equality, not equality of dress. Besides, we've been allowed to wear pants to church for a long time now. Really! There's no rule or commandment instructing women to wear dresses and skirts in church. In fact, back in 1971, the First Presidency said,

> The Church has not attempted to indicate just how long women's or girls' dresses should be nor whether they should wear pant suits or other types of clothing.[240]

We chose pants because they are a symbol of the feminist movement and because it seemed like a good way to test the strength of our feminist voices here in Whoville. Many of us knew we'd be alone in our congregations in bucking this cultural norm, and we viewed wearing pants as a way to say, "I am here." Perhaps we'd even start a few conversations with men and women in our wards, or at the very least our families.

Within hours of publishing the event on Facebook, it became clear that we underestimated the strength of our voices, as hundreds of responses, some supportive and some detracting, poured in. It's been a blessed opportunity to explain our frustrations and our worthy desires to our co-religionists, and the discussion has been vigorous.

We're still living on that dust speck, though. People can see what we're doing, but they don't understand why we are doing it. They can't hear us. That's no surprise. Mormon Feminism can be tricky to explain, and we've been silenced so many times. We can't go on living in Whoville, though. As loud as we may think we are, we're still quiet in the grand scheme of Mormonism. Too many women are leaving the church, or refusing to join, because there is no place for them. The ever-powerful social, cultural, and doctrinal messages about who women are and what they can be are threatening to boil our dust speck, or burn it, or just blow it away in the breath after a thoughtless word or a pointed question: Why don't you just leave? We don't want to leave. We are Mormons. We love the gospel. We are here.

I invite you to join us and wear pants this Sunday in solidarity with those of us who seek gender equality everywhere, including the LDS church. And when somebody asks you why you are dressed a little differently, take a moment to tell them. This is our opportunity to make it known: "We are here! We are here! We are here! We are here!"

Register your support for Wear Pants to Church Day here.

If you want to join All Enlisted, please contact me for an invitation. Right now it is just a private Facebook group, but big things are coming.

"POST PANTS: MORMON FEMINISM AND INTER-GROUP COOPERATION" BY TRESA BROWN EDMUNDS (DECEMBER 19, 2012)

I was talking with a very wise friend of mine the other day, a friend who is a professional activist and extremely schooled in how to create change in the world. I was filling her in on the big events in Mormon Feminism, the new groups being formed, the new actions taken, and sharing some of my thoughts about it all. She paraphrased a quote to me: "The great thing about critical thinkers is that they see problems in the world and want to come up with nuanced solutions. The problem with critical thinkers is that they can draw such nuanced distinctions and definitions that they tear their groups apart." Gloria Steinem said something similar in her book *Outrageous Acts and Everyday Rebellions*.[241] She said that certain radical feminists of the day became so obsessed with idealistic purity—did you actually marry a man? Did you have :gasp: children!!? — that there were maybe only three women who they could work with.

There are a multiplicity of approaches needed in activism. The press grabbing ones, the scholarly ones, the gentle pressure ones, the ones who have left to prove the problem and the ones who stay to try and work with leaders to fix it.

With the success of Wear Pants to Church Day, I think it's a good time for us activists to check in with each other, do a little homework, make sure we're humble enough to listen to each other, and then take our next steps as allies with different approaches, back to back and shoulder to shoulder fending off the critics.

I saw a lot of criticism of Mormon Feminism in the roll up to the big event, and what made me sad wasn't the total kookoo birds, although, yes, but the voices that mocked or criticized the efforts of what has come before. Here at FMH we're beyond used to hearing "all you do is talk." I think it's pretty close to white noise to us all now. But hearing it as people were preparing for activism, activism that had its roots on the FMH Facebook page, was disheartening. Hearing people criticize WAVE as ineffective was disheartening, particularly when WAVE's documents were then passed around to explain some of the problems. There were reasons why an endeavor like this couldn't work before, and one of the biggest was that we didn't have the numbers. Mormon Feminists had to put decades into education to radicalize enough people that a statement like this would get noticed, and more time in networking to bring them all together. Those things are dismissed only at the peril of the movement. Without further education and mentoring, we won't have our next generation of Mormon feminists.

What has come before wasn't "not enough," it was what was necessary for the time. Even two short years ago when we started WAVE, I got frantic emails over the threat to my membership. I lost friends who thought that I was going to bring the church stomping down on Mormon Feminism. Two years ago. And now the time is right for large scale demonstrations. It's amazing how things have changed so quickly, and that should offer us all a lot of hope for our future. But as Gloria Steinem says, "Hope is a very unruly emotion."[242]

Hope makes us see possibilities. It makes us see a day when we can move beyond education and into action. It makes us dream of a day when these dialogues are happening on a larger scale and when people are heard. It gives us courage to take a deep breath and take a bigger risk than we ever have before. And sometimes that hope and courage and dreaming makes us talk ourselves up as heroes, bigger heroes than the movement has ever seen. Willing to take "real" risks, unlike all those women of generations past who were too afraid to take a real stand. As maddening as that line of thought is, I don't think it comes from a bad place, I think it comes from hope. Unruly, wild, world changing hope. That needs a dose of education and humility to be transformed into faith.

So what does our friend Gloria suggest? She talks about feminine organizational structures and refers to the dynamic as "linking, not ranking."[243] Instead of ranking all our different organizations by how "radical" or "effective" they are, or by whatever other arbitrary value you want to name, we should link our organizations together, just as we intuitively ended up doing as the Pantsapocalypse unfolded. FMH and ExII provided support and networking and education, just as they have for years, WAVE provided support and materials, Zelophehad's Daughters provided their inimitable blend of education and snark, and All Enlisted provided the catalyst and the energy. Next time around we can think of ways to broaden our reach with the Mormon Women's Forum, or even Mormon Women Project, using our different techniques, skills, expertise and audiences to create something more far reaching and powerful than anything we could do alone.

This is how activism always works. Newly radicalized people are almost always disdainful of previous efforts. It's part of the radicalization process. We all have to work on rooting out the old scripts that still plague us, including the esteem we once had for women and feminists, unconscious or not.

> This is the most tragic punishment that society inflicts on any second-class group. Ultimately the brainwashing works, and we ourselves come to believe our group is inferior. If we achieve a little success in the world, we think of ourselves as "different," and don't want to associate with our group. We

want to identify up, not down. .... And this lack of esteem that makes us put each other down is still the major enemy of sisterhood.[244]

Sister Steinem has been at this longer than any of us. In her book she demonstrates that the work of feminism is just as much internal as it is external. Searching through beliefs you didn't know you had, choices you made that you didn't understand, reactions that took you by surprise. And as you excavate your true self out from under the weight of patriarchy, you can join the generations of women who have kept putting one foot in front of the other to get you where you are today. And then you can get walking down that road in preparation for the women who are coming.

Church leaders called Bonnie Oscarson as the Young Women's General President in the April General Conference. Missionaries began using social media to proselyte. In September, the Church released the first of the Gospel Topics essays: Race and the Priesthood.[245] This series attempted to explain challenging topics in Church history. The October conference brought news that the worldwide membership of the LDS Church had grown to 15 million.

Utah State legislators introduced a bill that would prohibit job and housing discrimination based on sexual orientation, but it failed before a vote took place. On December 20, a district court judge overturned Utah's ban on same-sex marriage on the grounds that it violated the US Constitution's Equal Protection Clause. The Church instructed local leaders not to perform same-sex marriages or allow such marriages in Church-owned buildings. For just over two weeks, same-sex marriage was legal in Utah, and many couples married during that window.

Claudia Bushman and Caroline Kline, both connected to the *Exponent II* community, edited a volume of academic essays titled *Mormon Women Have Their Say: Essays from the Claremont Oral History Collection.*[246] Jessica Finnigan and Nancy Ross surveyed the Mormon feminist online community, collecting information and stories from more than 1,800 individuals. They published the first of a series of articles and book chapters on the online Mormon feminist movement later in the year.[247]

Feminist Mormon Housewives Society, a closed Facebook group started in late 2012, grew rapidly this year. It provided a private place for Mormon feminist discussion that allowed people to use their real names instead of the pseudonyms that people tended to use as bloggers and commenters. It was also a key place to post news and to recruit organizers and participants for the activist events and organizations that took place throughout 2013 and beyond.

In the wake of Wear Pants to Church Day in December 2012, Young Women's General President Elaine Dalton gave a devotional at BYU where she said that Mormon women had no need to "lobby for rights."[248] Not long afterward, All Enlisted organized the letter-writing campaign Let Women Pray. Mormon feminists wrote to Church leaders asking that a woman be allowed to pray in a session of General Conference, which had not happened before. On April 6, Jean Stevens became the first woman to do so.

Lorie Winder Stromberg, Hannah Wheelwright, and Kate Kelly founded Ordain Women, whose website launched on the birthday of the Relief Society, March 17.[249] The website hosted profiles of women and men who declared their belief that women should be ordained to the priesthood in the LDS Church. Ordain Women organized a direct action where women asked to be admitted to the Priesthood Session of the October General Conference. Church officials denied the women entry to the meeting.

Activists created the website Mormonfeminist.org, which hosted profiles of Mormon feminists explaining their reasons for participating in the movement. Different members of the community took over the organization of the second Wear Pants to Church Day. Heather Olson Beal started the Equality is Not a Feelings series on the Doves and Serpents blog, which offered numerous responses to the challenge that many women felt equal to men in the Church. Mexican Mormon feminists held their first meeting, offering support to each other and identifying key goals for the group.

"A WOMAN'S PRAYER" BY ALICE FISHER ROBERTS (JANUARY 15, 2013)

When I was very small, before even my earliest memory, a counselor in the bishopric of our ward came down from the stand, walked down the aisle to where my grandmother sat, probably one row ahead of my family, and asked her to pray in our sacrament meeting. This may not seem like a big deal, but it was, because my grandmother became the first woman to ever pray in sacrament meeting in our ward.

35 years later, it is now common place for women to give prayers in sacrament meeting. Although even just a few years ago there was a clarification because many wards were still restricting women from giving either the opening or closing (it was different in different wards, depending on which "tradition" they were following).

For the last ten years of my life, I have paid attention to prayers in general conference, hoping, and always feeling the twinge of disappointment that it was a man again. Does it matter who gives the prayer? It shouldn't. But after so many years of noticing that women never pray in general conference, one eventually starts to wonder why? In 1978, President Kimball released a First Presidency statement saying,

> There is no scriptural prohibition against sisters offering prayers, it is permissible for sisters to offer prayers in any meetings they attend.[250]

The most common explanation I have heard as to why women are not asked to pray in conference is because "there are so many more men in leadership positions, and they want to give them all a chance to pray, so going off the numbers it wouldn't make sense to have women pray."

Ignoring the problem of "so many more men in leadership positions," let's look at the numbers, thank you to Heidi Doggett[251]...

> The number of General Conference prayers we've had since President Kimball lifted the 1960's ban on women praying in Sacrament meeting, and said that we should be able to pray in any church meeting: 560
>
> Number of men in the two main Quorums of 70, the Apostles, YM's and Sunday School Presidencies and the First Presidency: 163
>
> Number of female church authorities: 9, counting the Primary Presidency, YW Presidency and the RS presidency.
>
> The ratio of female to male General Conference prayers in the last 35 years is 0:560.
>
> The ratio of female to male church leadership is 9:163
>
> Saying that the reason women haven't prayed is because there are so few of them does not add up. Literally.

Would my life change if when I sat down to watch conference, I was greeted with a prayer given by a member of the young women's general board? Probably not, although my heart would burn with gratitude at having a quiet desire of my heart come to pass. I don't think my grandmother's life changed because she was invited to pray in sacrament meeting. What changed is that in my life, I've never had to wonder why women aren't allowed to pray in sacrament meeting. I've never wondered what is is about my prayers, or what it is about me or women in general that somehow makes it inappropriate for us to pray in sacrament meeting. I hope my granddaughters have the same experience with praying in general conference.

I hope and pray that as a church family, we can let go of traditions that, while they may not cause us pain personally, cause others pain. I hope that we can reach out and say, I don't understand why you hurt, but I love you, and I will stand beside you and do what I can do to fix the things that are hurting you.

"TRACY MCKAY SCHOLARSHIP UPDATE: A TRUE MIRACLE WROUGHT THROUGH YOU" BY TRACY MCKAY (FEBRUARY 5, 2013)

The Bishop's Storehouse has always been one of my favorite places in the Church. A million years ago, before life blew apart and school overtook me— back when my life looked like the cover of the Ensign, and we all find in a tight tidy little box— I would volunteer each Wednesday at the Storehouse. My job was to cook a hot lunch, using the food available to those being served, with enough for all the staff and whatever patrons wished to join us for the meal. It was a big job- usually cooking for around 30 people. I loved it.

My day would start early, arriving sometimes with a child in tow, while the produce boxes were still arriving for the day and the forklifts were busily moving pallets of wheat and sugar onto high racks in the other parts of the cavernous, cold warehouse. Heading first to the kitchen, I'd turn switches and knobs, and start the old industrial appliances warming up, and then make my way into the walk-in and the market area. Using up what was near date was important, but so was teaching people what delicious meals could be made from what the Storehouse offered.

One of my favorite parts of a wholly favorite calling was the prayer meeting we would have before we opened the doors to receive patrons. There were many of us that were there each week, and there was always a smattering of new faces, there to volunteer and learn. Each morning we would gather on church chairs in the office of the couple that ran the operation. We'd talk over the plans and goals for the day, answer questions, and have a brief scripture and prayer.

One morning, and new person spoke up, asking what we should do if someone looked like they might not need help. The storehouse manager, a gruff retired fireman with gnarled hands the size of leather mitts, who beat cancer (twice),turned his bright blue eyes towards the person. The room went quiet.

"Brothers and Sisters, in this Storehouse, we are called— commanded— to serve the Lord's children. We are not to look for anything beyond having our hearts open to seeing the person before us a child of the Lord, and we are to serve. It does not matter what anyone has or has not. If they show up here, we will feed them, we will love them, and we will send them away knowing their Heavenly Father cares about them, through our hands.

"We are to serve with our entire hearts, with everything we have. If you think you cannot do that, if that might be a problem, you cannot be here."

I have never, ever forgotten those words.

This is the spirit I carry with me. When the day came and I was unable to serve any longer, and I had to walk into the bishop's storehouse with my own yellow copy of a food order, hot tears in my eyes, I knew how I would be received.

When my life fell apart, my husband disappeared, my house foreclosed, my divorce final, kids and school on overload, and I had to depend on others to keep my head above water, I knew how I would be received.

And then the day came where I didn't know how I would be received anymore- where the safety net that had been provided me was now to be made ready for others. This was terrifying, and yet, was also part of a cycle of trusting, learning and having faith in not only God, but in the hands of his servants here in the world.

Because of what at first seemed like a panicked free-fall into desperation actually opened the window for something beautiful and utterly amazing to happen. I don't toss around words like "miracle' often... but in my case, in my last year of my undergrad, single with three kids, a true miracle was wrought in my life.

And it was wrought through you.

Tresa called me. She said, "Tracy, we got this one." My throat still tightens when I think of that day, and how those words changed the course of my life.

Your hands are the hands of the divine. Look down at them... they are so beautiful. They are made of the same molecules, stardust and atoms as God. And last year those hands reached out into the darkness and lifted not only me—through lifting me, they lifted my children, and quite possibly the generations to come.

My children will have a very different future now than they would have had if I had not managed to graduate from college, if I had not done well enough to be accepted into a graduate program. They have now seen their mother work hard, and they understand the value of education in a way that is not abstract, and is deeply meaningful.

The Feminist Mormon Housewives Scholarship[252] enabled me to pay for the last two semesters of college, apply to grad schools, and keep our heads above water until I was able to secure employment.

When you educate a mother, you educate the future.

Please join in supporting the FMH Scholarship as we solicit applications and find a new mother to grace with an amazing future full of opportunities.

****

Tracy McKay was the inaugural recipient of the FMH Scholarship, and Sara made her cry when she called to tell her they were naming it after her. She graduated Magna Cum Laude last year, and today lives outside of Washington DC, waiting for her grad program in Autism Studies to being in the spring. She's a Mormon, and a feminist. And she's chomping at the bit to give back

"ACTIVISM AND FMH: CAN WE CHANGE THE CHURCH?" BY NATALIE HAMILTON KELLY (FEBRUARY 26, 2013

Most everybody who reads or participates in FMH wants to see change come to the church. We all have long lists of the things we want to see changed. We're all united on that front. But we have more difficulty finding agreement when it comes to deciding how to go about creating that change. I spend a great deal of my day-to-day life negotiating with power structures, and developing/carrying out strategies for how to change the way things happen. I wanted to open a dialogue among Mormon feminists about strategy for approaching activism within the church, and also explain how FMH officially fits into that picture.

There are a few principles of building a strong, comprehensive campaign for change that I think are often overlooked. They are especially overlooked by people who desperately NEED change, for the good of their soul. Sometimes, our very valid, long overlooked emotions drive us to actions that feel really good, but maybe aren't that smart. So let's lay out some of those principles.

First principle: Know your goal. Know how your action will affect that goal. Don't be too proud to drastically change the action if you realize it will not aid in achieving your goal.

I'm sure most of us could think of 18 different ways to bring attention in a really loud public way about female inequality in the church. We could throw rocks in the windows of the Boy Scouts of America headquarters. We could send a group of vocal feminists to Thomas S. Monson's house to speak to him on his front porch. We could publish in the NY Times scandalizing exposes about all the bad stuff any Mormon leader has ever said about women.

But what are our goals? To shame leaders? To open minds about feminism? To challenge people to think differently about structures of power and prophetic authority? To get media attention? To speak authentically? To scare the church into change? To convince people to leave the church? To help teeny tiny new baby feminists decide that it's okay to speak up about their concerns?

These different goals will lead to very different actions. Delegating (when "delegating" is defined as when a group of people acting together demand an audience with a decision-maker in a way that is unscheduled, so as to control the setting and content of the conversation) Thomas S. Monson as he walks into a temple dedication would be awesome. It would feel super good and righteous. It would let people air a lot of legit grievances. But it would make those new baby feminists run the other way with their *skirt* between their legs. And it would make those old, faithful ladies, who love the church and the prophet but still see that things could change, discount the movement entirely. It would shame Monson, and make the church look bad in the public eye, so if that's your goal, there you go.

Personally, the two goals that I see as paramount are 1) organizing the base, developing more feminists, and 2) changing cultural beliefs about power and authority. Since goal #2 (which I really, really, really believe in) is a far distant, super-lofty, indirect goal, and since really, it can only be achieved through #1, I am comfortable staging my actions around goal #1. I also, incidentally, believe that this is how change will ultimately come to The Church of Jesus Christ of Latter-day Saints. What do we need to do to bring more people into this movement? How can we create community, build bridges, educate, change minds, and create the kind of environment that sparks beautiful, spontaneous action at the ward and family level?

Let's keep that goal (or whatever goal you have) always in mind when deciding next steps.

Second Principle: Always save something for escalation.

Many activists, in their desire to unleash all those years of rage, in the dizzying fervor of how it feels SO AWESOME to finally be taking action, want to stage the biggest, memorablest, badassest action possible. Because it's AWESOME. Speaking truth to power, baby! Pretty visual props! Exciting energy! News coverage!

But unfortunately, no real power structure worth its salt is going to change its ways because of one perfect, beautiful, memorable action. The first response of power to agitation for change is always, always, always retrenchment. Power only gives ground when it feels it has no other choice. Companies only let unions in if continuing to fight them will cost more than allowing them. Bullies only stop bullying if the risks of carrying on outweigh the perverse satisfaction that comes from the act. The church as a corporation will only change when it feels like failing to change is going to cost it more.

And a strong badass action will elicit a strong reaction. And that reaction might scare people. And those people might not show up for the next event. And if you already maxed out your creative strategizing, and you didn't get the outcome you wanted, and you lost support, how are you ever going to follow that up? What are you ever going to do next that will be even more powerful? Following up a powerful dramatic action with something wimpy makes you look, well, wimpy. And doesn't help you get taken seriously.

A smart strategy will start small, with safe, identifiable practices, that can build support, and lay out a clear moral high ground. Strategists should be well aware that sticking to the moral high ground could very well not get them what they want. They should do it anyway. Because when it fails, and they have a long track record of nice tactics to point to, and a swelling mass behind them that joined because those nice tactics really convinced them it was right, they can move much more confidently onto more aggressive militant strategies. And those will be beautiful and shiny.

Another advantage to taking the moral high road is that it allows the power structure to give in to your demands while still saving face. That is one of the single biggest considerations for the LDS power structure. So the moment they can no longer give in while saving face (by claiming it was all their idea), the likelihood that they will change or respond diminishes drastically.

But aggressive, militant strategies that are premature and that lack broad support are nothing more than self-satisfying gimmicks, if they actually undermine the goal of organizing more feminists.

Third principle: Don't polarize until it will work in your favor.

Taking strong, decisive, public actions will get attention. What we have learned from recent events is that the media (especially in Utah) is going to jump on ANY story about Mormon feminists. And if that happens prematurely, if we don't have a clear message, and disciplined participants, unified around a common goal (see principle #1), we are going to lose control of the conversation at that point. Any public action is going to get up the hackles of about 80% of active church members automatically. We have no interest in organizing them. It's the 20%, that may be sympathetic if they can be organized, that we need to focus on. Force an issue prematurely, take drastic action that makes people choose sides–well, if they're not organized, they're almost always going to choose the side that feels safe. And for much of that 20%, ditching feminism and sticking with the hierarchy is the default safe option.

But if we've done our work well; if we have clear goals; if we have publicly established that we are the good guys, that we are reasonable, that we have the same interests and beliefs as our audience; when those polarizing actions come, a few more people might be ready to pluck up their courage and stand on the side of change.

And THAT is what will make change happen.

****

So where does FMH fit in with all of this? I think looking at PANTS explains a lot. All Enlisted burst onto the Mormon feminist scene with this proposed action. Pants was hugely successful. It challenged thinking, but in a way that was safe enough for many, many fence-sitters to come over to our side. It was simple and direct and very high ground. It had thousands of supporters the world over.

That support did not suddenly exist because of one Facebook event or page. The smart strategy and effective messaging had to be paired with a decade of hard, unpaid, constant organizing. Feminist Mormon Housewives, Exponent II, Zelophehad's Daughters, By Common Consent, Mormon Women Project and countless feminists acting in their local congregations…. all these have been doing grunt work for YEARS to educate, educate, educate, and develop new theories, ideas, and leaders. PANTS was a brilliant step, and it was possible because of the diligent creative strategy of the planners at AE, and the years of groundwork by the larger community.

That's what FMH does best. FMH is not opposed to activism. A multiplicity of approaches is the best way to ensure a lively, creative, sustainable movement. Militant radicals in the trenches persuade the powers that be to negotiate with the less dangerous feminists. It's all vital. But what FMH does best is build that base; find those baby feminists; create solidarity; and host conversations about what the next steps should be.

FMH is not always going to be the one to carry out those steps. Since fingers point to us first at the bare mention of Mormon feminism, we are careful to preserve our cred and environment for a wide tent of MoFems. This does not mean we hate activism and think everyone should restrict their activity to online conversation. It does not mean that many of us wouldn't love to see the entire structure of the Church Office Building change in the twinkling of an eye. But it means that we have to maintain this place to do the work that should be at the heart of any good campaign strategy: ORGANIZING.

Put your shoulders to the wheels, sistren and brethren. There is much pushing to do. We gotchyo back.

"IT HAS BEEN CONFIRMED: WOMEN WILL PRAY" BY AMBER CHORUBY WHITELEY (MARCH 19, 2013)

(If you haven't read this article confirming in the SL Trib, you need to, NOW!)[253]

When we first began organizing "Let Women Pray" months ago, a question I had in the back of my mind was constantly bugging me: "Will this letter-writing campaign encourage progress?" I honestly answered, "I don't know."

I fully expected that no changes would be made, and understandably so. Leaders wouldn't want to appear like they conform to pressure. We even had several critics on the "Let Women Pray" page saying that they would be disappointed if the church leaders did allow a woman to pray in general conference. They didn't want their leaders to give in to protesting.

Of course, I had a different perspective. I thought that if a woman prayed in general conference, it would show Christ-like compassion on the part of our leaders. It would show me that this church isn't concerned as much about rules and politics as they are concerned about the well-being of their members.

I also thought, "This change is so small, why even bother? Why dedicate hours and days of my time to this?"

And then it came to me: change is change. And now a woman will be praying on behalf of the general population of the church—millions of men, women and children—for the first time in history.

Let me repeat myself: a woman will be praying on the behalf of millions for the first time in history!

I understand that for some, this is upsetting. I understand that having a woman pray isn't as big of a change as we all would like to see, but before anyone becomes upset with this small step, please understand the real meaning behind this: Church leaders are willing to listen to us. They are willing to make changes for us. They care about us.

They could have chosen to wait to allow a woman to pray until the fall general conference to appear not to have heard us, but they didn't.

Not only did they read our letters, YOUR letters, asking for a woman to pray, but they also read your letters and learned about the pain some of your experiences. They read and know about Mormon feminism, and they know that it is so much more than pants and prayers.

However exciting this is, in the back of my mind, I know that this isn't the end to my efforts. This is a small step towards equality. In fact, this is only the beginning, line upon line and precept upon precept, right? Now that we know that progress can be made, we should all take a collective step back and begin to ask ourselves, "What's next?"

We now know that our leaders and our Heavenly Parents will listen to our heartfelt pleas and our concerns, so I'd like to challenge all of you to be brave, to express yourselves, and engage open, honest conversations with anyone and everyone you feel comfortable doing so. One thing I have learned from my involvement with "Let Women Pray" is that I am most happy when I am brave enough to be my most genuine self with everyone I can. Speak up in Sunday School, engage in conversations with your bishops. When you start to feel scared, remember that you are not alone in this.

This is small progress with so much power, so much potential. Only time will tell what this small step leads towards. I'm excited to see what progress we will all bring forth together in the near future.

"Thoughts on the Ordination of Women? Our Diversity of Views" by Lisa Patterson Butterworth, Alice Fisher Roberts, Natalie Hamilton Kelly, Laurie Burk, Lindsay Hansen Park, Elizabeth Hammond, Nikki Matthews Hunter, Tresa Brown Edmunds, Derek Staffanson, Melissa Mayhew, Kimberly Fitzpatrick Lewis, Ryan Hammond, and Joanna Brooks (March 21, 2013)

It's an exciting time to be a feminist in religion! What with Catholic feminists pinking up the sky[254] above the newly-announced pope, and a new group dedicated to Mormon women being ordained to the Priesthood,[255] it seems the sky is the limit on what we can imagine and discuss. Ordination is a crucial issue within Mormonism, and feminists have a wide variety of feelings about what should be done. Just to give you a flavor, here are what some of your local FMH permabloggers have to say on the topic. Weigh in with your thoughts in the comment section below.

Lisa Patterson Butterworth: I understand why female ordination is important to many women, as a matter of simple equality or as a longing for access to great spiritual gifts, but I myself have never *felt* strongly inspired to take that stand.

I suppose ordination of women is one of my shelf issues, put it up on a shelf, keep on keeping on, and I'll think about it later. Would I love to see it happen? Yes. Do I think it's logical and necessary for true structural institutional equality? Yes. So why don't I feel a strong need to advocate for it? I suppose I should examine that. ... There is the obvious fear of judgement. I have always wanted to be a good and faithful Mormon woman (and am shallow enough to want to be seen as such by my family and friends), and it's no secret that publicly advocating for giving women the priesthood is the fastest road to being written off as a scary hairy-legged unisex-bathroom power-hungry women's lib-er.[256]

I think illustrative of this taboo is the fact that when asked, Mormon men are much more likely to be in favor[257] of female priesthood than women ourselves are. I'm sure there many reasons for this,[258] but ultimately men can favor women's ordination without fear of being labeled dangerous power-grubbers. The ladies, not so much.

Upon further examination, I suspect not having authority to exercise priesthood pains me a lot more deeply than I've ever allowed myself to explore. More than simply the "judgement" problem, I also genuinely do not want to be in opposition to the church, I don't want to set myself up as an enemy or to *be* unfaithful, because I do love the gospel and I do recognize the power of revelation and priesthood.

But my desire to be faithful does not negate the hurt and longing I feel every time my husband gives our children a blessing and I know that if I were to do the same thing I would be seen as a dangerous unfaithful rebel. Even the man I love with all my heart is deeply uncomfortable with the idea of me being involved in a blessing, and can I blame him, when I too am uncomfortable with it? Yet it seems so counterintuitive that something so rooted in faith, a longing to use the spiritual gifts we have been promised, the same spiritual gifts our foremothers exercised routinely,[259] would make me unfaithful. My husband has access to and connection to our Father's power through the priesthood, and he is celebrated and admired for using these gifts. But I have no (sanctioned) access to or connection to our Mother's power, and the very desire to connect with Her is taboo. It hurts but I don't generally let myself dwell on it (until right now I guess). (Please note that the standard responses "I don't feel that pain" or "Your pain is selfish/silly/unimportant" aren't very useful or Christlike.)

I know for many faithful Mormons the idea of women having the priesthood seems reasonable, and I think if the prophet announced this change tomorrow most would welcome it (I know my very conservative family feels this way). But the idea of women *advocating* for priesthood they find problematic, even offensive, because these kinds of changes should be directed by revelation, from the prophet, not from the desires nor pain nor logic of women like me. But the truth is our church has a long history of bottom up innovation,[260] and this fact should never threaten our belief in a living Prophet who directs the church. I do not think the women who advocated for the Primary program[261] intended to undermine the Prophet, they saw a need and felt called to fill it. The fact that the Prophet did not receive a direct revelation from the Lord outlining every minute detail, including the lesson plans and song book, does not make the Primary program less inspired.

It is our communities that make us strong, together as a church we make the body of Christ, the Prophet can't and shouldn't do all the thinking nor receive all the inspiration. I do not have the keys to have inspiration for the church, but I can be inspired to speak openly of my pain and the desires of my heart. It is likely that the Prophet did not see a need for a children's program because the Prophet spent far less time interacting with children and trying to meet their spiritual needs. And if taboo and fear prevent women from speaking, how is the Prophet to know our needs and our pain?

I have very confused feelings about the Ordain Women movement. I worry that this might cause schism between more moderate and more radical parts of the Mofem movement (thus our attempt here to model disagreement with love and respect), I worry that it might inspire retrenchment in the church bureaucracy, I worry for the women themselves and the consequences they may face in their communities and even from the church. I hope that these brave women will help lift the taboo against even talking about this issue, I do not believe that the current culture of silence and fear and judgment and shame helps anyone.

I deeply love and respect the women involved and I believe in their good intentions and I admire their willingness to face the taboo of asking for equality and seeking righteous power at great personal risk. Their pain is my pain and they are my sisters in Zion.

Alice Fisher Roberts: I'm excited that this movement is out in the open (and I think the website is beautifully done). I don't think women's ordination is an issue that can be lobbied for directly, I think any official change in regard to the priesthood would have to come from God through revelation. However, I also think that we rarely get revelation for questions we don't ask. I hope that taking President Hinckley at his word[262] and showing that there is a faithful agitation for change provides the needed nudge for our leaders to take the issue to God.

Several years ago, I had a newborn baby that wouldn't sleep, and as I walked laps around the living room in the dark of night, trying to soothe his crying, I prayed for him, as his mother, that he would be calmed and be able to sleep peacefully. Thinking about this, and many other times when I've had sick or injured children, I can't imagine that loving Heavenly Parents would listen to my prayers for my children less than they listen to my Mister when he gives them a priesthood blessing. That combined with blessings of the temple, and reading about my great great great great grandmother[263] who recorded in her journal blessings she gave to other women, make me think that there is something missing here. Something we don't understand, perhaps something different than the priesthood. Whatever it is, it is something that feels integral to my very person, I experience it at those times when I feel called upon by God to serve or lead or comfort, and I feel strong and capable and sure of my actions. Perhaps this is what priesshood is. I hope that we can ask for greater understanding and blessings and have the windows of heaven opened, because I truly believe that whatever the answer, God can soothe all troubled hearts.

nat kelly: First of all . . . YAY! We are talking about this! This conversation is not off-limits and should be treated seriously. I'm so happy so many Mormon women and men are feeling empowered to honestly explore and discuss their feelings on this issue.

In any conversation about women's ordination, I find it useful to start out clarifying what we're talking about. In Mormonspeak, Priesthood refers to two distinct things.

1. Spiritual gifts and ministering—healing blessings, rituals such as baptism/sacrament, receiving inspiration, etc.
2. Temporal authority to administer and lead and make decisions.

In the current church, these two iterations of Priesthood are completely conflated. In practice, they are inseparable, now more than ever before in church history. As time goes on, and they are more conflated, those without the official priesthood lose ever more authority to exercise the spiritual gifts aspect of priesthood.

I'll start by saying now that I see ample scriptural precedence for women's full and equal participation in both of these understandings of Priesthood. I see no doctrinal justification for blocking access to either category based on gender.

I believe the first category is something that is already available to all people. I believe any woman has the right to lay claim to her own spiritual power and spiritual gifts and exercise it as inspiration leads her. I also recognize that many women who feel inclined to do this are hurt by the institutional refusal to recognize their right to participate in official ordinances such as baptisms and public baby blessings. I unequivocally support their desire for ordination to gain access to these roles.

Even more troubling to me, however, is that exclusion from the Priesthood means total exclusion from the governing bodies of the church. Every final decision-maker at every level of the church is male. These men might have hearts of gold and be filled with love, but they can never fully understand women's experience in the church because they will never have it—they will never FEEL it. Invariably, then, these men making ALL the decisions will overlook women's needs. Sometimes this oversight is harmless, but sometimes it is devastating.

One solution to this is to change our current understanding of what Priesthood is. But if administrative authority and decision-making is decoupled from the Priesthood, I will advocate just as vigorously for women to have full access to whatever power structure exists.

The church proclaims equality. But as long as male leaders always have jurisdiction over the lives and roles of women, women's needs cannot be fully represented. And until the needs of women are represented in leadership, there cannot be equality.

And I believe that without equality, there cannot be Zion.

So I support the ordination of women to all the rights and responsibilities of the Priesthood.

Laurie Burk: I am not a joiner and I'm not one who likes to be constrained by a system or a quorum or a corporation. (Yes, I was born in the church. . . .) The whole structure of quora and obedience and hierarchy contained in the priesthood structure gives me the heebie jeebies. It's too much control: it's more hierarchy to place oneself in, and I don't like it. However, having said that, and as things stand now, as long as there is such a strong link between institutional power and the priesthood, there won't be a real voice for women in the church without priesthood.

Personally I'd be most happy if the management and decision making arms of the church were separated from the priesthood and if all the words obscuring and repressing female power and female blessings and female access to the divine would just get flushed down the metaphorical toilet of history. If the governance of the church could be de-linked from priesthood, and the power that we women have lost to patriarchy and history and correlation and to ourselves could be restored or taken back, and if we all would stop believing that a woman's power is weak or subservient or in need of permission from men—that would solve a lot of the problems of sexism in the church.

(I'd also add that at least the way I read the Doctrine & Covenants, what we call priesthood is a very very different animal than what most religions mean when they say priesthood. But that is a topic for another day.)

Lindsay Hansen Park: I'm pretty schizophrenic about my Mormonism, so it makes sense that I still haven't landed on a solid position regarding women's ordination. I've never firmly taken on the issue myself, but that doesn't mean I'm not supportive. My personal reservations include not feeling particularly "called" to it (but that could certainly be a product of my upbringing and cultural taboos) and seeing female ordination as yet another thing women need to ask permission for from men in the church. I realize that is neither a practical observation or a helpful one. The reality is, our church equates priesthood duties with administration duties, so women will never be equal to men in either visibility and participation or status until ordination is granted. And the usual excuses given for women not having the priesthood just don't cut it. Also, I've been spending a considerable amount of time with ordained women in the Community of Christ (formerly RLDS). These women are such a powerful example to me of leadership, love, holiness and ministry, and they really stir up feelings of sadness for the giftedness that is being robbed from women in our church. Women have many, many gifts that are just flat-out being wasted simply because our designated roles don't allow for women to use certain gifts. I say it's a spiritual tragedy. If women's ordination through men can rectify that, then it needs to happen. We are not living up to our full potential as a church.

Elizabeth Hammond Door #1: If I am to believe that there is no difference between women and men, then of course women should be ordained. I think this door has already been slammed in my face. Door #2: If I am to embrace the idea of gender essentialism, that women and men are inherently different, then I cannot believe that any man can give a woman her priestesshood. I don't believe a priest has priestesshood keys or the ability to bestow any divine power on a woman. In Mormon history, we used to think in terms of Father/Mother, God/Goddess, King/Queen, Priest/Priestess. I believe we have not yet emerged, as a covenant people, from the second Great Apostasy: we lie in darkness about the knowledge of our Heavenly Mother and our own eternal destinies as women and Female Creators in our own apotheosis. So do I think women should be ordained? Yes, by our Heavenly Mother, the great Eternal Priestess, and no amount of agitation to Church Headquarters can make that happen. I believe it has to happen like the restoration of the priesthood: that there is an awakening where people's hearts start to turn, as it were, to the mothers. Perhaps when enough of our hearts have done so, She'll respond and teach us Herself about what womanhood and priestesshood really mean. Door #3: On the other hand . . . if I were to believe I already have priestesshood through my temple "endowment" of power, I have no desire for my priestesshood to follow a hierarchical model like the priesthood does. . . . I'd much rather live in a church where women's priestesshood power is legitimated, but not controlled by leaders, keys, or committee. So right now, I am not in a hierarchy, and try to use this to my advantage. I like to try to live as though I have a priestesshood without a High Priestess—I give myself callings, establish some of my own individual and family rituals, I call upon my power, and I expect it to work. Those gifts of the Spirit are legitimate even for women (Healing! Tongues! Prophecy!) and will work for me whether I have a priestesshood or not. They may not be sources of administrative power, but they are still sources of ministerial power, and that's what matters to me most. I prefer to believe in door #2, but live door #3— because even if I don't have priestesshood yet, living like I do may best help prepare me to receive it. I look forward to when all the sistren can exercise our power together, while our husbands, sons, and daughters look on in wonder.

Nikki Matthews Hunter: My feelings about ordination are complicated, because I cherish the idea of a priestesshood, where women administer to each other and to their families, as in this beautiful account of women anointing and blessing both a pregnant woman and her soon-to-be born baby, from my own childhood home stake of Oakley, Idaho[264] (see p. 21), early in the 20th century. I grieve that we have lost this sacred, personal way of relating to and helping one another, and wish for its reclamation. On the other hand, because priesthood is now so attached to the idea of governance and voice in the institutional church, is a separate-but-perhaps-unequal authority enough to give women the voice needed to help the church progress toward institutional equality? As President Monson put it in a priesthood conference a couple of years ago, the priesthood is "the authority to act as God's servants, to administer to the sick, to bless our families, and to bless others as well. Its authority can reach beyond the veil of death, on into the eternities. There is nothing else to compare with it in all this world."[265] Why would desiring such a gift be unrighteous, regardless of gender? Spiritual gifts are given without regard to gender; why must this authority to bless and act be restricted? If the answer to ordination is "no," I can surely accept it, but I would like to know that the question has been brought before God with the seriousness and attention that it deserves.

Tresa Brown Edmunds: It's interesting to me to read so many of my fellow permas state that they don't feel a calling to the priesthood. Because I do. Not just out of a sense of fairness or equity, but a true spiritual calling to ministry.

It is hard to discuss this publicly without climbing up a rameumptom, but as I see all these women I love and admire, women who have completely dedicated their lives to ministry over the internet, say that they don't feel the calling, I wonder why that is. It's quite probable they can fulfill their missions without ever paying any attention to the formality of a priesthood. But maybe it's also the deep taboo that so often has us Mormon women denying ourselves. Maybe it's that nobody stands up and says, "You are not prideful, or a sinner. You are a devout disciple. And I feel it too."

Things in my ward have been tough over the last few years. I'm viewed with a great deal of suspicion, and until recently I tried to change that. But now I've decided that if I'm going to be viewed as a witch, I'm going to claim the freedom that gives me. Which means that I'm going to publicly state that I believe I have been called. I feel powerful spiritual gifts in my life, but I am constantly struggling to find ways to use them. I have given blessings (referring to the power of Jesus Christ, not the priesthood, because it is important to me to respect ordination I cannot claim) and they have been powerful, miraculous experiences. But my offers have been turned down as often as they've been accepted. One friend insisted we call it a prayer and that I just hold her hands. Another friend drove to an empty parking lot and had me crouch in her car, leaning over from the passenger seat, terrified her husband or a neighbor would see us but still desperate for some comfort.

A woman who has been blessed with the gift of revelation, or prophecy, or even differences in administration, has very very few opportunities to exercise that gift. It's like I've been given armfuls of food and set out to walk among starving people, but no one knows I'm there.

So women need the priesthood because it's fair. Women need the priesthood to have a voice in bureaucratic policies. But women also need the priesthood to be able to exercise their full expression of devotion to God, and to contribute all of their talents to the kingdom.

Derek: I feel somewhat sheepish making a statement. As a man raised in the Church, I am in no position to tell women what to do about the priesthood. I have no idea what it is like to be denied the priesthood, never to have a hope of seeing myself or someone else be in a position of authority—and frankly, I have never felt any special connection or even really a belief in the priesthood as anything other than a gateway to leadership. It doesn't mean anything to me personally. I believe women should hold the priesthood simply because it makes sense to me for all children of a loving Father in Heaven to share in those responsibilities and opportunities. I see no reason for priesthood and leadership to be the exclusive domain of men.

I am cautious about the idea of raising the issue of women in the priesthood. The issue seems to be one of the most charged in the Church. In my experience, your average Mormon responds with knee-jerk defensiveness to the issue, and shuts down any open conversation. I fear that the leaders of the Church, reactionary as they have often been in the past, are likely to become even more resistant to progress in women's concerns. I'm concerned about the impact this could have on those women who want their situation to improve within the framework of the Church. Caution seems the wiser course to me; continue to work with innocuous issues—pants, nursing, prayer in General Conference—constantly raising awareness and slowly but persistently ratcheting up the heat until ordination seems sensible to the mainstream and our leaders.

But again, I don't really know the intensity of the feelings of marginalization or disempowerment among the women in the Church. I am not in a position to tell them what is the right course on this issue. If women I trust feel the time is right to raise this conversation, to express their feelings to the leadership and to defang the issue, then I fully support them.

Melissa Mayhew: My thoughts on this are complicated, and in some ways ambivalent. I do not think that women in the church currently have anything equivalent to the Priesthood, in spite of the fallacious rhetoric of motherhood being its equal. It is a gap in authority, opportunity, and exercise of capacity that will someday need to be closed. What that will

224

eventually look like, be it ordination into the current priesthood or some change that we can't even imagine yet, I don't know, and I'm fairly agnostic on the ordination idea itself. I do think that this is a question that needs to be talked about and explored without people recoiling in fear, throwing out accusations of seekers being power-hungry or unrighteous, or feminist witch-hunting. And, quite frankly, I do hope that discussion does scare some people enough to shift their thinking on Mormon women's issues in general. If the Wear Pants to Church Day was enough to get them kicking and screaming and throwing a fit, maybe they need some exposure to even more radical and extreme ideas than Pants (because pants are so radical, dontchaknow) to give them a smidgin of chill out perspective. Sometimes you need to see what the ground closer to the edge actually looks like in order to realize that you're still miles from it, yourself, and can stop hugging the dirt in fear.

Kimberly: I'm in the prioritization phase of issues—where there are so many obvious things that can be fixed that are essential to dignity and fairness—aside from the more overwhelming concept of ordination. (Such as women praying in GC[266]—should have happened a long time ago.) However, I have often stated that I've already claimed my priestesshood (yes, I like the -ess in it, because to me, it feels as if it's issued directly from our Mother in Heaven), and I understand exactly why the lack of acknowledgement of our natural inheritance would wound women of our faith, even if I believe even more deeply that it isn't men's right to withhold it. I'm to the point where I don't need it acknowledged by men, but I do believe it would be to the spiritual benefit of both the sexes for the priesthood to correct the regression and re-restore what Joseph set out to organize for women to complement the men. It's a crucial step towards true equality.

Ryan Hammond: The recent Pew poll of Mormons revealed that men (13%) supported the ordination of women at a higher rate than did Mormon women (8%). As a feminist Mormon priesthood holder myself, I find this gender split sad. I can understand why a woman may not "want to be bishop" (most Mormon men agree), but I can't understand why she would not want to participate in family ordinances. My understanding of the priesthood is that it is about service and sharing, which makes arbitrary restrictions seem so out of line with its cosmic intent. If indeed the priesthood is the "power to act in God's name,"[267] then I find it hard to conceive of a Zion-worthy Mormonism where women are denied that power. I don't understand why we would want to limit that power in our families, in our wards and in the world. I would love to have the experience of laying on hands with my wife to give blessings to my children. I would love to hear her act as "voice" in giving a blessing. I would love to see her baptize our son or daughter while I then confirmed or vice versa. As someone who has participated in the administering of the beautiful ordinances of the gospel, I can't conceive of the inclusion of our wives, daughters, mothers and friends within the priesthood circle as doing anything but enhancing the experience. I have no desire to hoard it or exclude others from it.

I am also a big believer that we cannot have true equality in the church until women have structural equality within the ecclesiastical and administrative organization. Structural inequality breeds, exacerbates and buttresses all other forms on inequality. The evidence of this is legion within the church. While it is hard for me to conceive of structural equality within the church for women without some form of priestesshood/priesthood ordination, I am actually very open to many forms, some of which may not require big changes in priesthood ordination practices. I do think that the newly released Relief Society Minutes provide some pretty compelling evidence that Joseph Smith was moving toward a strong, robust female form of authority before his death. He thought of RS as a priesthood quorum and the women as something like priests. I hope that one day soon the church will seriously revisit the founding of the RS with deep questions regarding Joseph's intent. Until then, we need stronger roles for RSPs across the whole organization of the church from the general officer level, down to the wards. Give them more autonomy, more resources, more independence and put them on equal footing with priesthood quorums as much as possible. We need to model equality of governance in our homes. So while I hope for a day when I can baptize and bless with my eternal partner or watch my daughter and granddaughters pass the sacrament, I think there is much we can do within the current framework to expand the power and authority of women within our families and congregations. I try and focus on that.

Joanna: How do I feel about priesthood ordination for women in the LDS Church? Reading the writings of Mormon historians, I know that when Joseph Smith organized the Relief Society he "turned the keys"[268] to its leadership, and he patterned its early organization after the priesthood. I know that many Mormon women across the orthodoxy spectrum believe that temple endowments and sealings confer priesthood on women. These historical facts and widely held beliefs stand in tension with the way Aaronic and Melchizedek priesthood ordination is justified and explained in LDS communities today. There are many folk beliefs about gender in circulation. For example, one frequently hears that men as a group are inherently less capable of nurturing or service than women; I refuse to believe that God created his sons to be spiritually deficient, and so I reject this argument that men must hold priesthood in order to provide them with equivalent opportunities for selfless service. Fatherhood, I believe, is the equivalent of motherhood. Rhetoric like this about gender roles has hardened over the last thirty years, so much so that some LDS people have become more serious about the saving power of proper gender roles than they are about the saving power of the merciful atonement of Jesus Christ. I cannot find grounds for this in LDS scripture. I find it harmful and distracting. Having said all that, upon searching myself and praying about ordination, I personally do not feel moved to act on this question. But I know and love many women who do, and as a feminist, I am in solidarity. Last summer, on a national television program about Mormonism, in explaining Mormon feminism, I stated that for some Mormon feminists, equality in church participation and decision-making is an issue, while for others ordination is a pressing spiritual concern. The next day, strangers stopped me in the airport and told me how furious their friends and relatives were with me; others called for my excommunication on blogs and Twitter. Just for stating the fact that some Mormon women do care about ordination. Which is a fact. Some women really do. Including women near and dear to me. Including my own daughters. I do not believe that a healthy religious community will exile or ostracize faithful brothers and sisters for asking heartfelt questions about serious issues. That is a betrayal of the original seeking spirit of Mormonism—the spirit that led Joseph Smith to the sacred grove. I believe in a powerful, just, and merciful God, and I believe in the dream of Zion—a place where none shall come to hurt or make afraid, even each other. I believe that revelation is a continuing conversation between God and a people. I believe that a faith as beautiful and powerful as Mormonism both deserves and is capable of very rigorous and careful examination of history and doctrine. I fully support a more thoughtful, respectful, and open discussion of ordination. If there is doctrine, let us come to understand it better and not confuse it with traditional worldly ideas about gender roles, as we often do now.

"ATTN (EMERITUS) PRESIDENT DALTON: VIRTUE CANNOT BE STOLEN" BY LISA PATTERSON BUTTERWORTH (APRIL 8, 2013)

Yesterday in Conference, President Dalton[269] paraphrased from Moroni Chapter 9:9:

> For behold, many of the daughters of the Lamanites have they taken prisoners; and after depriving them of that which was most dear and precious above all things, which is chastity and virtue...

The next verse goes on to get even more graphic:

And after they had done this thing, they did murder them in a most cruel manner, torturing their bodies even unto death; and after they have done this, they devour their flesh like unto wild beasts. . . .

When President Dalton paraphrased this scripture, I think (and I very much hope) the part of the scripture that she wanted to use to make her point was the part that names chastity and virtue as dear and precious above all things. And for many people when they heard President Dalton quote that scripture, that is all they heard, chastity and virtue are of great value, dear and precious.

Problematically every woman and girl who has been raped, every victim of sexual assault listening to President Dalton didn't hear that simple message. As they imagined themselves in the place of those poor Lamanite women, and remembered the violations they too had suffered, as they were reminded of all the shame, fear and guilt that comes from having their innocence ripped from them—they heard the part of that scripture which Dalton probably gave very little thought to. They heard her say that their chastity and virtue had been stolen. That which was most dear and precious above all things had been ripped from them without their consent. They heard her message and they felt dirty, impure, and without virtue.

I do not think this is the message Dalton intended to send. Unfortunately it was the message she sent.

People ask us all the time why do we need feminism? Women in the church are happy. Most Mormon women aren't feminists. Why do you want to change things when most Mormons are happy with the way things are now?

This is the answer.

President Dalton sent a deeply hurtful and doctrinally incorrect message Saturday Morning, and she did it with no intention of hurting anyone. I think it happened because it just never occurred to her how her words would be heard by someone dealing with the pain and shame and horror of sexual assault.

We need feminism because until someone dares to break the silence, overcome the shame, and explain to her how much harm her words will do, then nothing will ever change.

As Mormons we hold the values of chastity and virtue as sacred, they are very important to us and it is very understandable that when we look to the scriptures we will cling to a scripture (even, tragically, include it in the current Young Women curriculum[270]) when it says exactly the words we want to convey: virtue and chastity are dear and precious.

Unfortunately while I will agree that virtue and chastity are dear and precious, this scripture is not about virtue or chastity at all.

It is clear that what is happening in this verse is rape, torture and murder. Those Lamanite women were deprived of something, something dear and precious. They were deprived of their innocence, their safety, their human dignity. They were deprived of their lives. They were not, however, deprived of their virtue or chastity.

Despite some problematic statements from Church leaders past, the Church's official position (in the handbook and website) is that rape is never the fault of the victim,[271] and that has been explicit for a rather long time now. Victims of sexual assault do not need to repent, there is no stain, no guilt, no blame, no loss of virtue or chastity. I think if one asked President Dalton if the women who felt shame for being raped when she quoted that verse, actually should feel shame for being raped, I think she would not only say no, I think she'd say heck no!

And yet the verse doesn't mince words, it clearly states that evil rapists deprived those women of their virtue and chastity before eating them.

So if rape is entirely the fault of the perpetrator, if these Lamanite women were not one tiny little bit responsible for the crimes committed against them, what are we to make of this scripture? What does it mean and why does it say the Lamanite women were deprived of their chastity when everything we believe as Mormons says that they were not?

Well, that's the thing about scripture. You have to read scripture in context, you have to use it in context, otherwise you run the risk of saying something really cruel and terrible when all you wanted to say was "yay virtue!"

That bit of scripture is part of a heartbreaking letter that Mormon wrote to his son Moroni, he's clearly shocked and heartbroken, as would any of us have been to witness these kinds of evil war crimes committed by our people. But these tragedies do happen, pick up a history book, just about any history book. But as part of history Mormon is also a man of his times. And that means that his understanding of what it means to be a woman, raped and murdered, was part and parcel to being a historical man. And not only that, Joseph Smith, who translated this letter, was also a man of his times.

And the way that rape was spoken of and understood throughout history is one of the great evils of humanity.

It wasn't so long ago in human history that a woman's value was entirely determined by her virginity. In some parts of the world this is still the case. It is still common for a young girl who is raped to be thrown out of her home, forced to marry the rapist, or killed to protect her family's honor. (Just read the Bible.) What is or is not her fault is beside the point. Her virtue/purity/chastity are dependent entirely on her virginity. Her choices, her morals, her human dignity, her value as a precious child of heavenly parents had NOTHING to do with it. When her virginity was gone, her value as a human being was also gone.

This seems like a distant and ugly concept to most of us. Even the most traditional of Mormons are no longer teaching that it is better that your daughter should die than to be raped. But this is the society in which both Mormon and Joseph were living when they wrote and translated those words.

This is not to say they approved of women being thought of or treated this way. It only means that they knew exactly what it meant for a woman to be raped within the culture that they lived, and it meant the end of her dignity, no hope for a decent marriage, and no possibility of a good respectable life. And when Joseph Smith translated those words, his culture informed him. 19th century men did not use words like "rape," they used euphemisms like "deprived of their virtue and chastity." And as Moroni lamented that they were deprived of what was most precious to them, he meant their virginity and their chance at a good life. Not their moral center, not their values, not those things *we* would call virtue and chastity.

A 19th century euphemism for rape (deprived of virtue), in a verse that laments the fact that these women's lives (that which was most precious) were ruined by that rape, is not meant to be used to praise what we 21st century speakers would call virtue and chastity. It's a terrible misuse of scripture, and it sends a deeply damaging message and we need to stop it.

"AUTHENTIC PRAYER AFTER A FAITH TRANSITION" BY DOROTHY HATCH WARD (MAY 9, 2013)

> Prayer is our sometimes real selves trying to communicate with the Real, with Truth, with the Light.
>
> — Anne Lamott[272]

I think a lot of us in the bloggernacle have gone through or are in the process of a "faith transition," or, as we used to call it, "a loss of testimony." But let's stick with the more positive and more descriptive "faith transition." After a faith transition, what happens to prayer? Particularly if that transition is so broad in scope that we start to question not just the LDS church, but also Christianity, organized religion, and the very concept of God? Does prayer cease? Does it morph into meditation and mindfulness practice? Does it dry up like a raisin in the sun?

My belief in a loving God capable of divine intervention is weak and often disappears completely, probably to Bali, or perhaps under the couch cushions. I should check. Yet, I have not lost my faith in prayer. My habit of prayer reminds me of the importance of quiet and of mental stillness; the act calms me and reminds me of my priorities. I meditate too, but for me meditation is best in addition to prayer rather than as a replacement for prayer. After and during my faith transition, I decided to just keep the practice and the form: *Dear God, Thank you for my kids. They're actually pretty fun. And thank you for leading me away from the temptation of getting in the car and driving alone to Vegas for the weekend; Netflix was indeed a better option. In the name of Jesus Christ, Amen.* Or: *Dear Heavenly Father and Heavenly Mother, Please help me to stop spending money on Kindle Books. May I be content with the twenty unread ones that I already have. In the name of Jesus Christ, Amen.*

These prayers—they're okay. They help me get outside of myself and remember what's important; it's unquestionably a beneficial mental exercise.

But then I read the following lines from Anne Lamott:

> My belief is that when you're telling the truth, you're close to God. If you say to God, "I am exhausted and depressed beyond words, and I don't like You at all right now, and I recoil from most people who believe in You," that might be the most honest thing you've ever said. If you told me that you said to God, "It is all hopeless, and I don't have a clue if you exist, but I could use a hand," it would almost bring tears to my eyes, tears of pride in you, for the courage it takes to get real—really real. It would make me want to sit next to you at the dinner table.[273]

When I read this passage, it really struck me. I thought I was being honest and authentic in my casual and slightly irreverent prayers, but Lamott's sample prayers take authenticity to a new level. I wondered if I could pray like that, as me, Dorothy, the inconsistent, confused human being who so wishes to be sure about belief one way or the other but who never is.

In the LDS church, we have this idea that the power of prayer is directly proportional to the faith of the individual or group praying. I think that by keeping the framework of the traditional LDS prayer, I was sort of clinging onto that idea. But Lamott in her wisdom has convinced me that it's not true. Faithful prayers do not necessarily have more clout with God. If we pray as though we believe, when in fact we don't, we are hiding something. We are lying to ourselves and God, and you can't pray a lie.

What matters in prayer isn't the measure of faith, but the measure of authenticity. So on the days when I believe that there is no higher power and humans are the only chance we have for ourselves, I'll still pray, and I'll say that in my prayers: *God, I don't think I can say I believe in you, but here is my plea to whatever is out there: help me to not eat my feelings.* And on the days when I decide to believe in God because why not, and while we're at it, why not Jesus and Joseph Smith and plates too? I'll still pray on those days, and I will pray as someone who recklessly believes all those things. Because when I pray honestly, prayer is more than a beneficial mental exercise. It's a spiritual exercise, too, and yields powerful spiritual benefits that I can't fully articulate because I don't know what I believe. This is all sort of fuzzy and hard to wrap my head around, which is, I suppose, to be expected; we're talking about God after all. My prayers of doubt feel really good, and I think that whoever or whatever God is, I'm (probably, maybe) getting closer through prayer.

"OPEN POLICY, CLOSED CULTURE" BY DEREK STAFFANSON (JUNE 21, 2013)

Several weeks back, we received an announcement in the mail. One of Luv's[274] cousins would soon be getting married.

"She looks East Indian," I noted as I looked at a photo of the cousin and his new fiancé, "Maya." Not only did she bear what appeared to me to be vaguely Indian features, but it looked like she wore a phul, the traditional stud many Indian women wear in their nose.

"She is," replied Luv. "Her parents converted to the Church from Hinduism when she was young, and moved here to Utah."

Last week, my wife came home from work indignant with the news she'd heard from the family. "Maya went to the temple for her endowment today, and they made her take the piercing out!"

"What?"

"The people at the desk wouldn't let Maya into the temple with the ring. She had to take it out. The temple president heard about it and ran down to stop it, but he was too late. She'd already taken it out."

This wasn't just as simple as switching out your earrings each night. As is customary in many Indian communities, she had been wearing the phul nonstop for several years. The skin had grown around it, and digging was required. By the time the temple president arrived, the phul was excavated. Maya had made a blood sacrifice at the altar of the temple.

As I suspected at the time, and as others have since pointed out explicitly, the Church policy on temple attendance does not support this turn of events.

> After carefully considering this very question, Church leaders have announced a ruling that preserves the need of an expanding church to both respect temple standards and accommodate itself to the demands of Christian love and understanding. The rule holds that the responsibility for teaching temple patrons about dress and grooming standards must rest upon the priesthood authorities who issue temple recommends. It is at the family, ward, and stake level, not at the temple, that the proper foundation for temple conduct and dress must be laid.
>
> Once a patron arrives at the temple in good faith and with a valid recommend, temple authorities are not to pass judgment on that person's worthiness nor upon the appropriateness of

his or her attire and grooming. Attire that seems inappropriate to those of more conventional tastes does not constitute grounds for refusing admission to the temple. Every faithful member, regardless of attire and grooming, is entitled to a satisfactory temple experience.[275]

The Church leadership, considering it the duty of the Church to roll forth to fill the whole earth, has long been conscious of the need to be flexible and accept diverse traditions and cultures. Policies have been crafted in several areas of the Church organization specifically to allow for cultural variation. Leaders have occasionally made official pronouncements about the need to be open to different cultural traditions among the saints. People like Sister Chieko Okazaki are well known for promoting core principles and flexible, contextual application instead of worldwide application of specific cultural practices, most famously in her April 1996 General Conference talk "Baskets and Bottles."[276]

Despite an institutional focus on multiculturalism, there is also within the Church a countervailing emphasis on ethnocentric cultural norms. Vaughn J. Featherstone spoke out in a 1999 session of general conference against "earrings for boys and men, tattoos, spiked hair,"[277] to be followed a year later by President Hinckley giving *two* addresses in General Conference (assuming the General Relief Society Meeting is part of General Conference) in which he denounced tattoos and earrings for men, and more than one set of ear piercings for women[278]—going so far as to apparently state this as official Church policy ("We—the First Presidency and the Council of the Twelve—have taken the position. . . ."[279]). His words were used more[280] than[281] once[282] in addresses by leaders in official capacities encouraging and applauding strict obedience to the words of the prophet in such matters. While perhaps not exactly policy, Church "guidelines" suggest that "ties and white shirts are recommended because they add to the dignity of [the sacrament],"[283] something true only to the extent that the local culture from which our leadership came dictates this is so. Dress and grooming standards of CES institutions continue to strictly enforce Western conventions of grooming, suggesting to the membership that such standards are some sort of higher law for which we should be striving. This particular incident with Maya calls to mind that of former FMH perm, Mfranti, who was unable to attend LDS Business college because she likewise has a nose stud. Her rejection was not error, but policy.

And so, frustrated as I am with the desk staff who refused to accept Maya's cultural trappings, I am uncomfortable blaming them. They were acting perhaps not according to the official policy, but according to what they had fairly logically deduced was part of the "unwritten order of things" so common within the Church. The official policies are quietly produced and disseminated, only occasionally mentioned, while the items which formed the basis for their understanding of the unwritten order of things are highly publicized and frequently reiterated. These staff members may have made a poor decision, but they should not be scapegoated when these attitudes are rather pervasive within the Church. This same undercurrent leads many members to encourage the universal adoption of these standards.[284] It led me to believe during the first couple decades of my life that long hair on men was inherently disrespectful to the Lord, led my father to give a sacrament talk when I was in my teens excoriating men for wearing anything but white dress shirts to Sabbath services or priesthood duties, led my mother to recently quietly condemn to us the parents of the toddler who was running around with the little mohawk. This attitude was the norm in my community growing up. It was the attitude which caused a high council speaker in our current ward to express sadness that the prophet should even have to warn us against such *obviously* degrading and offensive practices as tattooing. This atmosphere in the Church is generated by the same Church leadership crafting those more embracing policies and making those embracing statements. The buck stops not with the desk clerks at the temple, but with the institution and leaders and the non-policy messages they send.

I visited the temple yesterday with my son Tater to pick up Luv, and to offer my congratulations to the bride and groom after the sealing. I was delighted to see the wedding party taking the customary post-sealing photos on the temple grounds, all dressed in a splendid Indian fashion. The bride and her maids all wore colorful Saris, Maya sporting a new phul in her nostril. The groom, of Mexican-American heritage, wore a finely embroidered Indian sherwani. Wonderful that in this instance, everyone involved apparently accepted, even embraced, this unusual (for the location) celebration of heritage. This is what the Gospel to which I feel attracted is. Nothing I've read of Jesus suggests that maintaining middle-class wasp grooming models is a principle of the Gospel. An open mind to good found in whatever package it may be found is. I hope that the Church and its leaders change their messages to minimize the focus on superficial observances based on culture, and instead better encourage this shift towards inclusion within our communities. As they do, we will be more able to embrace the Gospel of the Lord of the *whole* earth.

"A Short History of My Breasts" by Franziska Schulze Patterson/Thunderchicken (August 20, 2013)

The other day I saw a beautiful picture of a naked woman in the woods. Surprisingly enough, when I saw the picture, it brought tears to my eyes. Apparently seeing someone the way they are, still smiling, even though another person is present to see their nakedness, to feel so comfortable to share yourself in such a way, was deeply touching to me. And also filled me a bit with envy. Because I'd rather die than have anyone see me naked. It got me thinking about my own discomfort with my body, and a life-long dislike in particular of my breasts. So, let me share with you a short history of my breasts.

When I was 11 years old, I got in a car with a strange man. He took me to a nearby forest, where supposedly an injured foal was laying, needing (my expert) help. Obviously, there was no foal. And as the man was walking in front of me into the forest, I suddenly realized the danger I was in, and thought I would get murdered in this forest. But the man turned around, said this was not the right spot, and we got back in his car. While sitting in his car, I noticed his penis hanging out of his pants. I also knew I had to get away and decided to jump out of the driving car. Unhurt, I got up and was heading for a corn field, when the man made one more attempt to lure me in, asking me to "do him some favors." I just ran off.

This experience set an early tone for how I would view my body—an object, wanted or needed by others for their own purposes. Maybe a year after this traumatizing event, I went to the public pool in my little home town. I do not recall the exact events, but remember wearing a modest one-piece swimsuit, and that I was standing in line for the slide, when some boys, maybe 14 years old, commented on my breasts. Even though I cannot remember if the comments were positive or negative, I can still almost feel the blush on my cheeks and the embarrassment I felt. There I was, with nowhere to hide, and my body had just become an object of public commentary, something to be noticed, talked about, critiqued, like the rest of me was not there.

Then, one day, after visiting a friend who was also a member of the Church, I came home with a bikini the mother of the family had given me to keep. I had never worn a bikini but appreciated the gift. Yet, when my parents found out about the bikini, it was promptly taken away. I did not understand my parents' actions then. I was unsure why the bikini was upsetting to them. Nonetheless, I did understand that wearing one was not ok, and I felt guilty for having wanted to wear it. I was thirteen.

As a teenager I started dressing in ways to hide the shape of my body, especially my ever-present and ever-sticking-out breasts. When I was looking for a dress for a dance, I found a beautiful dress that was luckily not emphasizing my breasts more than I wanted and that I felt looked beautiful on me. However, my parents strongly objected to my wearing this dress since the sleeves were half-off the shoulders. I ended up wearing a borrowed, simple dress from a friend, that fit too snuggly around my chest. The evening was spent self-consciously folding my arms in front of my chest.

I kept hiding myself under unshapely clothes, in hopes that no one would notice my body, or especially my breasts. That no one would comment. Maybe I was succeeding when a boy I really liked at age 16 called me fat. But I couldn't help thinking that part of my "fatness" was just my large breasts that would stick out and make the large clothes fall like a tent around me.

At 18 I was looking into breast reduction surgery. At the first appointment to schedule the surgery, I had to stand topless in front of a doctor, who analyzed the shape of my breasts, drew lines on them and took pictures of them. A normal medical procedure, I'm sure. Yet, I felt deeply ashamed and humiliated, wondering what this man was thinking as he drew on me and looked at me. The final obstacle to my surgery was having to see a gynecologist who approved of the surgery. Again, I was being seen by a man. He was kind and felt that I was pursuing the surgery merely out of desperation (I certainly was! I just wanted those evil breasts gone), and he encouraged me to wait a little, give the idea more time, and that as a professional, he felt my breast size was completely normal. When I came home from this appointment (that effectively prevented me from having the surgery), I grabbed a pair of scissors and chopped off my hair. I hated my body. I hated who I was. I hated the face looking back at me from the mirror. And in that moment, I wanted every part of my body to look as ugly and horrible as I felt.

Shortly before my twentieth birthday, I got endowed. Again, I remember the discomfort of not wanting my breasts to be noticed, and yet not wanting to look fat in the tent-like temple dresses rented out to patrons. My garments also complicated life as they kept riding around under my bra. Sometimes they'd get "sucked in" and slipped below my chest. I had now entered a new stage of life, where I'd be adding constant adjustments to a body part I already tried to not draw any attention to. Even further, for one part of my temple ceremonies, I could not wear a bra, and I tried to hide the embarrassment of walking around with completely uncontained full breasts with a humble look at the floor. They did not seem like receptacles of pure and virtuous principles. Instead, they were weighing me down with fear, shame and self-hatred. They seemed to make others uncomfortable in one way or another, and no matter what I did, they were always there. Doing what breasts do, without asking my permission.

I carried on, covering up, trying to hide the breasts God gave me, often times hating him for having burdened me in such a way. Why would he give me something that was impossible to hide, yet seemed to only bring out the worst in others, something that seemed to take over everything else I was? I hated God sometimes. Hated him for obviously being a man, because a woman never would have given me these breasts. A woman would have understood.

Then I met my future husband. When he brought me to a family reunion to meet his family, I later found out how some of them joked that he must be dating me for my breasts. There they were again, those breasts. They seemed to be what people noticed first. But I did not want my husband to notice them. I wanted him to see me, love me, talk to me. For a long time, I avoided any water activities, because I did not want my husband to see me in a swimsuit. I knew my breasts were being squished together into a big "monoboob" in a swimsuit and looked so unattractive along with being so very visible, that I couldn't bear the thought of a man I liked seeing me like that.

When I had to start looking for wedding dresses, terror filled my heart—terror that no dress would accommodate my chest, or that they would not fit well, making my breasts ooze out, take front and center stage, and possibly, on top of it all, make me look fat. I cried quite a few tears as I tried on dress after dress, trying to find one that worked with those hated breasts.

But there was a deeper-seated fear in my heart, beyond the fear of how I would look in a wedding dress. I was terrified of my husband seeing me naked. In my heart, I just knew he'd be disappointed. I knew I could not measure up to whatever he had hoped for. Even though society seemed to value large breasts, I knew that my breasts were ugly. And bad, because they made me feel so uncomfortable when others noticed them. The weeks leading up to our wedding, I would often stand in the shower, and end up crying on the floor of the tub as I looked at and felt my naked body.

During our wedding night, my husband left my breasts alone. Those hated breasts. Then I cried and cried the next morning, while my husband got us some food. I had faithfully hid them away all those years and tried to ignore the discomfort and embarrassment they brought into my life. But now, as much as I hated them, I still wanted someone to love them, or love me, despite everything those breasts seemed to entail. Luckily, it was just a misunderstanding, and my husband simply did not want to objectify me or make me think he only cared about my breasts. Because that's what we care about in society—breasts. And that's all I thought I was, for better or worse—a pair of breasts.

With marriage, eventually, came pregnancy, and the breast hiding continued. I was now constantly tugging at my bra as my breasts gained in size and didn't fit into my bras properly. They'd spill out on top, once again leaving me embarrassed as I tried to push the "double-boobs" back into a bra that refused to fit. No blanket seemed big enough to cover the space I needed covered when nursing. The first weeks of motherhood, I hid in my bedroom, too ashamed to have anyone see me, even my own mother. To make nursing easier, I now also wore my garment tops over my bra. Yet, an unpleasant side-effect was that my big breasts made pretty much any shirt a tight fit, and parts of my garments that I had covenanted to keep private were on constant display. I tried to remedy the situation by getting silk-screened tops, but the distribution center said they could not do that. Finally, during a flight my husband was trying to help me stay covered as I nursed our baby and had to endure my anger when he accidentally bared some of my breasts for a second. No one should have to see my breasts.

But if it was not pregnancy or nursing, it was always something else. About a year after my first child was born, I ran my first half-marathon. My husband took a video clip of me as I passed the 10-mile marker. When I saw the clip, I immediately deleted it. Even though I looked proud and strong as I passed mile 10, my breasts were clearly swinging side to side, despite two sports bras I was wearing. The image horrified me and overshadowed my accomplishments of a race well run with concerns of people having seen me with breasts bobbing all over the place.

Now my breasts just sag, almost down to my belly button (ok, maybe not quite), after having busted the buttons on many a shirt, moved garments up and down, exposed themselves by accident to various people, have been drawn on, felt and squished by various doctors and nurses, invited commentary, created inappropriate thoughts, fed 3 babies, pleased my husband, and met people before I did. My breasts—two parts of me that seem to define me, control me, and dictate what the world notices about me.

When I saw the picture of that naked woman, I thought of my breasts. My body. And how I feel I've never owned myself. I wish that I could experience that paradisiacal moment Adam and Eve experienced in the Garden of Eden. To be naked, to be without shame over my body, to push away the world that tries to own it, and see myself, the human God made, and know that this body I wear is "very good." "And I, God, saw everything that I had made, and, behold, all things which I had made were very good" (Moses 2:31).

"QUESTIONS ON CONNECTING TO HEAVENLY MOTHER SERIES" BY KIMBERLY FITZPATRICK LEWIS (SEPTEMBER 11, 2013)

I received quite a number of inquiries throughout the posts[285] (thank you for taking the time to contact me, I tried to respond in as timely a manner as possible). I appreciated the observations and the criticisms—and the reaching out from several sources.

It's clear that there is a lot of interest in Heavenly Mother and integrating her into an active faith practice for quite a number of you out there. One of the complaints I received was that I wasn't personal enough in addressing this concern.

That was intentional. I wrote the series for the initiate to Mother, the member who is trying to reach out to her and gain a personal relationship with her. I shared ways in which connection can be explored and deliberately kept it as broad as possible for there to be as many potential starting points as people need there to be.

We all approach personal relationships differently, which springs from individual needs and perceptions. For LDS members who love the doctrine of HM but struggle with the lack of practice, developing your own can be intimidating and frustrating. I hoped to emphasize that there is no one correct way of doing this, no one correct way of knowing her, no one correct perception of who or what she is. To a certain degree, I've shared some of what I've learned and tried to emphasize the fact that I'm continuing to learn every day too. Line upon line, precept upon precept applies in this case as much as it does to Father.

A reader submitted some questions I thought were thought provoking, and I have been mulling them over since I wanted to give them serious consideration:

> I'm finding myself increasingly hollow during church on Sundays. I feel lonely even when I do all the "right" things (which is what has led me to reach out for Mother). What I want to know is how do you find fulfillment in Sacrament, Sunday School, and Relief Society with your understanding of Mother?

I've always found fulfillment in the sacrament as the ritual pertaining to Christ and his atonement. As I see Mother in partnership with Father in the salvation the atonement makes possible, the inclusion alone affords me peace. This is where I spoke of inclusion being the first step in integrating Mother in practice. As it stands, we have nothing firm to grasp in our faith other than the fact she exists, and there are some negative cultural myths out there that aren't happy to contemplate that I don't find helpful. As Joseph did in the sacred grove, I had to be willing to ask Father for help in this since nothing tangible is currently being offered by leadership.

Relief Society is easy for me in this regard. These are my sacred sisters. We are Mother's daughters. That's what I see when I see other women now—fellow priestesses. Of course I'd love transformative and brave revelation that acknowledges that, but I'm not a novice anymore and I believe I already have that confirmation directly. It's not something I wait for men to confer upon me (it's not their place), it is my sacred inheritance to claim and I have done so. This makes me look upon my relationships with other women differently—we are responsible for each other.

Sunday School is what it is. Teachers and their level of preparation, depth of knowledge and open-mindedness vary in every ward. In every class, there is an opportunity to learn and grow. If I hear something derogatory, incorrect or otherwise harmful for members to take in, I most certainly comment—and that pertains to every topic, not only Heavenly Mother. Believe me, many people keep quiet when they'd like to speak up. I've had many people thank me later for rebutting something damaging.

Other church members probably find you strange (peculiar among the peculiar, ha!). How do you relate to them?

Actually, people who react like this are the ones who are afraid. I relate to them as frightened human beings; I try to be gentle and kind (it usually works). I recognize they need healing and are on their own journey. Yes, I have always been "strange" in LDS circles. I'm a convert of 20 years, I have a career I unabashedly love, I'm divorced and remarried, my older children are not members and that does not bother me. I've never fit the LDS female norm, didn't go through YW and so, remain an outlier in many respects. Add to the fact that I have a rich and rewarding relationship with Mother and of course, I am strange. Luckily, that hasn't rendered me unapproachable within my ward. I think people sometimes come to me because they know I won't judge them for exploring their own spirituality because I think it's a very healthy thing. Sometimes they just want permission to be weird too.

> While I understand that fear is not of God, I have a fear that exploring the Mother too openly will result in further isolation among my ward, especially with a Bishop who is very by the book. Have you experienced this? How do you still thrive—even among the shaking heads within your own ward family? (Reader question)

I don't tend to worry about who is shaking their heads at me because I live very close to my Heavenly Parents and the gift of personal revelation. I am a survivor of many things and have experienced recovery through this gift, and I do not allow anyone else's need to conform to interfere with that. It's precisely why I have the depth of spiritual confidence in my Parents and my savior that I require in my daily life. A huge part of claiming priesshood to Mother is in being confident in its gifts. I allow what others think to be their own problem; I'm not here to change other people's minds, they must do that of their own accord.

I'm trying to think of situations where Mother has come up with ward members lately. In my Sunday School class, when one of my students asked about my bracelets with a dove and tree, I told her that they stood for my Heavenly Mother. I have a necklace that has a labyrinth with a Goddess charm that I get asked about fairly often, and I claim her there too—it sparks a lot of discussion. If she comes up as a topic in classes, I add whatever information I know within the framework of the lesson because I'm not there to spout non-existent doctrine—I keep it in the framework of my experience or in research. Quite a few people have asked for more resources, which I am glad to share.

No, it's not wide open—it can't be. We don't have that yet, do we? It's part of what is so sad, because personally, I don't think religious equality is possible without a Goddess counterpart to God. I have no idea if our faith will develop this more or not, and I do not know if there will come a time that the lack of it might lead me in other directions. For now, this is my community and there is much I love about it. My incorporation in my personal practice of Mother has only enhanced it, and sure, I'd love for it to do that for others who ache for her, that's why I did the beginner series in hope of giving the seeker a starting point. But I am not a prophet who reveals truth to membership, I am only one person who has sought personal truth and lives within her love as a result of that journey. That is enough for now—I'll be told if there is anything else I need to do. One of those things is in having relationships with other people who love and know the Goddess, because it's nice to share that bond.

"LISTEN" BY NATALIE HAMILTON KELLY (OCTOBER 4, 2013)

When I served in the YW, the youth in my stake got a very special opportunity. Two apostles were going to hold a live teleconference to our ward building, where any youth in the stake would be able to ask them directly any question they had about life or the gospel. Our ward leaders encouraged us to talk through this opportunity with the youth, let them know how special it was, and make sure the questions they had in mind were relevant and appropriate.

One of my Beehives[286] surprised me with what she wanted to ask.

"Could I ask them about Heavenly Mother?"

"Sure."

At the event, the apostles really did engage with the youth. Kids asked them tips for the best way to prepare for missions, what their favorite scriptures were, etc. Most questions, both men took a turn answering and did a great job of connecting with the youth.

My Beehive waited her turn and got to the mic in front of the big drop down screen showing the two suit-clad apostles in SLC. She asked her question.

"Why don't we know more about Heavenly Mother?"

There was a brief pause. Then one of them answered with an apologetic shrug.

"I don't know."

The other chimed in to say, "I'd have to agree with him."

And that was that. Next question please.

She sat down, a little deflated after a super anti-climactic interaction with the top leaders of our church.

Their answer wasn't incorrect. It certainly could have gone much, much worse, with some horrible lines about protecting women, or putting her on a pedestal, or other terrible things people say about Heavenly Mother's absence. So I can't really fault them for it. They heard a simple question, and they gave a short, factual answer.

Here's the question they didn't hear. Why is a 13-year-old girl asking about the absence of her mother?

They didn't listen well enough to see the spiritual need. They didn't listen well enough to wonder why such a young girl would ask such a question, what the answer might mean to her, how important this moment might be for the development of her testimony and her identity as a girl in this gospel.

They didn't really hear her at all.

Too often, when church leaders are presented with people's concerns about the gospel, all they hear is the potential PR problems the concerns could pose. They have standard, safe, often dismissive answers.

The women standing with Ordain Women this weekend could present a huge PR problem for the church. Our leaders have already provided plenty of safe, evasive, PR-friendly answers to the concerns women raise about their place in the church. They've been engaging in plenty of damage control. They've gone straight to thinking about strategy before we finish getting our words out. Many, many members of the church see the OW event this weekend as an attempt to harm the church's public image. When some people hear about this movement, they hear danger and threats.

I hope our leaders don't hear that.

I hope they hear the intent, the sincerity, the hopefulness of the women standing at the door and knocking.

I hope they listen.

"When You Ask for Bread and Receive a Stone. Forgiving Our Leaders and Finding Ourselves" by Lisa Patterson Butterworth (October 5, 2013)

In the Saturday afternoon session Elder Ballard quoted from Matthew 7:8—10:

> For every one that asketh receiveth; and he that seeketh findeth; and to him that knocketh it shall be opened. Or what man is there of you, whom if his son ask bread, will he give him a stone? Or if he ask a fish, will he give him a serpent?

And it got me to thinking, I very sincerely feel that I've been asking very nicely for bread for nearly a decade now, and that made me pause as I contemplated what I have received back?

What has asking brought me?

I love the Gospel, I have never wanted anything but to be a good and faithful Mormon woman. But I must also be true to what I know about equality and justice and human dignity. I have asked, and asked nicely, for the nourishing hope that women's voices matter, that we can have a conversation about equality, that we will listen to the voices of thousands of Mormon women who quietly disappear, into despair, into inactivity, into other faiths, out of their Mormon home. They disappear rather than seeking, because asking and knocking are labeled faithless, contentious, and even evil.

I've made mistakes, I'm not perfect, but overall I feel like the bread I seek is righteous and nourishing: to improve the lives of Mormon women, to give Mormon women a voice, to include women who don't feel they belong in the narrow confines imposed by rigid cultural expectations. Goals squarely in line with strengthening the gospel and the Church.

And yet the responses we so often see from our fellow Mormons are rarely full of Christlike love. My own mother (in a moment of frustrated anger) asked me why don't I just leave the church. Angry Mormons on the internet say all manner of unkind and unfair things about us. And today Elder Christofferson condemned feminists,[287] and I assume he was talking to me (to us) even though the kind of feminism he described didn't actually describe any feminists I actually know, and I know a whole bunch.

And as I sit here contemplating bread ... and rocks, I realized something.

I don't think Elder Christofferson ever really heard me ask for bread. And I think, I truly do, that when he handed me that pile of rocks, he really for realz not-even-kidding thought he was handing me bread.

I know he hasn't heard me, because the feminists he heard, the feminists he described, the feminist he implied was like me is nothing like me at all. He has heard of feminists who devalue motherhood, motherhood is the best most valuable thing I have ever or will ever do. The feminist he heard of want to destroy the differences between men and women, I love Relief Society and I love it when my husband gets his beard on and then lifts heavy things. Rawrrrrr. The feminists he heard of want to be men, I look far too good in heels and twirly skirts, thanksanyway, nor do I hate men, see Rawrrr above. I spent the last two days straight canning applesauce, apple pie filling and pickles, I haven't even left the kitchen, I made an apple pie last night, I kid you not AN. APPLE. PIE. I'm that feminist.

But beyond continuing to be utterly transparent about who I really am, I can do nothing to convince anyone that my faithful yearnings are not selfish, power-hungry, rebellious and destructive. Until they are ready to look, until they are ready to hear, then the only thing I can do is to try my darndest not to return upon them that lack of seeing and hearing.

My mother doesn't want me to leave the church. She's scared, scared because she doesn't understand how I can love the gospel and still be so utterly honest about the flaws we have in our earthly organization. She's scared that she'll lose me and her forever family will come crashing down around her.

Those nasty internet Mormons are feeling deeply unsettled and insecure.[288] Their black and white world view doesn't hold room in it for women like us. They've never been where we are, they can't understand how we think, and trying to understand is often much too frightening to even contemplate. I've been there, I have great empathy for that desire to lash out to protect the most valuable sacred thing in your life.

And Elder Christofferson, as much as I'd like to believe that our leaders are super-human, they are in fact only human. And though I do believe our leaders to be inspired men, they are limited just like all of us by their experiences. He has never met me, he can't know me. Chance are he's never really sat down and had a deep open conversation with a feminist in which he really tried to understand, and chances are he never will. His days are spent surrounded by people who agree with him, people who believe their obedience to him is a sign of their own righteousness, people who probably see him perform kind and holy acts of service on a daily basis, who see his goodness and would never think to question or disagree and who have themselves probably never had a deep and meaningful conversation with a feminist.

And this is where I am at an advantage, I can understand them, I've been them. I can love them and try to hear them, because I used to think I was handing people bread, and I did not understand when people cast my bread away like it was a stone to them.

But even as I look at the rocks that I have been handed, rocks given to me with good intention and sincere love, rocks I can make no good use of ... I also realized that if I look in a different direction my life is overflowing with the nourishing bread the Lord has promised me. Ten years ago, I was alone, I wanted to be a Mormon, but I wasn't sure the church wanted me and my liberal views and quirky feminist beliefs. Today Elder Uchtdorf told me in no uncertain terms that "there is room for me,"[289] today Elder Caussé[290] said, "Our wards and quorums do not belong to us, they belong to Christ, everyone who comes should feel at home." But even more than the welcome I feel from my brothers, today I am no longer alone.

Today I am surrounded by my sisters. There is a whole world of Mormon feminism, a rich diverse community of love and support that overflows with so much awesome that it blows my mind. And this is only possible because we love each other, and we have the gospel to bind us. And this feeds me, nourishes me, every day. I have asked for bread, and I have received.

"AND I'M AFRAID OF NO ONE" BY LINDSAY HANSEN PARK (OCTOBER 12, 2013)

When I came to this blog I was afraid. I had questions and doubts and pain, and as a good Mormon girl, I was supposed to keep those quiet. Try as I might to calm the storms of dissonance, a voice inside me (which I would later discover was my inner compass) kept bubbling to the surface.

All was not well in Zion. There was hurt and institutional harm being done to the marginalized. There were things that didn't make sense. There was bigotry and homophobia and sexism amongst the saints, and it was wrong. I was afraid. When I questioned these problems, I more often than not internalized them. The confusion *must* be my fault. It must be my deficient faith or my dedication or loyalty that was flawed, it couldn't possibly be this perfect church, God's institution on Earth. It was me. I was the flawed one who just didn't have the eyes of understanding. My faith was lacking. My righteousness was faltering. The shame of my doubts kept me silenced. The doubting of doubts stilled my tongue. This is an old tactic in keeping oppressed[291] people oppressed. Like the caste system or other similar systems of oppression, the lowest class of people can be kept in their state of degradation by convincing them that they not only love it, but it's their Divine right.

> To hold a people in oppression you have to convince them first that they are supposed to be oppressed.
>
> —John Henrik Clarke[292]

I came to the blog and wrote under a pseudonym. I had to work out this divided heart, but I couldn't use my voice because too much would be risked. I could get into trouble! My bishop or ward might be upset. What if my family found out? I chose the name Winterbuzz from a childhood game. It was my voice of pretend and my voice of a small girl who could slip into one world and then back into another. I chose it because I didn't want anyone to know that the real me had questions or concerns. I was continually apologizing for my doubts and questions. I had an incredible amount of self-loathing. Why couldn't I just fall in line? Why couldn't I just trust my leaders? Where was my faith?

I was afraid.

Over the years of blogging here, I have gone on the most incredible journey. Feminism has empowered me beyond anything I have ever known or learned before. I have begun to find my voice and listen to my inner truth. While this is a journey and not a destination for me, feminism has taught me to stop seeking direction and authority from external voices and to start checking into my own truths. This is not selfishness as many Mormons, including myself, have been taught to suspect. It is called being responsible. I am a good person and I have values. I didn't trust any of that before, but I am learning to now.

Many of you have followed the story of the brave Malala Yousafzai, a Pakistani girl who risked her own life standing up against the Taliban to fight for her education and the education of those in her village. On October 9, 2012, a Taliban gunman boarded Malala's school bus and shot her in the head. She has survived and is now a global activist raising awareness for the education of girls. Here is a quote of hers below:

I don't mind if I have to sit on the floor at school. All I want is education. And I'm afraid of no one.[293]

Feminism has brought so many courageous women into my life. I have so many beautiful role models that exemplify courage, direction and a deep desire to fight for goodness. This is the gospel to me.

These examples of Womanhood do not sit idly by, content in what they are told they get. They do not doubt themselves or their doubts. They nurture the trust in themselves. They live with empathy and courage and don't take the world views given to them with blind obedience. They live their truth, sometimes risking great things for it, like Malala did. They do not encourage women to be satisfied with the status quo, they encourage women to check in with their hearts and ask important questions. These are the women that are helping change the world, even the small corner of our Mormon world.

Women like Lisa Butterworth who stepped into the abyss of the internet and created this blog that inspires thousands, or Kate Kelly and her call for Radical Self Respect,[294] or my hero Missy Lambert, who has dedicated her life to eradicating gender violence, or my best friend Malia, who stepped away from activity because of homophobic policies, even when I shunned her for it, or Joanna Brooks using a national platform to tell her story,[295] or Lorie Winder Stromberg, who isn't ashamed of power,[296] or Stephanie Lauritzen for using her questions to start a movement that has changed the lives of many.

They and hundreds and hundreds of other women every day who speak their truth and do good in the world. You are the women who inspire me. Women who challenge me. Women who wrap me in their arms when speaking my truth has caused me to be shunned from my community and those who once loved me. You are the women who have helped me find my Divine Nature, my Individual Worth and taught me about Choice and

Accountability, Good Works and Integrity and to stand for truth at all times and in all things and in all places.

It seems a strange thing that three years ago I was so afraid to even blog when younger girls than me, like Malala, can stand up to the Taliban.

I have been afraid for so, so long. Afraid to speak, afraid to act and afraid to believe the feelings I had were valid. I have been raised to not ask questions outside the realm of safety. I have been groomed to not trust myself but to seek validation and confidence of truth outside myself from leaders and my community, instead of listening to my inner voice. I have trusted leaders who continue to perpetuate discrimination and harm and have held my tongue for the sake of what I perceived was faith.

Since then, I have had a mighty change of heart. A change that allows me to look inside my heart and know the wrongs I see and to trust that they are wrong.

Seeing women like Malala and so many others have the courage to speak out on the wrongs in their world has inspired me to do the same.

Oppressing marginalized people is wrong. Telling them to be happy and content with their oppression is wrong. Telling them the burden of sin falls on them, because they are deficient for not fitting inside the rules, instead of calling attention to the deficient rule is wrong. Sexism is wrong. Racism is wrong. Homophobia is wrong. Institutional homophobia and sexism is wrong. Couching it in Mormon language like some of the language we heard at conference is worse because it increases the violence of the words. Harming people in the name of God is wrong.

Like courageous, beautiful Malala, I am Lindsay Park, and I am afraid of no one.

"On Idolatry, Institutional Repentance, and Grace" by Katie Langston (December 19, 2013)

Over the past few weeks, the church has been quietly releasing brief explanatory essays on a variety of controversial topics: race and the temple/priesthood ban,[297] multiple accounts of the First Vision,[298] and Utah-era polygamy.[299] Rumor has it that there are more to come.

On the one hand, I'm happy that the church is beginning to address the issues that have led many people to abandon the faith. On the other, I'm frustrated by the fact that these statements read like slickly-worded PR pieces intended to deny as much culpability as possible while still retaining a shred of historical credibility. In so doing, they neglect the heart of the issue—why people are leaving the church in droves over doctrinal and historical problems.

It's not because the church didn't have a blurb about this or that controversial topic on their website (though its refusal to officially acknowledge that the topics even existed was symptomatic of the problem).

It's because even into adulthood, we are taught to "follow the prophet" and all will be well—and when folks find out that our history is messy and teeming with human mistakes, it's a massive betrayal.

And that's the kind of thing that isn't going to be corrected with a few 2000-word carefully crafted essays. It will only be corrected with a major paradigm shift.

To put it another way, we don't need slick PR moves. *We need repentance.* The kind of repentance the church itself teaches: recognition of wrongdoing, confession of sin, restitution to those harmed, and a fervent commitment to never, ever do it again.

And what sin must the church repent of? To be frank, there are many institutional sins that weigh us down, including racism, homophobia, sexism, envy, greed, deception, and insularity.

But I believe there is one sin at the crux of it all—for repenting of any of these other sins will require the abandonment of the first: the idolatry of leader worship.

As I examine the history of our people, it seems as though leader worship has long been a temptation for Latter-day Saints—and right now is no exception. Lesson after lesson in Sunday services is devoted to obedience to leaders. In General Conference, we are exhorted to "heed the counsel of the Brethren." In order to receive temple recommends, we must affirm that we sustain the leadership of the Church. Children are raised singing "Follow the Prophet"[300] in Primary classes. The Church is so invested in a narrative of obedience to authority that there is very little room to acknowledge that leaders are flawed, that revelation is messy, and that sometimes we just plain get it wrong. (And no, Elder Uchtdorf's vague statement about unspecified leaders making unidentified mistakes[301] does not seem to me to be real engagement on this issue.)

This makes it very difficult for the institution to repent of its sins. So instead of repentance, we get shrewdly crafted statements and whitewashed history—disingenuous performances that allow pain to go unseen and unhealed—all in an effort to uphold the sanctity of a false god.

Take the statement on the temple/priesthood ban as an example. If the church now "disavows theories advanced in the past that black skin is a sign of disfavor or curse, or that it reflects actions in a premortal life; that mixed-race marriages are a sin; or that blacks or people of any other race or ethnicity are inferior in any way to anyone else"—all of which are concepts that were repeatedly taught by top leaders, sustained as prophets, seers, and revelators—*what does this mean for today's leadership? And what might they be wrong about now?*

This is a question that the church goes out of its way to avoid. The implications are too scary. The fear is that the "foundation of prophets and apostles" might crumble with the frank admission of error. And it's true that there will be backlash. Repentance hurts; and when you have encouraged people to place their trust in the arm of flesh for years, there is no way to say, "We're sorry, we were wrong" without consequence. The problem is, continuing in sin because repentance is difficult merely compounds the heartache.

Of course, the theology is right at our fingertips to release these heavy burdens, work through the pain, and find reconciliation and peace. We believe in Jesus, right? This means we believe in a God of forgiveness and grace.

About two years ago, my friend Ms. Jack wrote a compelling blog post[302] entitled "Can Grace Save Mormonism?" It's a piece that is extremely relevant in the wake of this statement's release. In it, she says:

> I propose that what the church needs is not a mere apology for its past wrongdoings and/or the past wrongs committed by its leaders. It makes little sense to call for such apologies when its current paradigm leaves precious little room for anything of the sort. What the church needs is a paradigm shift. . . . I propose that such an answer may be found in a more grace-centered theology (or ecclesiology, if you will). Grace can save Mormonism.

Her premise is that instead of clinging to the idol of infallible leadership, and compounding sins of deception upon leaders' mistakes in an attempt to cover their errors, Mormonism could be revolutionized by embracing a narrative that openly acknowledges our imperfection and says that we are called *despite* our weakness, not *because of* our worthiness.

Over the past few days, I've been thinking a lot about that. What might Mormonism look like if we acknowledged our faults and embraced the grace we so desperately need? I did a little thought experiment to explore what might be different. The results felt like a breath of fresh air.

- Leaders might go out of their way to meet with and receive counsel from the most marginalized among us—in order to understand how best to welcome them and minister to them
- We might drop excessively formal titles like "President So-and-So," and even the "greatest" among us would be "Sister Linda" and "Brother Tommy"
- Perhaps the institution would embrace financial transparency—to hold themselves accountable as much as anything
- Members might no longer live in fear of having their temple recommends revoked for honest disagreements
- As a people, we might apologize quickly when we make a mistake and seek to set things right just as soon as possible

- Even at the highest levels of church administration, there might be an air of openness as opposed to secrecy; perhaps we would pull back the curtain and show how and why decisions are made and invite feedback from the members
- As a church, we might recognize that "worthiness" is as much a false god as infallibility is—and we'd extend nothing but grace, love, and acceptance to sinners (HINT: that's all of us)
- Perhaps it would become okay to say in church services, "I really struggled with Elder So-and-So's talk in Conference"—sparking real discussions where people could feel free to come as they really are
- Maybe callings would be offered and discussed adult-to-adult; acceptance wouldn't just be assumed, and it would be okay to say, "No thanks, this isn't a fit for my life right now"
- Various life paths might become acceptable—and the church would become a support for people as they find their own way through life, as opposed to dictating what the way should be

When I imagine a church like this, I can hardly contain my joy. This is a church that could command my full engagement. This is a church that would look more and more like Zion. And the truth is, it's within our grasp.

The recent statements from the church on controversial topics are poignant reminders that we have a lot of repenting to do. Fortunately, we have a God of grace who can work miracles of reconciliation, healing, and forgiveness.

If only we find the courage to do the right thing.

"Family (Isn't It About Time?)" by Lindsay Hansen Park (December 23, 2013)

"Do what is right, let the consequence follow,"[303] is part of a hymn of our people that many of us grow up hearing from birth. I think it can take on multiple interpretations throughout our lives, but it has meant the most to me as a Mormon woman when speaking about LGBT issues. This week, our home state of Utah did what was right.[304]

My heart is full. I feel the deep-down burn of our Heavenly Parents' love for all of their children today.

Sara Burlingame, Joanna B., Nicole Christensen and many other awesome Mo's organized a flash-flower-drive so that a few of us could go to the courthouse and give flowers to gay couples as a wish of support and congratulations.

It was incredibly important to me that my children got to witness this event and know that their parents stood on the right side of history. Mostly they were just bored, and my 8-year-old accused me of embarrassing him with my enthusiasm. Other than that, they looked on the large crowds of people with nothing but acceptance. There was nothing strange or unusual about these couples embracing and wedding, except maybe their nutty momma hugging every stranger in sight and giving away roses with a little too much gusto.

Early in the day my husband was disheartened when a man at work said, *"I can't believe there are so many queers in Utah."* I had carried that dark image of bigotry all morning until I went to the courthouse and realized he was sort of right! The courthouse was filled with amazing gay couples from all walks of life, every race, economic status and appearance. Such diversity and numbers made my heart swell. There are so many couples in Utah who have been waiting for this day, a day many didn't think would happen. There are many. SO MANY. Today was such a beautiful day for them and for all of us who also *exercised our right* to share it with them.

As I handed out roses I said, *"A bunch of Mormons online organized a drive to let you know that many of us love you, support you and wish you congratulations with all our hearts."* This was met with tears of appreciation, surprise and hugs.

Many, many, many of these couples came alone and without friends or family. I told them that they have thousands of Mormons online who are rallying behind them today and love them, because it's true. There are literally thousands of us and more growing every day. We are moving inch by inch towards Zion's freedom, even though the consequences are hard, exhausting and sometimes painful.

Battle for freedom in spirit and might;

One couple, excited by my purpose, admitted that they were also Mormon and had been together for 35 years. They were as giddy as I was on my wedding day at 19. Another couple told me that they had met at Girls Camp (to which I squealed like an idiot and hugged them with awkward enthusiasm). There were so many Mormons getting married today, just like they had been raised to do. Mormons getting married. Our people! Remember the old Mormon ad, "Family, isn't it about time?"[305] The answer is YES! There's always time for families who love one another. The time is now! The time is here!

I am so utterly grateful my children got to witness this and will grow up in a state where goodness and equity blossom like a rose in the deserts of ignorance, hate and bigotry.

And with stout hearts look ye forth till tomorrow.
God will protect you; then do what is right!

It was such a blessing and an honor today to be able to share for a moment with them in this important history, both for our country and for their lives. It wasn't perverse, or "queer," or wicked—it was lovely. The courthouse was a holy temple within the hearts of all who were there. It was a consecrated feeling. I felt the greatest spirit of love, truth and genuine

Christlike acceptance in those walls today. A feeling that inspires me to try a little harder to be a little better, kinder and more gentle. To love one another as Jesus does and to swallow the beautiful taste of freedom and equity in the air in Deseret today and breathe it deep down into my lungs until it becomes more a part of me.

"Excommunicating Sexism" by Kate Kelly (December 30, 2013)

Recently I met with my stake president and my bishop at their request. They wanted to discuss my involvement with Ordain Women.

The most important, immediate takeaways from my encounter with leadership were:

1. They explicitly and emphatically assured me that I was not facing any type of disciplinary action for my founding of, and participation in, Ordain Women.

2. They told me there was no directive from any area authority or higher-level Church leader instructing them to meet with me, interview me or punish me in any way. Hence, they assured me when I asked, there is no concerted effort on the part of the Church to "crack down" on members of Ordain Women or target us specifically for our unequivocal calls for female ordination.

Clearly the power dynamic was not balanced, but I came away from the meeting feeling proud and satisfied. While they do not agree with me, I felt I spoke clearly and the discussion was a productive one. My friend Suzette and my dad[306] also recently met with their leaders. They both discussed their Ordain Women participation with candor and had their temple recommends renewed.

However, the results may not be this positive for every person. We have all known from the start of this movement that reactions from individual local Church leaders are impossible to predict or control. Recently, other members of Ordain Women have had less fruitful interactions with their leaders. In fact, feedback from different leaders has varied widely. Some women, due to geography, personal circumstances or just rotten luck, are at much greater risk than others. It is precisely this element of Russian-roulette-like unpredictability that has led to disparate results in the past and great trepidation today among many of my valiant sisters who dare to speak out.

Because of this uncertainty, the fear of Church discipline in our Mormon feminist community is palpable. The excommunication process— and the lingering fear that it could potentially occur, even if it never does— causes us great harm. It has what lawyers call a "chilling effect." The latent threat of sanction discourages our brothers and sisters who have legitimate questions and concerns from speaking up. Many are afraid of being punished for asking questions, even if they do so in faith and with complete sincerity.

This is not right.

A few weeks ago I attended a Conference sponsored by the Kairos Center[307] at Union Theological Seminary in Manhattan. One of the presenters, Charlene Sinclair, said something than rang so true to me it was a shock to my system, and I was amazed I had never thought the words before myself. It was like intellectual déjà vu. She said, "Do we have the power within to excommunicate the structure of institutionalized sexism?"

"Do we?" I thought as I met with my leaders. They seemed keenly invested in enquiring about my actions and views but seemed wholly uninterested in examining with a critical eye the system that puts them in a position of authority over me—over all women—because of a Y chromosome.

Perhaps we do, indeed, need a purge. But the purge we need isn't one of feminists, gays or intellectuals. It isn't of well-meaning, dedicated, faithful Mormon women with legitimate, sincere questions. The purge we need is of sexist practices that place all males above all females.

The oft-quoted leader Martin Luther King, Jr. gave one of his lesser-known, but most powerful sermons[308] one year before he died. In it he said,

> A true revolution of values will soon cause us to question the fairness and justice of many of our past and present policies.

Dr. King doubted if individual charity and intimate kindness were enough in the face of an altogether inequitable system and said,

> One day we must come to see that the whole Jericho road must be transformed so that men and women will not be constantly beaten and robbed as they make their journey on life's highway.

How can Mormons come together as a community to transform the institution we cherish into a more loving, inclusive and equal place? Do we have the courage to ask ourselves if we have a beam in our eye that needs to be cast out—a beam that blinds us to the ways in which we are hurting each other?

I find the words of LDS Church spokeswoman Ruth Todd to be both calculated and comforting.

When she met us on Temple Square as we attempted to attend the priesthood session[309] in October she said although she felt many would find our efforts divisive, "These are our sisters and we want them among us."[310] What a glorious day when the official spokesperson of the Church can look a group of feminists directly confronting sexism on Church property in the eyes and tell us we are wanted. Any church that can constructively coexist with those who persistently ask difficult questions and openly examine its own systematic inequality is a healthy and beautiful institution.

I hope that my recent experience, and the assurance of my leaders that I will not be disciplined, is a sign that the road to Jericho is under construction. Those with questions and sincere desires will not be disciplined, but will be taken seriously, and viewed as valued members of our faith community. Mormon men and women can now move beyond the fear of the past.

Together we can excommunicate, not those deemed to be "undesirable" for one reason or another, but sexism itself.

In March, the first General Women's Meeting replaced the annual Relief Society and Young Women meetings, welcoming all women and girls ages 8 and older. Ofa Kaufusi prayed at this meeting and in doing so became the first woman of color to pray at a session of General Conference. In October, Dorah Mkhabela was the first Black woman to pray in conference. The October conference also saw speakers delivering talks in languages other than English. The Church-produced documentary *Meet the Mormons* played in 200 US movie theaters that same month.

Conservative Mormon blogger Kathryn Skaggs received attention for her post that described the Disney movie *Frozen* as having an overt gay agenda. Apostles Henry B. Eyring and L. Tom Perry, together with Presiding Bishop Gérald Caussé, participated in an interfaith conference on marriage hosted at the Vatican with Pope Francis. Eyring stated, "We want our voice to be heard against all of the counterfeit and alternative lifestyles that try to replace the family organization."[311] This was repeated by Perry in a General Conference talk in April 2015.[312] Apostle M. Russell Ballard spoke at a devotional where he noted that "individuals do not choose to have [same-sex] attractions."[313] Rock star Tyler Glenn came out as a gay Mormon in a *Rolling Stone* magazine article.[314]

This year saw two significant publications by Mormon feminist authors. Neylan McBaine published *Women at Church: Magnifying LDS Women's Local Impact*,[315] which outlined a number of ways for local Church leaders to be more inclusive of women without changing Church policy. McArthur Krishna, Bethany Brady Spalding, and Kathleen Peterson wrote and illustrated the children's book *Girls Who Choose God: Stories of Courageous Women from the Bible*.[316]

FMH blogger and podcaster Lindsay Hansen Park started the podcast *Year of Polygamy* in January. The initial goal was to investigate the lives of Joseph Smith's plural wives for a year, but it grew into a multi-year project that included discussions of contemporary polygamy. In February, FMH added Kalani as a blogger.

Ordain Women planned a reprise of their 2013 Priesthood Session action for the April conference. Michael Otterson, the head of the LDS Church's Public Affairs department, made a public statement asking Ordain Women not to seek admission into the Priesthood Session. On April 5, five hundred Mormon feminists joined Ordain Women in City Creek Park in Salt Lake City before they marched to the Tabernacle, where Church officials refused them entry. The action drew local, national, and international media attention. As people sought information online, more people visited the FMH blog on April 6 than any other day prior or since.

A *New York Times* op-ed proclaimed the end of the Mormon Moment[317] as news emerged in early summer that Kate Kelly and John Dehlin would be facing Church discipline under charges of apostasy. Kate Kelly was one of the founders of Ordain Women and was frequently in the public eye, making comments about the role of women in the Church. John Dehlin hosted the popular Mormon Stories podcast and was a well-known figure in progressive Mormon circles. Kelly was excommunicated in June, and Dehlin's excommunication was pushed into early 2015. Both events signaled changes in the way that feminist and progressive Mormons viewed the LDS Church.

"FAIKAVA: ONE WOMAN'S THOUGHTS" BY KALANI TONGA (FEBRUARY 19, 2014)

It's Christmas evening. The kids have settled down from the sugar-and gift-high of the early morning, we've stuffed ourselves full of delicious Christmas treats, and we are relaxing together as a family, enjoying the last little bit of the Christmas season.

"We should go over to your mom's," my husband says. "I'll bet she would like to see the kids, and you guys could hang out."

Frankly, I'm floored. Things have been a little tense between my husband and me lately, and this is the very last thing I expect him to say. Excitedly, I bundle up our babies and pack everyone into the car. I'm looking forward to having a visit that didn't come at my insistence, with a fight brewing just beneath the surface. As we pull into my mom's driveway, my husband turns to me and says, "Since you guys are gonna hang out here for a little while, I'm just gonna run down the street and faikava."

And there it is.

This wasn't a gesture of goodwill after all, but, rather, a strategic move intended to pacify me so that he could go hang out with his male friends and relatives. I turn to him, eyes snapping with anger, and before I can utter a word, he says, "Come on, babe. It's Christmas!"

Funny, he took the words right out of my mouth. And yet, those words would have meant something completely different, had I said them first. Many women who are married to Polynesian men will understand the feelings that rioted through me as I got my children out of the car and marched us all into my mom's home, sans-husband, but the rest of the general population probably knows little about the word "faikava."

At the risk of drawing ire from most of my Polynesian brothers, and likely many of my Polynesian sisters, I am going to share my experience with the Pacific Island practice of faikava. In my observation, Tongan women seldom discuss the heartache and frustration caused by this tradition, but it is there. I know it is. I see it and I sense it, even when it is not spoken aloud. Our LDS church leaders have recognized it, too, and many areas with large Polynesian populations now have rules stating that faikava participation can keep otherwise worthy Polynesian men from serving in some leadership callings or receiving temple recommends. So, this in mind, I want to briefly explore its original island uses and then delve into the mutated form faikava has taken here in the United States. I want to look at what it says about Islander gender roles in general, and specifically, I want to tell the story of what this practice looked like for me, and the impact of this practice on my marriage and my family.

So. . .what is this mysterious ritual called faikava? In the words of the great Inigo Montoya, "Let me explain. No, there is too much. Let me sum up."[318] Kava is a root that, when ground to a fine powder and mixed with water, creates a drink that has narcotic sedative properties. In other words, it gives you a buzz without the use of alcohol. Originally, kava was used in ceremonies to mark important life events—weddings, funerals, milestone birthdays, formalized courtship, etc. Important cultural and genealogical information is passed from generation to generation during these faikavas. Young men learn from their elders, beautiful music is played and sung, and brotherly bonds are forged and cemented as the men sit together for hours drinking kava. To be honest, I really don't know a whole heck of a lot about traditional faikava ceremonies, having only been witness to a single event. A few years ago, my grandmother had a milestone birthday, and my grandpa honored her with a kava ceremony that we as a family were invited to observe. It was beautiful and special and unlike any other experience I'd ever had with this custom. What made it so lovely to me was that it focused on honoring my grandma. I felt and saw firsthand the love that my grandfather and others felt for her, and it opened my eyes to how beautiful this tradition COULD be.

However, as with many customs that cross the ocean to America, the traditional kava ceremony has mutated into a practice that mimics much of its traditionally intended use but lacks the subtle nuances that make it special and beautiful and sacred. These days, on any given night, you can find Polynesian men hanging out at the kalapu, or kava club. No longer used just during important ceremonial occasions, many Polynesian men now drink kava recreationally. As they sit around in a big circle, shiny brown cups carved from coconuts are filled with kava and distributed in "rounds" (as in, "this 'round' is on me, boys!"). Typically, only one woman attends this event—someone called a tou'a, whose job it is to dish out the kava and keep the men entertained with witty banter and small talk throughout the night. And when I say "throughout the night," I literally mean that these gatherings often last all night long. It was not at all unusual for my husband to stumble in at 3:00, 4:00, or even 5:00 in the morning after a night of drinking kava. But I'm getting ahead of myself.

Before I discuss the ways in which kava has affected me personally, I want to look briefly at what this practice says about gender roles in Pacific Island culture—specifically Tongan culture, as that is my heritage and I am thus most familiar with Tongan customs. As always, I want to issue a brief disclaimer and state that this is obviously something that I understand from my own unique perspective, and I do not claim to speak for Tongan women collectively. Furthermore, I acknowledge that my biracial background makes me even more of a weirdo in regards to my feelings about Tongan culture, and most certainly colors my perspective in ways that are different from a full-Tongan woman. So. . .take that for what it's worth, and let's proceed, shall we?

Okay, first I want to take a quick look at women's roles in the Americanized version of the faikava. I find it at once fascinating and infuriating that, with the exception of the tou'a, the participants in a faikava are exclusively male. Women are not just excluded from the faikava, they are shunned. Generally speaking, unless one wishes to be seen as a woman of low moral standards, one does not set foot inside a kalapu. I have admittedly little experience with the inner workings of faikava clubs, as I have always been told that it is not appropriate for a Tongan woman to have firsthand knowledge of these things, so I apologize if I inadvertently misconstrue any information. But, in my limited experience, and in speaking with others about the role of a tou'a, I feel comfortable saying that as the sole woman within the man's domain, the tou'a in most Americanized faikavas is seen as at once enticing and soiled. Much like the high school beauty that everybody sleeps with and then calls a slut, the tou'a typically has a reputation for being simultaneously attractive and repulsive—a woman it would be fine to sleep with, but who is not acceptable for marriage. Tou'as are "honored" with the attentions of all the men in the group, which, I'm told, often means that she fields inappropriate comments and questions from crusty old men for much of the night.

I'm hesitant to voice my opinions on Tongan cultural practices because I acknowledge that I do not understand the culture of my father nearly as well as I wish I did. I was raised in a small suburb in Texas where the only Polynesians for miles were my immediate family and my grandparents. In fact, because we did not live around any other Tongans, when I was very young I actually thought my dad was black. I distinctly recall coming home from kindergarten with a family portrait I had drawn, and having my dad sit me down, point to his likeness that I had drawn exclusively in black crayon, and explain that he was not, in fact, black. I remember feeling so confused because the only people I knew with skin even close to the same color as my dad's were blacks. Anyway, suffice it to say that due to my isolation, I was raised very differently from most other Polynesian girls, and this undoubtedly influences my feelings on some of the cultural practices I have encountered in adulthood. However, the lack of experience with faikava in my youth did not shield me from the effects of its presence in my adult life. Thus, although I may not understand everything about this custom, I feel more than qualified to discuss the ways in which faikava touches the lives of many women and their children. So, again, taking into account that I am writing from the perspective of an American-born half-Tongan woman, let me tell you what this aspect of Tongan culture felt like for me.

As a Tongan woman, I find the Tongan gender roles extraordinarily restrictive for women. Men, from a very early age, are permitted to kind of "roam free." It is expected that "boys will be boys" and that they will run around together and get into occasional mischief. Girls, on the other hand, are expected to stay home. Like, ALWAYS stay home. Men and women in the same family (extended family included) are not supposed to intermingle in most social situations. The men go off and do one thing, and the women typically stay home and cook/watch kids until the men return. If, heaven forbid, the men and women from the same family DO happen to find themselves in the same social setting (if, for example, unbeknownst to each other, each group happened to choose to attend the same dance club on the same night), the women are usually expected to leave since it is not proper for the men and women to be in the same social sphere. In light of these social norms, it is easy to understand how the faikava has evolved from a special, occasional ceremony to a recreational habit where the men get together to hang out and chat and sing and drink, leaving their wives and families home to fend for themselves while the men are off socializing together.

Under these circumstances, the word that bubbles to the top of the list when I try to characterize my feelings towards faikava is "forgotten." I felt completely and utterly forgotten when I sat alone in my house full of babies, changing diapers and making bottles and attending to feedings throughout the night while my husband drank his night away with his buddies and relatives. I felt forgotten the next morning when, since he had stayed out so late the night before, I woke up to once again face changing diapers and making breakfast and bathing my children alone while my husband slept until well into the afternoon. I felt forgotten on occasions like Christmas day when my husband dumped the kids and me at my mom's house and took off to go faikava.

It was bad when my husband would go faikava at houses that were an hour or more away—I worried constantly about him falling asleep at the wheel after drinking kava all night. But, it was almost worse when they would have their faikava at our home. On these occasions, all the men sat outside either in our garage or our yard, and I sat in my house alone (well … as the lone adult with 3 infants and a 7-year-old, anyway). Because Tongan culture is very strict about when and where men and women can be in mixed company, my presence outside would have been considered highly inappropriate and uncomfortable for all involved. So, when they would faikava at our house, I felt like a prisoner in my own home. I would sit inside by myself and listen to the laughter and music emanating from the kava circle mere feet from where I sat, and as I sat there all alone, I felt forgotten.

I used to ask my husband lots of questions about his kava drinking habits. "Why does it have to start so late? Why does it have to last for four or six or eight hours at a time, and why do you always have to stay until the very end? Why can't you do it at a normal time of day? Why can't we do something that allows us to interact as couples, rather than just in groups by gender?" I asked a steady stream of questions, and ninety percent of the time, he basically told me that this was just "the way it is," and that to try to change anything would be inappropriate, would be considered rude, and would be overstepping his bounds. I truly have no idea whether this point of view is accurate across the board, or whether these are just his feelings and beliefs, but I have a sneaking suspicion that the majority of Polynesian men would agree with his statements. Most Polynesians are raised with a deeply ingrained need to be culturally "correct," to live so that others look at them and say, "(He/she) knows how to act. (His/her) parents obviously taught (him/her) right." My husband was no different. I found it intriguing and more than a little discouraging that he valued the opinions of the other Tongan men at the faikava more than he ever valued mine as his wife.

Considering the fact that I felt both forgotten and devalued as a result of my husband's kava habits, obviously this cultural practice did not have a positive effect on my marriage. For various reasons, I am in the process of filing for divorce. And although this was not the sole contributor to the decision to file, I can honestly say that the underlying lack of respect I felt at being an unwilling bystander while my husband participated in this tradition most certainly and significantly contributed to my ultimate decision. The thing is, after taking a step back, I realize that much of the disrespect I experienced was unintentional. My husband didn't set out to hurt me; he just did what most Polynesian men are taught is acceptable and expected that I would act the part of a "good wife" and go along with it. But that forgotten feeling wouldn't allow me to feel okay about sitting passively at home. I know that I am not alone in feeling this way. I know that there are other women who are married to Polynesian men that feel as isolated and devalued as I did. For that reason, if for no other, I wanted to write this post. If this rings true to you, I am writing this for you. You are not alone. You are not forgotten. Your feelings matter.

I'm honestly not sure how to solve this problem. Because it is a cultural norm in most American Polynesian communities (I can't speak about the island communities, as I have no firsthand knowledge), I think many women have just come to accept it as an unfortunate but inevitable part of their life. I don't think this has to be true, but I think that in order for anything to change, we first need to acknowledge that this is, in fact, a problem. I do believe that this cultural tradition has a beautiful history and has an important function in the Tongan culture, but the bastardized form that faikava has taken here in the States leaves much to be desired. I don't know what the answer is. All I know is that I've been silent long enough, and I am no longer willing to sit passively and pass on this dysfunctional cultural practice to my daughters.

The struggle to sift through the cultural traditions of one's parents, hoping to separate the beautiful "wheat-like" aspects from the damaging and destructive "tares," is a universal dilemma. Although you may not deal with this specific challenge, have you dealt with something similar? And, if you have, how did you cope? Were there immediate solutions, or do you think I am preparing for a battle to be won for my daughters or my daughter's daughters, and not for me? Truly, I don't know the answer, but I know it is out there, and I would love to hear your thoughts. In the meantime, my hope is that this post will give another woman the voice I wish I had heard while I sat at home alone. You are not alone. You matter. We can make this right and it doesn't have to be an all or nothing ultimatum. Let's start the hard conversation and see where it leads.

"WHY 'LOVE THE SINNER, HATE THE SIN' DOESN'T WORK FOR ME" BY KALANI TONGA (MARCH 5, 2014)

These days, there is much ado about modesty rhetoric. People hotly debate both sides of the issue, with some claiming that "modest is hottest" and women should dress in a manner that will help young men keep their thoughts pure, while others believe that this concept is damaging and objectifying and is inappropriate to teach to young girls. Don't worry . . . this is not another modesty post. I don't know that I have anything to add to the conversation that hasn't already been said by a hundred other people in a hundred other ways on a hundred other blogs. But, a modesty debate on my friend's Facebook page did start the mental juices flowing in a different direction, and that eventually led me to write this post. The following is a small portion of the conversation we had. It is one person's response to the idea that leaders need to be more responsible for the content they teach young women/young men/Primary children.

> Ok, um, I had the lesson of the chewing gum[319] thing from my own bishop. But to me the lesson was about MY choices and to do your best to stay pure for temple marriage . . . My

point being, yeah you can blame the teacher, but you can also blame the taught. Because we are taught to pray for ourselves what is true and what is not.

For very personal reasons, this comment struck a chord deep in my heart. I posted a brief response on my friend's page and then left the conversation, but the feelings this comment stirred have been simmering inside me ever since.

"You can also blame the taught."

No. A thousand times no. And here's why.

When I was maybe 12 years old, a well-meaning young women's leader with some very outdated information taught us a lesson on temple marriage. To be honest, I don't remember the details of most lessons I learned in young women's, but for reasons that will soon be obvious, I recall the specific content of this one. On this particular Sunday, I heard something that changed the way I viewed myself and altered the way I viewed marriage. It was a concept I had not been exposed to previously: the idea that LDS men and women should seek to marry within their own race or culture.

As the product of an interracial marriage (my dad is Tongan and my mom's family is mostly Swedish), hearing that Heavenly Father did not approve of my parents' marriage was, as I'm sure you can imagine, rather distressing. I was a bright kid. I had been taught right from wrong and knew how to think for myself. Nevertheless, for reasons most Mormons can probably understand, I did not immediately question what my leader taught me at this time. Instead, I internalized this new knowledge and took it a step further by deciding somewhere in the deep, dark depths of my soul that if Heavenly Father disapproved of interracial marriages, this meant that any marriage I entered into would be unacceptable since I brought that interracial aspect into any relationship simply by being biracial. No matter who I chose to marry, we were already in an interracial relationship because I was interracial in and of myself. I remember feeling so confused and conflicted because on the one hand, I loved my mixed background and I was intensely proud of who I am, but on the other hand, I felt like there was a part of me that, through no fault of my own, made me inherently and irrevocably flawed.

I've often said that I wish I had more blind faith. I think my life would be so much easier if I didn't ask so many questions, if I could just take the "this is just the way it is" answer and run with it. But, alas, this is not who I am. I inevitably feel compelled to dig deeper in an attempt to satisfy my need to understand. So, as I puzzled over the idea that God doesn't approve of interracial marriages, I started digging. I was appalled by what I found. The following quotes were among those I happened across in my search:

Shall I tell you the law of God in regard to the African race? If the white man who belongs to the chosen seed mixes his blood with the seed of Cain, the penalty, under the law of God, is death on the spot. This will always be so.

–Prophet Brigham Young, *Journal of Discourses*, v. 10, p. 110

Your ideas, as we understand them, appear to contemplate the intermarriage of the Negro and white races, a concept which has heretofore been most repugnant to most normal-minded people from the ancient patriarchs until now. . . . There is a growing tendency, particularly among some educators, as it manifests itself in this area, toward the breaking down of race barriers in the matter of intermarriage between whites and blacks, but it does not have the sanction of the Church and is contrary to Church doctrine.

–LDS First Presidency (George Albert Smith), letter to Virgil
H. Sponberg (critic of the anti-black ban), May 5, 1947,
quoted in Lester E. Bush, *Mormonism's Negro Doctrine: An
Historical Overview*, p. 42

Although these quotes dealt specifically with black-white interracial marriages, in my heart I didn't differentiate. My dad was dark, my mom was not. In my mind, this put me in the same category as those Brigham Young said deserved "death on the spot." However, like every good Mormon, I learned to "shelve" these quotes . . . to set them to the side or put them "on the shelf" along with those other hard things I didn't understand. So, up on the shelf they went, to sit with the likes of polygamy, ministering angels, and "you will never be tempted past that which ye can bear," until some glorious future date when hopefully all would be resolved and I would understand. But, something happened fairly recently that caused me to take these quotes back down, dust them off, and reexamine them.

It took me years and, frankly, therapy, to realize that I have carried this sense of being innately flawed into my adulthood. After my marriage fell apart, I remember telling my counselor, "I feel like I can walk into a room full of perfectly wonderful, amazing, good men who all find me attractive, and the only one I will be attracted to is the one with the most emotional baggage." My counselor looked me in the eye and said, "Yes. Because you feel like their baggage makes yours okay." And, he was absolutely right. By choosing someone with more baggage than I had, I was essentially letting myself off the hook for being unacceptable (in God's eyes) for marriage. I learned at 12 years old that God wants us to marry within our own race, realized that because I was already biracial I didn't have the ability to marry within my own race, and so I subconsciously sought out men who had more undesirable traits than I did in an effort to make my inadequacy "okay." What I learned when I was 12 years old started me down a path that I truly believe has affected my entire life.

I know that this blog post is jumping all over the place. Modesty rhetoric, interracial marriage, and now I want to talk about homosexuality. This post is kind of a ticking time bomb filled with controversial Mormon topics. I've struggled with whether to divulge my feelings for several reasons, but all of those reasons boil down to fear. I've been afraid to disappoint my family. I think of my parents and my siblings and my children, and I desperately want to make them proud, to spare them from feeling embarrassment because of something I've said. I've also been afraid to lose my calling. I currently teach Relief Society, and I adore this calling. I feel like I am able to do good and uplift and serve my sisters. This calling makes me feel useful and competent in the adult world, which is something of a rarity in my daily life that is currently filled with diaper changes and feeding babies and substitute teaching at local elementary schools. I love teaching Relief Society, and I'm afraid to lose it. Along those same lines, I've been terrified that I could lose my temple recommend. I waited until I was 34 years old to become endowed. I fought my way through doubt and sadness and pain and confusion and emerged fully prepared to make the covenants required in the temple. I love the temple, even if it simultaneously brings me joy and sorrow. I want to be there, even though I have to once again "shelve" some of those things that I just don't understand. And, finally, I've been afraid of backlash from the LGBTQ community. Recently, I watched as comments from a couple of blog posts on LGBTQ/ally issues kind of blew up. Members of the LGBTQ community were divided, with some saying that allies should stop trying to monopolize the conversation when they don't really know how it feels or what the issues really are, and others saying that allies should continue to speak up. I almost used this upheaval as a cop out for remaining silent. I said to myself, "See?! Even those you hope to support don't want you to say anything. Seriously, you should just shut up." I took their feelings to heart, and I hope that those who feel that allies should wait to speak until spoken to do not see this post as an unwelcome intrusion. Voicing my opinion about homosexuality is scary. I feel like I have a lot to lose. But, I decided that I am no longer willing to let fear silence my voice, and I feel like I owe it to my 12-year-old self to speak up. So, here I am.

Here's the thing about the church's current stance on homosexuality: *it doesn't work for me.* As someone who has felt the pain and confusion of feeling like I am viewed by God as inherently flawed, "love the sinner, hate the sin" just doesn't work for me. As someone who has felt like no matter who I married, it would not be acceptable to God just because of who I am, this stance doesn't work for me. We tell our LGBTQ brothers and sisters, "I love you ... except for this big part of you that is completely and irretrievably interwoven into the fabric of your soul. I hate that part because it is sinful. But, really, I do love you." No, sorry, that doesn't work for me.

So, where does that put me? Am I still on the Lord's side? I hope that I am. I think there is a place for everyone in the church. I believe in erring on the side of love and on the side of compassion. I do not believe that homosexuality is a choice, and just like I don't believe that Brigham Young had the final word regarding interracial marriage, I have hope that our current stance regarding homosexuality is not the final word. The amazing thing about our church is its ability to adapt, to change, and to grow. I look at our current attitude towards interracial marriage, and I am so grateful for our ability to change and grow. I am grateful that my girls will not be taught by some well-meaning youth leader that loving someone of a different race is unacceptable. But, as peaceful as I feel about the fact that we no longer teach that those who intermarry should be put to death, years later I can still feel and see the effects of being inadvertently told that I was fundamentally defective. And, knowing how that felt for me, it absolutely crushes my soul to think about what we are telling our LGBTQ brothers and sisters. I know that this is an old topic. I know that the same things have been rehashed over and over and over again. But, if you could go back and take that young women's leader's place, what would you say to my 12-year-old self? Would you spare her years of feeling inadequate and unlovable due to circumstances beyond her control? I hope you answered yes. I love the church. I love the gospel. I don't understand the current stance we've taken on homosexuality, and yet I desperately want to be on the Lord's side. I don't want to be the cause of another person's belief that he or she is inherently flawed. I don't want to be the one that tells another brother or sister, "I love you, but. . . ." I cannot be the one to teach this, and we most certainly cannot "blame the taught" if our teachings cause them to grow up feeling like they are profoundly broken just by being who they are. I don't know what the answer is, but I believe that we can do better.

"Why the LDS Church's Statement on Ordain Women Convinced Me to Join OW at Temple Square on April 5" by Joanna Brooks (March 17, 2014)

Today, LDS Church Public Affairs wrote a letter to Ordain Women and released a statement about their planned April 5 event at General Conference.[320] You can read it here.[321]

Both the letter and the statement are an effort to discourage women like me (who care about women's issues but have mixed feelings about ordination) from joining OW's respectful, poignant, determined effort to advance equality within the LDS Church.

But I am not discouraged. And I hope you will not be either.

If anything, today's statements from the Church strengthen my commitment to be there April 5. I hope you will too.

The Church PR statement takes the defensive tactic of disparaging those it feels threatened by. It accuses Ordain Women of "detracting" from a productive "conversation" within the Church about women's issues. But it is plainly incorrect and inconsistent with recorded history for LDS Church Public Affairs spokespeople to state that there has been a good "conversation" in the Church about women's issues.

If there has been a "conversation" about gender equality in Mormonism, it is not because the Church has led or even supported it. It is because generations of Mormon feminists have continued to ask faithful but agitating questions of the faith we love, even when it has discouraged, rejected, and disrespected us. We've asked questions in our prayers, in our families, among friends, on our own blogs. The national media—including *The New York Times*—has done more to proactively acknowledge and advance serious conversation about gender issues in Mormonism than the LDS Church, which has been on the defensive on women's issues for decades.

If our faithful Mormon feminist questioning has penetrated the behind-closed-doors decision-making meetings at Church Headquarters, we are thrilled. But Mormon women are not involved in those meetings. Regretfully, we still have no authoritative role in making decisions of theological, policy, and financial consequence in the Church we love and serve. Our Church continues to function as an outdated, closed-door, gender-segregated bureaucracy—a model rooted in the secular conservative management models of the 1930s, 1940s, and 1950s, not in Mormon scripture and certainly not in the vision Joseph Smith had when he "turned the key"[322] to the women leaders of the Relief Society.

Ordination is not my bosom-burning cause. But I am tired of seeing women I love leave the faith because there is no serious, open, respectful conversation within the Church about issues that matter to them and because they are stigmatized and rejected when they dare to ask the questions. Today, again, the Church sought to push out women who are asking the questions.

I respect what OW has done to advance serious conversation about women's equality in Mormonism. I will stand with them this April 5. I hope you will join me.

"To the Saints Who Tell Heretics and Apostates to Leave" by Christa Baxter/christer1979 (March 25, 2014)

When I was a missionary, I pondered my purpose every day: To invite others to come unto Christ and receive His restored gospel through faith in Jesus Christ and His atonement, repentance, baptism by immersion, receiving the gift of the Holy Ghost, and enduring to the end. Never, not before, during, or after my mission for the church, was I asked to invite other people to leave it. Yet too often I see members of my church, in the name of their testimony and faith, inviting other members with questions and concerns to just leave if they're not happy here.

In a way, I can understand this impulse. Mormons sacrifice a lot for their faith. We live moral standards most people are baffled by. We attend hours of church meetings every week. As young adults, we even give up eighteen months[323] to two years of our lives, asking people every day to learn more about Christ and come unto Him. When you have done these things for God's church, to have someone come along and question it feels like a slap in the face—especially when that questioner is not some ignorant outsider but another member who has made these sacrifices too. It is painful and sometimes scary to see people so similar to me find fault with something I love so much.

And yet. I spent too much time inviting people to come feast on Christ's love to imagine ever inviting someone to leave it. To see a member of my faith casually undo what I've worked for my whole life by calling another member "heretic" and "apostate" stings more than those members' questions themselves. I cannot imagine standing before Christ and my Heavenly Parents at the judgment bar and trying to explain why I invited other people to leave their church and their love because I thought they were doing it wrong.

Instead, my responsibility is repeated over and over in the scriptures: to feed God's sheep—all of them. To love. To leave judgment to God, who will judge us not only by our works but also by the desires of our hearts.[324] In the words of President Uchtdorf, to "stop it!"[325] if I'm ever tempted to judge another, to shut someone out because I don't agree with who they are or the questions they're asking.

On my mission, I often studied The Worth of Souls in the scriptures. When I was feeling discouraged about tracting, these verses reminded me of each individual's vast potential and divine worth. Most scriptures were single verses, but there was one story in the New Testament that demonstrated how Christ felt about individuals' divine worth—even those who didn't seem to get the big picture. In this story, Christ's apostles are appalled because a group of Samaritans (of Samaritans!) aren't welcoming to their Savior and Lord. In Luke 9:51—53, it reads,

> And it came to pass, when the time was come that he [Jesus] should be received up, he steadfastly set his face to go to Jerusalem, and sent messengers before his face: and they went, and entered into a village of the Samaritans, to make ready for him [Jesus]. And they did not receive him, because his face was as though he would go to Jerusalem.

Can you imagine the sting? A group of lowly Samaritans (Samaritans!) choosing to slight your Savior and Lord. I think many of us can sympathize with how James and John felt (Luke 9:54):

> And when his disciples James and John saw this, they said, Lord, wilt thou that we command fire to come down from heaven, and consume them, even as Elias did?

Their response is similar to what I've seen among many friends: Lord, if someone has the audacity to question You and Your ways, should we lay the smackdown? Tell them how wrong they are? Make it clear that if they're not for the church they're against it? Invite them to just leave if they're so unhappy with things?

But look at how Jesus responds (Luke 9:55—56):

> But he turned, and rebuked them, and said, Ye know not what manner of spirit ye are of. For the Son of man is not come to destroy men's lives, but to save them. And they went to another village.

Christ wasn't interested in destroying the people who had disrespected him. His mission was to love, to convert, to bring peace and understanding. If he wasn't interested in driving away disrespectful Samaritans, how then can we assume he wants us to drive away people who are respectfully asking questions?[326] If he could cry, "Father, forgive them, for they know not what they do,"[327] how can we insist that they know very well what they do and they deserve to be cast out?

If you feel that Ordain Women and other church members with questions are a sign of crisis in the church, don't make it worse by inviting them to leave. We are part of the body of Christ; we have no business usurping God's role and deciding who is fit to stay and who should go. If you think that asking questions serves no purpose in God's church, then what can we do but approach people in love and invite them to Christ's love? And if they say, "But I do, and it is God's love and respect for all that compels me to ask these things," then remember that it was Jesus who said, "He that is not against us is for us" (Luke 9:50).

If you think you get to single handedly judge someone's worthiness to remain a member of the Church of Jesus Christ of Latter-day Saints, check your hubris and stop it. If you are tempted to forego listening and seeking to understand just to tell someone to go away, stop it. This isn't a political party, club, or country we're talking about. This is the gospel of Jesus Christ, with power to redeem human beings, and how dare we question who should and shouldn't partake of it? Furthermore, these interactions don't happen in vacuums, and many people who are barely holding on to their testimonies see your rejection of honest questioners as the final straw. I, for one, am too busy pleading with people to stay to ask anyone to leave. Will asking them to leave address their questions?[328] Or will it only address the discomfort you feel at those very questions?

Maybe President Uchtdorf wasn't speaking so much to doubting members as he was to their staunch family and friends when he said, "My dear friends, there is yet a place for you here."[329] If an apostle tells me there's room for those with questions and doubts, how can I insist they leave? Better to rejoice that they are still here and strive to love, even if their questions sometimes make me uncomfortable. After all, I don't have to agree with someone to love them. And there are many things I've been wrong about in life, but choosing to love others has never failed me.

"LDS Church PR and Ordain Women: Amputating the Body of Christ" by Katie Langston (April 7, 2014)

I walked to Temple Square yesterday, arm in arm and shoulder to shoulder with my sisters. I witnessed a quiet, peaceful, respectful action of love and yearning. There was no shouting. There were no demands. There was no disrespect. We were greeted warmly by a representative from church public affairs, Kim Farah, who hugged each of us and welcomed us and reassured us of the church's love for us.

I left the action renewed and even hopeful. The calm, peaceful expression of our desire for greater gender equality in the church seemed to have been met graciously and hospitably, with a tone and an approach that was mature and loving. Though it was clear that this didn't represent any sort of willingness on the part of church leaders to change or even consider a change to existing priesthood policies, there was a sense of camaraderie and friendship in the exchange. I felt as though the message Sister Farah conveyed was, "No, we don't agree with you, but you are still our brothers and sisters in Christ."

After the action, one friend even said, with tears in her eyes, "Look at how we were received. We're not going to be kicked out. The days of fear are over. We have nothing to fear anymore."

This is as it should be in the Body of Christ. Paul made it explicit that the Body has many parts, and each is needful—that no part can say to the other, "I have no need of thee," for just as a human body needs hands and feet, heart and lungs, even armpits and digestive systems to function properly, so the church needs each of us. This teaching reminds us that without all our perspectives, talents, and gifts working together for the good of the Kingdom, we are living below our privileges.

Currently, we Mormons are far from this ideal. Not only does 50% of the population lack basic representation at the table through systematic gender inequality, but more often than not, those with divergent views are pushed out, marginalized, and silenced. Yesterday's reception felt like a small step in the right direction—a sense that perhaps there is some loosening, some listening, some desire on the part of the institution to take this concept seriously.

Then last night, over pasta with some friends, we saw the church's official response pop up in our Facebook feeds.

It was a knife in the back.

From *The Salt Lake Tribune*:[330]

> Despite polite and respectful requests from church leaders not to make Temple Square a place of protest, a mixed group of men and women ignored that request and staged a demonstration outside the Tabernacle on General Conference weekend, refusing to accept ushers' directions and refusing to leave when asked," church spokesman Cody Craynor wrote in an email Saturday evening.
>
> While not all the protesters were members of the church, such divisive actions are not the kind of behavior that is expected from Latter-day Saints and will be as disappointing to our members as it is to church leaders.

This depiction of the action is disingenuous at best and dishonest at worst. I was there personally and never heard anyone ask us to leave. What's more, I have asked many people, including several official OW representatives, and none of them received a request to leave, nor did we fail to comply with any usher's requests. I repeat, the depiction from church PR in no way reflects the scene I observed.

But perhaps even more disappointing than the flexibility with the facts is the overall message the statement conveys to the membership. From their initial request asking OW to stand in the "free speech zones" to last night's heartbreaking spin, I am becoming increasingly concerned that their strategy is designed to give cues to the membership how to view us—as rabble rousers, outsiders, haters, disobedient apostates; people to be ignored or even ridiculed.

In a word: Other.

In so doing, I am concerned that they are trying to amputate us from the Body of Christ.

Whether or not that's their objective, that's certainly the effect. Search the #ordainwomen hashtag on Twitter or read the comments on Facebook. Church members feel they have permission to make personal, judgmental comments about their brothers and sisters in Christ as it relates to our testimonies and commitment to the gospel. Here is just a small handful of the kinds of things that are being said. . . .

"Satan is having a great day."

"Sisters, if you must hold office, start your own church."

"I am truly shocked to see that this group has formed among women that are active members. Obviously, their faith is lacking in their prophet & many other things pertaining to the scriptures & history of the church."

"So is this a new anti-Mormon group under cover?"

"You absolutely cannot have a testimony of the church and its leaders when you think you know better than they do. You really should be ashamed of yourselves, but even that is difficult to do when you are 'past feeling'."

"Apostasy is no new thing to have happened; what you are staging and carrying-on is no different than any apostate group that has ever rose up and left the church. If you do not agree with the doctrine, LEAVE."

"Why are Ordain Women still members of the church? Why don't you leave what you disagree with?"

I'm frustrated by these comments—they lack love and empathy. But I understand the people who say these things, and I have compassion for them. They are reading the script the institution has written for them. They are, devastatingly, following the example of their leaders and spokespeople.

Look, maybe women's ordination really isn't God's will. It's possible. I sincerely believe it is, but I could be wrong—wrongness is part of this whole mortality thing, after all.

But the challenge and promise of the Body of Christ is that we work together despite our differences. This doesn't mean marginalizing and shunning the already disenfranchised (the ones Jesus took special care to reach, I might add), but having difficult conversations with the people with whom we disagree most, and giving each other grace and space to disagree and *still claim each other*, as a token of our shared commitment to living out the message of Christ's love.

Who knows? Maybe Ordain Women is the butt of the church. I freely admit that could be the case. But as unglamorous as butts may be, we need our butts every bit as much as we need our hands, our eyes, our mouths, our feet. If we're the butt of the church, perhaps our role is to clear out some of the gunk that's accumulated in the Body, so that the entire Body can function more effectively and fluidly.

In any case, just like in life, when a Body part is hurting, the solution isn't to amputate—it's to attend to it with care. The church's response felt like a carving knife, when a lovetap and a comfortable chair would have done just fine.

"GLIMPSES OF HEAVENLY MOTHER: LESSONS OF FEMALE BLESSINGS" BY TRESA BROWN EDMUNDS (MAY 7, 2014)

You can call me Amanda, a name made up by the author of this *City Weekly* piece[331] to protect my real identity. That piece gives an excellent overview into why and how I started offering blessings, so I'll refer you there for the backstory. For today I want to say, I am a woman in the church in good standing, with a temple recommend, and I lay my hands on people's heads, or speak words over the phone, and offer them blessings through the authority of faith in Jesus Christ, in the same manner our pioneer foremothers did.

I think of those women daily, and I know they feel anger for me. I know they resent that I need to keep my identity protected when this power was something they claimed as their birthright. I have thought many times about coming out and calling the bluff of prominent voices who say that women don't need the priesthood, that we enjoy the blessings of the priesthood and access to spiritual gifts. I've thought about going public and asking them if they'd like me to give them a blessing, to exercise the gifts of revelation and prophecy and healing I've been given, but I really don't want to pay the consequences that come from proving those words false.

I've now been giving blessings for about two years, slowly at first, only a few that first year, and then more and more as word spread. I try my hardest to be available whenever I can for someone's first blessing and in times of emergency, and then after that I have to put people off and fit them in where I can to keep my family life going. I never want to turn anyone away, but I have to draw limits. There is such a devastating need for this kind of divine power with a woman as a conduit that I could spend every day from morning to night doing nothing else.

When I feel the push to approach someone that I'm not sure will be open to it, I usually say I'm "a little psychic." And then I ask if they've ever done Reiki or energy work or alternative healing. I view the blessings I give strictly in the Mormon framework, but this tells me if people will be scared off by it. It breaks my heart constantly that my own people are more open to claims of psychic power than the exercise of spiritual gifts we are exhorted to seek out, but that's the facts. People are so afraid of being inappropriate they'll deny themselves the power of heaven.

Offering these blessings has changed everything about how I interact with the gospel, but it's taught me so much about Heavenly Mother. I feel Her presence in these blessings every single time. I feel Her longing for Her children. I feel Her love, I see Her side by side with our Heavenly Father. I see Her reaching out. And She tells me to tell Her children of Her love for them.

I've learned that we can commune with Heavenly Mother in nature and through the companionship of animals. I am often directed to send people to the mountains to find Her. In those moments of appreciating creation, in quiet and solitude, that's when we can feel Her. In taking care of creation, protecting the earth, nurturing animals, creating gardens, that's how we worship Her.

And I've learned that She has a special appreciation for the gifts that aren't always so appreciated in our culture. She loves the shy and contemplative. She loves the people who would rather lay the framework than get the credit. She loves those that study and arrange and preserve. She sees the ones who aren't seen, and She treasures them.

Before these blessings I never felt a need for Heavenly Mother. Like many people say about women getting the priesthood, it wasn't my issue. But now I see what I was missing. Now I have Her in my life and I won't lose Her. Even if the day comes when I have to face consequences, I won't lose Her again.

"CLAIM YOURSELF: FINDING VALIDATION AND PURPOSE WITHOUT INSTITUTIONAL APPROVAL" BY TRINÉ THOMAS NELSON (MAY 15, 2014)

Much has been said about women's ordination, and while I don't feel called to hold the priesthood, I fervently support those who do. To my heart, if you desire to serve God you are called to the work, regardless of gender. I attended the action, but didn't ask for admission, on that premise. What I witnessed were women and men who feel called to serve and administer to their brothers and sisters.

For Women of Color, being marginalized, dismissed, and othered comes with the territory. Being involved in Mormon Feminism is often the same thing on a different day. We sigh deeply at the criticism and soldier on, doing what we must. We claim ourselves, we drive ourselves to succeed, and we derive our value from something greater than an institution.

I often have conflicting feelings regarding the movement for ordaining women when supporters equate it with the Civil Rights Movement and the Priesthood/Temple Ban. To me, the ban isn't some event in the past to use as a model for future actions. It's not something that should be subsumed by groups who have similar experiences. That is co-optation. It's about my parents; it's personal, and painful. The ban has been lifted for over 30 years, yet its effects can still be felt. As a child, I had Primary classmates, and the occasional adult, reassure me that I would be white when I was resurrected.

In college friends wondered if I would ever find an eternal companion because "the Church discourages interracial marriage."[332] Walking the halls at church, or in the temple, it is rare to see images that look like me, or my children, reflected.

Martin Luther King, Jr. often recognized Gandhi as one of his inspirations. He called Gandhi "the guiding light of our technique of nonviolent social change."[333] But while he used many of the principles of Gandhi in his own work, he was clear to point out the struggles of those who came before him and acknowledged their sacrifices and how they helped propel the movement in the United States forward.

Early in 1959 MLK was provided with the opportunity to visit India. Throughout his trip he had the privilege to see and learn from those who knew Gandhi, recognize their sacrifice, and to witness the progress that India had made towards greater equality. Upon his return, he used his platform not only to discuss what he learned and how it applied to the movement's next steps, but he also drew attention to the dire poverty in India and encouraged the world community to respond.

We can all be inspired by moments or movements in the past; however, it's important to acknowledge the pain or experiences of those who came before us or those who still experience the pain of oppression. Credit their wisdom for moving us forward, and then pay tribute to them by mentoring those struggling to reclaim themselves. To do less reduces the struggles of others to an academic discussion, which removes the humanity and sacrifice of those we profess to admire.

My father was a teen and young adult through the Civil Rights Movement. As a teen, he was told by his guidance counselor he would never make it to college. He went on to earn two graduate degrees. He was a Black Panther and served in Vietnam. The man knows conflict, he has experienced oppression, and he has overcome.

He joined the church at a time when he was not allowed to hold the priesthood. He experienced acts of racism from those who should have welcomed him into the Body of Christ. He repeatedly petitioned the leaders of the church to serve a mission and was denied. The burning desire to serve led him to serve an "unofficial mission" with a very recognized organization in LDS culture. My father did not hide his light under a bushel, nor did he allow "folk" doctrine to cloud his sense of self. He stopped asking and just followed where the Spirit led him to serve. This led him to meet my mother and touch countless lives with his dedication to the Lord.

My father talks of times where not having the priesthood or access to temple blessing was "like a slap in the face." In those moments he was comforted by the Spirit and remembered to "Be Still"[334] and recognize his worth as the son of a merciful God who would not bar any of His seeking children from exaltation. That legacy of faith and self-worth, that isn't dependent on an institution for validation, has been passed on to my siblings and me. I intend to pass it on to my children.

My parents didn't wait for the general body of the church to be ready for something that was never theirs to give. They sought their own personal witnesses and acted accordingly.

I use them as a template for how I live my life. I strive to be beholden only to my values; to live with integrity and be of service to my fellowman. My relationship with the institution has often been precarious. There have been moments of frustration, confusion, and contentment. The more confidence I gain in my inner voice, the more freedom I've experienced, and it's allowed me to create meaningful relationships within my community.

How can we claim ourselves while finding our place in an institution that is moving towards progress slower than we'd like? How can we leave a legacy for our children while paying tribute to those who suffered so we can be in our current place?

I look to my past, to my father, and remember to listen to the Spirit and follow that instruction. Relying on that wisdom has not led me astray. There are many lessons to be learned from those in the past who have experienced oppression and marginalization. I reclaim myself every time I honor those individuals and teach their lessons to my children.

"A Proper Church: On Mormon Women Stand, Church PR, and Listening and Engaging in the Body of Christ" by Katie Langston (May 22, 2014)

About five years ago, my world turned upside down.

Through a series of powerful experiences, I came to understand that the message of Jesus isn't one of strict obedience, rules and regulations, and worthiness. Instead, it's a message of reconciliation, of authenticity, of radical, challenging, heartbreaking, soul-stretching love.

When I caught the vision of the message of Christ, a Peaceable Kingdom expanding to fill the earth like yeast expands bread, I was transformed. I could never see the world the same way again. I wanted to be part of it. I wanted to fill my life and heart with it. I wanted to teach and preach and rejoice in the unbelievable weakness of a God born in a barn and murdered on a tree—a God who reached out to sinners and dined with prostitutes and healed lepers and called tax collectors as Apostles.

In short, a God who acted nothing like a proper God should.

This week,

> The LDS Church held a 90-minute video conference about global women's issues with leaders of Mormon Women Stand, an online-only group whose mission is to 'sustain the Lord's

prophet, the [faith's] Family Proclamation as doctrine and our divine role as covenant women for Christ.'[335]

I rejoice with my sisters who had a chance to be heard. They've reported that the experience was an outpouring of love and hope. I'm glad they feel loved and valued and cherished. They ARE loved and valued and cherished, by God, by *me*. That's how it should be in sacred community.

But why can't it be that way for all the women in our community?

In the *Salt Lake Tribune*, LDS Church spokesman Cory Craynor said:

> We are not planning to meet with activist groups whose demands are inconsistent with church teachings and doctrine.[336]

Look, I understand. They don't want to appear weak. They don't want to appear vulnerable. And that's fine and dandy, and it's what you'd expect from a large corporation.

But it's not what you'd expect from disciples of Christ.

I started by sharing my own conversion experience to Christ because of the radical, upside-down, topsy-turvy life He calls us to live. You see, the promise and challenge of the church, what Paul literally called the Body of Christ[337]—His hands and feet, His eyes and mouth, His heart and mind—is not just to hear those with whom we already agree; it's to embrace those with whom we don't. It's not to seek counsel from those who affirm our perspective; it's to seek out the perspective of those who challenge us.

We need to sit down together, Mormon feminists and Mormon Women Stand and church officials and everyone in between, and listen to one another. To engage with each other's experiences and see each other's pain. To make room for each other, to say, "You are mine, I claim you, I see you, I hear you, I want you, I love you, *just the way you are*."

That is what this whole Kingdom of Heaven thing is all about. That is the promise of Zion.

Jesus said,

> If you love those who love you, what reward will you get? Are not even the tax collectors doing that? If you greet only your brothers, what more are you doing than others? Do not even the gentiles do the same? (Matt 5:46–47)

Yes, it would turn the world upside down for the church to welcome divergent voices. Yes, it would be a sign of weakness and vulnerability. Yes it would. Yes it would. Yes, oh yes, it would.

But in so doing, it just might begin to reflect the life-changing teachings of the God whose name it claims.

A church that acts nothing like a proper church should.

"THE ALTAR AND THE FONT" BY MELISSA MAYHEW (MAY 22, 2014)

Friends, my heart is weary. Whatever the actual women's issue that arises, whenever a discussion addresses the inequalities and imbalances that are or ever have been, there is a particular thorn that seems to grow out of the conversation. To a lot of people, especially those who speak the words that have the thorn in them, it seems small. They barely notice it, if they do at all. It is expected, unquestioned, unexamined. It may not grow in a place that ever touches them, so they are never pricked by it, or don't notice or recognize it if it does. But it touches me, it pierces my heart, and it has done so frequently. I ache, I am wounded, and I mourn.

When we speak of imbalances and injustices that affect women (and I know this is echoed and multiplied across other groups and demographics that also experience oppression), it seems there is always a reason. It is so easy for so many people to posit and accept justifications for the Way Things Are, reasons why it is, and why it needs to be that way. It seems to be so easy for so many to list the known and supposed benefits for patriarchy, for not rocking the boat. There are some who do so with the hope or assumption that each and every thing listed, from the big to the small, will somehow make the pain of inequality, oppression, and neglect less in the hearts of those who feel that pain.

And sometimes, I am tempted to accept these justifications as a balm, because bearing the pain of the injustices and wrongs themselves is so exhausting and can be so overwhelming. There are times that I simply cannot hold it anymore, and my heart gives in and takes whatever comfort it can. I am tempted to surrender the fight and let my heart rest at peace that things are only the way they need to be, to accept that these offered words are indeed words of comfort and reason that make everything alright.

But justifications for inequality and oppression are not a balm. They are the thorn.

Every justification is an altar we are sacrificing women and girls on. Every reason we accept tells us what women's relative worth is; it tells us that whatever women are experiencing is a reasonable price to pay for whatever the supposed gain is. (And that choice is not theirs to make, only to accept.)

When people explain that the girls don't get as much support in terms of both time and money for their activities as the boys do because of any number of logistical tie-ups with Boy Scouts, or because the boys' needs for structure and recognition would then be neglected, they are saying that girls' needs don't matter as much as any of those things and are a reasonable sacrifice for maintaining BSA involvement or meeting goals that involve the boys.

When people explain that women in the church can't have a more prominent leadership role because then men from even more patriarchal countries would reject the gospel, they are saying that reaching every last recalcitrant man in the world is more important than the spiritual participation of righteous women who we can reach now, *and* that women's equality is not a crucial part of the gospel that needs sharing and acceptance.

When people explain that men have to preside because someone has to be in charge, they are saying that women's subordination is a just sacrifice for the purpose of maintaining a hierarchical order that can be taken for granted, and that it is better to sacrifice women to the default subordinate role than to ask that sacrifice of men.

When people explain that women staying in the home is a necessary ideal to keep society stable, they are saying that society is fundamentally founded on the sacrifice of women foregoing other possible pursuits, and on their unpaid work and isolation. They are saying that it is right that this sacrifice should come from women and women alone, as the rule. (There are other groups that are also routinely sacrificed for "stability," and it is sadly even less talked about. I speak here only of a common argument levied specifically against women having careers.)

There's always someone who has a reason. There is always someone ready to explain exactly what is more important than what women experience, feel, want, and need. There is always someone eager to point out exactly what altar they are willing to sacrifice women on, exactly what they are willing to spend women's worth on, exactly what they value more, exactly what they are willing to accept as a just return for someone else lying down.

The problems I have mentioned specifically are each relatively small first-world-problem examples (though those sorts of problems still add up to a lot altogether). There are so, so many worse things, so many worse pains and abuses at home and across the entire globe. And there is always a reason. It's so easy to find a reason. So many people accept the reasons.

And it is tempting at times for me to accept the reasons too, because if there's not a good reason, then the sheer wrongness of it all is crushingly overwhelming. Dealing with the thorn of the reasons given on top of the pain the immediate arrangements cause can be just too, too much.

But being willing to accept that women should be the sacrifice is the problem. Too many people on all levels in all places are far too okay with making women the sacrifice for everything, for anything, for every purpose. Too many people are too willing to devalue pain if it is women's pain and there is something else to be gained in allowing it. There are too many women on too many altars, from everything from the small matters of managerial logistics to all too literal matters of life and death.

It's everywhere. It is oppression, it is abuse, to accept that someone else's needs, desires, and lives be the thing that should give when there is tension.

In religious circles, this arrangement tends to be justified further by acknowledging the sacrifice exists and extolling it as Godly. God does ask us to learn to sacrifice, and there is virtue in a righteous sacrifice willingly given to Him. Women who complain about what is being asked of them are condemned as being selfish, unrighteous, willful, and wicked. Pushback against any sacrifice is viewed as rejection of all sacrifice. However, what is being asked of us in these cases is not to choose a righteous sacrifice, but to accept the sacrifice that someone else is making of us. Not all sacrifices are Godly, and it is not right that women should lay themselves down on any altar at all just because it is a sacrifice.

How many of us are asked, demanded even, to do just that? To allow ourselves to be offered as a sacrifice to any other concern, to accept that our own worth, autonomy, and involvement is a bargain price to pay for staving off instability, chaos outside of hierarchy, the loss of patriarchal power, loss of reproductive control of a population, damage to male ego, threats to masculine sexuality, competition for male opportunity, the loss of incentive for male good behavior, and whatever other supposed titans lurk in the water just waiting to rampage should their diaphanously-robed virgins decide to shake the chains off and go live their lives.

Sacrificing other people is a concept that is directly counter to Christ's teachings. Abraham was given an alternative to spilling Isaac's blood, and Christ's fulfilling of the law replaced the ritual of death in finality, moving us entirely away from the practice of taking from the life of another being. He gave us His baptism, where we instead receive new life from Him. Jesus wants the sacrifice we offer of ourselves to Him, not the sacrifice of one soul offered up by another's hand.

Jesus taught that all are alike unto God, specifically including male and female together. He still asks us all for sacrifice, to love those who spitefully use us, to turn the other cheek, and to go the second mile. He was a champion of using peaceful and loving methods to navigate the cruelties inflicted by social mores and injustices, and for acting with grace on a personal level towards your enemies. But He was never a champion of those injustices themselves, and Christians using His name to justify their own idolatrous altars, to justify exacting sacrifices from other people's lives, is blasphemy. We are to invite people to the font with love, not drive them to lie on our altars by teaching them constantly with ever-ready excuses and justifications that there is always one more thing, and it can be anything, that is more important than their experiences, needs, feelings, and desires.

We are all equal in the font, equal in Christ. What does gender equality look like? No more excuses. No more justifications. No more women on altars.

"#YesEvenMormonWomen" by Christa Baxter (May 29, 2014)

I was a sheltered child.[338] I had no idea what sexual assault looked like or what to do about it. So when it happened to me at 11, and again at 13, I told myself to pretend it didn't happen, and I did nothing about it. I wish I'd known there were other options.

My parents are outstanding, amazing people. They just didn't think I'd face this, particularly at such a young age. But I hit puberty young, and a ten-year-old girl-child with breasts gets noticed. The comments irked me. But the groping I just tried to pretend away. You see, nobody told me this happened, and I didn't know what to do with it when it did.

The first time was on a field trip in the fifth grade. I was 11. I fell asleep on the bus next to a male classmate. When I woke up, other girls told me he had nestled his head against my breasts. The second time was when I was 12 or 13, riding a school bus that included high schoolers. I tried to ignore the perverted graffiti and gross jokes, but one afternoon while walking to the exit, a hand reached out and squeezed my butt. I didn't know what to do. I whirled in shock, saw laughing faces, and fled.

I told no one. I did nothing. I pretended it would never happen again.

When I was just entering adolescence, all I associated sex with was sin. I knew eventually it would be okay, within marriage, but that was nothing like what had happened to me. Cleavage was bad; sex scenes in movies were bad; it was all bad. Being touched sexually against my will was also bad, in a different way. But I didn't know how to articulate the difference. So I just fiercely pretended it had never happened, and I saw that boy from my fifth grade class throughout middle school and high school, and I rode that bus for the rest of the school year.

The thing is, if I had thought to tell my parents, they would have fought for me. They would have confronted my teachers and principal, driven me to school, gotten me out of those situations. I know that now. Yet somehow I didn't know it then, and I was too ashamed to tell. What happened to me was bad, even though it was a bad I hadn't chosen. And like any good Mormon kid, I avoided bad things. Furthermore, I didn't know anyone who actually had been assaulted or raped. I had narratives of repentance for sexual sin. I had no narrative of recovering from sexual violence.

It was a long time before I ever heard a church story about recovering from sexual violence or abuse. In the meantime, chastity and modesty were touted as shields and protections. And believe me, I was modest; after all, I was completely uninterested in ever, ever getting attention for my body again. I never wanted to risk it again. But I had been perfectly modest and perfectly chaste my whole life, and that didn't stop other people from sexually assaulting me. (It took me until I was 27 years old, reading about the BYU groper travesty,[339] to actually call it that—sexual assault. I had to read a legal definition before I recognized myself as the one out of the three.)

When I was older, a BYU student, I wondered why we hadn't all been taught more about consent. I knew all about boundaries that the church and God set (no necking, no petting, no French kissing according to some), but no one ever told me I could set my own boundaries. And no one ever told me that my consent mattered, or what to do if a boy ignored it or violated it. I figured all Mormon boys knew to respect women and not to push boundaries—a myth I was disabused of as roommates and friends told me their stories—so that was why we never addressed it in church. Because we all knew not to abuse other people.

What I didn't realize was that my church pews are filled with women aching from the consequences of abuse, of rape, of incest, of assault. So why don't we talk about this more? Why don't we make it perfectly clear, for 11-year-olds to 99-year-olds, that our bodies are not the receptacles of other people's shame? That if someone hurts me, I ought not be embarrassed but ought to feel like I can demand help until I get it? That sex in the wrong context is bad, but sex in a violent, coercive context is infinitely worse?

Our faith community needs to hear this issue addressed publicly. The statistics in Utah[340] are damning. We are worse than the national average, with one in three women being sexually assaulted in her lifetime. (In the United States, it's one in four.) Even worse, nearly a third of sexual violence victims are abused by family members.

The young adults in our faith community need to hear this issue addressed publically. According to BYU's Women's Services and Resources, BYU students often don't recognize rape when they see it. In a survey of 150 students (results reported at a BYU Women's Studies conference in November 2012), 13 percent of students thought it isn't rape if the couple is married, even if the wife doesn't want to. 10 percent of men think if you spend money on a woman and she says no to sex, she's partly to blame. Over 40 percent of men and nearly 30 percent of women thought an immodestly dressed woman is partially to blame if she is raped. We need clear guidelines on consent and on accountability.

But BYU and Utah are not the church. We are a worldwide church, and this is a worldwide problem.[341] Think of the good we could do if we mobilized. We can't prevent every assault, but we can warn youth that it happens, and we can promise to stand up for them when it does. We can teach them about consent so they don't cross someone's boundaries and think aggression is manly or romantic. We can teach the law of chastity so that not crossing your date's boundaries is just as crucial as not crossing God's boundaries. We can just be there.

But if we keep on pretending this doesn't happen, that Mormons don't commit and aren't harmed by sexual violence, then we will continue to fail our daughters and sons. There will be more young children and teens who don't even know they can ask for help. And there will continue to be victims scarred and scared and hurting.

Let us address the issue that so pervasively hurts us, not just through an occasional conference talk, but through clear guidelines in the *For the Strength of Youth*[342] pamphlet, in wedding prep classes, in youth lessons and singles wards. Let's tell young men that keeping the law of chastity isn't only about staying worthy to serve a mission but just as much about respecting a child of God and that person's autonomy. Let's explicitly encourage parents to prepare their kids for sexual violence. Let's promise to be there for our Primary children and youth. Let's follow the law and report these crimes to the police when our children trust us enough to tell us.

But first, let's mourn with those who mourn. In the past few days, many women have documented their experiences with sexual violence with the hashtag #YesAllWomen. I am asking all LDS women who have survived sexual violence to also document it with the hashtag #YesEvenMormonWomen. I invite our leaders to read these accounts and prayerfully consider how to address this gaping wound in the body of Christ. I'm pleading with all of us to take sexual violence seriously and do something about it. Because the efforts we've put forth thus far simply aren't enough.

"WE SHALL FIND KINDNESS: ORDAIN WOMEN AND A WOUND TO THE BODY OF CHRIST" BY LISA PATTERSON BUTTERWORTH (JUNE 11, 2014)

> Two Mormons who have gained national attention for pushing their church to ordain women to the priesthood and to accept openly gay members have been notified this week that they face excommunication for apostasy."[343]

Old wounds, reopened.

Ten years ago when I started a blog called Feminist Mormon Housewives, I was a little nervous to use my real name when the *NYT* reporter[344] asked it of me, but really I had little sense of Mormon feminist history. When September Six happened, I had been young and orthodox; it was all distant and shadowy. Even as a newly emerging feminist with a shiny new blog, I only had the vaguest notion of what had happened.

Slowly I began to understand the toll those excommunications took on Mormon feminists and all Mormon women and on all Mormons. Mormon feminists went underground, there were splits, there was fear—a whole generation just before me hid in silence, or secret listservs, or left the church entirely. A whole generation of Mormons never dared to call attention to unrighteous dominion, no matter how severe, because they knew that the consequence could be losing everything—their families, their friends, their whole way of life. So they were silent.

I did not understand that I would have a part in rebuilding all that was lost. I don't think I would have dared, had I known.

But over these years, as I have become more educated about our feminist Mormon history, I not only learned about what had happened, I also met the women to whom it had happened. There was a part of me that wondered if there was something bad about these women; I was scared of them. The decade passed slowly and the more time I spent with Lavina, and Maxine, and Janice, and Margaret,[345] the more it became clear to me that these women are beautiful to the core of their souls, and deeply deeply spiritual, with the kind of glowing spirit that wraps a person in love and has no fear. The kind of love that cuts across boundaries and destroys labels and makes everything a little more sacred. They strengthened my testimony, urged me to stay, helped me find my own spiritual gifts. I started to wonder if there was something about excommunication that made them more holy, somehow. I still don't know what to make of that.

Perhaps there is something about losing that which is most precious to you, perhaps there is something about being rejected and cast out and stripped bare and humiliated that is like a refiner's fire. The pain purifies and makes stronger. No one wants to go into that fire, but the result is unparalleled beauty.

Today in class I learned about a woman named Sally Gross.[346] Sally was born intersex but did not know this. She was raised as a man, became a Catholic priest, and it wasn't until she had some medical testing at the age of 40 that she discovered that she is genetically a woman. She had to decide if she would be honest about who she really is, and potentially lose everything she had, or to hide her true self in order to maintain her place in her community. I can't imagine having to face such a difficult choice. There is nothing more painful than being rejected by those we love.

Sally chose to be vulnerable, to risk everything. And she lost everything. She was stripped of her priesthood, she was ejected from the church, she was not allowed to participate in any church capacity including taking communion. And she holds no bitterness.

Watching an interview with her today, she glowed with the same refiner's glory. Her goodness shone like a fire. She was an anti-apartheid activist, part of why she chose the priesthood, and she was kicked out of

South Africa, losing her country as well. She now organizes safe spaces for intersex individuals all over the world. She turned her pain into beauty and kindness and love. She does not hide under a bushel; her candlestick gives light to all. Her good works shine, glorifying our Father in Heaven.

Today there is so much fear and so much pain. We have lost so much. And today we feel like we are losing our sisters and brothers in Christ. We feel rejected, ejected, unwanted. Losing our delicate trust in our community, the beloved home of our faith and the gospel we love. Losing our hope in the church our foremothers built with their sweat and blood and tears.

I felt it cut across my heart. I felt my guts rip open. I thought I'd mourned enough. I was wrong. I want to run from it. I want to bury myself in some faraway island and pretend I never knew it. But that pain has something important to teach me, and I am strong enough to bear it. I believe we can all bear it, I believe we can learn those lessons. Find that unparalleled beauty.

Today we, the Body of Christ, face hard choices.

1 Corinthians 12:12:

> For as the body is one, and hath many members, and all the members of that one body, being many, are one body: so also is Christ.

We, every single one of us, we are the Body of Christ.

> For by one Spirit are we all baptized into one body, whether we be Jews or Gentiles, whether we be bond or free; and have been all made to drink into one Spirit. (1 Corinthians 12:13)

The feminists, the Primary teachers, the intellectuals, the Quorum of the Twelve, the gays, the PR Department, the Ordain Women, we drink into one Spirit.

> For the body is not one member, but many. (1 Corinthians 12:14)

We will all make different choices. And that is hard, but still we are the Body of Christ.

> If the foot shall say, Because I am not the hand, I am not of the body; is it therefore not of the body? (1 Corinthians 12:15)

Many women will find Mormon feminism too scary today, their circumstances not secure enough to take risks. We must love them. We are the Body of Christ.

> And if the ear shall say, Because I am not the eye, I am not of the body; is it therefore not of the body? (1 Corinthians 12:16)

Many of my dear friends will write letters resigning their memberships soon. I fear we may lose a whole generation of young Mormon women and men. They are unlikely to silence their voices and to hide like their grandmothers did. We must love them. We are the Body of Christ.

If the whole body were an eye, where were the hearing? If the whole were hearing, where were the smelling? (1 Corinthians 12:17)

Without all of us, the meek and the bold, we are incomplete, we are diminished. We are the Body of Christ.

But now hath God set the members every one of them in the body, as it hath pleased him. (1 Corinthians 12:18)

We are, every one of us, wanted and needed by God. No one can tell us we are unwanted, no one can invite us to leave. We are the Body of Christ.

And the eye cannot say unto the hand, I have no need of thee: nor again the head to the feet, I have no need of you. (1 Corinthians 12:21)

There are no essential members vs. untouchable members. They CANNOT say they have no need of us. We CANNOT say we have no need of them. We are the Body of Christ.

Nay, much more those members of the body, which seem to be more feeble, are necessary: (1 Corinthians 12:22)

There are no true believers vs. false believers, all believers are necessary. We are the Body of Christ.

And those members of the body, which we think to be less honourable, upon these we bestow more abundant honour; and our uncomely parts have more abundant comeliness. (1 Corinthians 12:23)

There are no good Mormon feminists vs. bad Mormon feminists. We are the body of Christ.

For our comely parts have no need: but God hath tempered the body together, having given more abundant honour to that part which lacked. (1 Corinthians 12:24)

This fire burns; this testing strengthens. We are the Body of Christ.

That there should be no schism in the body; but that the members should have the same care one for another. (1 Corinthians 12:25)

This painful divide hurts us all. And we must all care for each other, even when our brothers are unnecessarily causing this pain. The men who opened the schism, they are our Brothers. We are the Body of Christ.

And whether one member suffer, all the members suffer with it; or one member be honoured, all the members rejoice with it. (1 Corinthians 12:26)

After I have mourned with our sisters, I hope I can find it in my heart to feel mercy for our brothers in Christ, who took this step to sever our beloved body, thus wounding us all.

Now ye are the body of Christ, and members in particular. (1 Corinthians 12:27)

I believe this. I believe it with all my heart. But today our body is wounded, we have cut ourselves and we bleed, and we cry, and we mourn.

Mosiah 18:9:

Yea, and are willing to mourn with those that mourn; yea, and comfort those that stand in need of comfort, and to stand as witnesses of God at all times and in all things, and in all places that ye may be in, even until death.

Kindness by Naomi Shihab Nye.[347]

NOTE ABOUT THE COMMENTS: We are commanded by Jesus Christ to mourn with those who mourn. Comments that do not express that sentiment will be deleted. Commenters that insist on repeatedly posting comments with judgment and derision will be banned. This blog provides many posts where we welcome respectful disagreement; basic manners (and the scriptures) should inform you that a post calling for mourning is NOT an appropriate time or place.

"LET IT BE DIFFERENT THIS TIME" BY JOANNA BROOKS (JUNE 13, 2014)

it happens almost every time i speak in public.

almost every time i am in a group of mormons, people of faith, new friends, strangers.

during the Q&A or after the event, someone takes me aside and asks, "you're a mormon feminist. the church excommunicates people like you. have you ever been called in for church discipline?"

and i look them in the eyes and say, in all truth, "no. i've never been called in. i've been left totally alone. my ward welcomes me. i think the church may be outgrowing the urge to hold courts for mormon feminists. i just don't think it's going to happen anymore. i really believe mormonism is big and strong enough to absorb difference and honest questioning."

without fail—whether the person is progressive or conservative, mormon or not mormon—they smile and their face relaxes.

i have said this—that i believe mormonism is outgrowing the urge to purge—even when i have been afraid. i have said this almost as a dare, willing, hopefully willing, that the religion i love is capable of moving beyond its historic repression of mormon feminists.[348]

i am putting my arms around kate kelly and everyone facing discipline. i am hoping, hoping, hoping the church doesn't prove me wrong. not because it will matter that i was wrong. but because outgrowing a spirit of control and repression is, i believe, so important to mormonism.

in every generation of mormon women, women have asked and will continue to ask the questions kate kelly and others have bravely raised. the questions continue to come up because our doctrine and practices around gender are contradictory and incomplete. disciplining kate accomplishes nothing to resolve that.

i am hoping this turns out differently than it did for sonia johnson in 1979 and for lavina, lynne, and maxine in 1993, and janice in 1995, and margaret in 2000.[349] these women, my friends, kate, my friend. and the men who sat in those small rooms and did what they had to do, bearing unspeakable pressure, all those men, my brothers.

i am hoping this turns out differently for us all.

"AM I OBLIGED TO STAY?" BY DEREK STAFFANSON (JUNE 17, 2014)

Now that the hammer has come down on two of the more visible members of our heterodox Mormon community, feelings have been running high. Alienation abounds, and many have been calling this the last straw in their relationship with the Church. Others implore us to stay and continue to play the "long game" in our work to bring about change. Among those of a more conventional mindset, some[350] few[351] have likewise been calling on us to stay, recognizing a value in some diversity and in the less comfortable conversations that we spur in the community. While they may not agree with our positions or ultimate goals, they appreciate some of the more moderate developments that are results of our prodding, or just having the conversation. They see the diversity we bring as a benefit to the Church.

But at what personal cost to Mormon Feminists and other Mormons with differing visions of the faith? Is the value we bring to the Church worth the pain that the alternative thinkers suffer in it?

Historian Greg Prince has made an interesting observation a few different times. In an interview with Chieko N. Okazaki, he noted the younger generations within the Church.

> They have so many competing voices that if you don't make it relevant to them, you're going to lose them. ... We haven't done the job of making the gospel interesting and relevant. ... Your generation, my generation, and earlier generations all looked upon religion as a duty, that there was to be discomfort as part of it. And we accepted that. In some cases, it was a hair shirt that we wore, and that was just part of the deal. Not with the generations now! They are not willing to do that.[352]

He made the same point at the end of his address at the Washington DC Mormon Stories Conference, "Big Tent Mormonism" (Mormon Stories Podcast 295[353]).

It poses an interesting question of perspective on the nature of religion. "Earlier generations all looked upon religion as a duty." To them, it is something that must be done. The outcome is irrelevant; what matters is fulfilling the obligation.

What Prince seems to be describing about the more recent generations is a focus on religion as self-improvement or renewal. It isn't that they need to be entertained as some less understanding critics suggest. ("Kids these days! Too soft, always need a song and dance to compete with the internets.") These people tend to be just as disinterested in the glib and amusing Mormon circuit speakers at youth firesides or EFY[354] as they are by the onerous duties and boring meetings focused on external observances. They want to experience the sort of things that uplift their spirits, that challenge their assumptions and make them think; that increase their capacities to love and serve; that help them become better people and more at peace with life.

These are not, of course, mutually exclusive categories. I think some level of duty is expected by any person sincerely striving to grow and to consider something beyond themselves. Many of these heterodox thinkers voluntarily seek out opportunities to serve. The difference lies in how they view duty. The old guard will tell you that one finds ultimate happiness and growth in fulfilling the Lord's commands for his servants, regardless of how much sense these duties make, or whether there is any apparent impact of the service. Immediate peace and happiness are concerns far lower in priority than fulfilling the Lord's will. It may not make any difference in this life, but that's okay; what matters is cultivating obedience like that of Abraham with Isaac. For these younger generations, duty is only valid to the extent that it appreciably helps us grow or serves to lift our sisters and brothers in meaningful, direct ways.

Which is the more correct perspective? That of the old guard certainly makes a lot of sense. If God is God, and he is leading the Church as its leaders claim, then His will is logically paramount. It doesn't matter what we feel about X, Y, and Z. Heavenly Father is omniscient and omnipotent. He will eventually be our judge, and whether we like them or not, what he required of us is logically what those judgments will be based on. The only positive outcome will come through surrendering our will to his, regardless of what trials we face.

Yet.

Jesus told us that we would know them (institutions, groups, people, ideologies, etc.) "by their fruits" (Matthew 7:20), because "even so every good tree bringeth forth good fruit; but a corrupt tree bringeth forth evil fruit" (Matthew 7:17). We are encouraged by the Book of Mormon prophet Zenos to try "an experiment upon my words" [or, we can infer, any teachings, concepts, ideologies, or organization claiming truth] (Alma

32:27), to exercise our faith, however faint, and then evaluate by the results of that faith, whether it "enlarge[s] my soul" (Alma 32: 28) or "swelleth and sprouteth and beginneth to grow" (Alma 32: 30). If it does not grow or enlargen our soul, we are told that "therefore it is cast away" (Alma 32:32).

Most of us either have in the past or now go to services each week, the Sacrament Meetings, Sunday School, and Relief Society/quorum meetings, and fulfill our callings as an exercise of sincere faith, in hopes of being spiritually nourished, uplifted, expanded. We want to be challenged mentally and spiritually. But if the fruits of these meetings are spiritual depletion, a withering of our souls, a parching of joy, a narrowing of minds, and increased weight of shame and guilt, then what good are they? We diligently attempt to honor and sustain the hierarchy of the Church, hoping for a greater understanding and embrace of love, for a better perspective on the big picture to help us chart our courses. But if the words and directives of the leaders result in more exclusion and scorn, more focus—even obsession—on minutia and arbitrary rules, more feelings of inadequacy or being pressured to fit in a box that stifles our innate—dare I say divine?— individual nature, and if the directives and policies of the Church are contrary to the dictates of our conscience, then why should we continue to accord power over us to those leaders and the organization they head? Is the potential benefit of starting community conversations which may refine the Church worth the malnourishment we feel?

I appreciate these more traditional members expressing empathy and extending invitations to remain. But I would invite them in return: if you appreciate our presence, and want us to continue to provide diversity in the Church, will you help bear our burdens? You may disagree with us, but will you stand against those harsher voices who mock or judge us in your wards? When we express less popular or alternative ideas, do you take the opportunity, privately or publicly, to express appreciation for our thoughts? It gets very lonely out here on the fringes, and leaving becomes more attractive when you feel unwanted.

I want more than anything for my son and daughter to feel love and feel loved, to pursue those things that expand their horizons and capacities for good and for joy. I do not believe any loving Divine Parents would expect us to wear hairshirts to prove anything to them. The core Gospel is incredibly beautiful and soul expanding. If the Church is not doing an effective job in helping us embrace that, and if our leaders, who claim direct revelation from heaven, cannot make the Church relevant, and duty is the primary reason to stay, should not the seed be cast out?

"THE POWER OF PAIN: MOURNING WITH KATE KELLY" BY LISA PATTERSON BUTTERWORTH (JUNE 23, 2014)

My lungs don't want to function and I can't see the computer screen through the tears. A raw pit has taken over my stomach and I feel gorge rising.

It seems so illogical that I could have known this was coming and still feel so shocked, so utterly horribly shocked. So cruel. So cruel. How can they be so cruel?

We have lost so much today, our hearts will never be the same. Our hearts are broken, they cut our dear dear sister, Kate Kelly, violently from the body of Christ. We feel rejected, too. Unloved. Unwanted. It hurts so much.

What do we do with all this pain?

Our whole lives we've been told that our feelings don't matter, and *that message* is at the core of every oppression that we have accepted as our lot. We've been told not to be sad or angry, we've been told to smile and be attractive or else no one will love us, and deep down in our deepest soul we believed it.

When we cry we say, "I'm sorry to be so silly." Because our sadness is just silly, it doesn't really matter. We feel our anger rise up and ruthlessly stamp it out, and put on a bigger smile. We can't be one of *those* bitter ugly women. We've pushed the anger down so far we forgot it was even there, and when we looked for it, we couldn't find it. Only a big empty pit.

Today we find our anger, and our anger is important. God cares about our anger.

Today we grieve and we rage, and we don't apologize for our feelings. We don't have to protect everyone from our feelings, WE MATTER TOO! Our PAIN matters!

I can't breathe right now, shallow breaths rip from my chest and I shake and I type and tears stream down my face and land on my chest. And the silent tears turn loud, the silence is no longer satisfying, I wail, I sob with loud awful sounds of grief.

It's scary to let it out, I've held it in for so long. I'm scared of letting it out, scared of how I look right now, how I sound in my grief. Afraid I'll get stuck there in pain, I'll get trapped in bitter wallowing.

But don't be scared, trust yourself, lean into the pain. Believe your pain matters. It's the most important thing of all. It's the lesson our Heavenly Parents sent us here to learn. Because until we believe our pain matters, we do not believe that we matter. And until I believe that I matter, I cannot love myself, and I can't truly love anyone else.

You may not grieve like I do, with tears and wailing and shaking sobbing breaths. You may grieve in your thoughts, you may grieve in your actions. The only wrong way to grieve is to tell yourself you're doing it the wrong way. Let yourself feel what you feel. Go deep, deep into your body and feel all the feels and think all the thinks. Go into your angry place inside and say all the angry words to all the menz who abuse us and call it love. It is safe there, no one can hear.

And tomorrow, and the next, and the next. And as you do this work the day will come when you can lift up your voice, and your words will ring out, you will tell your story and we will hear it and your safe spaces will expand both within you and outside you.

And when you embrace yourself, and decide you matter enough to let yourself grieve, the unexpected gift at the other side of this painful journey will be that you will find you love yourself enough to let yourself be free and bold and happy.

"THESE MEN ARE NOT THE ENEMIES" BY LINDSAY HANSEN PARK (JUNE 27, 2014)

The past week's events have sent shock waves of despair throughout our community. Prominent Mormon Feminist Kate Kelly was excommunicated[355] by a group of men in white shirts and ties in an act hauntingly named "A Court of Love."[356] Many of us have called out the spiritual violence of the process. We had no idea the sting we would feel, even if we anticipated this decision. Some of us can barely harness the grief. It just seems so wrong. Many, many of us are hurting and deeply grieving. Some of us are angry and some want to make the Church or Kate's local leaders the enemies.

But they are not the enemies. We have a heritage of fear[357] and a legacy of violence that predate the events of the last week. Among the many spiritual legacies handed down to us, we have a birthright of deep Mormon shame,[358] and that birthright extends around and especially to the male leaders in authority. It is a system that every living Mormon today has inherited and one that is so ingrained in our Mormon psyche, it is second nature to us.

We Mormons are an End-of-Days bunch, a community that since 1830 has been convinced that the Second Coming[359] is just beyond the cusp of our own generation. Ours is a fiery people.

On a quiet Ohio night on March 24, 1832, Joseph Smith had fallen asleep next to his sick child. Little Murdock, one of the twins, had contracted measles sometime in the night, and his father's strong arms wrapped around his tiny, fevering body. Joseph would be woken by the sound of an angry, drunken group of men just outside the home.[360] Fawn Brodie explains:

> Fortified by a barrel of whiskey, [the mob] smashed their way into the Johnson home on the night of March 24, 1832 and dragged Joseph from the trundle bed where he had fallen asleep while watching one of the twins. They stripped him, scratched and beat him with savage pleasure, and smeared his

bleeding body with tar from head to foot. Ripping a pillow into shreds, they plastered him with feathers. It is said that Eli Johnson demanded that the prophet be castrated, for he suspected Joseph of being too intimate with his sister, Nancy Marinda. But the doctor who had been persuaded to join the mob declined the responsibility at the last moment.[361]

This would mark a beginning of a culture of violence for our people.[362] Within a few years, the Mormons were organized and effective at returning violence for violence, intimidation for intimidation, and meeting cruelty and fear with retaliation.

We became a persecuted people. But things were not so simple.

Our brethren fau[gh]t like tigers. They cl[e]ared the ground at the time in knocking down and dragging out" Joseph proudly wrote in his journal after another conflict (dubbed the Gallatin Election Day Battle) where Mormons had fought back after being harassed by local citizens.

By the night of October 24, 1838, Mormons were in full-on war with their neighbors.

Sidney Rigdon would deliver this famous, ominous speech[363] calling for the extermination of Mormon enemies:

We take God and all the holy angels to witness this day, that we warn all men in the name of Jesus Christ, to come on us no more forever. For from this hour, we will bear it no more, our rights shall no more be trampled on with impunity. The man or the set of men, who attempts it, does it at the expense of their lives. And that mob that comes on us to disturb us; it shall be between us and them a war of extermination; for we will follow them till the last drop of their blood is spilled, or else they will have to exterminate us: for we will carry the seat of war to their own houses, and their own families, and one party or the other shall be utterly destroyed.—Remember it then all MEN.

We will never be the aggressors, we will infringe on the rights of no people; but shall stand for our own until death. We claim our own rights, and are willing that all others shall enjoy theirs.

No man shall be at liberty to come into our streets, to threaten us with mobs, for if he does, he shall atone for it before he leaves the place, neither shall he be at liberty, to vilify and slander any of us, for suffer it we will not in this place.

We would continue on, fighting back, and sometimes initiating violence against our enemies. Our narrative would be that of wronged innocents, but we were not always so innocent.[364] Our hymns[365] would reflect the narrative of God's chosen people, exiled and victimized by apostates and gentiles. We would create stories,[366] legends and an entire culture around the idea that we were always God's persecuted people, and how it entitled us to exclusive blessings beyond the reach of our enemies.

Persecuted and peculiar, we adopted strange new doctrines[367] that laid claim to ancient entitlements. These sacred curiosities would fuel even more isolation and contempt from outsiders. The provocation was the oven our community was baked in, and it solidified us into a hard, brittle biscuit that we would spend decades trying to sweeten. We transitioned from phrases like "Mind Your Business"[368] to "Service with a Smile." We would draw strength from the hardness of our pioneer grandmothers and soften ourselves with modern virtue.

We would take our history of double-speak[369] and bend the rules[370] in the name of righteousness.[371] To survive,[372] we sometimes had to smile through our pain to shelter the world[373] from the realities[374] of God's restored gospel.

The culture of secrecy and putting-our-best-face-forward[375] has evolved over time. Most contemporary members wouldn't see any similarities in church public relations tactics between Orson Pratt's *The Seer*[376] and Ally Isom's Radio West interview.[377] Yet, like any organization seeking growth and understanding, the parallels are there. We want to remain peculiar, but we also want desperately to fit in.

Our culture of violence—of both being victimized by violence and responding through violence—would also evolve. We would no longer raid neighboring towns or form militias, but we became electrically efficient at in-group favoritism,[378] and often our harsh community boundaries[379] have hard consequences.[380]

The Strengthening the Members Committee doesn't flash the glint of a bowie blade,[381] but they don't have to. Their very function is like the eerie tune of a Whistling Elder. We know they are there and that they are watching, keeping our people in line, monitoring the words of the Saints.[382] The rumor of the group is enough to keep a people like us, with generations of boundary policing, scared to speak publicly. We might even mistake these tactics for the ingredients of Zion and call them blessings.[383]

There has been debate on who initiated the excommunication of Kate. Was this the result of a directive from Salt Lake City brass? Was it local?[384] Truthfully, the answer is more blurry than that. The decision came from a system we are all complicit in. The burden is one we all shoulder. We as a people have continued for generations to perpetuate a victim mythology with an unchecked acknowledgement of our own involvement in our past. We have allowed ourselves to believe our bad deeds are justified because of the violence brought against us in days gone by. We hold in our hearts the harshness of the 19th century frontier and write it down, year after year, as if it were a branch on our family group sheet.

Somewhere, deep down in our spiritual DNA, are the bruises of Joseph Smith, the blood on our hands at Crooked River and the fanaticism of 1857 Southern Utah. Our history speaks to us like the whisper of a prophetic, still, small voice: *"Keep quiet. Don't express doubt publicly. Stay in line. Niceness instead of kindness. Obedience. Loyalty. Obedience."*

The men who excommunicated Kate Kelly are not the enemy; they too are our people. Our biggest enemy is our collective, unchecked self, and the bleeding scars of our history. We are a fiery people and we are still burning from the open wounds of our past. These wounds will not heal until we can all stand together as a people and change our mythology to one of strength, honesty and empowerment—one of a checked humility and joint responsibility, one that allows for our mistakes both past and present. Until then, we will not escape the abiding heirloom we have weaved for our people who truly believe that spiritual violence is an act of love.

We are all responsible.

Special thanks to Joe Geisner and other historians for helping out with the resources linked here.

"WHEN YOUR FEARS COME TRUE" BY TRESA BROWN EDMUNDS (JULY 10, 2014)

> Freedom's just another word for nothing left to lose.
>
> —Kris Kristofferson

For years and years those of us public about our feminism have been asked, "Aren't you afraid of being disciplined?" And for years and years we've said, "Things are different now. We have the internet. They wouldn't dare." Well, they did. What we've all been afraid of has happened to Kate, and it's happening over and over again in ways large and small with rising frequency all over the nation. Temple recommends revoked, hostile interviews, callings stripped, friends attacking in the name of righteousness. All of us who are public about our feminism are suddenly facing pressure from all sides that is unprecedented in the internet age.

I haven't been very public about a lot of my experiences, but for the past four years I've been dealing with those consequences myself. In my last ward my bishop just decided, without speaking to me at all, that I was trouble. He had me released from my callings, refused every request to call me to a new position, wouldn't let me speak in sacrament or be called on to pray, and when I chose *The Book of Mormon Girl*[385] as my selection in our RS Book Club, he insisted on attending to supervise the discussion. (The book club ended up disbanding in protest shortly after that because those women are awesome.)

I've had book deals fall through because I was viewed as too radical—me, not the project. My creative living blog—where I write about craft projects and my son—has been the target of haters. I've been left out and rejected from professional opportunities. The mommy blogging world and the craft world are both run by Mormons. It would have been better for me if I was flat out no longer practicing than to be what I am.

I had a pregnancy before Atticus that resulted in miscarriage, but before catastrophe, when we first got the news that after seven years of trying we were pregnant, we called Bear's[386] parents, and then we drove over to the house of a couple in our ward to share the news. They called Bear "son." We attended all the family birthday parties. They told us that if they got to choose kids they would choose us. They've since unfriended us on Facebook and haven't spoken to us in years.

I'm not sharing any of this for sympathy, but because suddenly my experiences aren't unique. Every hour we're hearing another story of someone being called into her bishop's office for something she wrote on Facebook, or being released from her callings because she has an Ordain Women profile, or having her temple recommend threatened because she supports marriage equality. The excommunication of Kate emboldened leaders all over to pull the boundaries in and leave those of us on the borders outside.

So when you're faced with these threats, when you no longer feel safe, when people who once loved you are now causing you pain, what do you do?

The first step is safety. Grieve fractured relationships, mourn the loss of your place in the community—these are serious, painful events that you are right to take seriously. Self care. Self care. Self care.[387]

But once you find stability, you'll discover something surprising.

When your world has come crashing down around you and everything you've feared has happened, and you're still standing? You feel unstoppable. When you have lived through your fears and come out the other side, you have nothing left to fear.

I've jokingly referred to this as "Abused Child Privilege." When strangers on the internet line up with their torches and pitchforks I say to myself, "My own parents don't love me. Who the hell cares what *they* think?" It's never as simple as that, of course; losing your community is not something to make light of, your children losing friends is not something to make light of, having it affect your employment is not something to make light of, but there are ways through all of those trials. And once you're through, you find power.

People who are ignorant of Mormonism or activism will often say, "Why do you have to ask for power? Just take it!" And those of us who have been doing this for a while have dents in our heads from slamming them against our desks. Religion has never dealt well with revolution. We can't take institutional power by just seizing it, but we can take personal power by walking over the hot coals of fear and coming out the other side marked, scarred, weary, but invincible.

"A Lost & Tired Generation" by Sara Katherine Staheli Hanks (July 25, 2014)

There's a lost generation of Mormon feminists.

In the early 1990s, with the discipline levied against the September Six and the crackdown on troublesome professors at Brigham Young University and the generally unfriendly climate towards people who loudly questioned the status quo, a lot of Mormon women bowed out. It was all too much. Or maybe it was all too little. According to the handful of conversations I've had with women who remember those days, the Mormon feminist community went underground. It certainly didn't die, and important work was still being done, but many members of that community distanced themselves from the church or from fellow feminists or both, leaving a gap in our matriarchal ancestry.

I thought I knew why these women went away. I assumed that they did it out of fear. With such obvious examples of formal church discipline being brought against their brothers and sisters, who could blame them? It was reasonable to fear that they could be next, if they spoke too loud or wrote too controversially. It was reasonable to fear that they'd need to sacrifice authenticity and integrity to remain active church members. Fear can be a prison, but it can also be a gift, telling you deep down in your gut to steer clear or run like the wind. I didn't blame these folks for being afraid and for using that fear however they saw fit.

I figured that fear motivated them to leave. Maybe I was right and maybe I wasn't. But I look at where I am right now and I have a new hypothesis:

Maybe they didn't leave because they were afraid. Maybe they left because they were tired.

I bring up this possibility because it reflects my own situation. We're in a tough moment,[388] us Mormon feminists. Even for those (like me) who have received a lot of kindness and understanding and little-if-any personal ugliness over feminist issues in the last few months, we still have sisters and brothers who haven't been so fortunate, and we mourn with them. (My goodness, the tears I've shed and the frustrated journal entries I've written for people who are not me.)

And I find it necessary for my spiritual and physical health to leave. For a little while, anyhow. I don't want this leaving to be permanent. I can't tell you how much I would rather be at church on Sundays, but between the anxiety spells and panic attacks and spiritual promptings and disturbing dreams, I've felt it best to take a purposeful break.

I'm not leaving because I'm afraid. In fact, I'm not afraid. I'm not afraid of being second-guessed by my bishop. I'm not afraid of whether my name is brought up in ward council meetings. I'm not afraid of gossip. I'm not afraid of formal discipline. I'm not afraid of what would happen if I lost my temple recommend. I'm not afraid of being too loud or of being too timid. I'm just not afraid.

But I am tired.

I'm tired of wondering if I've saved up enough social capital to make the contrary comment in Sunday School. I'm tired of strategizing about how I'll protect my son from damaging, false ideas that are so often perpetuated at church.

I'm tired of listening to Jesus's parables twisted into unrecognizable versions. I'm tired of "hastening the work"[389] lessons where I'm guilt-tripped for not inviting people to a church that hurts me on a regular basis. I'm tired of hearing stories of such blatant unrighteous dominion and knowing that victims have little or no recourse. I'm tired of lessons that focus on the motes in others' eyes and overlook the beams in our own.

I'm tired of hearing nothing about Heavenly Mother. I'm tired of believing heart and soul in the doctrines of salvation and seeing them prioritized underneath rules about earrings and white shirts.

I'm tired of discussions about the temple that leave no room for a less-than-gorgeous experience. I'm tired of having the most plain and precious things ripped away from me.

I'm tired of being able to fit in with the Relief Society sisters so easily—because I look the part and I know the lines—while hearing those same sisters say such mean things about the person they don't realize I am. I'm tired of wanting church to be a place of rest and learning and soul-sharing when I find mostly stress, stagnation, and superficiality.

And can I tell you, this is not about being in a bad ward or a bad family. I have had wonderful wards; I belong to a wonderful family. This is partly about the way I've been operating, the way I've been approaching church. I've gotten defensive and bitter, and I've had some good reasons for that, but the way I've damaged my own church experience is totally on me. And it's not sustainable, not in the long run. I'm trying to regroup and get back to basics, as they say. My testimony still burns inside me. I'm not tired of Jesus, of the Holy Ghost, of forever families, of repentance, of faith, or of love. I'm not tired of saying my prayers or reading my scriptures. But when it comes to church, I am tired.

It's not just church, either. I've pulled back somewhat from my involvement in online Mormon feminist communities—because, dangit, *I'm tired*. I find myself scrolling right past most of the blog posts and tuning out of the Facebook conversations. I'm tired of processing the anger and frustration and disillusionment over and over again. I'm tired of trying to scrounge up some optimism about "how far we've come!" and so forth.

To everything there is a season. I'll probably look back on this as my Tired Season. And it'll pass. I'll find renewed energy and cycle back through to hope. My personal Tired Season matters to me, but it's only notable insofar as it fits into the larger story of where we are as Mormons right now, where we are as a church family. And if you want my guess, a lot of people are gonna bow out for some length of time. If you want my guess, we're going to lose another generation. And it won't be because we're afraid. It'll be because we're tired.

"THE TROUBLE WITH FEMINISM" BY ALICE FISHER ROBERTS (AUGUST 22, 2014)

There's major road construction going on near my house. At the hardware store a neighbor asked my husband and me if we had noticed the wonky data lines strung across directly in front of the new signal lights. We hadn't. On the drive home we sure did though. Those lines (four of them, all lined up) hung directly in front of the signal lights, just like he said, and you know what? It looked ridiculous. I hope it doesn't stay that way, because it looks like some seriously shoddy work, considering how much money the city is paying for this "city upgrade."

I hadn't noticed until it was pointed out to me, but now I can't unsee it.

That's the trouble with feminism. In a recent discussion on another blog, I was told that the trouble with feminism is that it's packaged up so nicely and logically, but that it's a slippery slope to apostasy. I don't quite view it the same way, but you know what? Once you notice the inequality and the injustices, you can't un-notice them. And sometimes, noticing them over and over while people around you are blissfully unaware can make you feel all sorts of stabby. Noticing them when other people don't can make you feel alienated from people who used to be your friends, because it's hard to not be understood. It's hard to have friends think, "Well she went off the deep end." I didn't go off the deep end, I just noticed some stuff that I can't un-notice. And it's lousy. It ruins all sorts of formerly good books and movies.

So yeah, sometimes I'm an angry feminist. Because injustice makes me angry. It's pedestals, and chewed gum, and porn shoulders, and holding girls responsible for the thoughts of boys, and letting boys think that it's normal for them to objectify girls who don't dress modestly, and women being barred from callings (even those that don't require the priesthood) just because they're not men. There are so many little things we do without thinking about them that don't have to be that way, doctrinally. We could

298

be a church that is a woman's church AND a man's church. We could be a liberal's church and a conservative's church.

I'll admit that I grew up in a home where compassion for the underdog was part of our family creed. My siblings are all working in fields where they help people who are struggling. It's in our blood. So I was probably a bit susceptible to "teh feminism" based on my upbringing.

What can we do about this? This trouble with feminism? Sometimes it feels like a self-fulfilling prophecy. If feminism is dangerous because it leads to apostasy, then we should distance ourselves from feminists. If we distance ourselves from feminists, those feminists aren't going to feel very welcome at church. People who don't feel welcome at church are going to have a hard time continuing to go, no matter how strong their testimonies are, because people don't really like being in places where they aren't welcome (oddly enough). Then we say, "See! Feminism leads to apostasy, I told you so!"

If I could go back and un-see all the inequalities, I wouldn't. It's harder to feel peaceful at church now than it was when I didn't notice things, back when "they didn't bother me," but I also feel like they have taught me so much and made me a more loving, accepting person. I no longer judge people who aren't doing things just the way I think they should, because I recognize that things are messy sometimes and we're all just doing the best we can. I feel like feminism has forced me to take more responsibility for my own spiritual wellbeing. For me personally, that means that when I find myself focusing on the things that frustrate me to the point that church is a chore every week, I have to figure out how to recalibrate so that I can see the love and beauty that keeps me firmly rooted as a Mormon. For you that may mean something very different.

Feminism has meant that I can no longer pick up my feet and be carried along in the current of other people's testimonies. I have to figure it out myself, and that can be scary and more spiritually satisfying that anything else I've ever done.

REFLECTIONS

In late 2017, the editors asked several members of the community to reflect on the role that FMH played in the development of their Mormonism and their feminism. The personal essays that follow reflect a just a handful of viewpoints and experiences of the thousands of bloggers, commenters, and readers that have engaged with the blog since its founding.

ON AGENCY, ADVOCACY AND AMPLIFICATION BY LORIE WINDER STROMBERG

There is a tendency to see Mormon women as either victims of an oppressive, patriarchal religious tradition or completely autonomous agents committed to their faith. Both narratives are problematic. The latter fails to recognize the very real constraints on women's agency within a patriarchal community, while the former insists that women can only demonstrate agency by resisting the norms of such a community. Contemporary feminist scholars wrestle with the problem of agency within conservative religious traditions. Since resistance to patriarchal norms is generally equated with agency among feminists, asserts Mormon scholar Amy Hoyt, "women's acts [and attitudes] that sustain traditional religions are not viewed as constituting agency."[390]

Drawing on the work of Saba Mahmood, Hoyt suggests that agency can be evident both in resisting and maintaining norms within a community, though she admits "it is often difficult to locate autonomy . . . when one is compliant." Still, Hoyt posits that agency often includes a simultaneous "spectrum of behaviors . . . that fall between the poles of autonomy and limited freedom." Though *Feminist Mormon Housewives*, as its name implies, leans toward the feminist perspective, its pages contain attempts by Mormon women to inhabit, negotiate, and resist the gendered norms of Mormonism.[391]

When Lisa Butterworth founded FMH in 2004, she, like many of us, struggled to negotiate that space and sought a community where such a negotiation could safely take place. FMH was her attempt to create a supportive, feminist-friendly platform within the LDS community, hoping, also like many of us, that the two were compatible. By exploiting the then nascent but far-reaching potential of social networking on the Internet, she also worked to provide, in her words, "a respectful space that allowed women to safely wrestle with the consequences of defying Mormon social norms."

Throughout the 1970s, 80s, and 90s, independent LDS forums and publications, such as *Dialogue, Sunstone*, the Sunstone Symposium, *Exponent II*, and the Mormon Women's Forum, provided invaluable, though by their very nature limited, public platforms for the discussion of Mormon feminist issues; however, the Internet was a game changer in terms of its ability to reach a much broader audience and facilitate feminist activism through online organizing, discussion lists, blogs and websites. Many believed its reach and transparency would also protect Mormon feminists from the excommunications and institutional retaliations of the past that tended to dampen feminist activism and led *Salt Lake Tribune* religion writer Peggy Fletcher Stack to ask in 2003, "Where have all the Mormon feminists gone?"[392]

What Stack overlooked in her article was that Mormon feminism was establishing itself online. The process, however, was not seamless, nor would the Internet's scope prove to be universally effective in uniting the Mormon feminist community or protecting individual feminists from institutional reprisal. A significant split in the Mormon feminist community emerged between so-called "good Mormon feminists"—those who wanted more expansive opportunities for women in the Church but stopped short of advocating for significant structural change, none of whom had been excommunicated—and "bad Mormon feminists,"—those who called for full structural equality and were willing to risk institutional reprisal. Female ordination was the flashpoint. At FMH, Lisa resisted the "good Mormon feminist vs bad Mormon feminist" paradigm. Since FMH bloggers themselves were divided over the issue of women's ordination, she explained, she wanted to make sure FMH remained a space for "both women who felt passionately in favor of ordination and women who had reservations—those who needed more time to think about the issue, those who refused to work within a male paradigm of authority, those who rejected hierarchy, those who accepted a complementarian view of gender roles but wanted more opportunities for women, or those who were transitioning from one view to another."[393]

Over the last 40 years, my feminism has always been activist, and much of it has been devoted to advocating for women's ordination in the LDS Church. I remain concerned about how gender inequality negatively impacts all of us and convinced that the fundamental inequality of an all-male priesthood within Mormonism is such that anything less than ordination for women is insufficient. Too, an exclusive priesthood policy seems at odds with what I understand to be foundational to Mormonism itself, namely, the expansive belief that God does not hoard power as if it were in short supply or reserve it for an elite few but shares it liberally and makes it available to all. I still believe Mormonism at its best can help liberate rather than subjugate women and other marginalized groups. However, it must be held accountable when it does not. Inequality cannot go unchallenged, and as Mormons, we are called to a moral activism that holds us responsible for our choice either to perpetuate inequality through silence and inaction or to work for justice and equality.

In an essay about the birth of the decidedly activist organization Ordain Women, I wrote, "A significant social movement could not coalesce around the issue of women and priesthood ordination in Mormonism until a profound shift in attitudes and expectations about gender equality emerged—one sufficient enough to create a critical dissonance between Mormon women's lived experience and LDS cultural norms. There also had to be an effective, far-reaching social platform to facilitate communication and collaboration among enough of those troubled by the dissonance that they, through an alchemy of personalities and social networks, were compelled to confront it."[394] FMH provided a hospitable forum to facilitate that profound shift in attitudes and expectations about gender equality, even when many Mormon feminists were unconvinced or afraid to consider the question of women's ordination.

When we launched the Ordain Women website on March 17, 2013, FMH as a platform was essential to both facilitating its inception and amplifying its message. Not only did FMH bloggers increasingly tackle the issue of female ordination in surveys and blog posts, they graciously gave our guest blog posts space on their website, and many went public with their support for female ordination in profiles on the Ordain Women website.[395]

What I appreciate most about FMH's contribution to Mormon feminism is that it has consistently built community, facilitated activism, and provided a place for women's voices to be preserved and amplified. "[W]omen who may have once felt isolated in their congregations," wrote Joanna Brooks of online Mormon feminist forums, "... found a safe space to communicate and collaborate."[396] Further, FMH offered a place where feminists could work out how to stay or how to transition out of Mormonism without losing the sense of community—whether inherited from Mormonism's communitarian roots or intuited from its insistence on lay participation—vital to every Mormon's experience.

Though not primarily a forum for advocacy, what FMH does best, writes FMH blogger, activist and community organizer Nat Kelly, is provide the years of groundwork and a multiplicity of approaches necessary "to ensure a lively, creative, sustainable movement." It "build[s] that base; find[s] those baby feminists; create[s] solidarity; and host[s] conversations about what the next steps should be" in facilitating change.[397]

Amplification as a feminist strategy was identified by female staffers in the Obama White House who were tired of being ignored or overlooked. They "adopted a meeting strategy they called 'amplification': When a woman made a key point, other women would repeat it, giving credit to its author. This forced the men in the room to recognize the contribution — and denied them the chance to claim the idea as their own."[398] In a broader sense, FMH functions as a platform for the amplification of Mormon feminist thought and experience and an essential online archive to preserve the collective memory of Mormon feminists in the twenty-first century.

THE FAITHFUL DISSIDENT BY CLAUDIA FOX REPPEN

It's been interesting to look back at some of my old blog posts under the pseudonym *The Faithful Dissident*, a name which came to me one day when I was out jogging and trying to release the frustration I was feeling as a result of my personal struggles in the LDS Church. I had always been "faithful" by the usual standards employed to measure one's faithfulness in the Church: I was active and attended meetings, held callings, paid a full tithe, held a temple recommend, obeyed the Word of Wisdom and the Law of Chastity, etc. But as I was knee-deep in the messy process of learning the non-correlated, nuanced version of LDS Church history, and simultaneously witnessing troubling aspects of contemporary Mormon history and culture unfold, I was also becoming more aware of the "dissident" within me – and she was dying to be heard.

I suppose I was always aware of my inner dissident, which probably surfaced as soon as I started the Young Women's program in church. Being the oldest child and a tomboy with four younger brothers, I hated the lessons about motherhood and gender roles. I knew already then that I didn't want to be a mother. But I knew I was supposed to want to, and so the cycle of endless guilt began. It would be compounded when I chose to marry a non-member (a decision for which I would be very grateful only after leaving the Church), despite years of almost weekly reminders of how important it was to marry in the temple. Never mind the fact that I couldn't have married a kinder, more loving, more supportive man, or that having children just wasn't for us. Never mind the fact that my record was pretty squeaky clean when it came to sins of commission. It was these Mormon cardinal sins of omission – temple marriage and childbearing – that consumed me in how I viewed myself.

As I read my old blog posts, I'm reminded of just how hard I really tried to justify myself not only to other Mormons, but to myself and to the God that I believed in. I'm also struck by just how angst-ridden I was during that time, with feelings of anger, betrayal, and loneliness as I tried to make sense of everything I had learned about the origins of the LDS Church and various troubling doctrines. Since I had no in-person support network, the online Mormon blogosphere (known as the bloggernacle) became my lifeline, of which Feminist Mormon Housewives would play a major part.

Later on, I would embark on a humanitarian journey that would change my life and educate me immensely on other people, culture, religion, circumstance, personal experience, psychology, and how each and every one of these affect who we are and what we believe. This experience and the knowledge that I have acquired since has presented me with existential and philosophical questions that transcend Mormonism, Christianity, or religion altogether.

When I was writing as The Faithful Dissident, I was desperate to reconcile my faithful self with my dissident self, and to claim what I felt was my rightful place in the Church. I failed in this endeavor, but gained a wealth of knowledge that I simply could not have attained in any other way. Now, as a non-believer, I am ambivalent as to whether there will be any continuation of life or consciousness after death. But if there is, perhaps I will discover the Mormon adage that "knowledge is the only thing we can take with us" to be true. And as the catalyst that spurred me on my journey towards further knowledge, I will be grateful to my inner, angst-ridden faithful dissident.

A Collective Voice Reminding "You Are Not Alone" by Rachel Hunt Steenblik

I stumbled upon the Feminist Mormon Housewives blog by accident in April 2008. I had just graduated from Brigham Young University in philosophy and accepted a short term—but full-time—research position from one of my professors. My work would be to study Heavenly Mother.

I started at lds.org and searched terms like "Heavenly Mother" (approximately six results), "Mother in Heaven" and "Eternal Mother" (approximately three more results), and "Heavenly Parents (a few hundred results). Frustrated that there were not more specific references to Heavenly Mother, and not quite knowing where to look next, I turned to Google. A smattering of things came up, including many personal essays written as blog posts for Feminist Mormon Housewives by women who wanted to know more about their Heavenly Mother and feel closer to Her.

Many questioned the seemingly "sacred silence" surrounding Her, surmising that the silence might not be all that sacred. I still remember reading words written with sincerity, longing, seeking, and (sometimes) anger and sadness. I didn't necessarily resonate with every post or feeling, but I appreciated that the authors asked the questions and that they were speaking. Their voices witnessed almost from the wilderness that I was not alone; it felt simultaneously comforting and powerful.

A few years later, I wrote a post on my personal blog about physical and mental illness and George Albert Smith. A friend, Ashley Mae Hoiland, suggested I submit it to some of the Mormon blogs. I asked her which ones and she suggested the Exponent, By Common Consent, and FMH. I didn't know how submitting guest posts worked so tried all three. The Exponent and FMH ended up publishing my post the same day, February 3, 2012.[399] While I later became a permanent blogger at the Exponent, I remained grateful that FMH co-welcomed me into the bloggernacle and allowed me a space to ask my own questions and to speak, perhaps witnessing to new readers that they were not alone.

A few years after that, an FMH writer reached out to me to see if they could repost a piece I published at the Exponent called "What I First Learned About Heavenly Mother." FMH's blog was running a series on Heavenly Mother and they thought it would be a good fit. I was honored to have it included and grateful for the sisterhood between the Mormon feminist blogs. It felt especially sweet because the post was written about the same BYU research period that introduced me to feminist Mormon housewives.[400]

I was deeply moved by Sara Katherine Staheli Hanks' contribution to that same series, titled "Heavenly Mother and the Baader-Meinhoff Phenomenon." She applied the well-known (though not always known the name of) phenomenon where you hear, or see, or notice, or learn about something and then start hearing, or seeing, or noticing, or learning about that thing everywhere to Heavenly Mother, that being who is not often heard, or seen, or noticed, or learned about. After Sara had reasons to notice Heavenly Mother during her early twenties, she started seeing Her, in the very old, the middle-aged, the very young, the freckled, the expressive, the serene, the, the, the. She also included beautiful picture after beautiful picture, helping me see Heavenly Mother too. I smiled and cried and smiled and cried as I scrolled through the stirring words and images. It inspired me to look harder for my Mother in the faces and characteristics of people around me.[401]

That same month, my heart was cracked open by another FMH post, though for much more harrowing reasons: the predecessor to 2017/2018's #MeToo movement, #YesAllWomen, that Althea memorialized as #YesEvenMormonWomen.[402]

It made room for Mormon women to tell their stories of suffering sexual harassment and abuse, oftentimes at the words or hands of Mormon men (including Mormon leaders), and to bring dark things to light. The comments overflowed with hurt done to Mormon women. I read and cried and read and cried before writing my own. Layers of loneliness broke down as we shared "we too."

Around this same time, I was working with FMH's own Joanna Brooks and Young Mormon Feminists' Hannah Wheelwright to edit what would become Oxford University Press's *Mormon Feminism: Essential Writings*. The Feminist Mormon Housewives blog was an essential space to glean and garner Mormon women's writings. One such piece was Elizabeth Hammond's "The Mormon Priestess (The Short Version)."[403] I first learned about it from what I can only describe as hushed but hurried emails, asking "Have you read it yet? Have you read it?" I hadn't, but did so. It hurt to read (*devastated* might be more accurate) and opened up important, challenging conversations. My co-editors and I knew that we wanted to publish it, but also knew that we didn't have as many words to offer it as we would have liked. (We chose to curate and cut within individual pieces so we could include more voices.) Liz and I went back and forth many times until both parties felt satisfied. It never became less painful to read. Still, I was grateful for Liz's patience and flexibility and that she allowed her important post to be disseminated, offering deeper understanding to those who have felt hurt by holy places.

More broadly, I feel a deep sense of gratitude for FMH's blog, which offered me first a space to read brave questions and answers about Heavenly Mother and a sense of comfort and solidarity as I formed my own, and second a welcome space to write. I'm grateful too for numerous FMH posts, which have inspired, blessed, and challenged me. So many are essential. So many are worth preserving. So many whisper, or shout, from the rooftops: You are not alone.

BEING A BUCKET BY MICA MCGRIGGS, PH.D

During the first month of my first year of graduate school at BYU, I sat with classmates in the graduate lounge discussing issues of feminism in the church. While I had spent my college years reading the womanist and feminist classics, I had not involved myself in the Mormon Feminist community. I had read a few of the must-reads, like Elna Baker's memoir and *The Book of Mormon Girl* by Joanna Brooks. In fact, prior to school starting, I tracked down Joanna's book tour and stalked her like a whacka-doo! Like most people within progressive Mormonism I was smitten with her. I started showing up at all of her events, and once I even brought her a brownie from the BYU Creamery because she had mentioned she enjoyed them at a previous event. Yeah … stalker-ish, I know! Clearly I was yearning for a community and conversation that validated my questions and concerns.

Back in the lounge at the Lord's University, I made an impassioned argument about the nuances of benevolent Mormon patriarchy. A classmate of mine asked, "Mica, are you in FMH on Facebook?"

"No, what's that?"

My classmate told me about the blog and the group and how I would love it! I sent a request to be added to the Facebook group later that day and began reading the blog that evening. Whoa, these women are discussing the exact things I am chatting about with close friends!

I loved it! I began posting questions or crowdsourcing for feedback on a daily basis, watching for the latest blog post, and discussing the content with friends and classmates. I began watching the trends of conversation and identifying the women in the group whom I felt were producing the best of dialogue.

A few weeks later I was again in the lounge having one of my Mormon feminist debriefs, and I mentioned a post that made an impact on me written by a woman named Sara Burlingame. "Did you know she's not even Mormon?" one of the men in my cohort stated. I did not know this, and I was shocked to say the least. How did this crazywomancreek capture the experience of a Mormon woman so perfectly and from an intersectional lens?

While I was enthusiastic about the content in the group and on the blog, I noticed that something was missing: the voices of women of color. The group reeked of white lady feminism, and there seemed to be a narrow and privileged lens through which the majority of the content was filtered. A dialectical tension came as a result of feeling that the FMH community related to so much of my experience and at the same time erased or was simply blind to other parts of my experience. There was a small contingent of the community doing intersectional work, but the majority was white-washing history, tone policing, and debating the appropriateness of a Pocahontas costume for Halloween among micro and overt racial aggressions. While I was often annoyed or disappointed, I was invested (similarly to the way I felt with the church itself) and wanted to see the FMH community grow into a place where I and other women of color would want to be.

I shifted my focus from just posting questions and general concerns within the church to reframing or calling-out violations in conversations in the group. As I asserted my voice, I was creating space at the table for myself and hopefully for other Mormon women of color. I began inserting myself in not only dialogue but also in physical progressive spaces, and people began to take notice. There were white Mormon Feminist who were thirsting for knowledge from the margins whether they realized it consciously or not. I was determined to become a bucket in the well for my white progressive sisters, and while I couldn't force anyone to drink, I could deliver the water.

I believe what started as pressure to have diversity in the leadership of FMH grew into genuine appreciation for me and my perspectives. I became a moderator in the Facebook group, a regular contributor on the blog, a guest cohost on the FMH Podcast with Lindsay Hansen Park, and eventually was voted on as a board member for FMH's non-profit, which organized and managed a scholarship foundation.

Part of my role as a bucket in the well was not only to call white lady Mormon feminists on their racism, but it was also to really understand their experience. While I had been raised in a White Mormon community, it was a mainstream orthodox community, where for most part women were satisfied with the status quo (or at least presented themselves to be). A poem I wrote and performed in Mormon feminist spaces in honor of Emma Smith was not only a tribute to her but a recognition of my white sisters in the church.

Am I Enough: a spoken word for Emma

Do my arms not wrap around him completely? Does my heart fail to greet him?
Do the words of comfort that flow from my lips reach him, or do they fall short and hit th
e floor, only to be crushed by the strong feet of men coming and going each day.
Am I enough?
I smile, I dance, I love, I write, I laugh, I teach, I serve, I bless, and still I wonder…
Am I enough?
I know the Father, I know the Son. I have burned with spirit and dressed in white.
Yet I find myself walking through the valley of the shadow of doubt.
Am I enough?
In the quiet moments, in the stillness of the night, in the glow of the fire,
fitting perfectly in his infinite embrace,
I feel peace, I safe, I feel loved. Then the morning breaks, and the coat,
hat, and scarf leave, as well promise goes.
And again I walk through the world, and never truly know.
Am I enough?

I saw white Mormon women's pain surrounding the history and doctrine of plural marriage; I spent long hours discussing the topic with close friends. As a black woman, the issue was not at the forefront of my concerns about problems in the church. The more time I spent with Lindsay, the more I understood the complexity of emotions produced by the problematic practice. There was real pain, feelings of betrayal, and confusion surrounding polygamy for white women in the church. After spending countless hours in conversation with Lindsay and others who spend time studying polygamy, I developed a concern for those still living in Mormon Fundamentalism today. Like many others, I saw fundamentalists as our cousins who (particularly those who were living in the FLDS community) had been isolated from the mainstream LDS. Their isolation and marginalization created an environment that evil leaders exploited and plundered. I learned this firsthand when I traveled to Short Creek, an FLDS community located on the border of Utah and Arizona. Again I placed my body and empathy with a group of White Mormons to act as a bucket. Most living in this isolated community had not seen a Black person in real life, let alone interacted with one; my presence in town would certainly garner a response. A few of our contacts from the community thought it might be unsafe for me, but when I arrived with Lindsay, we were both welcomed warmly and enthusiastically. That first trip to the crick and the several trips since then provided an opportunity for mutual understanding.

As I involved myself more and more in White progressive Mormon spaces, I became more disconnected from my Black Mormon community. Many from my squad did not understand why I wanted to educate and work on White lady issues when they so often erased my experiences and sometimes even enacted violence onto myself and other Mormons of color. They were right; being a bucket was depleting me, and the water supply from the well was not endless. There was certainly richness and renewal in many of my relationships with Mormon Feminists, yet at times, the work of advancing intersectionality in my Mormon Feminist/Progressive Mormon community was exhausting in ways that seeped to the marrow of my bones. I needed to drink from my own bucket.

I continue to participate with the FMH community in a multiplicity of ways, and I've worked to find balance by focusing on my own self-care and finding refuge from my white and brown sisters in and out of the gospel. FMH provided me an environment to test my bandwidth and emotional energy. Not only have I grown spiritually during my time in the Mormon Feminist community; I have grown professionally, socially, personally, and most importantly, I have learned to drink from my own bucket. This lesson will serve me for years to come.

My work in intersectional equity did not begin in progressive Mormon spaces and it will not end there, but these spaces and the people in them have shaped my bucket in ways that are sacred to me. Happy Birthday, Feminist Mormon Housewives. My wish is for you to continue to host dialogue and create space for many more budding feminists to come.

A Journey From Mormon "Feminist-Ally" to Feminist Mormon by Kalani Tonga

For the entirety of my youth, I was an "ideal" Mormon:

- I came from an intact, sealed family, and both my mom's and my dad's families have been members of the church for several generations.

- I served in various callings and watched my parents serve in leadership callings in our wards.
- I attended and graduated from BYU.
- I didn't drink or smoke, and I was honest in my dealings with my fellow man.

In short, based upon my life experiences, I believed I had no reason to question the status quo within the church. I don't know that I ever would have questioned it, if not for the fact that my "ideal Mormon" status changed when I entered adulthood.

When I was in my 20s, my (now ex-) husband committed the (nearly unpardonable) sin of murder. He served time in prison, and while he was there, I searched relentlessly for information about how his choices would affect my own eternal salvation. I believed that binding myself to him in marriage also bound me to whatever eternal fate was reserved for those who commit serious sins while in the flesh. I had always heard that murder was second only to denying the Holy Ghost in terms of severity, and everything I read and heard about Mormon doctrine led me to believe that I could never progress to the highest degree of eternal glory while married to my husband because his choices affected my eternity. I loved him. I WANTED to be married to him. But, I felt like I had to make the impossible choice of tying myself to a sinking ship for eternity or letting go of the father of my children, a man that I still loved with my whole heart. It was a hopeless and heartbreaking time, and I remember thinking to myself, "I just can't believe that a loving Heavenly Father would force me to choose between my marriage and the highest degree of eternal salvation. It doesn't make sense to me that the consequences of loving someone who committed a serious sin would stunt my spiritual growth forever. I just don't understand this at all."

In trying to find my place within the church as the wife of a man convicted of homicide, I ravenously consumed all sorts of essays and conference talks and books about church doctrine. During this search, I stumbled upon the FMH blog, and it was like a tiny light flickered in my otherwise dark and hopeless existence. I found FMH at a time of immense loneliness, hopelessness, and confusion, and the essays I read brought the balm of Gilead to my tender, wounded soul. Suddenly, I found an entire community of "others" who didn't quite fit in. Their stories made me feel less alone. Their questions echoed my own. Their power and confidence in their own abilities gave me strength and hope that I, too, could voice my concerns and be met with compassion and understanding. Nevertheless, as a lifelong member of the church and a traditional believer of the doctrine I had been taught, I cringed at the word "feminist" and initially viewed myself as more of an ally/sympathizer to the feminist cause, as opposed to a feminist myself.

I distinctly recall reading a comment one day where someone spoke negatively about feminists, and I thought to myself, "Hey! They're talking about US!" And then, I immediately thought, "Wait…US? I mean 'THEM,' right?" As I worked it out in my mind, I realized that, no, I didn't mean "them." I saw myself as a feminist, and I felt personally attacked when someone spoke negatively about feminists. It was both eye-opening and liberating to accept and embrace "feminist" as an adjective that described myself. The Feminist Mormon Housewives blog directly influenced my transformation from "ally of feminism" to "feminist."

I think, though, that the FMH blog most profoundly influenced my life by giving me a community of women who were at once fierce and powerful and strong, but also possessed gentleness and grace and kindness. I had never in my life seen women claiming spiritual power unapologetically, and their security in their own unorthodox spirituality strengthened me and gave me permission to step up and be spiritually strong in my own way. I'm a lifelong athlete and participated in team sports, so I knew what physical strength looked like, but for the first time in my life, I witnessed women who possessed spiritual strength and unapologetically wielded spiritual power. As I read the blog and interacted with the authors who wrote about ideas that gave me much needed light during a very dark time in my life, hope and excitement bloomed within me and I felt a sense of inner peace and power that I didn't even realize I had been missing.

The lessons I learned from reading and writing for the FMH blog have completely transformed my life. I credit FMH – both the ideas from the blog and the women themselves who wrote the words – for helping me survive a divorce, a faith crisis, the incarceration of my partner, and raising five small children on my own. Through my interactions with the FMH bloggers, I have learned about racial identity, feminist theory, and sisterhood. We have struggled with betrayal, dealt with disagreement and disappointment, and suffered immense losses. But, we have also celebrated life together and supported and loved each other through the good times and the bad. Both my feminism and my Mormonism have grown in ways I never imagined possible because I happened to wander across the FMH blog as I searched for truth and comfort. I hope I am a wiser, kinder, more loving person because of my experiences with FMH. My life has been forever changed for the better.

A Love Letter to FMH by Ziff, a blogger at Zelophehad's Daughters

I didn't begin reading the Feminist Mormon Housewives blog regularly until it was almost two years old. When I did, though, I quickly found that it was the most consistently compelling of all the blogs in the bloggernacle. What struck me the most, and it struck me repeatedly, was how participants on the blog, both bloggers and commenters, shared their experiences of sadness and disappointment and frustration and anger in such raw and moving ways.

As FMH is a feminist Mormon blog in particular, naturally much of the frustration that writers expressed was directed at problems in the LDS Church. I went into reading the blog as a feminist-leaning person, but as a straight, white, cisgender, and most importantly male person, my sympathies for feminist positions were largely general and theoretical. Of course women are people just like men are, I thought, but what I hadn't thought about were the realities of the endless concrete ways that women were being pedestalized, condescended to, dismissed, or outright ignored in the Church. Reading the FMH blog gave me a window to women's experience in the Church that I had never had before. Writers opened my eyes to the myriad of large and small ways that Church doctrine and practices put them down.

A particular type of comment on the blog always stood out to me, and I saw it over and over. A new reader, who had typically just come by after having a friend refer her, or after Googling a difficult question, would express how happy she was to find that she wasn't alone in being disturbed by an issue like the sexism of the temple, or the endless quoting of the Family Proclamation and its attempts to shoehorn all of women's lives into a single role. This was in the years before the rise of Facebook and other social media allowed for people on the fringes of Mormonism to connect on other online platforms, and the FMH blog served a unique role in not only discussing all kinds of feminist issues in the Church, but also in just communicating to women who found themselves not fitting the Mormon women's submissive mold that there were others like them.

In the years since I began reading FMH, I feel like I've moved from not just being sympathetic to feminism in theory or in general, but to feeling like I have a much better grasp on some of the major issues in feminism, particularly in a Mormon context, and considering myself a feminist. I think much of the credit for that change goes to the opportunities I've had to read so many women's experiences discussed on the FMH blog. I owe a debt of gratitude to Lisa and to her co-bloggers for the tremendous amount of work they have put into the blog over the years. I appreciate that I have had the chance to learn so much from them by listening in.

I LOST MY FAITH BUT FOUND MY VOICE: FMH AND COMMUNITY BY MARISA MCPECK-STRINGHAM

I discovered Feminist Mormon Housewives when I worked at LDS Family Services and was longing for a like-minded community. I was raised by feminist, egalitarian parents and I bristled at the confining patriarchal structure of the church. Over the course of my many years commenting at FMH, I went from an active, temple-recommend holding -- albeit rebellious and progressively liberal -- member in good standing to what I lovingly refer to now as a disaffected feminist apostate. If it hadn't been for FMH, I don't know if I would have been able to articulate and process my feelings of disillusionment with the church. I struggled against patriarchy and gender roles, and FMH helped me give voice to that. I am a member of a family that believes in equality and a member of a church who doesn't. Feeling like the church believes my highest calling as a woman is that of mother has always weighed heavily on my heart as I believe my highest calling is that of disciple of Christ.

FMH was my lifeline after my mother died and gave me a life raft and a place to belong while my emotions were adrift on the troubled waters of motherless daughterhood. The anonymous women behind the most creative handles on the internet were my closest confidants during a particularly trying time in my life. For the first time I felt something that I had never felt on the cushioned seats in Relief Society: sisterhood. Eventually I met some of my new online friends at various "snackers" and felt a community within this group of mostly women, some men, that I had never felt in a ward, wards where I was always the troublemaking liberal. I spent hours reading the finely crafted and thoughtful essays of women who were discovering their feminism in spite of being told their whole lives that feminists were evil man-haters who want to destroy families. I commented often, sometimes too much, as I spewed everything I had felt for over 30 years and never had a safe place to express outside of the confines of my immediate family and husband.

Although I considered myself a life-long feminist, I learned about being a better intersectional feminist from FMH and confronted all of my biases, and not just the ones I felt comfortable confronting. I learned how to become a better ally to all marginalized groups, in word and in action, through this incredible group of women. It was this identifying of my values that made me realize that my values did not, and never had, aligned with the values of the church. This was a painful realization and thrust me deep into a faith crisis. Having a faith crisis while you work for your church is awkward and painful, and sometimes, career-ending.

My time commenting on FMH was always fraught as I walked a careful line of wanting to express all my feminist feelings and dissatisfaction with the role of women in the church and maintain my career at LDS Family Services. I loved working with my clients as an adoption/birth parent caseworker and I didn't want to jeopardize that, but I also couldn't fathom continuing to work there without an outlet to express my frustration. Eventually when push came to shove, I was forced to choose between FMH and my job when comments I made online were sent to

LDS Family Headquarters. My supervisor told me that I needed to leave all Mormon feminist/progressive Facebook groups and stop commenting on Mormon feminist/progressive blogs if I wanted to continue to work there. It felt like a knife through my heart because FMH was the one thing keeping me in the pews. It was the one place I could turn to when church culture and doctrine went against my morals as a person. Of course, it didn't help that the moderators of FMH let people speculate that I wasn't in trouble at work for my participation in Mormon feminism but because I violated my clients' confidentiality, a rumor I still haven't forgiven as it could have cost me my professional license and my livelihood. The leaders of the Mormon feminist movement at that time were in denial that the church would ever punish them because they believed erroneously that the internet kept them safe. Kate Kelly's excommunication absolved them of this notion.

Six months after my last child was born, I realized that I could no longer say that I believed the leaders of the church were prophets, seers, and revelators. I could no longer sustain them in their callings and because of that, I was no longer worthy to hold a temple recommend. The cognitive dissonance wasn't worth my spiritual health anymore. I knew LDS Family Services was actively dismantling their adoption program and I didn't want to be a part of the demise. I went to the temple for the last time in August 2013 with a former client of the agency to support her as she took out her endowments. She had relinquished two of her children to adoption and attended our weekly support group and wanted me and my coworker there by her side. I knew when I was there it was my last time attending a temple session and I soaked it all in realizing that I no longer believed any of what happened there was necessary for my salvation. Being able to participate in Mormon feminism was a Godsend until it wasn't. The next summer Kate Kelly was excommunicated and I came to the conclusion I no longer belonged in a church where women are punished for asking to be treated as equals.

My soul was liberated the day I realized that my priesthood leaders only had as much power over me as I decided they did. Once I recognized they had no power in my life, I was free. My faith shelf was already broken into pieces by the time the exclusion policy was announced. The new policy set my shelf on fire. That's the day I realized the church wasn't worthy of me.

I credit Feminist Mormon Housewives with helping me to wake up to the reality that was all around me but I was too blind to see. Growing up in a part-member family, all I ever wanted was to be sealed to my family and live forever with them. "Families can be Together Forever" is a powerful drug to a girl who just wanted to be good and belong. This desire clouded me to the realities of chicken patriarchy, soft misogyny, homophobia, and racism in the church. FMH shone a light on all of those issues for me and I could no longer justify my participation in a church that has hurt, and continues to hurt, those on the margins -- those who Jesus commanded me to love without exception. For those reasons, I will always be grateful for the forum Feminist Mormon Housewives provided when I needed it most.

NOTES

[1] Thomas S. Monson, "Stand in Holy Places," General Conference talk, October 2011.

[2] The group of excommunicated individuals and the events of their excommunications in September 1993 are known as the September Six. Peggy Fletcher Stack, "Where have all the Mormon feminists gone?" *Salt Lake Tribune*, October 4, 2003; Frieda Klotz, "The Rise of Mormon feminist bloggers," *The Guardian*, March 19, 2012; Joanna Brooks, "An Introduction," in *Mormon Feminism: Essential Writings*, ed Joanna Brooks, Rachel Hunt Steenblik, and Hannah Wheelwright (Oxford University Press 2015), p. 18-19.

[3] Peggy Fletcher Stack, "Where have all the Mormon feminists gone?" *Salt Lake Tribune*, October 4, 2003.

[4] Margaret Toscano, Moderator; Lisa Butterworth, John Dewey Remy, Jana Bouch Remy, "Mormon Feminist Bloggers: Can Blogging Help Mormon Feminism," Sunstone (podcast), January 1, 2006. https://www.sunstonemagazine.com/mormon-feminist-bloggers-can-blogging-help-mormon-feminism/

[5] Lorie Winder Stromberg, "The Sacred and the Mundane: Mormon," Sunstone (podcast), January 1, 1997. https://www.sunstonemagazine.com/the-sacred-and-the-mundane-mormon-feminism-on-the-internet/

[6] Jessica Finnigan and Nancy Ross, "Mormon Feminists in Social Media: A Story of Community and Education," in *Voices for Equality: Ordain Women and Resurgent Mormon Feminism*, ed Gordon Shepherd, Lavina Fielding Anderson, and Gary Shepherd (Greg Kofford Books, 2015), 335–376.

[7] Ibid.

[8] Jessica Finnigan and Nancy Ross. "'I'm a Mormon feminist:' How social media revitalized and enlarged a movement." *Interdisciplinary Journal of Research on Religion* 9 (2013): no 12; Nancy Ross and Jessica Finnigan. "Mormon feminist perspectives on the Mormon digital awakening: A study of identity and personal narratives." *Dialogue: A Journal of Mormon Thought* 47, no. 4 (2014): 47–75.

[9] Jessica Finnigan and Nancy Ross, "Mormon Feminists in Social Media: A Story of Community and Education," in *Voices for Equality: Ordain Women and Resurgent Mormon Feminism*, ed Gordon Shepherd, Lavina Fielding Anderson, and Gary Shepherd (Greg Kofford Books, 2015), 335–376.

[10] Ibid.

[11] Nancy Ross and Jessica Finnigan. "Mormon feminist perspectives on the Mormon digital awakening: A study of identity and personal narratives." *Dialogue: A Journal of Mormon Thought* 47, no. 4 (2014): 47–75.

[12] Jessica Finnigan and Nancy Ross, "Mormon Feminists in Social Media: A Story of Community and Education," in *Voices for Equality: Ordain Women and Resurgent*

Mormon Feminism, ed Gordon Shepherd, Lavina Fielding Anderson, and Gary Shepherd (Greg Kofford Books, 2015), 335–376.

[13] Peggy Fletcher Stack, "Where have all the Mormon feminists gone?" *Salt Lake Tribune*, October 4, 2003.

[14] Margaret Toscano, Moderator; Lisa Butterworth, John Dewey Remy, Jana Bouch Remy, "Mormon Feminist Bloggers: Can Blogging Help Mormon Feminism," Sunstone (podcast), January 1, 2006. https://www.sunstonemagazine.com/mormon-feminist-bloggers-can-blogging-help-mormon-feminism/

[15] "Mo" is an abbreviation for Mormon.

[16] The Relief Society, sometimes abbreviated RS, is the LDS Church-wide women's organization that meets for an hour during the regular Sunday church service.

[17] Lisa Patterson Butterworth, "Career as a Lonely Bed Partner," Feminist Mormon Housewives (blog), October 21, 2004. http://www.feministmormonhousewives.org/2004/10/career-as-a-lonely-bed-partner/

[18] Times and Seasons, another Mormon blog.

[19] "The Family: A Proclamation to the World" (1995) is a document that outlines the LDS view of the family, gender roles, and expectations of monogamous heterosexuality. It is often referred to as the Proclamation on the Family or simply the Proclamation.

[20] See Butterworth's essay "Moral Authority" in the chapter titled 2004.

[21] Richard Lyman Bushman, *Joseph Smith: Rough Stone Rolling* (Knopf, 2005).

[22] "Mission Statement + Beginnings," Segullah (website). https://segullah.org/about/

[23] Debra Nussbaum, "Faithful Track Questions, Answers and Minutiae on Blogs," *New York Times*, March 5, 2005.

[24] *Desperate Housewives* was a scripted drama-comedy series that ran on the ABC network from 2004–2012.

[25] Julie in Austin, comment, "Are Powerful Women at a Disadvantage?" Times and Seasons (blog), January 15, 2005. http://www.timesandseasons.org/index.php?p=1858#comment-42717

[26] Jan Shipps. "Dangerous History: Laurel Ulrich and Her Mormon Sisters," *The Christian Century* 110, no. 29 (1993), 1012–15.

[27] Jan Shipps, *Sojourner in the Promised Land: Forty Years among the Mormons* (University of Illinois Press, 2000).

[28] Jan Shipps. "Dangerous History: Laurel Ulrich and Her Mormon Sisters," *The Christian Century* 110, no. 29 (1993), 1012–15.

[29] Betina Lindsey, "Why Don't Women Hold the Priesthood? A Brief but Insightful Interview," *Mormon Women's Forum Quarterly* 1, no. 1 (October 1989): 5.

[30] Gordon B. Hinckley, "Ten Gifts from the Lord," Relief Society General Women's Meeting, September 28, 1985, published in *Ensign*, November 1985, 86; Patricia T. Holland, "A Woman's Perspective on the Priesthood," *Liahona*, 6:5, June 1982, 21; Russell M. Nelson, "Woman—of Infinite Worth," *Ensign*, November 1989, 20.

[31] Russell M. Nelson, "Woman—of Infinite Worth," *Ensign*, November 1989, 20; Barbara B. Smith, "The Legacy Remembered and Renewed," Relief Society General Women's Meeting, March 27, 1982.

[32] Kate Kirkham, Todd Britsch, Olani Durrant, Mack Lawrence, and Steven C. Walker, "Relating to the Other: Building Bridges, Working Together," BYU Women's Conference, April 29, 1993.

[33] Bruce Hafen was an emeritus General Authority for The Church of Jesus Christ of Latter-day Saints and author of several books on LDS doctrine.

[34] Bruce Hafen, "Women, Feminism and the Blessings of the Priesthood," BYU Women's Conference, March 29, 1985.

[35] Bartchy, Scott, "Jesus, Power, and Gender Roles," Sunstone Symposium, Session 190, August 18, 1994.

[36] See "Power Hungry" by Lorie Winder Stromberg earlier in this chapter.

[37] Lorie Winder Stromberg, "The Sacred and the Mundane: Mormon ," Sunstone (podcast), January 1, 1997. https://www.sunstonemagazine.com/the-sacred-and-the-mundane-mormon-feminism-on-the-internet/

[38] Sonia Johnson was excommunicated in 1979 for her activism in the Mormons for ERA movement. See Amanda HK, Kris, and Andrea, "A History of Women's Excommunication," Juvenile Instructor (blog), June 12, 2014. http://juvenileinstructor.org/a-history-of-womens-excommunication/

[39] Peggy Fletcher Stack, "Where have all the Mormon feminists gone?" *Salt Lake Tribune*, October 4, 2003.

[40] Laurel Thatcher Ulrich, *A Midwife's Tale: The Life of Martha Ballard, Based on Her Diary, 1785–1812* (Knopf, 1990).

[41] Laurel Thatcher Ulrich, *The Age of Homespun: Objects and Stories in the Creation of an American Myth* (Knopf, 2001).

[42] Laurel Thatcher Ulrich and Emma Lou Thayne, *All God's Critters Got a Place in the Choir* (Aspen Books, 1995).

[43] Laurel Thatcher Ulrich, "A Pail of Cream," *The Journal of American History* 89 (2002): 43–47.

[44] Claudia L. Bushman, Nancy Dredge, Carrel H. Sheldon, and Laurel Thatcher Ulrich, "My Short Happy Life with *Exponent II*," *Dialogue: A Journal of Mormon Thought* 36, no. 3 (Fall 2003): 178–192.

[45] Ulrich is referencing changing tables for changing a baby's diaper.

[46] Jan Shipps, "Dangerous History: Exploring the Role of Mormon Women." *The Christian Century* 110, no. 29 (October 20, 1993), 1012–15. The essay can also be found in Shipps's book of collected essays, *Sojourner in the Promised Land: Forty Years Among the Mormons* (University of Illinois Press, 2000).

[47] Salt Lake City.

[48] Celestial Kingdom, the highest of the three kingdoms of heaven in Mormon cosmology.

[49] At the time of putting this book together, these posts were no longer available on the blog By Common Consent.

[50] *Improvement Era*, vol. 10 (1907): 308.

[51] Carrie A. Moore, "Debate renewed with change in Book of Mormon introduction," *Deseret News*, November 8, 2007.

[52] "Church Responds to Questions on TV Series," Mormon Newsroom (website), March 6, 2006. https://www.mormonnewsroom.org/article/church-responds-to-questions-on-tv-series

[53] Maxine Hanks (ed), *Women and Authority: Re-emerging Mormon Feminism* (Signature Books, 1992).

[54] Kate Chopin, *A Pair of Silk Stockings and Other Stories* (Dover Thrift Editions, 1996).

[55] The LDS Church is headquartered in Salt Lake City, Utah. The Church's offices in Salt Lake City are kept running by paid employees, volunteers, and official church leaders. Since many decisions that come from the Church are the result of processes and procedures that are unclear to church members, involving unknown people and committees, a reference to "church headquarters" is often meant to mean the general collection of leaders and bureaucrats who have a hand in such decisions. The same can be said of the term "Church Office Building" (sometimes abbreviated as COB), an actual building in Salt Lake City where many church departments have offices.

[56] In the temple endowment ceremony, participants are asked to make sacred promises in exchange for certain pieces of information. At one point, men are asked to pledge obedience to God, while women are asked to "hearken unto" the counsel of their husbands. Prior to 1990, the wording of the covenant for women used the more explicit language of "obey" rather than "hearken unto."

[57] In my opinion.

[58] This question was part of a short informal survey.

[59] Linda King Newell and Valeen Tippetts Avery, *Mormon Enigma: Emma Hale Smith* (Doubleday, 1984).

[60] Wearing or displaying a cross as a symbol of belief in Jesus Christ is frowned upon in LDS culture and discourse. In the church-published book *True to the Faith* (The Church of Jesus Christ of Latter-day Saints, 2004), readers are told that "because the Savior lives, we do not use the symbol of His death as the symbol of our faith" (pp. 45–46).

[61] In her blog posts, Butterworth used nicknames for her children and referred to her son as "Brick."

[62] Ezra Taft Benson, "The Honored Place of Women," *The Ensign* (November 1981): 105.

[63] *Doctrine and Covenants*, often abbreviated D&C, is a book of scripture in the Mormon tradition.

[64] Eve, "Leading A Secondary Life," Zelophehad's Daughters, September 26, 2006. http://zelophehadsdaughters.com/2006/09/26/leading-a-secondary-life/

[65] See p. 52.

[66] "Interview With Elder Dallin H. Oaks and Elder Lance B. Wickman: "Same-Gender Attraction,"" Mormon Newsroom (website), undated. https://www.mormonnewsroom.org/article/interview-oaks-wickman-same-gender-attraction

[67] The content of these talks is typically seen as authoritative instruction. Julie B. Beck, "Mothers Who Know," general conference talk, October 2007.

[68] Priya Jain, "More than a Mormon: feminist Mormons speak out," *Bust*, June/July 2007.

[69] Todd M. Compton, *In Sacred Loneliness* (Signature Books, 1997).

[70] In the parlance of internet abbreviations, DH can stand for "dear husband" or "damn husband," as the case may be.

[71] See p. 59.

[72] Gospel Doctrine is a Sunday school class for adults in the LDS Church.

[73] Bruce Hafen and Marie Hafen, "Crossing Thresholds and Becoming Equal Partners," *Ensign*, August 2007, 24-29.

[74] Boyd K. Packer, "For Time and All Eternity," *Ensign*, Nov. 1993, 22.

[75] Bruce Hafen and Marie Hafen, "Crossing Thresholds and Becoming Equal Partners," *Ensign*, August 2007, 24-29.

[76] Lisa Patterson Bitterworth, "BUSTed,", Feminist Mormon Housewives (blog), May 21, 2007. http://www.feministmormonhousewives.org/2007/05/busted/

[77] See p. 15.

[78] Julie B. Beck, "Mothers Who Know," General Conference talk, October 2007.

[79] Ibid.

[80] Utah State University.

[81] Davis Bitton and Maureen Ursenbach, "Riding the Herd: A Conversation with Juanita Brooks," *Dialogue : A Journal of Mormon Thought* 9, (1974): 11–33.

[82] Julie B. Beck, "Mothers Who Know," General Conference talk, October 2007.

[83] What Women Know (website). http://www.whatwomenknow.org/

[84] Jesse McKinley and Kirk Johnson, "Mormons Tipped Scale in Ban on Gay Marriage," *New York Times*, November 14, 2008.

[85] Gospel Principles is an adult Sunday school class for recently converted Mormons.

[86] *Gospel Principles* (The Church of Jesus Christ of Latter-day Saints, 1981), Chapter 2.

[87] "Article 27—Work and Employment," Division for Social Policy and Development: Disability, United Nations. https://www.un.org/development/desa/disabilities/convention-on-the-rights-of-persons-with-disabilities/article-27-work-and-employment.html

[88] Janet, "Happy New Year!" Feminist Mormon Housewives (blog), January 1, 2008. http://www.feministmormonhousewives.org/2008/01/happy-new-year/

[89] Stay-at-Home Mom.

[90] A letter from the Church's First Presidency (regarding California's Proposition 8) was sent to LDS congregations to be read during Church meetings on June 29, 2008.

[91] Wikipedia contributors, "Coverture," *Wikipedia, The Free Encyclopedia*, https://en.wikipedia.org/w/index.php?title=Coverture&oldid=813058574

[92] In her blog posts, Lauritzen uses the nickname "Marigold" for her oldest daughter.

[93] FMH readers and others contributed to an online fundraiser in honor of Grace.

[94] Mormons for Marriage (website). http://mormonsformarriage.com/

[95] Many LDS meetinghouses have a room called the cultural hall, which is used for ward events (such as classes, sporting events, or dinners) and, less frequently, can be reserved for family gatherings or community events. The cultural hall typically includes a basketball court and a stage.

[96] Sara Burlingame is a long-time participant in the FMH community, but she has never been a member of the LDS Church.

[97] David Stevens, *The Sum of Us/Play* (Samuel French Inc Plays, 1991).

[98] "Larry King Live," Transcript of interview with Gordon B. Hinckley, http://www.lds-mormon.com/lkl_00.shtml

[99] Dallin H. Oaks, "Criticism," *Ensign*, February 1987.

[100] BYU-TV is a television station operated and funded by Brigham Young University, available in the United States through cable and satellite distributors and worldwide through its own website. BYU-TV airs religious programming, documentaries, BYU sporting events, classic films, and original content.

[101] "California and Same-sex Marriage," Mormon Newsroom (website), June 30, 2008. https://www.mormonnewsroom.org/article/california-and-same-sex-marriage

[102] Wikipedia contributors, "September Six," *Wikipedia, The Free Encyclopedia*, https://en.wikipedia.org/w/index.php?title=September_Six&oldid=806547097

[103] Korihor is a character in the Book of Mormon who is described as an "anti-Christ" (Alma 30).

[104] Allison Pond, "A Portrait of Mormons in the US," Pew Research Center, Washington, D.C. (July 24, 2009). http://www.pewforum.org/2009/07/24/a-portrait-of-mormons-in-the-us/

[105] Tamu Smith and Zandra Vranes, *Diary of Two Mad Black Mormons: Finding the Lord's Lessons in Everyday Life* (Ensign Peak, 2014).

[106] Lisa Patterson Butterworth, "So What's Your Beef (Mormon) Ladies?" Feminist Mormon Housewives (blog), December 12, 2009. http://www.feministmormonhousewives.org/2009/12/so-whats-your-beef-mormon-ladies/

[107] Tresa Brown Edmunds, "On the Other Hand …" Feminist Mormon Housewives (blog), December 14, 2009. http://www.feministmormonhousewives.org/2009/12/on-the-other-hand/

[108] Scott Peck, *A World Waiting to be Born: Civility Rediscovered* (Bantam, 1993), 170.

[109] In some areas, the church organizes dances for Mormon teenagers to attend. Tickets to attend the dances are called "dance cards," and they're obtained from priesthood leaders after an interview to confirm the young person is living by the standards of the church.

[110] The pamphlet contains this quote: "There is a falsehood that some are born with an attraction to their own kind, with nothing they can do about it. They are just 'that way' and can only yield to those desires. That is a malicious and destructive lie. While it is a convincing idea to some, it is of the devil. No one is

locked into that kind of life. From our premortal life we were directed into a physical body. There is no mismatching of bodies and spirits. Boys are to become men—masculine, manly men—ultimately to become husbands and fathers. No one is predestined to a perverted use of these powers." See Boyd K. Packer's talk "To Young Men Only" in the October 1976 General Conference.

[111] Affirmation is an organization founded in the 1970s to serve the needs of LDS people who identify as lesbian, gay, bisexual, transgender, or same-sex attracted.

[112] This post mistakenly identifies the church's efforts to *stop* Proposition 8; the church supported Proposition 8.

[113] Ibid., 141.

[114] See Fox's Reflection essay on page 291.

[115] The Faithful Dissident (blog). http://thefaithfuldissident.blogspot.com/

[116] Hebrews 13:8; 1 Nephi 10:18.

[117] The privacy settings have changed for this blog and it is no longer possible to link to the relevant post.

[118] Scott, "LDS Gay History Timeline [Unabridged]," Dichotomy (blog), November 20, 2008. http://mormoninthecloset.blogspot.com/2008/11/lds-gay-history-timeline-unabridged.html

[119] Gay LDS Actor (blog). http://gayldsactor.blogspot.com/

[120] Michele Madigan Somerville, "Born Again in Brooklyn," *The New York Times* (blog), June 27, 2009. https://opinionator.blogs.nytimes.com//2009/06/27/born-again-in-brooklyn/

[121] Ibid.

[122] Beehive Clothing is a clothing production and sales company owned by The Church of Jesus Christ of Latter-day Saints, offering clothing used in temple ceremonies as well as the garments worn daily by endowed members of the Church.

[123] Simon Maloy, "Glenn Beck called hurricane survivors in New Orleans 'scumbags,' said he 'hates' 9–11 families," Media Matters (website), September 9, 2005. https://www.mediamatters.org/video/2005/09/09/glenn-beck-called-hurricane-survivors-in-new-or/133786

[124] Jason Linkins, "BeckWatch: As Wildfires Burn, Beck Flames Victims," Huffington Post (website), October 22, 2007. https://www.huffingtonpost.com/2007/10/22/beckwatch-as-wildfires-bu_n_69466.html

[125] Ali Frick, "Glenn Beck: I was wrong. We're not marching to socialism, we're marching toward fascism," Think Progress (website), April 1, 2009. https://thinkprogress.org/glenn-beck-i-was-wrong-were-not-marching-to-socialism-we-re-marching-toward-fascism-669717ecd875/

[126] Lawrence Delevingne, "More Advertisers Dump Glenn Beck over Obama Remarks," Business Insider (website), August 18, 2009. http://www.businessinsider.com/glenn-beck-quickly-losing-advertisers-for-2009-8

[127] "Glenn Beck Interview," video, 8:24, October 22, 2006. https://www.youtube.com/watch?v=wKtAPT9KEfM

[128] Matthew Neeley, "The Family Is of God," *Friend*, October 2008.

[129] Caroline Eyring Miner, "Home," *Children's Songbook* (The Church of Jesus Christ of Latter-day Saints, 1989), 192.

[130] Carri Jenkins, "BYU Women's Research Institute discontinued; BYU reorganizes women's studies program," BYU News (website) October 28, 2009. https://news.byu.edu/news/byu-womens-research-institute-discontinued-byu-reorganizes-womens-studies-program

[131] Various WRI Faculty Affiliates, "A Farewell Salute to the Women's Research Institute of Brigham Young University," *SquareTwo*, Vol. 2 No. 3 (Fall 2009). http://squaretwo.org/Sq2ArticleWRIFarewell.html

[132] This blog is no longer open to the public.

[133] Joanna Brooks, "Mormon Leader: 'I'm Sorry' for Hurtful Legacy of Prop. 8," Religion Dispatches (blog), October 4, 2010. http://religiondispatches.org/mormon-leader-im-sorry-for-hurtful-legacy-of-prop-8/

[134] Ibid.

[135] Maxine Hanks (ed), *Women and Authority: Re-emerging Mormon Feminism* (Signature Books, 1992).

[136] Simone de Beauvoir, *The Second Sex* (Alfred A. Knopf, 1953).

[137] See p. 41.

[138] While there is no official dress code for LDS Church meetings, traditions and cultural expectations can often impose a dress code of sorts. The specifics will vary largely across different countries and communities, but in many cases, women are expected to wear a dress/skirt while men are expected to wear a button-up shirt (preferably white), a tie, and possibly a suit jacket.

[139] Mfranti, "Dear fmh: Why are some members so preachy?" Feminist Mormon Housewives (blog), July 12, 2010. http://www.feministmormonhousewives.org/2010/07/dear-fmh-why-are-some-members-so-preachy/

[140] Harvard Divinity School, "Strange Fruit: The Cross and the Lynching Tree," video, 1:30:48, June 2, 2014. https://www.youtube.com/watch?v=ZngcqqgQyzo

[141] James H. Cone, *God of the Oppressed* (Seabury Press, 1975).

[142] Jesse McKinley and John Schwartz, "Court Rejects Same-Sex Marriage Ban in California," *New York Times*, August 4, 2010.

[143] "Church Statement on Proposition 8 Ruling," Mormon Newsroom (website), August 4, 2010. https://www.mormonnewsroom.org/ldsnewsroom/eng/news-releases-stories/church-statement-on-proposition-8-ruling

[144] Michael Aaron, "Utah's Gay Community Reels from Recent Suicides," *Q Salt Lake Magazine*, August 22, 2010. https://qsaltlake.com/news/2010/08/05/utahs-gay-community-reels-from-recent-suicides/

[145] General Authority, a priesthood holder who has ecclesiastical and administrative authority in the LDS Church. Many Mormons view statements made by general authorities as official and binding.

[146] The Mormon Women Project (website). https://www.mormonwomen.com/

[147] Holly, "Our Visions, Our Voices: A Mormon Women's Literary Tour— Schedule of Readings," Mormon Women Writers (blog), March 8, 2010. http://mormonwomenwriters.blogspot.com/2010/03/our-visions-our-voices-mormon-womens.html

[148] Tresa Brown Edmunds, "Getting Down to Work," Patheos (blog), December 1, 2010. http://www.patheos.com/resources/additional-resources/2010/12/getting-down-to-work ; Tresa Brown Edmunds, "Mormon, and feminist too," *The Guardian*, August 9, 2010.

[149] Peggy Fletcher Stack, "Where have all the Mormon feminists gone?" *Salt Lake Tribune*, October 4, 2003.

[150] LDS WAVE. http://www.ldswave.org/

[151] See chapter introduction.

[152] In her blog posts, Burlingame calls her son by the nickname "Noodle."

[153] Lynette, "Why I Do Want to Believe in Heavenly Mother," Zelophehad's Daughters (blog), October 23, 2010. http://zelophehadsdaughters.com/2010/10/23/why-i-do-want-to-believe-in-heavenly-mother/

[154] James Olsen, "In Praise of Heavenly Mother," Times and Seasons (blog), October 6, 2010. http://www.timesandseasons.org/harchive/2010/10/in-praise-of-heavenly-mother/

[155] Lisa Patterson Butterworth, "13 Articles of Healthy Chastity," Feminist Mormon Housewives (blog), November 3, 2010. http://www.feministmormonhousewives.org/2010/11/13-articles-of-healthy-chastity/

[156] The LDS Church publishes and periodically updates a two-volume guide called the Church Handbook of Instructions (commonly called the CHI or Handbook) to give instruction on various policies and procedures. The first volume is specifically intended for use by stake presidents (the priesthood leader called to preside over a group of wards) and bishops (the priesthood holder called to preside over a single ward); though copies have been leaked on the internet, the Church itself doesn't widely share the content of this volume. The second volume is distributed to male priesthood leaders over smaller organizations, and in November 2010, it was also made available to the general public on the church's website; coincidentally, that change occurred just a few weeks after the publication of this blog post.

[157] In LDS congregations (called "wards" or "branches," depending on their size), decisions often need to be made about events, lessons, local policies, budgets, and so forth. The Church's hierarchy, even on the local level, is innately patriarchal, and in some cases, no female leaders are present at meetings where important matters are discussed, even though the decisions made in these meetings will impact the women, girls, and children these female leaders have been designated to serve and represent. This post from Natalie Hamilton Kelly suggests that such instances be eliminated, and in the years since it was published at FMH, Church policy has encouraged greater inclusion of women on various councils. Still, there remain regular occurrences of meetings affecting the entire ward where female leaders are not included.

[158] See p. 125.

[159] Edwin Brown Firmage, "Reconciliation," in *Women and Authority: Re-Emerging Mormon Feminism*, ed. Maxine Hanks (Signature Books 1992), 335–349.

[160] Quoted in Angela Davis, *Women, Race, & Class* (Vintage, 1983), 51.

[161] Audre Lorde, *Sister Outsider: Essays and Speeches by Audre Lorde (Crossing Press Feminist Series)*, (Crossing Press, 1984).

[162] The Articles of Faith are an outline of thirteen key doctrinal points, originally written by Joseph Smith in 1842 in response to a newspaper editor who asked to know what members of the church believed. The Articles are now included in official LDS scripture. The 13th Article of Faith reads, "We believe in being honest, true, chaste, benevolent, virtuous, and in doing good to all men; indeed, we may say that we follow the admonition of Paul—We believe all things, we hope all things, we have endured many things, and hope to be able to endure all things. If there is anything virtuous, lovely, or of good report or praiseworthy, we seek after these things."

[163] JohnR, "For Those Who Struggle with Eating Disorders and Self Injury," Feminist Mormon Housewives (blog), January 12, 2007. http://www.feministmormonhousewives.org/2007/01/for-those-who-struggle-with-eating-disorders-and-self-injury/

[164] Family Home Evening is a program supported by the LDS Church that encourages family members to gather on a Monday night to share faith-based lessons and activities.

[165] "Endure to the end" is a common LDS expression used to encourage Church members to remain faithful and hopeful through the trials of life. The expression is found repeatedly in LDS scripture; for example, in the Book of Mormon in 2 Nephi 31:20, the prophet Nephi states, "Wherefore, ye must press forward with a steadfastness in Christ, having a perfect brightness of hope, and a love of God and of all men. Wherefore, if ye shall press forward, feasting upon the word of Christ, and endure to the end, behold, thus saith the Father: Ye shall have eternal life."

[166] Walter Kirn, "The Mormon Moment," *Newsweek*, June 5, 2011. http://www.newsweek.com/mormon-moment-67951

[167] Stephenie Meyer, *Twilight* (Little Brown, 2005).

[168] Ibid.

[169] "Romney's Mormon Faith Likely a Factor in Primaries, not in a General Election," Pew Research Center, Washington, D.C. (November 23, 2011). http://www.pewforum.org/2011/11/23/romneys-mormon-faith-likely-a-factor-in-primaries-not-in-a-general-election/

[170] David L. Paulsen and Martin Pulido, "A Mother There: A Survey of Historical Teachings about Mother in Heaven," *BYU Studies* 50, no. 1 (2011): 70–97.

[171] Jonathan A. Stapley and Kristine Wright. "Female Ritual Healing in Mormonism." *Journal of Mormon History* 37, no. 1 (2011): 1–85.

[172] Jana Riess, *Flunking Sainthood: A Year of Breaking the Sabbath, Forgetting to Pray, and Still Loving My Neighbor* (Paraclete Press, 2011).

[173] In 1997, Australian journalist David Ransom interviewed LDS Church president Gordon B. Hinckley. In the interview, Ransom addressed issues of dissent in the

LDS Church, the concept of Heavenly Mother, baptism for the dead, Hinckley's relationship with God, and the 1978 revelation extending priesthood ordination to males and temple ordinances to men and women of African descent, among other topics. The most well-known statement from Hinckley in this interview had to do with the possibility of LDS women being ordained to the priesthood: "[God] could change [the rules], yes ... But there's no agitation for that. We don't find it. Our women are happy." This acknowledgment that a new revelation on the subject of women's ordination was possible, but that there was no agitation for it, was part of the inspiration behind Dane Laverty's Agitating Faithfully project. A transcript of the interview can be found here: http://www.abc.net.au/compass/intervs/hinckley.htm

[174] Jeffrey R. Holland, "A Prayer for the Children," *Ensign*, (May 2003).

[175] Agitating Faithfully (website). http://agitatingfaithfully.org/

[176] http://www.mormonstories.org/228-agitating-faithfully-for-gender-equality-within-the-lds-church/

[177] Ask Mormon Girl was the title of Joanna Brooks's blog, where she asked and answered questions about Mormonism. She cross-published some of these posts on FMH. https://askmormongirl.wordpress.com/

[178] ECS, "Are Mormon Girls Dementors of the Priesthood?" Feminist Mormon Housewives (blog), March 27, 2011. http://www.feministmormonhousewives.org/2011/03/are-mormon-girls-dementors-of-the-priesthood/

[179] Peggy Fletcher Stack, "Loss of members spurred LDS singles ward changes," *Salt Lake Tribune*, April 29, 2011.

[180] David Stewart, "Trends in LDS Church Growth," *The Law of the Harvest: Practical Principles of Effective Missionary Work* (online book), Section 01 Chapter 01. http://www.cumorah.com/index.php?target=law_harvest&chapter_id=4

[181] The term "laurel" refers to an LDS Church class for girls ages 16–17 (within the Young Women organization) or to an individual member of the class.

[182] Richard J. Maynes, "Establishing a Christ-Centered Home," General Conference talk, April 2011.

[183] Dieter F. Uchtdorf, "The Love of God," General Conference talk, October 2009.

[184] Dieter F. Uchtdorf, "You Are My Hands," General Conference talk, April 2010.

[185] Caroline Winter, "How Mormons Make Money," *Bloomberg*, July 18, 2012. https://www.bloomberg.com/news/articles/2012-07-18/how-the-mormons-make-money

[186] Matthew Bowman, *The Mormon People: The Making of an American Faith* (Random House, 2012).

[187] Hokulani Aikau, *A Chosen People, a Promised Land: Mormonism and Race in Hawai'i* (University of Minnesota Press, 2012).

[188] Terry Tempest Williams, *When Women Were Birds: Fifty-Four Variations on Voice* (Sara Crichton Books, 2012).

[189] Joanna Brooks, *The Book of Mormon Girl: A Memoir of an American Faith* (Free Press, 2012).

[190] Timothy Pratt, "Mormon Women Set Out to Take a Stand, in Pants," *New York Times*, December 18, 2012.

[191] Joanna Brooks, "I'm pretty sure Mormons still believe in polygamy. Am I wrong?" Ask a Mormon Girl (blog), January 22, 2012. https://askmormongirl.wordpress.com/2012/01/22/im-pretty-sure-mormons-still-believe-in-polygamy-am-i-wrong/

[192] This was a series on the FMH blog that commemorated the lives of Joseph Smith's plural wives.

[193] Todd M. Compton, *In Sacred Loneliness* (Signature Books, 1997).

[194] See p. 155.

[195] Rebecca J, "Unclean! Unclean! Unclean!" By Common Consent (blog), February 10, 2012. https://bycommonconsent.com/2012/02/10/unclean-unclean-unclean/

[196] "LDS Temple Baptistry Policy: A Crowdsourced Database." https://docs.google.com/spreadsheets/d/1ZuDefD1xKjCTOVeF0uK4hHuagNr kFUI_J5A2qI980t8/edit#gid=0

[197] Sonia Johnson was excommunicated in 1979 for her activism in the Mormons for ERA movement. See Amanda HK, Kris, and Andrea, "A History of Women's Excommunication," Juvenile Instructor (blog), June 12, 2014. http://juvenileinstructor.org/a-history-of-womens-excommunication/

[198] Nadine Hansen, Lorie Winder Stromberg, Paula Jensen Goodfellow, and Margaret Toscano.

[199] The original blog post contains the poem, removed for lack of permission to reprint. http://www.feministmormonhousewives.org/2012/02/facing-fear-as-mormon-feminists-a-call-for-elderwomen/

[200] Urbanrenewalprogram, "Joy Harjo A Poem to Get Rid of Fear," video, 2:44, August 30, 2010. https://www.youtube.com/watch?v=DAYCf2Gdycc

[201] Shesare Er Villano, "StaceyAnn Chin, 'Not my fault,'" video, 1:44, February 27, 2011. https://www.youtube.com/watch?v=Zk2DNSllHeQ&feature=related

[202] Audre Lorde, *Sister Outsider: Essays and Speeches by Audre Lorde (Crossing Press Feminist Series)*, (Crossing Press, 1984), 44.

[203] See "Call to Action: Addressing the Temple 'Issue,' Period" by Elizabeth Hammond, published earlier in this chapter.

[204] See Layne Huff, "Blood in the Water" by Layne Huff, published earlier in this chapter.

[205] Rebecca J, "Unclean! Unclean! Unclean!" By Common Consent (blog), February 10, 2012. https://bycommonconsent.com/2012/02/10/unclean-unclean-unclean/

[206] Gloria Steinem, "'Women's Liberation' Aims to Free Men, Too," *Washington Post*, June 7, 1970.

[207] Eliza R. Snow, "O My Father," *Hymns* (The Church of Jesus Christ of Latter-day Saints, 1985), no 292.

[208] David L. Paulsen and Martin Pulido, "A Mother There: A Survey of Historical Teachings about Mother in Heaven," *BYU Studies* 50, no. 1 (2011): 70–97.

[209] An LDS periodical written almost exclusively by Orson Pratt for a non-

Mormon audience. It was published 1853–1854.

[210] Carol Lynn Pearson, *Mother Wove the Morning* (Pearson, 1992).

[211] Gordon B. Hinckley, "Daughters of God," General Conference talk, October 1991. https://www.lds.org/general-conference/1991/10/daughters-of-god?lang=eng

[212] Janice Allred, *God the Mother* (Signature Books, 1997).

[213] Sharon M. Haddock, "BYU Professor Is Appealing Her Termination," *Deseret News*, June 12, 1996.

[214] This blog post references angry responses to Joanna Brooks's appearance in Brian Williams's documentary *Mormons in America*, which aired on television August 23, 2012.

[215] Peggy Fletcher Stack, "Mormon women seeking middle ground to greater equality," *Salt Lake Tribune*, August 23, 2012.

[216] "How LDS faith could raise women's profile," *Salt Lake Tribune*, August 20, 2012.

[217] Sheri Dew and Virginia H. Pearce, *The Beginning of Better Days: Divine Instruction to Women from the Prophet Joseph Smith* (Deseret Book, 2012).

[218] Laura Brotherson, *And They Were Not Ashamed: Strengthening Marriage Through Sexual Fulfillment* (Inspire Book, 2004).

[219] Boyd K. Packer, "The Fountain of Life," BYU Multi-Stake Fireside, March 29, 1992. http://emp.byui.edu/OpenshawR/Family%20Foundations%20Articles/Packer%20The%20Fountain%20of%20Life.doc

[220] Proverbs 5:19.

[221] Spencer W. Kimball, *Faith Precedes the Miracle* (Deseret Book, 1972), 130–31.

[222] The smashed cupcake lesson is a variation on the chewed gum object lesson, see note 319.

[223] Natasha Helfer Parker is a certified sex therapist within the Mormon community.

[224] Articles of Faith 1:2 reads, "We believe that men will be punished for their own sins, and not for Adam's transgression." Also, see note 97.

[225] Laura Brotherson, *And They Were Not Ashamed: Strengthening Marriage Through Sexual Fulfillment* (Inspire Book, 2004).

[226] Cynthia L., "Editing Photos to Add Cap Sleeves is a Bad Idea," By Common Consent (blog), September 3, 2012. https://bycommonconsent.com/2012/09/03/editing-photos-to-add-cap-sleeves-is-a-bad-idea/

[227] Ziff, "A Modest Bit of Data," Zelophehad's Daughters (blog), July 27, 2011. http://zelophehadsdaughters.com/2011/07/27/a-modest-bit-of-data/

[228] Jennifer Abbasi, "Why 6-year-old Girls Want to be Sexy," Huffington Post (blog), July 16, 2012. http://www.huffingtonpost.com/2012/07/17/6-year-old-girls-sexy_n_1679088.html

[229] Dallin H. Oaks, "Pornography," General Conference talk, April 2005.

[230] Tracy M, "Perverting Modesty," By Common Consent (blog), July 9, 2011.

https://bycommonconsent.com/2011/07/09/perverting-modesty/

[231] Piper Anderson, "Modesty Part One of Four," Feminist Mormon Housewives (blog), November 9, 2010, http://www.feministmormonhousewives.org/2010/11/modesty-part-one-of-four/

[232] Piper Anderson, "Modesty Part 2 of 4: Between You and God," Feminist Mormon Housewives (blog), November 10, 2010. http://www.feministmormonhousewives.org/2010/11/modesty-part-2-of-4-between-you-and-god/

[233] Piper Anderson, "Modesty Part 3 of 4: Between You and the Neighbors," Feminist Mormon Housewives (blog), November 12, 2010. http://www.feministmormonhousewives.org/2010/11/modesty-part-3-of-4-between-you-and-your-neighbors/

[234] Piper Anderson, "Modesty Part 4 of 4: Just for You," Feminist Mormon Housewives (blog), November 14, 2010. http://www.feministmormonhousewives.org/2010/11/modesty-part-4-of-4-just-for-you/

[235] *Daughters in My Kingdom: The History and Work of Relief Society* (The Church of Jesus Christ of Latter-day Saints, 2011).

[236] Heather Whittle Wrigley, "Church Leaders Share More Information on Missionary Age Requirement Change," Church News (blog), October 6, 2012. https://www.lds.org/church/news/church-leaders-share-more-information-on-missionary-age-requirement-change?lang=eng

[237] Maxine Hanks (ed.), *Women and Authority: Re-emerging Mormon Feminism* (Signature Books, 1992).

[238] Theodor Seuss Geisel, *Horton Hears a Who!* (Random House, 1954).

[239] The contents of this blog are no longer public.

[240] "Policies and Procedures Newsletter," *Ensign*, July 1971.

[241] Gloria Steinem, *Outrageous Acts and Everyday Rebellions* (Holt McDougal, 1983).

[242] Ibid., 120.

[243] Ibid., 173.

[244] Ibid., 125.

[249] Lorie Winder Stromberg, "The Birth of Ordain Women: The Personal Becomes Political," in *Voices for Equality: Ordain Women and Resurgent Mormon Feminism*, ed Gordon Shepherd, Lavina Fielding Anderson, and Gary Shepherd (Greg Kofford Books, 2015), 3–26.

[254] Dominique Mosbergen, "Pink Smoke Billows Over Vatican as Protestors Challenge Church's Women Ordination Policy," Huffington Post (blog), March 13, 2013. https://www.huffingtonpost.com/2013/03/13/pink-smoke-vatican-protest-women-ordination_n_2868433.html

[255] Kate Kelly, "Organizing women after the manner of the priesthood," Ordain Women (blog), March 17, 2013. http://ordainwomen.org/organizing-the-women-after-the-manner-of-the-priesthood-2/

[256] Caroline, "Good Mormon Feminists vs. Bad Mormon Feminists: The Dividing Line," Exponent II (blog), June 18, 2009. http://www.the-exponent.com/good-mormon-feminists-vs-bad-mormon-feminists-the-dividing-line/

[257] Deborah, "Who Thinks Women Should Hold the Priesthood? Men, Apparently," Exponent II (blog), December 20, 2010. http://www.the-exponent.com/who-thinks-women-should-hold-the-priesthood-men-apparently/
[258] Grant Hardy, "Why Do Mormon Men Want Women to Have the Priesthood More Than Women Want It for Themselves?" Flunking Sainthood (blog), December 2012. http://www.beliefnet.com/columnists/flunkingsainthood/2010/12/why-do-mormon-men-want-women-to-have-the-priesthood-more-than-women-want-it-for-themselves.html
[259] Jonathan A. Stapley and Kristine Wright, "Female Ritual Healing in Mormonism," *Journal of Mormon History* 37, (2011): 1–85.
[260] Heidi Doggett, "Revelation Through Innovation," Feminist Mormon Housewives (blog), October 2, 2012. http://www.feministmormonhousewives.org/2012/10/revelation-through-innovation/
[261] The Primary organization is the LDS Church's program for children. Each year, the Primary children lead the service, and this is referred to as the Primary program.
[262] See note 119.
[263] Alice Fisher Roberts, "Patty Bartlett Sessions: Remembering the Forgotten Women of Joseph Smith," Feminist Mormon Housewives (blog), September 23, 2011. http://www.feministmormonhousewives.org/2011/09/patty-bartlett-sessions-remembering-the-forgotten-women-of-joseph-smith/
[264] Linda King Newell, "A Gift Given: A Gift Taken: Washing, Anointing, and Blessing the Sick Among Mormon Women," *Sunstone* 10 (1981): 17–25.
[265] Thomas S. Monson, "Priesthood Power," General Conference talk, April 2011.
[266] General Conference, see note 38.
[267] Dennis L. Lythgoe, "Giving Priesthood Blessings," *Ensign*, February 1982.
[268] "Nauvoo Relief Society Minute Book," p. [40], *The Joseph Smith Papers*, http://www.josephsmithpapers.org/paper-summary/nauvoo-relief-society-minute-book/37
[269] Elaine S. Dalton, "We Are Daughters of Our Heavenly Father," General Conference talk, April 2013.
[270] "Why Is Chastity Important?" Young Women Lesson Outlines. https://www.lds.org/youth/learn/yw/marriage-and-family/chastity?lang=eng
[271] "Abuse," LDS Church. https://www.lds.org/topics/abuse?lang=eng
[272] Anne Lamott, *Help, Thanks, Wow: The Three Essential Prayers* (Riverhead Books, 2012), 7.
[273] Ibid., 6.
[274] In his blog posts, Staffanson uses the nickname "Luv" for his wife.
[275] David S. King, "Is there a dress and grooming standard for temple attendance?" *Ensign*, Feb 1993, 29–31.
[276] Chieko N. Okazaki, "Baskets and Bottles," General Conference talk, April 1996.
[277] Vaughn J. Featherstone, "One Link Still Holds," General Conference talk,

October 1999.

[278] Gordon B. Hinckley, "Great Shall Be the Peace of Thy Children," General Conference talk, October 2000.

[279] Gordon B. Hinckley, "Your Greatest Challenge, Mother," General Conference talk, October 2000.

[280] M. Russell Ballard, "'His Word Ye Shall Receive,'" General Conference talk, April 2001.

[281] Sharon G. Larsen, "'Fear Not: For They That Be with Us Are More,'" General Conference talk, October 2001.

[282] David A. Bednar, "Quick to Observe," *Ensign* (December 2006).

[283] *Handbook 2: Administering the Church* (The Church of Jesus Christ of Latter-day Saints, 2010).

[284] Gramps, "What is the Mormon Church policy regarding dress codes for priesthood ordinances," Ask Gramps (blog), February 3, 2008. https://askgramps.org/what-is-the-mormon-church-policy-regarding-dress-codes-for/

[285] Lewis wrote 13 posts as part of this series, offering suggestions on how readers could honor and learn more about Heavenly Mother through rituals, traditions, sexuality, and engaging with nature.

[286] The term Beehive refers to an LDS Church class for girls ages 12–13 (within the Young Women organization) or to an individual member of the class.

[287] D. Todd Christofferson, "The Moral Force of Women," General Conference talk, October 2013.

[288] fMfLisa, "On Nastiness: Why nice Mormons can be so very very mean (about Pants)," Feminist Mormon Housewives (blog), December 13, 2012. http://www.feministmormonhousewives.org/2012/12/on-nastiness-why-nice-mormons-can-be-so-very-very-mean-about-pants/

[289] Dieter F. Uchtdorf, "Come, Join with Us," General Conference talk, October 2013.

[290] Gérald Caussé, "Ye Are No More Strangers," General Conference talk, October 2013. https://www.lds.org/general-conference/2013/10/ye-are-no-more-strangers?lang=ase

[291] Tom Head, "12 Types of Social Justice Oppression," ThoughtCo, updated March 17, 2017. https://www.thoughtco.com/types-of-oppression-721173

[292] John Henrik Clarke, "Concept of Deity," Department of Africana & Puerto Rican/Latino Studies, Hunter College. http://www.hunter.cuny.edu/afprl/clarke/concept-of-deity201d-by-dr.-john-henrik-clarke

[293] Malala Yousafzai and Christina Lamb, *I Am Malala: The Girl Who Stood Up for Education and Was Shot by the Taliban* (Little, Brown and Company, 2013).

[294] Kathryn Peterson and Kate Kelly, "The House She Lives In," The Mormon Women Project (blog), September 12, 2013. https://www.mormonwomen.com/interview/the-house-she-lives-in/

[295] Jon Stewart and Joanna Brooks, "Exclusive - Joanna Brooks Extended

Interview PT. 1," The Daily Show with Jon Stewart, August 9, 2012. http://www.cc.com/video-clips/i5ahwr/the-daily-show-with-jon-stewart-exclusive---joanna-brooks-extended-interview-pt--1

[296] This essay is included in the chapter titled 2005.

[297] "Race and the Priesthood," The Church of Jesus Christ of Latter-day Saints (website), 2013. https://www.lds.org/topics/race-and-the-priesthood?lang=eng

[298] "First Vision Accounts," The Church of Jesus Christ of Latter-day Saints (website), 2013. https://www.lds.org/topics/first-vision-accounts?lang=eng

[299] "Plural Marriage and Families in Early Utah," The Church of Jesus Christ of Latter-day Saints (website), 2013. https://www.lds.org/topics/plural-marriage-and-families-in-early-utah?lang=eng

[300] Duane E. Hiatt, "Follow the Prophet," *Children's Songbook* (The Church of Jesus Christ of Latter-day Saints, 1989), 110.

[301] Dieter F. Uchtdorf, "Come, Join with Us," General Conference talk, October 2013.

[302] Bridget Jack Jeffries, "Can Grace Save Mormonism?" LDS and Evangelical Conversations (blog), March 8, 2012. https://ldstalk.wordpress.com/2012/03/08/can-grace-save-mormonism/

[303] George Kaillmark, "Do What Is Right," *Hymns* (The Church of Jesus Christ of Latter-day Saints, 1985), no 237. The scattered quotes in this post are all from this hymn.

[304] Marissa Lang and Brook Adams, "Judge denies Utah AG's request to halt same-sex marriages," *Salt Lake Tribune*, December 23, 2013.

[305] "Family (isn't it about time?)" video, 1:09, September 5, 2009. https://www.youtube.com/watch?v=56v8uqetN_E

[306] Jim Kelly, "Hi, I'm Jim," Ordain Women (website), April 19, 2013. http://ordainwomen.org/project/hi-im-jim/

[307] Kairos Center (website). https://kairoscenter.org/

[308] "Rev. Martin Luther King, Jr. - April 4, 1967 - Beyond Vietnam: A Time to Break Silence [Full Speech]," video, 56:48, January 15, 2011. https://www.youtube.com/watch?v=OC1Ru2p8OfU

[309] Sunlight Cinema, "Mormon Women of October 5," video, 9:40, October 16, 2013. https://vimeo.com/77027706

[310] Kristen Moulton, "Mormon women shut out of all-male priesthood meeting," *Salt Lake Tribune*, October 18, 2013.

[311] L. Tom Perry, "Why Marriage and Family Matter—Everywhere in the World," General Conference talk, April 2015.

[312] Ibid.

[313] M. Russell Ballard, "The Lord Needs You Now!" *Ensign*, September 2015.

[314] Caryn Ganz, "Neon Trees' Tyler Glenn: Gay, Mormon and Finally Out," *Rolling Stone*, March 25, 2014.

[315] Neylan McBaine, *Women at Church: Magnifying LDS Women's Local Impact* (Greg Kofford Books, 2014).

[316] McArthur Krishna, Bethany Brady Spalding, and Kathleen Peterson, *Girls Who*

Choose God: Stories of Courageous Women from the Bible (Deseret Book, 2014).

[317] Cadence Woodland, "The End of the 'Mormon Moment,'" *New York Times*, July 14, 2014.

[318] *The Princess Bride* (movie, 1987).

[319] Object lessons and analogies are frequently used in LDS classes to teach a certain principle. Many women who grew up LDS report being taught to abstain from sex before marriage and having the importance of doing so reinforced by comparing women to chewing gum. Since no one wants to have a piece of gum that's already been chewed, girls are meant to understand that unrighteous sexual behavior will leave them similarly used and unwanted. The harmful consequences of this common object lesson include perpetuating the objectification of women, communicating a double standard, minimizing the power of repentance, and shaming victims of sexual abuse.

[320] "Ordain Women Requests Tickets to the Priesthood Session," Ordain Women (website), March 16, 2014. http://ordainwomen.org/ordain-women-requests-tickets-to-the-priesthood-session/

[321] Tad Walch, "LDS Church: Aims of 'Ordain Women' detract from dialogue," Deseret News, March 17, 2014.

[322] "Nauvoo Relief Society Minute Book," p. [40], *The Joseph Smith Papers*, http://www.josephsmithpapers.org/paper-summary/nauvoo-relief-society-minute-book/37

[323] Jodi Cantor and Laurie Goodstein, "Missions Signal a Growing Role for Mormon Women," *New York Times*, March 1, 2014.

[324] Doctrine and Covenants 137:9.

[325] Dieter F. Uchtdorf, "The Merciful Obtain Mercy," General Conference talk, April 2012.

[326] "Mission Statement," Ordain Women (website). http://ordainwomen.org/mission/

[327] Luke 23:34.

[328] "How Can I Improve My Teaching Skills?" *Preach My Gospel: A Guide to Missionary Service* (The Church of Jesus Christ of Latter-day Saints, 2004), 175–94. https://www.lds.org/manual/preach-my-gospel-a-guide-to-missionary-service/how-can-i-improve-my-teaching-skills?lang=eng

[329] Dieter F. Uchtdorf, "Come, Join with Us," General Conference talk, October 2013.

[330] Kristen Moulton, "Mormon women again turned away from priesthood meeting," *Salt Lake Tribune*, April 11, 2014.

[331] Eric S. Peterson, "Restoring the Priesthood," *City Weekly*, October 2, 2013. https://www.cityweekly.net/utah/restoring-the-priesthood/Content?oid=2304765

[332] Newell G. Bringhurst, Darron T. Smith, *Black and Mormon* (University of Illinois Press, 2004), 5.

[333] Mary King, *Mahatma Gandhi and Martin Luther King Jr: The Power of Nonviolent Action* (UNESCO Publishing, 1999), 118.

[334] Psalms 46:10.

[335] Peggy Fletcher Stack, "Mormon women's group meets with LDS Church PR officials," *Salt Lake Tribune*, May 23, 2014.

[336] Ibid.

[337] 1 Corinthians 12:27.

[338] #Yesallwomen was a social media campaign, popular in May 2014, where users shared stories of violence against women and experiences of misogyny. #YesEvenMormonWomen was the Mormon version of this.

[339] Pat Reavy and Sandra Yi, "New cases have BYU police suspecting serial groper," KSL (website), March 19, 2014.https://www.ksl.com/?sid=29122830&nid=148

[340] Paige Fieldsted, "Sexual assault survivors open up about experiences," *Herald Extra*, April 4, 2013. http://www.heraldextra.com/news/local/sexual-assault-survivors-open-up-about-experiences/article_5a585594-85b5-52fc-b9d6-94c0383745ed.html

[341] "Violence Against Women fact sheet," World Health Organization, updated 2017. http://www.who.int/mediacentre/factsheets/fs239/en/

[342] *For the Strength of Youth* (The Church of Jesus Christ of Latter-day Saints, 2011).

[343] Laurie Goodstein, "Two Activists in Mormon Church Threatened With Excommunication," *New York Times*, June 11, 2014.

[344] Debra Nussbaum, "Faithful Track Questions, Answers and Minutiae on Blogs," *New York Times*, March 5, 2005.

[345] The LDS Church excommunicated Mormon feminist writers Lavina Fielding Anderson and Maxine Hanks in 1993 as part of the September Six. It excommunicated Janice Allred in 1995 and Margaret Toscano in 2000.

[346] Wikipedia contributors, "Sally Gross (South African activist)," *Wikipedia, The Free Encyclopedia*, https://en.wikipedia.org/w/index.php?title=Sally_Gross_(South_African_activist)&oldid=814273666

[347] We do not have permission to reprint the poem here. It is still on the original blog post. Lisa Patterson Butterworth, "We Shall Find Kindness: Ordain Women and A Wound to the Body of Christ," Feminist Mormon Housewives (blog), June 11, 2014. http://www.feministmormonhousewives.org/2014/06/we-shall-find-kindness-ordain-women-and-a-wound-to-the-body-of-christ/

[348] Amanda HK, Kris, and Andrea, "A History of Women's Excommunication," Juvenile Instructor (blog), June 12, 2014. http://juvenileinstructor.org/a-history-of-womens-excommunication/

[349] Ibid.

[350] Kylee Shields, "An Open Letter to Mormon Feminists," Kylee Shields (blog), June 11, 2014. https://web.archive.org/web/20160303035648/https://www.kyleeshields.com/2014/06/an-open-letter-to-mormon-feminists.html

[351] Neylan McBaine, "Blessed Are the Peacemakers," Neylan McBaine (blog), June 11, 2014. http://www.neylanmcbaine.com/2014/06/blessed-are-the-peacemakers.html

[352] Greg Prince, "'There Is Always a Struggle:' An Interview with Chieko N. Okazaki," *Dialogue: A Journal of Mormon Thought*, 45, no. 1 (Spring 2012): 112–140.

[353] John Dehlin and Greg Prince, "295: Greg Prince on 'Big Tent Mormonism,'" Mormon Stories (podcast), October 20, 2011. http://www.mormonstories.org/295-297-2011-washington-d-c-conference-with-greg-prince/

[354] Especially for Youth (EFY) is a summer camp experience with LDS speakers and faith-promoting activities.

[355] Kristy, "Reaction to Kate Kelly's Excommunication," Ordain Women (website), June 23, 2014. http://ordainwomen.org/reaction-to-kate-kellys-excommunication/

[356] Robert L. Simpson, "Courts of Love," General Conference talk, April 1972.

[357] Peggy Fletcher Stack, "Sunstone: Paying the Price of Intellectualism," Beliefnet, August 2001. http://www.beliefnet.com/faiths/christianity/latter-day-saints/2001/08/sunstone-paying-the-price-of-intellectualism.aspx

[358] Joanna Brooks, Phyllis Barber, Timothy Weymann, D. Jeff Burton, Katie Langston, and Robin Linkhart, "Sunstone Navigating the Borderlands Part 6," video, 15:00, April 11, 2011. https://www.youtube.com/watch?v=8WT_2tD1A18

[359] "Revelation, September 1830–A [D&C 29]," p. 36, *The Joseph Smith Papers*, http://www.josephsmithpapers.org/paper-summary/revelation-september-1830-a-dc-29/1

[360] Scott Gemmell, "Tar and Feathering of the Prophet Joseph Smith," O Say What is Truth (blog), October 24, 2010. http://scottgemmell.blogspot.com/2010/10/tar-and-feathering-of-prophet-joseph.html

[361] Fawn M. Brodie, *No Man Knows My History: The Life of Joseph Smith* (Alfred A. Knopf, revised and expanded 1971), 119.

[362] D. Michael Quinn, "The Culture of Violence in Joseph Smith's Mormonism," *Sunstone* (October 2011): 16–37.

[363] "Oration delivered by Mr. S. Rigdon, on the 4th of July, 1838 : at Far West, Caldwell County, Missouri," L. Tom Perry Special Collections, Harold B. Lee Library, Brigham Young University. http://contentdm.lib.byu.edu/cdm/compoundobject/collection/NCMP1820-1846/id/2816

[364] Wikipedia contributors, "Mountain Meadows Massacre," *Wikipedia, The Free Encyclopedia*, https://en.wikipedia.org/w/index.php?title=Mountain_Meadows_Massacre&oldid=816084050

[365] Robert Keen, "How Firm A Foundation," *Hymns* (The Church of Jesus Christ of Latter-day Saints, 1985), no 85. https://www.lds.org/music/library/hymns/how-firm-a-foundation?lang=eng

[366] Sherrie Johnson, "Persecutions in Missouri," *Friend*, July 1993. https://www.lds.org/friend/1993/07/persecutions-in-missouri?lang=eng

[367] Year of Polygamy (podcast). http://www.yearofpolygamy.com/

[368] Michael Hicks, "Minding Business: A Note on 'The Mormon Creed,'" *BYU Studies* 26, no 4 (1986): article 8.

https://byustudies.byu.edu/content/minding-business-note-mormon-creed

[369] Lindsay Hansen Park, "Episode 10: Polygamy in Nauvoo," Year of Polygamy (podcast), Jan 29, 2014. http://www.yearofpolygamy.com/year-of-polygamy/year-of-polygamy-polygamy-in-nauvoo-episode-10/

[370] Wikipedia contributors, "Reed Smoot hearings," *Wikipedia, The Free Encyclopedia*, https://en.wikipedia.org/w/index.php?title=Reed_Smoot_hearings&oldid=818500562

[371] 1 Nephi 4:17–18.

[372] Jessie L. Embry, "Exiles for the Principle: LDS Polygamy in Canada," *Dialogue: A Journal of Mormon Thought* 18 (1985): 108–116.

[373] Loren Franck, "Ten Lies I Told as a Mormon Missionary," Mormonism Research Ministry (website). http://www.mrm.org/ten-lies

[374] Nightingale, "Please help me, I'm in shock," Exmormon (website), July 5. http://www.exmormon.org/mormon/mormon049.htm

[375] Kathryn Skaggs, "Excommunication All the Rage," Well-Behaved Mormon Woman (blog), June 25, 2014. http://wellbehavedmormonwoman.blogspot.com/2014/06/kate-kelly-excommunicated-mormons-respond.html

[376] Wikipedia contributors, "The Seer (periodical)," *Wikipedia, The Free Encyclopedia*, https://en.wikipedia.org/w/index.php?title=The_Seer_(periodical)&oldid=788644294

[377] Doug Fabrizio and Ally Isom, "Latter-day Saints and Excommunication," Radio West (podcast), June 16, 2014. http://radiowest.kuer.org/post/latter-day-saints-and-excommunication-part-ii

[378] Wikipedia contributors, "In-group favoritism," *Wikipedia, The Free Encyclopedia*, https://en.wikipedia.org/w/index.php?title=In-group_favoritism&oldid=807356527

[379] Alison Moore Smith, "Shunning the Unbelievers," Times and Seasons (blog), September 4, 2011. http://www.timesandseasons.org/harchive/2011/09/shunning-the-unbelievers/

[380] Eric Ethington, "Gay Mormon, excommunicated from his church, commits suicide," LGBTQ Nation (website), September 22, 2011. https://www.lgbtqnation.com/2011/09/gay-mormon-excommunicated-from-his-church-commits-suicide/

[381] Wikipedia contributors, "Danite," *Wikipedia, The Free Encyclopedia*, https://en.wikipedia.org/w/index.php?title=Danite&oldid=814053334

[382] Joanna Brooks, "The Real Mormon Moment," Religion Dispatches (blog), June 24, 2014. http://religiondispatches.org/the-real-mormon-moment/

[383] M. Russell Ballard, "A Chance to Start Over," *Ensign*, September 1990.

[384] "Church Responds to Church Discipline Questions," Mormon Newsroom (website), June 11, 2014. https://www.mormonnewsroom.org/article/church-responds-to-church-discipline-questions

[385] Joanna Brooks, *The Book of Mormon Girl: A Memoir of an American Faith* (Free Press, 2012).

[386] In her blog posts, Edmunds uses the nickname "Bear" for her husband.

[387] Lindsay Hansen Park and Julie de Azevedo Hanks, "Episode 114: Self Care with Julie de Azevedo Hanks," FMH Podcast, June 30, 2014. http://fmhpodcast.org/2014/06/30/episode-114-self-care-with-julie-de-azevedo-hanks/

[388] Lindsay Hansen Park, "Woman, Know Thy Place," Feminist Mormon Housewives (blog), July 20, 2014. http://www.feministmormonhousewives.org/2014/07/woman-know-thy-place/

[389] "Hastening the Work of Salvation," Worldwide Leadership Training (website), 2013. https://www.lds.org/training/wwlt/2013/hastening/a-new-vision?cid=HPL1P01W01031&lang=eng

[390] Amy Hoyt, "Agency and the American LDS Woman," paper presented at *Women's Lives, Women's Voices: Agency in the Lives of Mormon Women*, Claremont Graduate University, February 5, 2011, p. 2.

[391] Ibid, p. 5-6.

[392] Peggy Fletcher Stack, "Where have all the Mormon feminists gone?" *Salt Lake Tribune*, October 4, 2003.

[393] Phone discussion with Lisa Butterworth, February 27, 2018.

[394] Lorie Winder Stromberg, "The Birth of Ordain Women: The Personal Becomes Political," in *Voices for Equality: Ordain Women and Resurgent Mormon Feminism*, ed Gordon Shepherd, Lavina Fielding Anderson, and Gary Shepherd (Greg Kofford Books, 2015), 3–26.

[395] See pp. 209 and 258; Lindsay Hansen Park, "Tell us how you REALLY feel about women and priesthood," Feminist Mormon Housewives (blog), March 23, 2013. http://www.feministmormonhousewives.org/2013/03/tell-us-how-you-really-feel-about-women-and-the-priesthood/; Sara Katherine Staheli Hanks, "MoFems in 2016: How do you feel about women's ordination?" Feminist Mormon Housewives (blog), May 30, 2016. http://www.feministmormonhousewives.org/2016/05/mofems-in-2016-how-do-you-feel-about-womens-ordination/; Kate Kelly, "#peakpatriarchy," Feminist Mormon Housewives (blog), August 21, 2013. http://www.feministmormonhousewives.org/2013/08/peakpatriarchy/; Lorie Winder Stromberg, "Agitating Faithfully," Feminist Mormon Housewives (blog), September 30, 2015. http://www.feministmormonhousewives.org/2015/09/agitating-faithfully-2/

[396] Joanna Brooks, "Mormon Feminism Is Back," *Religion Dispatches*, September 22, 2010. http://religiondispatches.org/mormon-feminism-is-back/

[397] See p. 204. /

[398] Juliet Eilperin, "White House women want to be in the room where it happens," *The Washington Post*, September 13, 2016.

[399] Rachel Hunt Steenblik, "On physical/mental illness and George Albert Smith," Feminist Mormon Housewives (blog), February 3, 2012. http://www.feministmormonhousewives.org/2012/02/on-physicalmental-illness-and-george-albert-smith/

[400] Rachel Hunt Steenblik, "What I first learned about Heavenly Mother," Feminist

Mormon Housewives (blog), April 29, 2014.
http://www.feministmormonhousewives.org/2014/04/what-i-first-learned-about-heavenly-mother/

[401] Sara Katherine Staheli Hanks, "Heavenly Mother and the Baader-Meinhoff Phenomenon," Feminist Mormon Housewives (blog), May 6, 2014.
http://www.feministmormonhousewives.org/2014/05/heavenly-mother-and-the-baader-meinhoff-phenomenon/

[402] See p. 269.

[403] Elizabeth Hammond, "The Mormon Priestess (The Short Version)," Feminist Mormon Housewives (blog), April 6, 2014.
http://www.feministmormonhousewives.org/2014/04/the-mormon-priestess-the-short-version/

CPSIA information can be obtained
at www.ICGtesting.com
Printed in the USA
LVHW03s0620140618
580710LV00001B/176/P